MAGIC CITY

BURGIN MATHEWS

MAGIC CITY

HOW THE BIRMINGHAM JAZZ TRADITION SHAPED THE SOUND OF AMERICA

THE
UNIVERSITY OF
NORTH CAROLINA
PRESS
CHAPEL HILL

This book was published with the assistance of the
Fred W. Morrison Fund of the University of North Carolina Press.

Cover illustration: *Clockwise from center:* Sun Ra in a 1973 publicity photo; Erskine Hawkins, courtesy Birmingham Public Library Archives; John T. "Fess" Whatley, courtesy Birmingham Public Library Archives; Ethel Harper, publicity photo from the collections of the North Jersey History and Genealogy Center, the Morristown and Morris Township Library.

Library of Congress Cataloging-in-Publication Data
Names: Mathews, Burgin, author.
Title: Magic City : how the Birmingham jazz tradition
shaped the sound of America / Burgin Mathews.
Description: Chapel Hill : The University of North Carolina Press,
[2023] | Includes bibliographical references and index.
Identifiers: LCCN 2023029861 | ISBN 9781469676876 (cloth) |
ISBN 9781469676883 (paperback) | ISBN 9781469676890 (ebook)
Subjects: LCSH: Jazz—Alabama—Birmingham—History and criticism. |
BISAC: MUSIC / Ethnomusicology | HISTORY / United States / State &
Local / South (AL, AR, FL, GA, KY, LA, MS, NC, SC, TN, VA, WV)
Classification: LCC ML3508.8.B57 M37 2023 |
DDC 781.6509761/78—dc23/eng/20230627
LC record available at https://lccn.loc.gov/2023029861

For Glory

CONTENTS

ILLUSTRATIONS

MAGIC CITY

INTRODUCTION

I n July 1985, Erskine Hawkins came home to Tuxedo Junction, the place where he had first heard jazz.[1] Just north
of Birmingham, Alabama, surrounded by steel mills and
smoke, the Junction had once been a flourishing dance
spot for the local Black community, a block of bandstands and nightclubs
that had dazzled young Hawkins many years before. He had become a
trumpeter and bandleader, one of the high-note heroes of American swing,
celebrated in the 1930s and 1940s as the "Twentieth Century Gabriel." Now,
for Hawkins's seventy-first birthday, Tuxedo Junction welcomed him home
for an outdoor concert in celebration of his legacy. Afternoon rains erupted
but the faithful remained, cramming into a sweltering school gymnasium,
setting up metal folding chairs, spreading out all over the floor, and fanning themselves with wilted programs. Backed by local musicians, a few
longtime bandmates, and some of his oldest hometown friends, Hawkins
blew his way through his greatest hits, a repertoire that stretched back
half a century. The climax, of course, was "Tuxedo Junction," the tune
that had made famous both Hawkins himself and this little spot on the
map. He had played it by now all over the country, in bright-lit cities and
dusty small towns, had blasted it far and wide over the airwaves and set it
multiple times to wax. The tune's infectious, unmistakable groove had sent
a generation of dancers across New York's swankiest ballroom floors and
had rallied American GIs on their way to take down the Nazis. In recent
years, Hawkins had settled into a cushy permanent gig at a Catskills resort,
entertaining each night's crowd with that signature theme and evoking in
the gray-headed vacationers nostalgia for bygone years. But today "Tuxedo
Junction" had come home, and the local crowd savored every note. Verna

Chambers—a retired schoolteacher, eighty-two years old—could not keep from dancing, and the room cheered her on as she gyrated and bounced all over the basketball court.

"Honey," she said, "when I hear that music, I have to get up and move."

Hawkins struggled to put into words his feelings for the Junction. "It's hard for me to explain," he confessed. "It means everything to me. The place itself taught me my music. And I'll never forget it." All through the performance he was beaming, a man wholeheartedly in his element. He cracked jokes with the crowd and broke into a few dance steps of his own. And he vowed to come back each year for his birthday.

"Home," he said, "is home."

But home can be a complicated thing.

Jazz iconoclast Sun Ra came back to Birmingham in February 1988.[2] He had booked a show at the Nick, a grimy rock and roll dive tucked into the shadow of a highway overpass. Like Hawkins, Sun Ra had grown up in Birmingham. But unlike Tuxedo Junction's most celebrated son, he never quite claimed it as his own.

He had really come, he said, from Saturn.

The crowd that turned out to see Sun Ra that night at the Nick was unlike the hometown crowd that had clamored for Hawkins three years before. Sun Ra was greeted with enthusiasm but met by no old friends or family, no life-long fans who remembered the band he had led in town four decades before. The fans who did gather were younger, they were white, and they were, every one, a stranger to him. Many belonged to Birmingham's bohemian crowd: long-haired artists, poets, and record-store junkies, Southside radicals and self-proclaimed weirdos. Others had come to the Nick from sheer curiosity, unsure of just what to expect. As the show got underway, a few gasped aloud.

The performance opened with a wild explosion of sound—an onslaught of horns, percussion, and strings—furiously wrought by Sun Ra's band, the Arkestra, billed that night as the Cosmo Jet Set Love Adventure. As the chaos reached a crescendo, Sun Ra strode through the room, eliciting from the crowd rambunctious, intoxicated applause. He was outfitted in a spar-kling silver gown with flowing rainbow sleeves; he wore a bright red goatee and an elaborate homemade headpiece that suggested both ancient Egypt and a science-fiction future; and he moved back and forth dramatically, waving his arms like some kind of mystic conjurer. After the initial barrage of sound, he took his place behind the keyboards and launched into an ec-static, swinging rendition of one of the band's signature tunes, an original anthem called "This World Is Not My Home." The song borrowed its name and central idea from an old gospel standard—"This world is not my home," the old lyrics went, "I'm just a-passing through / My treasures are laid up somewhere beyond the blue"—but it shifted that earlier song's heavenward glance toward the dark infinity of the cosmos. Sun Ra half-crooned, half-chanted the lyrics, his bandmates echoing each phrase behind him. "This world!" he proclaimed,

Is not my home!
My home!
Is someplace else!

Just where that someplace was, Sun Ra made clear—"In outer space!" he shouted—and he invited the Nick's ragtag crowd to go there with him.

Erskine Hawkins and Sun Ra seemed to have come from different worlds entirely. Everything about them—their music, their wardrobes, their worldviews, their fans—suggested the gulf between them. But both were born (or, Sun Ra would say, "arrived") in Birmingham in 1914, both died ("departed") in 1993, and between those bookends their lives were full of intersections and parallels. Both were reared in the band rooms of the city's segregated Black schools, played their first gigs at the same local venues, entertained dancers at the same "society" dances, performed alongside many of the same musicians. Both enrolled after high school in teacher training colleges but abandoned the path of the classroom to make music, leaving Alabama for long careers as bandleaders and maintaining for decades big ensembles of loyal musicians. They would pay tribute to their hometown in landmark compositions—Hawkins with "Tuxedo Junction" and Sun Ra with his sprawling, experimental "The Magic City"—and would allude to the place they had left in other tunes throughout their careers. Late in life, they returned to the city of their youth with increasing frequency: Hawkins made good on his promise to come home each year for his birthday, and Sun Ra's performance at the Nick was only the first of several now-legendary local shows. In the end, both their bodies were laid to rest in Birmingham's Elmwood Cemetery, buried in the same red earth.

Histories of jazz tend to map a predictable geography, one in which a handful of places loom large: New Orleans, Chicago, Kansas City, New York. But since the very beginnings of jazz, local communities of players developed their own variations on the music, their own repertoires, conventions, and traditions, their own homegrown heroes and scenes. For much of the twentieth century, the city of Birmingham was home to one of the music's most essential unsung communities, a thriving network of musicians whose lives helped shape the culture and sound of jazz as we know it. Nurtured in the social institutions of the city's Black middle class, these musicians carved out a distinctive identity, forging an active tradition at home and sending out ripples all over the world.

At the center of it all was the man they called "Fess": John T. "Fess" Whatley, the larger-than-life high school printing instructor and bandleader who retooled the restrictions of the Jim Crow classroom to craft a far-reaching culture of ambition and achievement. Thanks in large part to Whatley, Birmingham's jazz tradition was linked inextricably to the segregated Black schools, whose innovative approach to music instruction churned out a teeming army of professional players. Creatively adapting Booker T. Washington's philosophy of industrial education to the purposes of instrumental music training, Whatley turned his city into a deep wellspring of professional talent, all while promoting an ideology of self-determination and community pride. His rigorous training in reading and arranging music, in instrumental versatility, in professional discipline and personal principle became the basis of a homegrown tradition—and provided vital means to survival and empowerment in an oppressive, often dangerous society.

Music also provided access to the world outside. To make their careers, many local players left home, taking their Birmingham training on the road and into the nation's jazz capitals. Birmingham musicians tended to exert their influence from the margins, behind the scenes, or in the shadows—as sidemen, arrangers, businessmen, mentors, and teachers—and perhaps for these reasons, the city's influence has long been overlooked; but as early as the mid-1920s, a steady stream of homegrown talent had already joined the tide of the larger Great Migration, fanning out across the country in search of opportunity. The city's musicians backed Bessie Smith on stage and on record and helped populate the bands of Duke Ellington, Count Basie, Cab Calloway, Louis Armstrong, Fletcher Henderson, and Billie Holiday. When the country went to war, they took leadership roles in the army, navy, and air force bands that crafted the soundtrack for the cause. Others helped usher in the birth of bop or went on to push the music to its furthest-out, most adventurous extremes.

The musicians carried the city with them everywhere they went: no matter where they traveled, their mutual roots made for a kind of portable community, a permanent sense of family and home reconstituted anyplace two players might meet on the road. Musicians looked out for each other. They helped each other find jobs, make connections, and score places to stay or play. They created a network that stretched across the country.

Others stayed at home. They made music on nights and on weekends while working other jobs, most often as teachers. Many became bandmasters and music directors in local schools, passing their tradition to new generations. They became constants in the city's Black community: they were civic leaders, role models, pillars. Their music would play an essential role in the development of the city's Black community, contributing to a culture of racial and regional pride and helping define Black Birmingham's sense of identity and possibility. Indeed, if Birmingham helped make the world of jazz, so too did jazz help to make Birmingham; without each other, neither the city nor the music would have been the same.

It is not for its music that Birmingham is typically known. In 1963, the city emerged as a central battleground in the country's civil rights struggle, and its image ever since has been locked in time, defined by the events (and iconic black-and-white photographs) of that year. Martin Luther King Jr. penned his famous letter from the Birmingham jail that April, declaring the place "the most thoroughly segregated city" in America. In May, hundreds of schoolchildren marched and sang in the streets, faced down fire hoses and police dogs, and crowded the same city jail past capacity. In September, a Klansman's bomb blew a vicious hole in the Sixteenth Street Baptist Church, killing four young girls. Through a long season of conflict and courage, the Black people of Birmingham would change the course of the nation's history—their protests would lead directly to the passage of the Civil Rights Act, declaring segregation illegal—and, ever since, oppressed people all over the world have looked to the city and its legacy for models of resistance.

But Birmingham's quest for freedom did not spring fully formed from the climactic events of the civil rights era—and a portrait of the city that begins and ends in 1963 obscures not only the much longer path to civil rights but, just as essential, deep local traditions of Black joy, excellence, exuberance, and art. Decades before the modern movement took shape, a vibrant, independent, and forward-looking Black community took root in Birmingham. Its members built a rich web of churches, social clubs, fraternal organizations, and schools; established an active, self-contained commercial and entertainment district; and nurtured tight-knit families and proud residential communities. They advocated for progress, solidarity, and uplift. They threw parties and hosted dances. The city's jazz musicians helped make this world, stylizing and reflecting back to it its own values and ambitions, projecting vital images of Black success in the heart of the segregated South.

During the swing years, especially, musicians set out in their teens and soon returned—sometimes only months later—as heroes, playing the city's ballrooms and stages and fueling the dreams of countless young hometown admirers. With their fresh tuxedoes, their glistening conks and golden horns, their customized tour buses and cross-country radio broadcasts, their names emblazoned on big-city marquees and roll-called in the pages of the country's leading Black papers, these Birmingham celebrities were possibility made manifest, the living embodiments of sophistication, success, and style. They were proof that a Black man could overcome in this world after all, proof the horizon was not so unreachable as it seemed. Sun Ra would in time declare himself an emissary from another universe entirely, proclaiming to the inhabitants of this sad planet that there were greater, freer, stranger worlds than we had ever known down here. But Sun Ra only exaggerated and spun into myth what he had seen musicians do, since his youth, on Birmingham's Fourth Avenue. It was a profound truth he had discovered, early on: that the members of a Black big band were, every one of them, messengers and prophets from other planes of experience.

"Sometimes," Sun Ra liked to say, "music becomes more than music."[3]

Certainly, it had always been that way in Birmingham.

The story that follows reveals a long-neglected but vital music community and, through it, explores key forces and phenomena whose influence on the development of jazz, nationwide, are often overlooked or underplayed. *Magic City* foregrounds the contributions of public educators, society dance orchestras, circus sideshows, musicians' unions, fraternal lodges, southern Black colleges, and street parades. It presents a musical ethos devoted more to discipline than to freedom, a tradition more of communal than individual expression and identity. It is a story that grows from the deepest South and, like so much of American culture, from there branches outward in every direction.

Like a lot of migration stories, this one comes full circle, returning in the end to the place where it started. For much of the twentieth century, Birmingham musicians rode their music into the cities of the North or hit the open road, living on buses or circling the globe; but if some musicians left the South for good, many others had come back home by the century's end, settling down, raising families, passing their music on to young players. This book roughly follows that trajectory. Part 1 examines the contexts, personalities, and places that built a distinctive Birmingham heritage; part 2 follows a few of the bearers of that heritage into the larger world, as they navigate—and help define—the wider culture of jazz; part 3 comes home, as a circle of veteran players seeks to preserve and perpetuate a waning tradition, explicitly promoting their city's music as key to a better Birmingham, one capable of transcending its legacy of racial injustice and division.

Readers should remember that for every Birmingham-bred musician sketched in these pages, dozens more traced their own epic journeys through the dance halls and nightclubs of the country, logging innumerable touring hours and lending their sounds to countless recording and jam sessions. Names that appear here once or twice represent unique legacies of their own; other deserving artists are absent altogether, their stories left for others to tell. A few key players who first appear near the end of this book's chronology—notably Cleve Eaton and Arthur Doyle—deserve much deeper dives, even books of their own. Rather than log an exhaustive, definitive catalog of Birmingham musicians, I have tried to get at the larger community heritage by sketching the careers of a few essential and illuminating personas, fleshing out the contexts in which they lived and made music.

Special attention is due to the Erskine Hawkins Orchestra, a band *full* of Birmingham players, including (besides Hawkins himself) brothers Paul and Dud Bascomb, Haywood Henry, Sammy Lowe, and pianist Avery Parrish, creator of the enduring standard "After Hours." The Birmingham tradition's clearest personifications and ultimate ambassadors, these musicians in their collective, decades-spanning journey offer unique insights into the history of jazz. And while the life and music of Sun Ra—originally Herman Poole "Sonny" Blount—has inspired the detailed attention of scholars and fans, few have reckoned with the ways in which the city of his arrival actively nourished his own musical and philosophical sensibilities, establishing themes he would pursue for the rest of his life. Also overlooked or misunderstood has been the nature of Sun Ra's ongoing, lifelong relationship with the city.

Other key figures are the drummer Jo Jones, a giant of the genre whose rhythms remade the soul and sizzle of swing; his mentor Wilson Driver, a forgotten pioneer of jazz music's earliest days; and bandleader and businessman Teddy Hill, who fostered a new breed of talent and—as longtime manager of Minton's Playhouse in Harlem—set the stage for the bebop revolution. Like so much in the culture of jazz, the tradition begun in Birmingham band rooms was decidedly male, a *brotherhood* (deliberately and exclusively) shaped by interconnected conventions of gender and class. The story of singer Ethel Harper, however, reveals one woman's unrelenting drive—amid controversy, compromise, and challenge—to carve out an independent space in a field dominated by men. There are tragedies here, too, and broken potentials, as the life of bebopper Joe Guy makes clear. But the cliché of the tortured, tragic jazz hero finds little room in these pages; the Birmingham story is one more of adventure than adversity.

I was a stranger to this story when, in the summer of 2008, I first set foot in the Alabama Jazz Hall of Fame, a museum and performing arts center on Birmingham's historic Fourth Avenue North. The tour guide was Dr. Frank "Doc" Adams, one of the last surviving elders of the community tradition and a tireless champion of its history. Born in 1928, Adams had played as a teenager in the Birmingham bands of both Fess Whatley and Sun Ra; after attending Howard University and picking up jobs with Duke Ellington and others, he returned to Birmingham, where he served for decades as a beloved and influential music educator and led his own local band. In 1978 he was inducted to the then-new Alabama Jazz Hall of Fame, for which he later served as executive director and then as director emeritus of education and community outreach. He was, besides all this, a consummate storyteller—warm, engaging, hilarious, and insightful—and thus a natural tour guide. The day we met, Adams walked me (his morning's sole visitor) through two floors of exhibits, unspooling an extraordinary history that he illustrated with personal anecdotes and, on his saxophone, elegant instrumental asides.

A year later, Adams and I sat down with a tape recorder in his office at the hall of fame. I had requested an interview, proposing a magazine article but mostly seeking an excuse to soak some more in his company. That meeting led to another the next week, and another the week after that, then another and another, and by the time we finished eighteen months of weekly interviews, our "article" had become a book, *Doc*, an oral autobiography drawn from our hundreds of pages of transcripts. Even after the book was published, in 2012, we continued to meet almost as often as before, sometimes with the recorder still running (Doc could always find more to tell), sometimes to plot new projects, from school presentations to radio broadcasts to a series of Sun Ra tribute shows. Though the larger Birmingham jazz story had served as a backdrop to the book Doc and I had created, it became clear that there was much more of that story still demanding to be told. Before his death in 2014 at the age of eighty-six, Doc Adams read and offered his notes on some of the earliest, roughest drafts of this book (it was he who insisted this was an "adventure story," above all). In the years since, I have turned frequently to his original voice and vision, his inspiration, insight, and interpretations—and to all those mountains of transcripts and tapes—as I have continued to work my way through this history.

The rest of the world may not have recognized Birmingham's significance as one of the birthplaces of jazz, but the musicians themselves knew they

Dr. Frank "Doc" Adams with his students at the Alabama Jazz Hall of Fame, 2012. Photo courtesy Jessica Latten.

belonged to something big, and a few were determined to set the record straight. *Magic City* is indebted to a few especially dogged preservationists and flame keepers: Frank Adams, my friend and mentor; J. L. Lowe, who developed both the Alabama Jazz Hall of Fame and the Birmingham Heritage Band in an effort to honor the community legacy; his brother, Sammy, trumpeter and arranger for the Erskine Hawkins Orchestra, who set down his life in a thick, unpublished manuscript; Tommy Stewart, a former Bama State Collegian and a passionate chronicler of that group's long history; and Jothan Callins, a son of Tuxedo Junction and cofounder of the Alabama Jazz Hall of Fame, a trumpeter, bassist, educator, and ethnomusicologist whose 1982 dissertation on Birmingham's jazz roots helped preserve a faded past.[4]

Through the efforts of these and other witnesses, we can uncover a secret, century-spanning history of jazz, an untold story of how a single, unlikely community changed the shape, soul, and sound of American music.

It begins with the birth of the city.

PART I

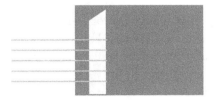

BEGINNINGS

The city of Birmingham seemed to erupt out of nowhere, an industrial boomtown in the depths of the agrarian South. It began as a monument to what was called the *New* South, a region refashioned in the wake of civil war to better meet the needs of the future. To the city's founders, its potential seemed limitless. Jones Valley, where Birmingham was built, was uniquely equipped for the new economy: the region boasted rich deposits of limestone, iron ore, and coal, the three ingredients essential to the making of steel. The arrival in 1870 of two intersecting railroad lines made the spot ripe for development, and a year later, the city incorporated. Migrant laborers, Black and white, arrived to fill the new steel mills and mines. The population swelled. Touting this sudden, remarkable growth, local boosters declared the place the "Magic City."[1]

Central to all this growth was the influx of African Americans from all over the state. In 1870, Birmingham's Jefferson County was home to 2,500 Black residents, roughly 20 percent of the total population. By 1900, the number had shot to 56,917, some 40 percent of the county's inhabitants. Birmingham and the smaller mining and mill communities that grew up around it drew a new class of laborers who exchanged grueling and dangerous work for the lowest possible wages. Years later, Jothan Callins would describe the contributions of Birmingham's Black workers to the city's earliest development: "They wielded axes, sledge hammers, spades, hoes, shucked and husked, loaded and unloaded ships, rowed boats, dug ditches, lined railroad tracks, picked crops, poured steel, and mined the ore." They raised families and put down roots. In the new century they would build their own businesses, banks, social clubs, churches, and schools.[2]

They also made music. Out of Birmingham's Black community emerged a rich tradition of musicianship and, in the century to come, a powerful jazz heritage. In the dance halls and the schools, in stage shows and street parades, Birmingham musicians would help shape the culture of the city. And all over the country, in big bands and nightclubs, over the airwaves and on records, they would help shape the world of jazz.

From the beginning, there was money in Birmingham for hardworking musicians, a living sometimes more substantial than could be eked out of the plants, mills, and mines. The city's earliest musicians, Black and white, found employment in a nightlife culture well known for its lawlessness. On Second Avenue North, around Fifteenth and Sixteenth Streets, was the Scratch Ankle District, home to gambling houses and boardinghouses, crowded bordellos and raucous saloons. A culture of drink, gambling, dance, and sex thrived in places whose names made a poetry of vice: the Rabbit's Foot Saloon, the Slide-Off, the Hole in the Wall, the Bucket of Blood, Bear Mash, Dry Branch, Buzzard's Roost, Pigeon's Roost, the Big Four, the Gambribrus. Segregation did not yet dictate all arenas of social life in Birmingham; Black and white workers intermingled, after their shifts, in many of the city's dives. Music was always in demand. A solo player might pound the piano, strum a guitar, saw a fiddle, or pick the banjo. A cappella vocal groups harmonized on pop songs. There were string bands and brass bands and little combos made up of whatever instruments were available: a cornet and a drum, perhaps, or a mandolin, string bass, and rusted trombone. Musicians played a mix of sounds: marching band staples, parlor songs, country dance tunes, and the earliest blues. Popular by the turn of the century were pianists and combos steeped in the new sensation of ragtime, the syncopated dance sound that prefigured the growth of jazz.[3]

Vaudeville singer and comedian Coot Grant grew up in one of Birmingham's honky-tonks; her father ran the place, and it left its stamp on her memory. "I guess I was kind of smart for my age," she said, "because when I was eight years old—that would be 1901—I had already cut a peephole in the wall so I could watch the dancers in the back room. . . . They did everything," Grant said of her father's customers, recalling the dances of the day: "I remember the Slow Drag, of course, that was very popular—hanging on each other and just barely moving. Then they did the Fanny Bump, Buzzard Lope, Fish Tail, Eagle Rock, Itch, Shimmy, Squat, Grind, Mooche, Funky Butt, and a million others. And I watched and imitated all of them." One dancer stood out in Grant's memory, six decades later: "a tall, powerful woman" named Sue "who worked in the mills pulling coke from a furnace—a man's job. . . .

When Sue arrived at my father's tonk, people would yell 'Here come Big Sue! Do the Funky Butt, Baby!' As soon as she got high and happy, that's what she'd do, pulling up her skirts and grinding her rear end like an alligator crawling up a bank."[4]

Later generations of Birmingham musicians would hone their crafts in venues more refined—by the 1920s the city's jazz scene would be shaped by the genteel soirees of the social elite—but in Birmingham's earliest years, musicians found work where they could. In the late 1880s, the "Magic City" earned a less congratulatory nickname, "Bad Birmingham," and by the turn of the century it could claim a higher murder rate than any American city its size. Local reformers and churches railed against the saloons, where prostitution, crime, and deadly violence flourished. Certainly, the mixing of the races, both socially and sexually, confirmed for many whites the undesirability of the spots. More than once, music was caught up in debates over the city's reform. At least one group of reformers argued, unsuccessfully, for outlawing music in the saloons. Cutting the "social feature" from these places, they hoped, would make them less-appealing destinations: simply abolish entertainment, and the drinking and crime would dry up, too. On one occasion, the Anti-Saloon League held a downtown parade in its push for Prohibition. The leaguers hired a ragtime band for the event, but opponents of Prohibition also showed up with a band of their own, and the two groups squared off in the street, each side doing its best to drown out the other.[5]

The papers failed to record which band outplayed which, the temperance group's or the drinkers'. But the saloons stayed open.

Before the advent of radio or record, music traveled by way of itinerant musicians, mobile performers who picked up songs and styles and scattered them wherever they went. One early wanderer into Birmingham was William Christopher Handy, a native of Florence, Alabama, still in his teens and just beginning a long career in music. His stay in the city was brief, but his activities there resonated for years. The influence ran both ways: W. C. Handy could trace his own interest in the trumpet to a Birmingham player who had passed, a few years before, through Florence, performing with a Baptist choir and inspiring Handy to get his own hands on a horn.[6]

Handy arrived in Birmingham in 1892 with plans of becoming a teacher, but he quickly found he could make more money ($1.85 a day) at a pipe works in the neighboring town of Bessemer. There he started his first brass band, teaching the players to read and play music. After that, "a small string orchestra" approached him, asking him to serve as both music teacher and leader. The gig was a good one. "Folks around Bessemer began calling me Professor," Handy later wrote, "and I began to cut a figure in local society." He charmed the girls, singing and accompanying himself on guitar, and he played trumpet for an area church. "Everything was fine" until the Panic of 1893 slammed local industry: his pay was cut to a daily wage of ninety cents' credit at the pipe works' commissary, his schedule reduced to three days a week. He left the pipe works, returned from Bessemer to Birmingham, exhausted his savings, and "began to walk the streets aimlessly."[7]

He continued to take aspiring musicians under his wing, training them to read music and organizing them into little ensembles. One night in a saloon he overheard a vocal quartet, introduced himself, and offered to teach the singers some arrangements, working up a mix of popular, sentimental, and comic novelty tunes. He printed business cards for the group and set his sights on something big: the World's Columbian Exposition, slated to open in Chicago in the fall of 1892. Handy and his latest act left Birmingham with just "twenty cents in the treasury," hopping trains and singing for their supper at stops along the way; but when they reached Chicago, their plans unraveled. "The Fair," they discovered, "had been postponed for a year." They drifted to St. Louis, but a depression was on and work was scarce. The quartet disbanded.[8]

Handy continued to pursue music however he could—in military brass bands and with a traveling minstrel show; as a solo performer, music instructor, bandleader, and composer. In time he would become the first publisher of original blues compositions, the creator of "The Memphis Blues," "St. Louis Blues," and other standards of American popular music. Eventually he would be touted as a full-fledged musical celebrity, an icon of Black professional success, and the avuncular, near-saintly "Father of the Blues."

Back in Birmingham, it was one of Handy's protégés, a multi-instrumentalist named Ivory Williams, who would pick up where Handy left off, fostering the birth and development of a thriving music scene. Unlike Handy, Williams would not become a star, but his quieter legacy was nonetheless profound. In jazz, nicknames carry a special weight of authority, and "Pops" Williams, grandfather to a unique tradition, could not have been better named.

Jothan Callins called him the "primary perpetuator for the development of jazz in Birmingham," a one-man "vanguard for training and developing young musicians." Pops Williams laid the groundwork for everything that followed. He initiated a system of musical apprenticeship, mentoring younger musicians and helping establish formal music instruction in the

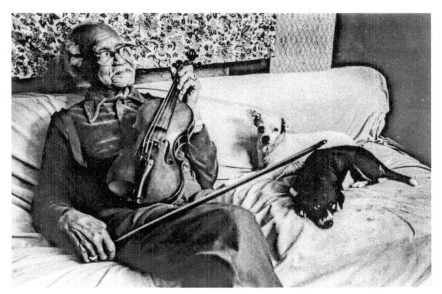

Ivory "Pops" Williams, grandfather of the Birmingham jazz community, pictured late in life, at home with his violin and his dogs. Courtesy the Alabama Jazz Hall of Fame.

schools; he oversaw "the rise in jazz professionalism" in Birmingham, setting standards not only of musicianship but of punctuality, dress, and union membership. He helped build an active network of musicians, one that connected local players to one another and to musicians across the country. Through his wide-ranging travel and his far-flung connections, Williams served as vital link between Birmingham and the rest of the world.[9]

He lived into his second century and in the last decades of his life was revered by many, especially musicians, for his depth of experience and insight. "He was a living history," his friend Frank Adams said, "because he was *there*." For Birmingham musicians reared in the swing years or later, Pops was a link to earlier eras, to the days *before* jazz was born. He toured with circus bands and medicine shows and played Mississippi steamboats and vaudeville tents. In the 1910s and 1920s, he provided violin accompaniment for the silent movies; like a lot of musicians in those days, he lost his job when sound came in, and he took the loss personally, the new technology a betrayal. Though he lived into the 1980s, he refused all his life to go back to the movies.[10]

Pops's specialty was the stringed instruments—he played violin, upright bass, tenor banjo, mandolin, and cello—but he was proficient also on trumpet, trombone, piano, and drums. He played classical music, marches, ragtime, blues, and jazz, and he insisted younger players develop an appreciation not only for brass bands and "hot" music but also for symphonic music and string arrangements. He learned to read music early on and would always be a stickler for the printed score. He was, besides musician, an odd-job man, undertaker, house-painter, and barber—and, Frank Adams recalled, "sort of a bootleg doctor," concocting and prescribing herbal and home remedies for any number of ailments. He had a quick sense of humor, smiled all the time, and called everybody "Hon," male and female alike.

Williams continued making music into his nineties, when finally he hung up his last violin, his hands too unsteady to play. Still, he remained a cherished presence in the community he had helped create. In 1985, director Sandy Jaffe produced a documentary film about the local jazz tradition, *Jazz in the Magic City*, and in it Pops can be seen, ancient but spry, reminiscing over a century of music. As the film ends, a friend, the music teacher George Hudson, leans over Williams's shoulder and shouts into an ear all but deaf, "How old are you, Pops?"

"One hundred," the old man answers. He stretches out his index finger and crooks it into a wriggling hook. "Reaching for another." He speaks in short sentence bursts and cracks a sly grin. "Think I'll make it?"[11]

He made it to May of 1987—just a few months shy of his one hundred and second birthday.

Williams was born around 1885, outside of Tuscaloosa, Alabama.[12] His parents meant for him to be a preacher and sent him to a seminary to study— "but," he later said, "I liked the music better than I did the preaching." His father had had some early training in music but gave it up when he joined the church; a brother briefly fooled with their father's old trumpet, but his interest faded, too, and the instrument found its way to Ivory's more receptive hands.[13]

He spent his childhood between Tuscaloosa County and his grandmother's home in the new city of Birmingham. Details on Williams's family history are scarce, but he cited Native American blood in his veins and proudly remembered his grandmother as a woman of real social standing: she had been a "free Negro" in the days before emancipation, had bought her own property and owned her own home. Birmingham itself was only eight years Ivory's senior, and the city and the boy would grow up together.

Barely a teenager, Williams played "bass fiddle" in a quartet of musicians his age; soon they were joined on cornet by W. C. Handy, who gave them some musical training, helping expand their repertoire and polish their sound. After Handy left Birmingham, he and Williams stayed in touch for decades. Once Handy settled in Memphis, he brought Williams up from time to time to play in his bands—most notably to perform on the luxury steamboats that cruised up and down the Mississippi from Memphis to New Orleans. Through Handy, Williams met Bessie Smith, whom he also considered a friend.[14]

In Birmingham, Williams made music for all sorts of occasions. He learned to play some ragtime piano; he formed a duo with a drummer, George Earl; he led his own combo. On some weekends he might pick up as many as four or five house parties, and the gigs provided steady income. "Anything more than two or three dollars," he said, "was considered good"; a high-paying engagement might bring in as much as ten. City parks offered additional work, and during the holidays—on the Fourth of July and through the Christmas season, especially—the parks brimmed with festivity. "During these times," Williams recalled, "people in the community would donate a hog, goat, or calf to be barbecued. Everyone was invited, Black and white alike, to eat, drink, and have a good time." It was not until the close of the nineteenth century that legal segregation, in Birmingham and across the South, began officially to restrict the mingling of the races. The city's first park opened in 1874 and others quickly followed, all of them providing recreation for anyone who wanted it. Two decades passed before the city, in an effort to keep the most popular neighborhoods exclusively white, began to designate separate "Negro parks," all of them positioned outside the city limits. Under the new social order, green spaces like the Colored Attraction Park (nicknamed "Traction Park") would develop into crucial sites for Black recreation, music making, and community building.[15]

It was not just the parks: segregation would soon pervade all aspects of life. In 1896, *Plessy v. Ferguson* made Jim Crow the law of the land. Alabama's new constitution, adopted in 1901 and explicitly designed to maintain white supremacy, further entrenched segregation into the culture of the state. Both by custom and by law, Black and white would create separate, parallel worlds.

Williams spent much of his early life on the road, chasing the music wherever there was work. With one foot always planted in Birmingham, he connected his city's growing music scene to the latest developments from outside, importing new sounds, tunes, and ideas each time he came home. He spent a season in New Orleans, covered the Midwest in tent shows, toured across Texas and Arizona, trekked all the way San Francisco, even sailed to Honolulu. In later years, he described how, on the night of his own wedding, he left Birmingham—and his new bride, "Miss Ida"—with a road show and did not come back for a good two years. When he finally returned, Ida was waiting, furious, in the home they had never shared. After that, he said, he stayed put.[16]

A highlight of Williams's travels was his work with P. G. Lowery, a bandleader whose influence on American popular music, though mostly forgotten today, was enormous. Born in Kansas, Lowery by the mid-1890s had built his reputation as a cornet player like no other; in his own youth, W. C. Handy confessed, "My great ambition was to outplay P. G." Lowery reveled in his prowess: in 1896 he declared himself "the greatest colored cornet soloist on earth" and publicly issued a "Challenge to the World," inviting into competition any players who thought they had him beat. In 1899 he began his long association with the circuses, and until his death in 1942 he worked with the biggest names in the business—Sells and Forepaugh, Wallace and Hagenbeck, Barnum and Bailey, Ringling Brothers—playing the segregated sideshow annex tents that soon outdrew their white counterparts. Lowery's bands mingled operatic overtures with military marches and popular tunes, but ragtime and eventually jazz were the heart of the Lowery repertoire. An expert and untiring entrepreneur ("Good Things Cometh to He Who Waiteth," he advised, "so Long as He Hustleth while He Waiteth"), Lowery published in the Black press not only updates on his own band but also musical criticism, bits of instrumental pedagogy, and encouragements to hopeful musicians. As his band rolled through the country it left in its wake a multitude of converts, young Black spectators whose worlds expanded as they witnessed the band in action. Wherever Lowery played, it seemed, new players remapped their horizons.[17]

Ivory Williams joined the Lowery group around 1903, playing tenor banjo, mandolin, and trombone with the band for a decade. At a stop in Des Moines, the team picked up a trumpeter with whom Williams struck a close friendship: Sam Foster, a Georgia native whose ability to hit the high notes had earned him the nickname "High C." Louis Armstrong would make such feats a hallmark of his own performances in the 1920s, inspiring a generation of followers; but in the first years of the twentieth century, few players were reaching so high with their horns, and the high C—as performed by both Lowery and Foster—was an exhilarating stunt.[18]

Williams and Foster hit it off right away, and when they grew weary of the road, Williams proposed a solution: he had a home and connections in Birmingham, where there was always plenty of work. Soon the two friends and their music were constants in the city's late-night drinking and dance spots, and—on Williams's recommendation—Carrie Ann Tuggle, founder and president of Birmingham's Tuggle Institute, hired Foster as her school's first band instructor. In time, the city's Black schools would become the indispensable training grounds for generations of musicians, the first and most influential nurturers of a unique jazz community. Foster's arrival at Tuggle marked the start of the tradition, the beginning of instrumental music training in Black Birmingham schools. More famous in the history of jazz is the Waif's Home in New Orleans, where a young Louis Armstrong learned to play cornet, or the Jenkins Orphanage in Charleston, South Carolina, remembered today as feeder for some of the nation's top bands; paralleling those histories, and deserving an equal reputation of its own, Tuggle Institute would become an important early incubator of jazz. And in the Tuggle band room, John Whatley, a protégé of both Foster and Williams, would pick up and play his first horn.[19]

From these beginnings an entire culture would spring.

AN INDUSTRIAL EDUCATION

John T. "Fess" Whatley became a musician by accident, in the crawlspace beneath his family's home. Rooting around below the floorboards as a boy, he came across an old loose spring; he plucked it, and it gave out a twang. He stretched the wire and released it, bent it back and let it go again—and found himself, there in the dark under the house, letting loose a series of notes. That little bit of cast-off, coiled wire, he would later say, was his introduction to music.[1]

All of Whatley's earliest instruments were homemade, improvised, and imaginative: expanding from his discovery of the spring, he fashioned a guitar from a wooden cigar box and some wire. Soon he was blowing his first solos through the hollowed-out cow horn his father used to call his hunting dogs. If the possibilities of musical sound ignited John Whatley's imagination, his fate was sealed when the circus came to town, bringing with it P. G. Lowery and his celebrated team of musicians. Whatley was entranced by Lowery's virtuosity, his piercing high notes, and his personal showmanship; but equally impressive was his greater role as bandmaster, his ability to direct an entire unit of top-notch musicians, corralling this great assemblage of players into a single, cohesive whole. When the circus left town, the boy organized the neighborhood kids into his own little ensemble and led them around the block in a ragged and raucous parade. Young Whatley marched out front, blowing into that hunting horn his best impression of Lowery.[2]

It was in that moment that the bandleader was born.

In 1966, writer Bertrand Demeusy published in the British magazine *Jazz Monthly* the first detailed profile of Fess Whatley, a figure Demeusy championed as one of jazz music's great unsung heroes. The recognition was a long time coming: Whatley had recently retired from nearly half a century in the classroom, and over the course of his career he had molded legions of musicians, establishing a unique Birmingham tradition and sending out into the world a rich diaspora of homegrown talent. "It is difficult," Demeusy observed, "to think of any major band that at one time or another has not had a former pupil of Mr. Whatley among its members." And yet, he marveled, Birmingham's "Maker of Musicians" had been thoroughly neglected by historians, his name unknown to jazz fans, a group well known for their obsessive poring over the names and minutiae of the music. Maybe the neglect lay in the fact that Whatley never recorded, leaving no artifacts for future audiophiles to cherish—or in the fact that he never migrated, himself, out of his native South and into the nation's jazz centers, preferring instead to work his influence from the schoolrooms and society dances of Birmingham. In a way, Whatley was not alone in this neglect: even today, more than fifty years since Demeusy's tribute to Fess, historians have never fully reckoned with the influential role played by Black music teachers in shaping the development of jazz.[3]

In Black communities across the Southeast, however, Fess Whatley had been a legendary figure for years, and jazz musicians all over the country—bandleaders, especially—had certainly known his name. In 1934 the *Chicago Defender* had declared him "one of the most outstanding band teachers in the country." By then, he had already "turned out scores of excellent musicians who have made their way into many of the country's leading orchestras." The bandleader's protégés were ubiquitous: "In the East, West and South, wherever you go, you can find musicians who are musicians because of Fess Whatley." In the 1980s, Dizzy Gillespie reminisced with writer Albert Murray about the reputation Whatley once held among Black musicians: "Everybody was talking about him," Dizzy said.[4]

The Whatley reputation was so highly regarded, musicians claimed, the Whatley product so consistent, that bandleaders were said to hire Birmingham players on the spot, often even without audition. "Wherever they went," Fess himself bragged of his players, "they went to play—not to try out." Writing to Demeusy in the 1960s, he explained the source of his and his players' reputations: "My boys all was given a real foundation in music and when they left me to join other orchestras or bands they did not have to pass tests or examinations. All they had to say: 'I am from Fess Whatley.' This was even true during the war when the boys were drafted or volunteered, the Navy, Army and Air Force accepted my boys without any test. When they were asked where they were from, if they said from Birmingham, then

[they] were asked who taught them, all they had to say was Fess Whatley. They were told to: pass on!"[5]

"Fess" was short for "Professor," an informal designation bestowed in southern Black schools on the most respected of educators. Once you were Whatley's student, they said, you were his student for life. A 1941 article in Birmingham's *Weekly Review* illustrated the point, reporting that Whatley had just returned from a monthlong summer road trip, covering more than 7,000 miles "in his brand new 1941 Cadillac" and visiting former students "in every port" along the way: St. Louis, Denver, Boise, Seattle, San Francisco, Los Angeles, Phoenix, Abilene, Dallas, Fort Worth, Shreveport, Jackson. Fess was said to chastise grown men, years after they had left high school, for behavior he considered beneath them, going so far as to show up at their doorsteps in some city halfway across the country. By the same token, he sent money to former students in need, and he discreetly helped pay the college tuition of students unable to foot their own bills. His students returned the generosity: anytime Fess visited New York, they gave him tickets to Broadway shows—Whatley players were fixtures in Broadway's pits—and awarded him VIP treatment at their most prestigious gigs. They sent him postcards from their travels and flooded his mailbox each year on his birthday.[6]

Whatley cut a striking presence. Tall and lean, he dressed sharp and stood erect, walked with purpose, and spoke with an authority challenged by none. He was famous for those Cadillacs: he always owned two or three at a time—each year he traded in an old one for the latest model—and he kept each of them spotless and shining. In his younger years, he could be seen driving down Fourth Avenue, a pet poodle perched in his lap; later, he hired a "lady chauffeur" to get him around. At school he roamed the hallways with a fraternity paddle or ruler, and he snapped it across the knuckles or bottom of any student who spoke out of line, dressed out of code, or blew his horn out of tune or time. Everything with Whatley came down to time; he even walked, students said, with the built-in timing of a human metronome. He was a first-rate musician in his own right, too, pouring out of his trumpet a crisp, clear sound the locals called the "Whatley tone." In addition to directing the student band, he led Birmingham's first jazz orchestra, the Jazz Demons, and for more than thirty years that group and his later ensembles dominated Birmingham's elite social functions, Black and white alike.[7]

Certain extraordinary teachers—the most beloved, the most eccentric, the most feared—have always made for good stories, and Whatley's own classroom helped forge not only a musical tradition but a kind of tale-telling tradition on the side. Entering freshmen heard Whatley stories before they set foot in his classroom; veteran musicians swapped and embroidered well-worn favorites long after their graduation. As his influence spread and legend grew, Whatley became de facto dean for Black orchestras across the state. Sometime in the 1920s, a group of musicians in Gadsden, Alabama, decided to start their own community orchestra, the first of its kind in their town. They hired Fess Whatley to drive up once a month from Birmingham and help develop the band. Trumpeter Tommy Stewart, grandson of one of the original players, loved retelling his grandfather's story of the band's first practice: Whatley walked in and announced, "I want to hear some *music*. I don't want any mistakes"—and, Stewart said, "*pulled out his .45*," which he kept visible on a table all through the rehearsal. "He carried a .45 with him all the time," Stewart added, laughing. "Never shot nobody, but he always kept everybody intimidated."[8]

The stories and their superlatives might be dismissed as pure hyperbole were not the realities themselves—the man's outsize personality, wide-reaching influence, exacting standards, and furious temper—so truly extraordinary. He was an icon in Birmingham by the time he turned thirty, a civic leader and homegrown celebrity—and a source of nerve-racking anxiety for the students subject to his ferocious brand of discipline. An image that recurs in story after story from his students is this: A roomful of musicians is practicing in the band room, unobserved, they think, by Fess, who also taught printing in the workshop immediately downstairs. Suddenly Whatley appears in the door; from the room underneath he has heard a wrong note, or he has heard a student getting creative and deviating from the printed score. Whatley, students claimed, had his ears tuned at all times to the band, could recognize each student's instrument from the floor below, and would listen intently even as he oversaw his printing class downstairs. Without warning he would emerge, his punishment swift and exact: a printing mallet would fly through the air, straight at the offending student.[9]

Whatley's aim, they said—just like his ear—was dead-on, every time.

John Lewis Whatley—the middle initial *T* came later—was born in Tuscaloosa County around 1895, son to Samuel and Lucy Whatley and one of seven siblings. When he was twelve, his parents sent him some sixty miles east to Birmingham, where they had friends who could give him a leg up in the world. One of these was Carrie Ann Tuggle: an educator, social reformer, philanthropist, and newspaper editor (she ran the weekly *Birmingham Truth* from 1902 to 1910) widely revered as guardian angel to Birmingham's neediest Black youth. In 1901, Tuggle convinced the courts to give her custody of a young boy, orphaned and homeless, who had been sentenced to ten days in jail; before long, she was taking in additional outcasts. Seeking to give a home, education, and moral foundation to Black youth with no place to go—the motherless, the fatherless, the destitute, and those who had had trouble with the law—Tuggle garnered financial support from Black women's groups and fraternal organizations, as well as a base of white supporters. Her Tuggle Institute formally opened in 1903 and for close to three decades provided its pupils a balance of academic, industrial, and religious training, advocating middle-class values, Christian virtues, and a strict sense of personal and civic responsibility. The *Birmingham News* dubbed the school's founder the "female Booker T. Washington." Her students called her "Granny Tuggle."[10]

For her board of trustees, Tuggle recruited women from two statewide secret societies she oversaw, the Independent Order of Calanthe and the Knights and Ladies of Honor of Alabama. John Whatley's mother, Lucy, was a friend of Tuggle's, a Lady of Honor, and a board member; a firm believer in the school's mission, she arranged for John to enroll. Another family friend was Ivory Williams, who offered to keep an eye on the boy—and, through this mentorship, Pops Williams again would prove essential to the creation of the city's jazz culture. With the older musician as his guide, John Whatley discovered a world of music that captivated his imagination and ignited his passion, pushing him further along the path begun under his parents' home. For his formal training, Whatley received instruction from "High C" Foster, who handed him a cornet and taught him to read music. Meanwhile, Whatley picked up another sort of education in the downtown venues where Williams and Foster performed at night. "I wanted to introduce Whatley to the orchestra business," Williams said, so "I used to slip him out of the Tuggle Institute dormitory and have him perform with my band." Afterward, Williams would bring his charge back to campus, sneaking him through a window back into the locked dormitory. When Carrie Tuggle found out what was going on, she threatened to have Williams arrested, and, Williams said, she resented him for the rest of her life.[11]

Whatley would grow into the strictest of disciplinarians, but as a student he was willing to bend the rules or put off his studies to immerse himself in music. P. G. Lowery's circus band remained an essential inspiration and its own education. "I didn't go to school at all when the circus was in town," Whatley later confessed. "I hid my books somewhere and followed the band all day."[12]

Barely a teenager, Whatley befriended the young Arthur George (A. G.) Gaston, another Tuggle student who in time became Alabama's leading Black entrepreneur, a multimillionaire and behind-the-scenes patron of the civil rights movement. In those early days Gaston was a drummer in the Tuggle band, and he and Whatley were both favorites of "Granny." One night the band played a Knights of Pythias convention, and Tuggle introduced her players to the audience, heaping on them her characteristic praise. Gaston, she predicted, was "going to be a great man" and Whatley "a great musician." Young Whatley, Gaston recalled in his memoir, "stood grinning at the audience with his cornet stuck under his arm. He had a lip and he could blow." When the music began, Whatley "threw his cornet to his mouth and blasted out the first bars of 'The Saints Come Marching In.' We all picked it up," wrote Gaston, "and I admired the flash of my cymbals under the hot spotlight. The muscles in John's neck stood out as he hit a high one." Half a century later, A. G. Gaston still basked in the thrill of this and similar memories: the invigorating heat of the spotlight, the public acclaim bestowed on the boys by their "Granny," and, always, the exhilarating "blare of the band."[13]

In more ways than one, the year 1913 marked Whatley's sudden entry into adulthood: in a few months' time, he graduated from high school, started his long professional career, and married his sweetheart, Alice Foster, who would be his wife for more than half a century. Carrie Tuggle kept Whatley on at the school, hiring him to teach printing and assist Foster with the music program. For the next four years, Whatley toured the state with the school band, expanding the institute's reputation and, in the process, his own. Upgrading from the cornet he played as a student, he sold scrap metal to buy his first trumpet. He worked sometimes without pay, conscious of the debt he owed the school. All his life he would express his gratitude to the Tuggles—to Granny and her husband, John—and to the institute itself. Before he was twenty, John Lewis Whatley changed his middle name in tribute to his adoptive family: for the rest of his life, he was John *Tuggle* Whatley, and he never omitted the new initial from his name.[14]

In later years, Fess would say his early road had been a rough one. He remembered, as a schoolboy, covering the holes in his shoes with paper and making do with only one set of clothes: one night he would sleep in his underwear while his shirt and pants dried on the line; the next night he would wash the underwear and sleep in his clothes. At Tuggle he had made a late-night, prayerful deal with God, that "if He would help me learn . . . I would do all I could, when I grew up, to help and give to others."[15]

Near the end of his life, Fess Whatley packed a thick scrapbook with photos and bios of his many successful students, tracking their progress through the world of music. Their lives meant everything to him. They were the proof that he had kept that promise to God.

The site of Whatley's greatest influence was Birmingham's Industrial High School (renamed A. H. Parker High School, after its founding principal, in 1939). For nearly forty years, Whatley served as the school's printing instructor and unofficial band director, a central figure in shaping not only the music but the culture and reputation of the school. For many students and alums, Fess Whatley and the "spirit" of Industrial were synonymous.

The seeds for the school had been planted in 1899, when members of Birmingham's Black community drafted a petition, appealing to the board of education for the establishment of a public high school for Black students. Spearheading the campaign were William Pettiford, president of the first Black-owned bank in Birmingham, and Hattie Hudson, one of the bank's employees. With the school board's cooperation, Negro High School opened its doors in the fall of 1900, operating out of a single room on the second floor of a Black elementary school. Arthur Harold Parker, a transplant to Birmingham from Ohio and the son of former slaves, served as the school's principal and sole instructor.[16]

Enrollment began with eighteen students and by the end of the year had grown to forty-five. In its early years the school relocated frequently in search of adequate facilities, moving five times in two decades before the construction of a permanent home on Eighth Avenue North, where Parker High remains today. Hailed as "the world's largest high school for Negroes," Industrial brought Black families to Birmingham from across Alabama. By the start of the 1940s, as Birmingham's jazz culture reached its pinnacle, nearly 4,000 students were in attendance.

The name change, a few years after its founding, from "Negro" to "Industrial" reflected the school's central purpose and the thrust of its curriculum. Like other southern Black schools, Industrial High was rooted in the educational philosophy of Booker T. Washington, who famously championed a "practical" training for Black students: to prepare graduates for the kinds of manual, menial jobs society would most likely afford them, industrial schools taught pupils to work with their hands. Claiming Washington as his "patron saint," Parker insisted that "our boys and girls should be taught in the schools how to do thoroughly and well the everyday duties that they find right around them"—casting down their buckets where they were, as Washington had put it, and training to undertake what the school board called "the work of life." Each student received, in addition to the usual core studies, intensive instruction in a single selected field. Boys could specialize in such areas as shoe repair, automotive repair, printing, carpentry, or tailoring; girls might study cooking, sewing, millinery, nursing, or cosmetics. The goal was to balance academic learning with the practical work of a trade.

Industrial High School shoe shop and cooking class, c. 1930. Fess Whatley's innovation was to introduce music, like shoe repair or cooking, as an industrial trade. Courtesy Birmingham, Ala. Public Library Archives.

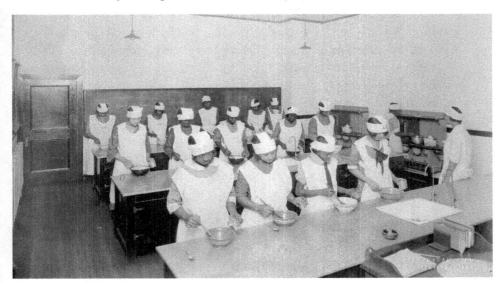

"It makes no difference who they are," Parker told a white reporter; "when they enter high school they know that they're going to have to work with brooms as well as books."[17]

For all its emphasis on "industrial arts," the school boasted a unique agenda of academic training and cultural development. Teachers found creative ways to merge academic and industrial studies: in a chemistry class students devised a hair straightener and shampoo for the girls to use in their cosmetics courses. Meanwhile, students received instruction in citizenship and Black history and produced a first-rate school newspaper. There were 4-H and science clubs and programs in oratory, drama, and debate. Students attended chapel services and each morning gathered for assemblies in which their peers, faculty, or visiting guests presented on a range of civic-minded themes. Each homeroom featured its own student government in miniature: homerooms elected their own presidents, who collaborated to address student concerns. The school maintained community garden plots around the city, and students delivered the harvest to families in need.[18]

A major source of pride for the school was its music, which served as running complement to, and relief from, the demands of industrial labor. Students began their mornings by singing in the campus chapel, and each aspect of the day's work, one white reporter observed, seemed "touched with the tempo of that chapel singing." The school's administration was "doing a wondering work," the writer continued, "exploiting the deep harmonies of their race to make rhythm of routine." This reputation for vocal music began as early as 1903, when Ms. Orlean Kennedy directed the first annual student musical showcase, an event that became a favorite public tradition. When reporters from the *Birmingham News* visited the school that year, they swooned over performances of "old plantation songs," which the students performed alongside a repertoire of "popular and up-to-date selections." "The singing of 'Old Folks at Home' by upward of 65 voices was superb," one writer gushed, adding, "What the Negro High School needs more than anything else are larger quarters and better equipment."[19]

School leaders recognized a correlation between the singing program and the support of white benefactors; calls like this one for greater resources were often linked explicitly to descriptions of the students' singing. Musical performances offered an effective tool for fundraising, especially among white patrons who found a seductive romance in the students' repertoire of "plantation melodies," harmonized spirituals performed alongside sentimental southern airs and Stephen Foster chestnuts. As early as 1871, Fisk University in Nashville had discovered the fundraising potential of the spirituals: the Fisk Jubilee Singers had helped save their school from bankruptcy, touring the country and raising money with their formal arrangements of the songs, preserved and adapted from slavery. Just as Fisk had been saved by its singers, so could Industrial High harness the artistry and emotional pull of its own singing students to generate support for its other programs, capitalizing on the inherent appeal of "Old South" themes to wealthy white donors. "You will get an instructor of orchestra on one condition," Superintendent John Herbert Phillips told the graduating class of 1914, "and that is that you will always sing these old songs."[20]

For Black students, teachers, and community members, the "old songs" served a different purpose, appealing for other reasons. What the songs evoked was not a nostalgia for earlier times but a pride in Black history, identity, and beauty, a continuity with the long quest for freedom. The songs also offered a form of community expression and bonding. Malachi Wilkerson, a carpentry teacher and singing instructor, served on Industrial's faculty from 1911 to 1934, and as the student body expanded to more than 3,000 he organized the swelling group into a single choir of harmonized voices. At daily assemblies, students sat according to their vocal parts, and Wilkerson (who never needed a pitch pipe, his admirers bragged) directed each part from the stage.[21]

The performances attracted an impressive stream of visitors. President Teddy Roosevelt, education pioneer Mary McLeod Bethune, social reformer Jacob Riis, and opera singer Lawrence Tibbett each came to Industrial in the first decades of the twentieth century, and each was greeted with song. After witnessing more than 2,500 students singing "It's Me, O Lord," and four other spiritual songs, Tibbett, in tears, proclaimed the moment one of the most emotional experiences of his life. For years to come, students proudly recounted Tibbett's remarks, as well as those by Eleanor Roosevelt, who visited in 1937 (the singing was by then under the direction of Wilkerson's successor, Harold White McCoo) and remarked that she had never heard anything like the performance. "Music," the First Lady promised students, "is one of the things which will help to smooth the way for all of you."[22]

One student singer, Ernestine Diffay, shared at 1914's commencement exercises her own appreciation of the music program, citing the many famous guests who had enjoyed the students' songs. But, Diffay insisted, "Honored as we feel by the plaudits of these distinguished people, we prize our melodies for a deeper reason. They are part of our life and history as a race and our contribution to the world of music. They are evidences of our power to create a music of our own, based on our experiences and reflecting our ideals." Diffay noted that the school's singing program had fostered a musical culture beyond Industrial's doors, filling the choirs of Birmingham churches with well-trained student harmonizers. But if the school found a source of racial identity and community pride in the singing of spirituals, other sounds were less welcome. "Our school has made a constant fight," Diffay continued, "against ragtime music and the suggestive and oftimes openly coarse popular song. No such music is permitted at any time or on any program." The attitude reflected the school's emphasis on polite and refined cultural values, a desire to stand above the cheap, unbecoming, tawdry, or crass—a tendency that would also shape the school's complicated, often contradictory relationship with jazz.[23]

What was missing, for now, was an instrumental music program. Already the faculty had begun, piece by piece, to build a collection of instruments, in hopes of starting a band. "We have been trying hard for three years to build up an orchestra," the student newspaper observed in 1916, but one problem remained. "We have the instruments, we have the boys and girls, but we need a teacher."[24]

John T. Whatley, fresh from Tuggle, joined Industrial's faculty in 1917, all of twenty-one years old. He would remain there until his retirement in 1956. Officially Fess taught printing—but, his students liked to say, he "bootlegged" band into the school in the process. "He did it illegitimately and illegally," one former student, J. L. Lowe, explained, "and without the professed approval of the board of education." Initially Whatley taught the band before and after school and on weekends, building the program without compromising his obligations as printing instructor. Once the band had proven its success, practice was added to the school day, and a band teacher, George Hudson, was hired. Even with Hudson's arrival and lengthy tenure at the school, Whatley closely oversaw the band's activities and remained the public face of the program.[25]

Whatley's first task was to build on the school's collection of instruments. As the program got started, he dedicated a portion of his salary toward the purchase of used instruments for the band. Principal Parker required each class to raise ten dollars for instruments, and students sold peanuts to contribute to the cause. Meanwhile, Whatley appealed to white benefactors like Williams Music House, which donated cast-off horns in various degrees of disrepair, instruments that Pops Williams helped mend for student use. As was so often the case in the history of southern Black schools, the resources provided were hand-me-downs and rejects from the white community, but from those discards Fess Whatley built his empire. After five months of practice, the band gave its first public performance. By the end of Whatley's first year on the job, the school had built an outdoor bandstand from which

Industrial High School band, c. 1917. Fess Whatley stands in center at back.
Courtesy Birmingham, Ala. Public Library Archives.

the orchestra offered Sunday afternoon concerts and "Community Sings,"
whenever the weather permitted.[26]

The Sings showcased a variety of vocal and instrumental soloists, rec-
itations of poetry and oratory, and performances by local orchestras and
gospel quartets. Providing a stage for Black Birmingham's achievements
and arts, the events became an important venue for community expression
and pride. Oscar Adams, editor of the city's leading Black newspaper, the
Birmingham Reporter, championed the sings as soon as they were introduced
in the spring of 1918, declaring them "an innovation that is elevating, inspiring, educative, entertaining. The crowds that have thronged the campus
and street in front of the school for the past two Sundays attest to the popularity of this new feature. It shows too that our people really appreciate a
community sing of their own, where they do not have to be 'jim-crowed.'"
The sings presented an affirming alternative to the demeaning dominant
culture. When Malachi Wilkerson directed the huge, generation-spanning

crowds in a harmonized spiritual, just as he did the students in assembly, the effect was a powerful enactment of community itself. "The Community Sing," said J. L. Lowe, "contributed a lot so far as culture was concerned. It became a showcase for orchestras in the city," most notably Whatley's own inspiring ensemble. "Everybody loved to hear the band," Lowe continued, speaking to writer Carolyn Marzette-Bolivar in the 1990s. "I don't think we'll ever reach a point where a type of music will be as popular and at the same time promote culture as Fess Whatley's did. We have popular bands now that are, in many instances, doing little to promote culture. . . . That wasn't true of Whatley's band." This emphasis on "promoting culture" reflects what would become, through Whatley's example, an essential theme in the Birmingham jazz tradition: through their public personas and performance, Black Birmingham musicians would reflect and instill in the community a set of values that transcended the musical. The bands were models of self-respect, sophistication, and style. They were expressions of unity, reflections of Black self-sufficiency. For Lowe and other products of the Whatley era, later musical forms paled in comparison: if music was *only* music, if it did not serve to uplift and affirm, it missed its essential purpose.[27]

At Tuggle Institute, High C Foster had introduced instrumental music instruction to Birmingham's Black schools; Fess Whatley expanded that instruction into a homegrown cultural movement. What made Whatley's work at Industrial so widely influential was the revolutionary approach to the philosophy and requirements of "industrial education" he pioneered: with Principal A. H. Parker's encouragement, Whatley advocated for band as one of the industrial disciplines. Like auto or shoe repair—like sewing, cooking, and hat making—*band*, Whatley argued, was a manual discipline; a trade, like any other, to be plied with one's hands; a practical, technical skill that with the proper training could ensure successful employment after graduation. Students enrolling in the school's band program were signing up for no extracurricular "add on," no mere elective or after-school hobby. They were learning to make a living, building the skills for their very survival.

For members of the band, a full third of the school day was spent in practice, the same intensive "time on task" other students might devote to printing or carpentry. But for the band there were the before- and after-school practices, too, as well as school assemblies, parades, and evening and weekend dances. Musicians went to their own proms without dates and watched the dancing from the bandstand. But the extra commitment was worth it: if you belonged to the band, students felt, you were somebody.

Remarkably, as the Whatley revolution made clear, the very restrictions of segregated, industrial education—a system designed to reinforce the social structure, perpetuating Black subservience—could be refigured as a means to empowerment and opportunity. Whatley's training generated an era of musicians who would shape the course of jazz history; but the same training did more, even, than that. Whatley passed on to his students strategies of community affirmation and individual agency, tools for ensuring their livelihoods and their manhood.

Frank Adams, a budding saxophonist, came to Industrial and Whatley in 1941. The city's schools were separate and fundamentally unequal; but, Adams would say, "sometimes something that's not the way it *should* be can work to your advantage. If it had been equal, I wouldn't have learned as much about music as I did. I wouldn't have had the opportunity! Those were times when certain people would say, 'My goodness. I'm going down in the mines and digging coal, and this guy's going to New York City—playing a doggone horn!'" It is a piece of historical wisdom that would often be repeated by musicians of the Whatley era: that through much of the twentieth century, if you were Black in Birmingham and aspired to middle-class status—if you hoped for a life outside the mines and mills—you had only a couple of options. You could be a teacher or a preacher.[28]

Or, thanks to Fess Whatley, you could blow a horn.

MAKER OF MUSICIANS

Almost immediately, Fess Whatley's student band became a fixture in Birmingham's Black community. Its musicians were on display at school assemblies and student variety shows; they marched in civic parades and provided backdrop to the luncheons and teas of elite women's clubs. When Black soldiers left for the First World War—and, again, when the survivors came home—Fess's players marched with them in the streets. Some gigs became reliable, anticipated rituals. Each year on January first, the band played an Emancipation Day program of speeches and performances devoted to Black history and achievement. And a new school year really had not begun, students maintained, until the band's annual end-of-summer matinee dance. During the Christmas season, the band worked tirelessly, playing as many as three or four engagements in a day.

Like the singing student body, Whatley's band entertained whatever dignitaries or celebrities came to town. In 1921, on the occasion of the city's semicentennial, students played for President Warren G. Harding, who shocked the crowd of 40,000 citizens—white and Black, in segregated seating—when he called for equal educational and economic opportunities, along with equal access to the vote, across racial lines. "Whether you like it or not," the president told Birmingham, "unless our democracy is a lie, you must stand for that equality." White spectators sat in stony silence, as the Black section erupted with applause. Band members dared not break their stillness, but for decades they would brag that they had been there, that they had played for that historic occasion.[1]

Other visitors were no less notable. Whatley's own childhood hero, P. G. Lowery, arrived a year after Harding, and Whatley played the role of

John T. "Fess" Whatley, Birmingham's "Maker of Musicians."
Courtesy Birmingham, Ala. Public Library Archives.

beaming host: his Cadillacs shuttled Lowery and his men all over the city, and his wife, Alice, served them a feast in the Whatley home. After a performance by the Industrial band, Lowery presented students with one of his own handwritten charts to play at their future engagements; later he hired one of Whatley's star pupils, Calvin Ivory, for his band (Ivory would return to Birmingham as an assistant band teacher). Fess was building connections with the nation's top Black bandleaders, and he brought heroes from the ranks of entertainment royalty to the school. W. C. Handy had left Birmingham in 1892 with next to nothing in his pockets; Whatley brought him back now, a full-fledged celebrity, the world-renowned "Father of the Blues," and students honored him with a performance of his most famous composition, the "St. Louis Blues." What other bands in the country could say they had done *that*?[2]

Bandleaders across the country came quickly to know the distinct Birmingham brand that issued from the school. Whatley musicians could read and play any printed music on sight; many could also write and arrange. They were versatile, proficient on more than one instrument, and fluent in the widest range of styles. They were professional, punctual, disciplined, and sober. They knew how to dress, and they kept their union memberships up to date. They were, in short, consistent, dependable products of Birmingham industry.

Membership in Fess's band was a sacred honor, and the group's tuxedo uniforms symbolized it all. Fess "reminded everybody that they were supposed to be in uniform at all times," said singer Jesse Champion. "And along with the uniforms came your personality as to what you were supposed to be about, and how you were supposed to carry yourself." "He taught us the meaning of sacrifice and he set the example for us," added trumpeter Frank Greer. "In fact, he taught us a way of life. He gave us a sense of respectability and achievement." From Whatley, Greer learned the pride of owning one's own horn. Since Greer could not afford an instrument, Whatley helped him secure his first jobs, busing tables and delivering newspapers, until he could buy his first trumpet.[3]

Whatley's training encompassed its own code of conduct and its own way of moving through the world. Fess preached what he called the "Golden Dozen Traits of Character," a list his students committed to memory: love of God, humility, self-esteem, self-respect, self-reliance, ambition, integrity, cooperation, love of the beautiful, respect for others, responsibility, thrift. Whatley required more than lip service to these traits; each was an imperative for living, not only a key to one's character but a key, too, to surviving—even thriving—in a world that seemed bent on holding a Black man back. These traits defined students' personas, shaped their reputations, seeped through their every interaction. Musicians knew to address every man they met, regardless of race or age, as "mister" and "sir" and every woman as "ma'am." The rule was about more than manners: it was a means of navigating the waters of race in the South, where each Black person addressed each white person with a title or else risked the consequences. By calling everyone "sir" or "ma'am," students granted everyone, Black or white, the same respect; it was a way of holding on to their own dignity, of refusing to give whites special treatment just for the sake of their whiteness. Such formal address may have suggested deference to those who demanded it, but Whatley—a master of nuance in matters of race—was adept at investing prevailing conventions with their own, secret forms of empowerment. Moreover, if Fess addressed his pupils themselves as "Mister"—"Mr. Ivory," "Mr. Champion," "Mr. Greer"—it did more than "sort of needle them," as one student put it: it acknowledged in them a social power and prestige they could proudly own, no matter who else might try to deny it.[4]

To enforce his standards Whatley relied on a system of fines, intimidation, and physical upbraiding. His corporal reprimands were legendary. In the band room, he would count off a tune, said saxophonist Amos Gordon—"One, two, three, four"—and "if you didn't come in, he'd crack you across the head with a stick." J. L. Lowe also recalled the ritual of Fess's rappings: "He hit me three times a day. One was to start me off, the second lick was if there was a mistake, and the third lick meant 'that's enough.'" In the town of Gadsden, sixty miles east of Birmingham, trumpeter Tommy Stewart faced the famous Whatley discipline when his mother arranged a private lesson. "When I first came in, he hit me on my knuckles—I hadn't even played. He said, 'I know, Mr. Stewart, I'm going to have to get you for something, so hold your hand out.' *Bap!* He hit me on the knuckles and told me to start playing."[5]

Whatley's band was the embodiment of order. Students marched single file to their seats at the bandstand and sat or stood in unison, their bodies coordinated with military precision. Each man had a designated job: "One guy," explained trumpeter Sammy Lowe, "would set up the music stands, another would put the music out—and by the way, each fellow had to keep his book in numerical order or risk a fine." There were fines for every conceivable infraction, withholdings for a litany of potential offenses. The band traveled in Whatley's Cadillac caravan, each player assigned a seat determined by his weight. Whatley's own car brought up the rear, so Fess could keep his eyes on the cars in front. If either "swerved just one iota," said saxophonist Frank Adams, "he would stop it and change drivers."[6]

Tardiness was the greatest sin. For the rest of their lives, students would remember what they called "Whatley time," the strict adherence to the clock that Fess ingrained in his players, an unbending punctuality they would carry through their careers. Fess fined musicians for every minute they arrived late, was known to pull out from the school with a barely delinquent musician chasing the caravan in vain. Gigs began—and, just as important, no matter how well the night was going, no matter how eager the audience, gigs *ended*—on the precise minute advertised; with a few refrains of "Home Sweet Home," Fess and the band signaled the end of each evening's performance, ushering dancers off the floor, out the door, and back to their own sweet homes. "If I had an appointment with the devil himself," Whatley barked at his pupils, "I'd get there fifteen minutes early—to find out what *in hell* he wanted!" It was a funny line, maybe, but you dared not laugh.[7]

The hours could be grueling as the band covered the state and parts of Mississippi, often getting home just before sunup. On the latest nights, Fess would drop off his musicians one by one at their homes and then head to the school for a quick nap in his classroom, stretched out on the printing slab. When students arrived, a few hours later, he would be there to greet them—awake, alert, and neatly dressed—and all day he would check up on them, appearing in classroom doors, disciplinary stick in hand. Fess withheld each night's pay until the end of the next school day: first, to give himself time to calculate the deductions—the "ducks," students called them—and second, to ensure his musicians' academic performance. If they missed school the day after a gig or if Fess caught them nodding off in class, they forfeited their pay.[8]

There was always, students grumbled, *some* kind of duck withheld, always some fresh necessity or improvement—mouthpieces, derby hats, bandstands, *something*—that required a chunk of cash be withdrawn from each player's earnings. When the Rhythm Club in Natchez, Mississippi, made headlines for a deadly fire, Fess equipped each of his players with a small ax. When they arrived at a gig, musicians unloaded the ax cases first, followed by their instruments. At the end of the night, the axes were the last things loaded back onto the trailer. That way, if a fire broke out, each man could chop his way out.

"Fess was very enlightened about safety," Frank Adams explained. Some of those rural dance halls were little more than rickety shacks, pure kindling for disaster; the axes and their cases constituted a necessary expense, and they did not pay for themselves. For weeks to come, gig by gig, the musicians' ducks paid off the axes.[9]

It is no wonder the Natchez fire weighed heavily on Fess Whatley's mind: the 1940 tragedy was widely mourned in Black America, memorialized in song, discussed at length in the press, and grieved for generations. More than two hundred Black women and men lost their lives, including swing bandleader Walter Barnes and members of his orchestra. Also among the dead was Woodrich McGuire, beloved bandmaster at Natchez's Brumfield High School, a teacher whose reputation in many ways mirrored Whatley's. Like Fess, McGuire viewed music not as entertainment but as a means to racial uplift and an expression of community values. He had urged his students to attend the dance, and many of them—particularly seniors, their graduation just a week away—perished with him in the flames.[10]

For Whatley, the tragedy hit much too close to home.

The first, most important thing, musically, was the ability to read, to pick up and play any score on demand. "You couldn't play in his damn band unless you read," growled drummer Wilson Driver. It was one of the hallmarks of the Whatley training, a key piece of the Whatley brand. "When guys would get to New York, they'd say, 'You from Birmingham? You one of them Fess Whatley men? Yeah, okay, you can read.'" It was like Fess always bragged: *no audition necessary*.[11]

For the "Maker of Musicians," jazz improvisation was irrelevant: in the dawning swing era, what mattered most was an immediate and nuanced mastery of the printed charts. Bands were expanding to twelve, fourteen, fifteen, pieces, whole sections of saxophones and trumpets and trombones, each part tightly orchestrated. The new "big bands" were a far cry from the early free-for-alls that had exploded out of New Orleans, with each player riffing off the other; they were a far cry, too, from the bebop to come, where bold soloists pushed the limits of a tune's structure, inventing unlikely harmonies and rhythms. In the big bands, Frank Adams explained, "every man couldn't go for himself. You had to have harmony. You had to be in a section. You had to have an arrangement—and that called for the reading of music." And that, Adams said, "was Fess Whatley's forte."[12]

At Industrial High, students' art was, more than art, their trade; reading was an essential employable skill. But if reading was the mark of the tradesman, it was the mark of the gentleman, too, a skill that signified refinement, education, and prestige. Reading was a status symbol that separated Whatley disciples from a world of run-of-the-mill, self-taught players. *Anyone* with half an ear could improvise, Whatley maintained: adherence to the score demonstrated "legitimate" musicianship. The score was perfection, a song's original, ideal type, to be faithfully recreated with each performance. So Whatley stalked the band room, stopped before a random student, and pointed to a random passage, expecting to hear it just as it was written. "If you couldn't read," said J. L. Lowe, "you are illiterate so far as the music is concerned . . . and that's where he would discover you and then use the stick."[13]

Whatley expected students to show off the skill and the virtue of literacy with dutiful, predictable precision—no embellishments or elaboration. "I was trying to syncopate every damn thing," Wilson Driver remembered, "and then I'd hear, 'Mr. Driver . . . Is that what's on the paper? No? Well don't go improving things. Just play the notes on the paper.'" All of this added up to the great irony of Birmingham's growing jazz tradition. Fess Whatley—the city's first jazz bandleader, the man who launched a thousand jazz careers—forbade in his own classroom any hints of improvisation, experimentation, or syncopation. Students mastered military marches, "sweet" dance tunes, and complex classical pieces—but jazz itself was off limits, and Whatley whacked with his stick any player who crossed the line.[14]

Whatley's policies were not so much a rejection of jazz as a question of priorities, his rigidity a means to an end. One day students could play whatever, however they wanted, and Fess made them hungry for that day, recounting the successes of his many far-flung graduates.

Fundamentals, however, came first. First, they had to master the score.

Under Whatley's influence, a tradition of music instruction spread through the schools. A few blocks from Industrial, the Lincoln grade school replicated the upper-level curricula in miniature. Behind the main academic building, a row of wooden shacks housed the workshops for the industrial trades, and in a rickety band room, heated by a wood stove and plagued by a leaky roof, bandmaster Benjamin Smith gave students their first exposure to reading and playing. Like Fess, Smith did not mind using physical force to get the results he desired. "He'd say, 'Try it again,'" remembered Sammy Lowe, "and at the same time he'd get a handful of the upper part of your thigh and squeeze. . . . Or he would take the little paddle he carried and jab you lightly in the rear," producing from his tearful victims' horns what students came to call "the crying tones." By the mid-1930s, Smith had been succeeded by W. W. (William Wise) Handy, nephew of W. C. and a skilled composer in his own right, a soft-spoken intellectual whose nurturing style contrasted that of Smith or Whatley. As Jefferson County added additional schools for Black students, each facility hired its own bandmasters, most of them trained and recommended to the school board by Whatley himself. While other graduates pursued careers across the country, those teaching jobs helped support a core of musicians in Birmingham, providing financial security while helping develop an active musical culture at home.[15]

Whatley's professional band, the Jazz Demons, organized as early as 1921, consisted entirely of former Whatley students—and entirely of teachers. At first, the group's music echoed the freewheeling sounds coming out of New Orleans, but over the years the sound shifted with the times. In the 1930s, the group expanded into a fourteen-piece big band, Fess Whatley's Vibra-Cathedral Orchestra; in the 1940s, it continued in the big band vein, now as Fess Whatley's Sax-o-Society Orchestra. In all its incarnations, the group catered to Birmingham's society dances, white as well as Black: debutante balls, fraternal dances, swanky holiday soirees. "The orchestra became so much in demand," recalled J. B. Sims—a Whatley protégé, bandleader, teacher, and local entertainment columnist—"that to get a date with them you had to put in your bid months and, on occasions, a year in advance of your scheduled party event." If the band was not available, Fess could send his student orchestra instead. Some years, he sponsored additional, semiprofessional, student-led groups, lending his name and his clout (the

Fess Whatley's Jazz Demons, early 1920s. *Left to right:* Wilson Driver,
Fess Whatley, Joseph Britton, Walter Blythe, Carl Bunch, Shed Harris,
Edward Whatley (Fess's brother), Murray Harper, Calvin Ivory. Courtesy
Birmingham, Ala. Public Library Archives.

phrase "Fess Whatley Presents" could guarantee a crowd), arranging their
transportation, and organizing their tours and their money.[16]

The Jazz Demons' membership reflected the inseparable ties between
jazz, formal education, and middle-class notions of respectability in Birmingham. Across the country, the Black press made much of the professional bond that linked Whatley's musicians. "Every man in the band is an
artist," the *Chicago Defender* announced, "and, something more, each man
is an instructor in some particular branch of learning in high schools in
Birmingham." On another occasion, the *Defender* declared the group "in its
make-up probably the most unusual band in the country. Composed of a
group of talented musicians teaching in the public schools of Birmingham,
the band plays more for the real love of music than for the financial remu-
neration received. This set-up assures the vast field of admirers two things:
first, a high type of music, modern and up-to-date; second, intelligent, cultural discipline that commands the respect of all classes of patrons."[17] In
short, the "promotion of culture."

In the classroom and on the bandstand, Whatley's music was framed by
the ideology of racial uplift and steeped in a politics of respectability. In a

newspaper advertisement, Whatley promised "A REAL JAZZ ORCHESTRA —BUT NOT THAT 'EAR-SPLITTING,' 'NERVE-RACKING' KIND." The musicians—"DISPENSERS OF SOULFUL WALTZES, PEPPY ONE STEPS, [and] IRRESISTIBLE FOX TROTS"—were, the ad proclaimed, "A NEAT APPEARING GROUP OF MEN WITH GRACE AND FUNCTION CATERING TO LOVERS OF MUSIC." The message was clear: the Whatley crew was professional, clean-cut, entertaining, and unoffending; their repertoire was vast; they promised "real" jazz, yes, but promised not to get carried away, not to split any ears or rack any nerves.[18]

Even if they were teachers now themselves, the men in Whatley's band were still and always his students, and he ruled them with the same rigidity they had come to know in school. Fess insisted his players resist the temptations of drink but admonished them to be polite to drunks. His players knew not even to accept food offered them by a dance host. It was a matter of professionalism, Fess explained: they were hired to entertain, not to be entertained, not to eat or drink or have a good time. They could eat when they got home.[19]

Musically, Fess told his men to "stay in the front yard," avoiding unexpected or adventurous terrain. Some players chafed against this conservatism. "We looked and sounded like Guy Lombardo or one of them other straight white bands," grumbled Wilson Driver. "Oh, now and then, if it was the right kind of setting, we'd play the 'St. Louis Blues' or something like that, and he'd let each man go for himself and swing it to death. But if we were playing a dance or a social function, he didn't want nothing but was on that damn paper—especially if we were playing for some white people."[20]

There were two kinds of dance music, the "sweet" and the "hot," and while plenty of bands could and did play both, the distinction reflected competing approaches to performance. Hot music was fast-tempo, hard-driving, high-energy stuff; it celebrated the freedom of improvisation and catered to those uninhibited dancers who really wanted to swing, jump, and sweat. Sweet music was slower to mid-tempo, melody-driven, unaggressive, pretty, and sentimental; at its extreme it veered into the saccharine schmaltz known as "corn." Sweet music catered to dancers, too, but to dancers of a more restrained sort, society types who preferred to glide gracefully—or to bounce, lightly and innocuously—across the floor. These audiences were Fess Whatley's bread and butter.[21]

And still, as master of diverse styles, Whatley could play whatever the evening demanded. His jazz arrangements of the spirituals particularly endeared him to Black audiences, who recognized in the old tunes a history of resilience and resistance—stories of hidden meanings, secret meetings, and escape routes north—that was lost on white ears. And if Fess may have leaned most nights on the sweet and predictable, now and then he would "go back in the alley," as he put it, to showcase a bluesier, hotter sound. As other jazz bands began to crop up in the region—the Black Birds of Paradise in Montgomery, Wilson's Red Hots in Mobile, a slew of Whatley-trained bands right there at home—Fess faced off the competition in fierce but friendly "jazz battles," staged musical showdowns that left no question of his prowess. The battles were contests of showmanship and endurance, and Whatley—for all his serious stiffness, for all his "grace and function" and genteel decorum—emerged from battle after battle the victor. It was a well-known fact, across Alabama, that no one could beat him on the bandstand.[22]

Not yet, they couldn't.

In the summer of 1934, Whatley set out on his most extensive tour, his band's most ambitious venture beyond the South. "Running true to form," recalled Sammy Lowe, "Fess had the summer tour organized down to the very last detail. He had two men travel two weeks ahead of us to book the dates, to make arrangements for the places we were to eat and sleep." Fess set a curfew for the road and performed frequent bed checks to keep his men in line—and to make sure they kept away from women, particularly white women and prostitutes, they might meet along the way. The band played Chicago, Wilson Driver said, "and when we got back to the hotel all these prostitutes were sitting around the lobby and talking about, 'I'm in Room 1420' and all that. But we couldn't get around Fess, because he took bed check every half hour." "When did he sleep?" Driver was asked, and he exclaimed, "That's what I'm trying to tell you. . . . He didn't sleep. And neither did we. We had all damn day to sleep. So, every half hour there'd be a knock at the door. 'Mr. Driver?' 'Yeah, Fess, I'm here.' Isn't that something?

"He was too much," Wilson Driver insisted, many decades after the tour, "but he was a hell of a man, and a hell of a teacher."

And, Driver added, "I'm *still* his student."[23]

The history of jazz rests on the shoulders of Black teachers, many of them from southern Black schools, almost all of them unsung, consigned to footnotes or erased altogether from the official record. In Houston, brothers Russell and Percy McDavid launched a fertile music program that in many ways paralleled Birmingham's, establishing their city's Phillis Wheatley and Jack Yates High Schools as important incubators of jazz. At Garnett High in Charleston, West Virginia, Maude Wanzer Layne, author of *The Negro's Contribution to Music*, produced professional players known for their skills at arranging. Mobile boasted E. B. Coleman, bandmaster at

Booker T. Washington High School, along with Central High's Fred Wesley Sr. (father of James Brown's celebrated trombonist-arranger, Fred Jr.); like Whatley, both led their own orchestras in addition to training young players. A rich lineage of public school teachers meanwhile shaped the course of jazz in New Orleans, their long-overlooked legacies unearthed in author Al Kennedy's invaluable study, *Chord Changes on the Chalkboard*. In the late 1920s Jimmie Lunceford turned Manassas High School in Memphis into a musical powerhouse; Lunceford's student band would grow into one of Black America's top dance orchestras, while the musical culture sparked by Lunceford flourished for years in the city's Black schools (in the 1960s, students and grads from the rival Manassas and Booker T. Washington High Schools would form the creative heartbeat of Stax Records, creating some of that era's most exhilarating popular music). Most famously, perhaps, from 1931 to 1962, at Chicago's Wendell Phillips and DuSable High Schools, "Captain" Walter Dyett produced a remarkable roster of jazz players, including key members of the Sun Ra Arkestra.[24]

No educator, though, was more prolific than Birmingham's Whatley. His influence extended, too, into the musical culture of historically Black colleges and universities across the South. Frank Greer would serve twenty years as band director at Tennessee State University, often looking to his old teacher for fresh recruits to his program. At Alabama State, Thomas E. Lyle, another Whatley pupil, would build the 144-piece Marching Hornets, whose televised appearances in the 1960s brought national attention to a dynamic style of high-stepping half-time entertainment, helping establish a tradition that continues today; a prolific composer and arranger, Lyle also directed the school's 100-piece symphonic orchestra. Other Whatley protégés would leave their marks on the music programs of Tuskegee University, Tuscaloosa's Stillman College, and Birmingham's Miles College.

Whatley also helped formalize and organize his city's—and the surrounding region's—musical culture through the creation of an active Black musicians' union. Birmingham's existing local, 256, admitted only white members, so, with Pops Williams and a few of his own former students, Whatley formed a new local, 733, establishing union membership as an essential requirement for any Birmingham player. For thirty years, Whatley himself served as secretary-treasurer to Local 733, and he traveled the country as delegate to national conventions. In 1937 he addressed the floor of national delegates, both Black and white, delivering an impassioned lecture on the contributions of Black musicians to the whole of American culture; back home, reports of that address were added to Whatley's ever-growing lore.[25]

As a teenager, Frank Adams would ride shotgun in one of Whatley's Cadillacs as the two covered Alabama, collecting dues from the small-town musicians who belonged to 733. When they hit an open stretch of country highway, Fess would look at his pupil, then back at the road. The path ahead of them clear—of white drivers, police, and all other obstacles—Fess would hit the accelerator hard, watch the speedometer shoot forward, and listen with pride to the engine's roar. He would tell his young passenger to listen to it, too. Then he would speak a simple message.

"*Power*, son," he would say, his eyes fixed on the road. "*Power!*"[26]

SMITHFIELD

When J. L. Lowe joined Fess Whatley's band, he did not have the money for the required tuxedo uniform. Fess gave him one of his own, and Lowe never forgot it. In time, Lowe would himself become a teacher and musician and then an elder statesman of the Birmingham jazz community, a devoted champion of the Whatley tradition. Decades later, he would develop the Alabama Jazz Hall of Fame as monument to his old mentor and to the music that sprang from his classroom. And it all began with that handed-down tuxedo.[1]

Whatley was not the only source of Lowe's lifelong passion for music; much of the credit also went to the Lowe family itself: "Mother Dear" and "Papa Lowe"; his sister, Leatha; and brother, Sammy. J. L.'s experience, in this regard, was typical: "Most of the musicians came from the same type of families," he said of Birmingham's jazz players. They were the children of hardworking parents who imbued in them a respect for industry, a commitment to education, a love for family, and a pride in community. Fess sought out those sorts of families when recruiting his students; if they came from some "background," he knew he had something to work with. ("Background" for Fess need not represent financial security or social standing but, more important, a foundation of character, rooted in the home.) For years, Birmingham brimmed with musical families: the McCords, the Grimeses, the Greers, the Bascombs, the Parrishes, the Clarkes, the Lowes. The schools may have been training grounds for the city's jazz heroes, but the music was nurtured first in the more intimate space of the home sphere, in parlors and on porches, in family bands and at neighborhood get-togethers. For many members of Birmingham's Black middle class, especially, music was an essential component of family life. And in no place was this truer than in the Lowes' own neighborhood of Smithfield.[2]

Birmingham planners first developed Smithfield in the 1880s, establishing in its 500 acres the city's pioneering suburban residential community. The site, before the Civil War, had been home to corn and cotton fields—and to dozens of enslaved laborers whose hands made the Smith family rich. After the war, Joseph Smith—an ex-slaveholder, physician, newspaper publisher, and perennial businessman—divvied up the family land into residential lots. A father of twelve, he named the Smithfield streets for his children: Virginia, Mary, and Sarah Avenues ran east to west; Mortimer, William, and Thomas Streets ran north to south. When he ran out of children, he borrowed the names of his ancestors.[3]

Both Black and white residents bought up and built on the first Smithfield lots. Many of the settlers there were recent European immigrants, drawn to the smoking, smoldering promise of the New South's Magic City. Others were leaders in the local Black community, prominent and ambitious families who built their first homes along the avenues and streets that bore the names of Smith's daughters and sons. Birmingham's new suburb offered them all a welcome retreat from the city's confines and noise, and what the twentieth century would dub the "American Dream," Smithfield introduced proudly to Birmingham: its settlers embraced the opportunity to put down roots, to raise a family, to own a home. Smithfield land offered the suburban-utopian promise of both independence and community, the chance for families to carve out personal spaces for themselves and, at the same time, to participate meaningfully in a larger social network.[4]

By the twentieth century's start, the community's racial diversity was already on the wane. More and more Black families moved in; more and more white families moved out. Some immigrants, Italians especially, held on—both Italian and Black Americans faced prejudice in Birmingham, and they sometimes formed tentative alliances—but by the 1920s Smithfield's population was almost entirely Black. It was, in particular, the heart of the city's rising Black middle class, a home to doctors, bankers, preachers, lawyers, Pullman porters, and entrepreneurs. The community took special pride in its many educators, whom parents held up to their children as models of success. Industrial High and Lincoln School were both situated on the neighborhood's edge. Fess Whatley walked to work from his Smithfield home, and Principal A. H. Parker lived nearby, in a grand, two-story home of his own.[5]

Haywood Henry grew up down the street from the Lowes and would make music with brothers J. L. and Sammy all his life (he and Sammy would be core members of the Erskine Hawkins Orchestra for two decades). "I'm so glad that I grew up in Alabama, in Birmingham," he explained. He knew it sounded outlandish to any outsider, but he was emphatic on the point. "I did nothing but play," he said of his Smithfield childhood: "no work, just play. . . . Played music, played sports, go to church, knew everybody. I lived in a whole Black neighborhood for blocks—and miles—around. And," he repeated, "*knew everybody!*" It was a complete, self-contained universe, an oasis of autonomous Black culture in the deepest heart of the South. Whatever happened outside its borders—and Henry would become well acquainted with the cruelties of prejudice—Smithfield itself was a safe space, a playground and homeplace, where Black identity was celebrated, youthful ambition encouraged, and deep relationships nurtured.[6]

Frank Adams grew up steeped in the same culture. Born in 1928, fifteen years after Haywood Henry and J. L. Lowe, ten years after Sammy, he grew up in one of Smithfield's most prominent families, and he idolized those older musicians. His father, Oscar Adams, was owner and editor of the *Birmingham Reporter* newspaper, Grand Chancellor of the Knights of Pythias fraternal organization, national secretary to the AME Zion Church, and an outspoken, often controversial champion of race pride. He preached to his two sons the principles of homeownership, which Booker T. Washington had advocated as a key to racial uplift. "Get you a brick house on a corner lot," Adams instructed the boys: the bricks bespoke both prominence and permanence, and the corner lot anchored the block. It was the duty and honor of the privileged to set an example for the community.[7]

There were other lessons, too. When J. L. Lowe walked by the house, Oscar Adams called his boys to the window and told them to take a good look: here, he said, was someone they should emulate. The confident cut of his stride, the dapper perfection of his dress, the professorial heft of his talk—Mr. Lowe may have been barely past twenty, but just to watch him go by was an inspiration.[8]

When their time came, Frank Adams and his brother, Oscar Jr., would become Smithfield role models as well. Frank became a musician and educator; Oscar became a civil rights lawyer and, in 1980, the first Black justice of the state's supreme court. Both men raised their families in brick, corner-lot homes of their own, a few blocks from where they had been born. And while Frank Adams grew up to become J. L. Lowe's friend, colleague, and bandmate, he never forgot the awe he felt seeing him pass by the window. Smithfield, Adams said, was full of such inspirations. "When a person like Mr. Lowe would . . . walk down the street, the children would *know* that he was something. He was something special. And you got that in your system.

You got that in your blood." If Lowe's brother, Sammy, sold a million records, you only thought, "Why not?"

After all, said Adams, "he's from *here*."[9]

There was music everywhere in the neighborhood, and, as in the schools, that music tended to reflect the ideals and aspirations of the community. Sundays set the tone, beginning with church. "Sunday was the *day* in Birmingham," said Sammy Lowe. "You only had to stand in front of your house and somewhere you could hear the voices of a congregation raised in song." Smithfield families attended the city's most prestigious Black churches, like the elegant Sixteenth Street Baptist Church downtown or Fourth Avenue's Metropolitan AME Zion Church. Favorite soloists, quartets, and choirs worked the circuit of local churches, drawing crowds each week. Many of the city's burgeoning jazz musicians practiced their horns in the choir lofts, blowing out sacred song for the worshippers below. After church came the Community Sings, which, Sammy pointed out, were "enjoyable for all, the believers and the non-believers in God. . . . My parents, though God-fearing, never forced us to go to church," which meant the Lowe siblings attended only when some good music had been advertised. "But I don't remember us ever missing a Community Sing."[10]

Smithfield's most elite homes boasted a Victrola record player and a piano, and those furnishings were on central display, not just a means to entertainment but valuable objects in and of themselves, symbols of culture, class, and clout. Frank Adams recalled that his mother spent the first money she made as a teacher to buy a piano, even though he never once saw her play it. Just *having* it was the thing. Sammy Lowe wondered how his father procured a piano on a carpenter's modest salary, but it was considered a necessary investment for the family, something for which a parent worked and saved.[11]

Private students, mostly girls, learned classical music in the Smithfield home of Minnie Chambliss, founder of the Chambliss School of Music and the Chambliss Music Study Club. An active figure in local women's clubs—the Periclean Club, the Twentieth Century Club, the City Federation of Colored Women's Clubs—Chambliss was organist, for decades, at St. Paul Methodist Church. Founded in 1921, hers was the first formal music school for Black children in Birmingham, and it produced a wealth of music teachers and church organists. Surveyed in 1960, Chambliss could claim among her former pupils forty-two active organists at churches across the state, fifty-plus working music teachers, and countless amateur players who performed at home for family and friends. Other private studios followed the Chambliss mold.[12]

Conventions of both gender and class shaped the musical destinies of Smithfield's residents. The three Lowe children were reared on the family piano, but only sister Leatha stuck with the instrument into her teens, working her way through a battered copy of the *Gospel Pearls* songbook and enrolling in lessons with Chambliss. As in other communities, the piano was perceived as a "girl's instrument": its entertainments belonged to the parlor and the hearth, spaces that suggested domesticity and, it followed, femininity. Girls were encouraged in their study of the instrument but were restricted from the music that consumed so many Birmingham boys. In elementary school at Lincoln, Leatha played clarinet until her mother insisted she quit. The reason, her brother Sammy explained: "Mother Dear said girls—all girls—looked too ugly playing a wind instrument." By the time they got to high school, the bias was official school policy: Fess Whatley refused to allow girls in the band, claiming they lacked the stamina to march and adding that they only stirred up drama with the boys. So Leatha continued her classical training instead—and in time opened her own studio for girls.[13]

For boys, early training in piano was useful for learning the fundamentals of music, but those who continued too long with the instrument risked being called "sissies," so most boys—including Sammy and J. L.—gave it up early. The few who stayed with it often compensated by building bluesy, risqué repertoires that showed off their masculine bravado. In the schools, of course, the blues were strictly forbidden; associated in the minds of many with illiteracy (musical and otherwise), rural poverty, even slavery, the music represented everything an educator like Whatley was working to combat. The formalized, blues-*inspired* orchestrations of W. C. Handy, which adapted and "elevated" folk tradition to high art, were one thing. But by the 1910s an earthier style of blues and rollicking boogie-woogie piano had also found a home in Birmingham, pioneered by the likes of Clarence "Pine Top" Smith and Charles "Cow Cow" Davenport, both of whom arrived from smaller Alabama towns, made a temporary home in the local honky-tonks, and finally migrated north, where in the 1920s they cut seminal records (Davenport's "Cow Cow Blues" and Smith's "Pine Top's Boogie Woogie" became standards and helped define the boogie-woogie sound). Davenport had arrived in Birmingham after being expelled from a theological seminary in Selma (he had incorporated a "raggy" dance rhythm into his accompaniment to a school march, and "the girls got so frisky they couldn't march in time"). He drifted to Birmingham and developed his percussive, propulsive boogie-woogie style in the seedier venues of Eighteenth Street: "joints," he said, "where the nice people did not go." The "nice people"—preachers, teachers, and middle-class strivers, the most upright citizens of Smithfield—preferred a music more refined.[14]

Some of that boogie and blues seeped inevitably into Smithfield, all the same; not all the neighborhood's music was so high-minded or "polite" as a Fess Whatley or Minnie Chambliss might have liked. Scattered through the community were the shot houses where neighbors could buy a few drinks of bootleg liquor and dance to the sounds of a bluesy piano pounder. Ragtag jug bands and loose-knit groups of "midnight serenaders" roamed the residential streets some nights, playing for tips. "You'd see guitar players walking around with singers," said J. L. Lowe; "they'd come to your house to serenade you . . .with blues." In a couple of empty Smithfield lots, a traveling Holy Ghost revival sometimes set up its tents, filling the air with a rawer sort of music than was common in the middle-class churches, ecstatic cries to glory accompanied by nothing but a bass drum and handclaps. On other occasions, itinerant carnivals pitched their own tents in the same lots, presenting sideshows of "colored dancing girls" and their red-hot backing bands. Preteen and teenage Smithfield musicians could pick up some change "ballyhooing" for the carnivals, blowing their horns on the street to draw up a crowd. If they were good enough, they might get hired to play behind the dancing girls—or even, in the summers, to join the show on the road, sending their earnings home to their families.[15]

At school dances, Fess Whatley barked from the bandstand at any students he thought were dancing too close or with too much shimmy or grind in their hips; predictably, teenagers found, or created, opportunities for more sensual dancing. "Practically every week," Sammy Lowe wrote, "there was a house party going on. These parties were called jooks, all you needed was an invitation, and 5¢–10¢ was the admission price." Entertainment was provided by a couple of older piano players, most notably a gritty blues player named Shepard. "When you pack fifteen or more kids in a living room there wasn't much you could do in the way of dancing except grind," Lowe recalled—that is, "holding your partner as closely and tightly as possible and just moving your hips. The object was to do this as much as possible without being obvious. Of course, there were couples who didn't care whether anybody was looking or not. They'd stand there glued to one spot perspiring profusely, their hips going like mad, rotating from right to left, up and down, and round and round. This would inevitably cause someone to remark, *All they need is a bed and a towel*." By the time the night was over, the air would be thick with sweat, teenage hormones, and cheap perfume. It was the first time Sammy Lowe heard the work "funk": at those sweaty jooks, they said, you could "cut the funk with a knife."[16]

For the members of many Smithfield families, music started in earliest childhood. "My mother wanted all of us to be musicians," Sammy explained. As kids, the siblings formed "a little family orchestra," with Leatha on piano, Sammy on trumpet, and J. L. on saxophone; a neighborhood friend played drums, and they built a repertoire of stock arrangements. Their parents took them halfway across the state, instruments strapped to the car's running board, to play five nights of dances in their old hometown of Livingston, a few miles from the Mississippi state line. Papa Lowe printed advertising placards and tacked them onto trees: *Dancing, 25¢, Music by the Lowe Family*. "The little country towns were evidently starved for dancing," Sammy said, since a single day's notice was enough to crowd the halls and homes where the band performed. From their little tour of west Alabama, the Lowes took in almost fifty dollars; after paying back their expenses and giving nine dollars to the drummer, the family still reaped thirty dollars.[17]

J. L., from the beginning, was a champion of his siblings' and friends' musical talents. He schooled his younger brother in reading music and hounded him to practice daily, whether Sammy wanted to or not. "So I'd climb the chinaberry tree that stood in our front yard and practice," Sammy said. "It must have been a ludicrous sight—the other kids playing ball, and I'd be blowing like mad." Occasionally a neighbor complained about the noise, but Sammy stayed up in that tree, blowing his heart out.[18]

Other sounds pervaded the Smithfield air. Another teenager, Wilbur Hollins, led a band called the Dreamers, and the sounds of their practice sessions wafted from the Hollinses' home. Some nights around twilight Haywood Henry could also be heard, improvising on his clarinet or flute. Haywood was an athlete, heavily built and always active; he had a reputation for trouble, for skipping school and starting fights—once he had broken another boy's collarbone in a wrestling match, and adults called him "Peck's bad boy" after a popular series of novels and films—but it was easy to see he was gifted. He had an analytical mind and an intuitive grasp of the inner workings of things, could take apart and fix a broken watch or radio, could make a baseball glove from a bunch of old rags, and could outwit almost anyone on a checkerboard. And, said J. L., "he was playing music that we did not understand," complex melodies and riffs he picked up by ear or made up on the spot. In later years, Haywood's blend of physical power with sophistication and grace earned him a nickname, the "Gentle Monster." A natural musician, he wanted nothing to do with *reading* music: in high school he faked the reading as long as he could, until Whatley's paddle finally changed his mind.[19]

Haywood, too, came from a home full of music. His older stepsister, schoolteacher Mabel Barker, was organist at the Sixteenth Street Baptist Church, where their father was a deacon; she had her own radio program and taught classical piano to many Birmingham girls. Much like Whatley's, Haywood's musical development began with homemade instruments, crafted beneath the floorboards: "I used to go under the house, take a cigar box, cut a hole in the back of it, put pegs in it, and make a guitar." When he was seven, he saw a flute for sale and was inspired to make his own: "I went in the woods and took a cane and made myself one. . . . I bored six holes through it and started playing songs." He graduated to a ten-cent flute from Woolworth's and picked out the popular tunes of the day: "Yessir, That's My Baby," "The Sheik," "Yes, We Have No Bananas." When Haywood got to Lincoln School, Mabel (who was also his homeroom teacher) offered to buy him a clarinet if it would keep him from playing hooky and getting into fights. The bribe worked, and in Benjamin Smith's band room Haywood and the Lowes made music with other lifelong collaborators, including trumpeters Wilbur "Dud" Bascomb and Marcellus Green, saxophonist Cornelius Aiken, and bassist LeMeyer Stanfield. Outside of school, the friends found ways to create their own musical culture, on their own terms.[20]

The benefits of making music quickly became apparent. Haywood played his first gig with a classmate, pianist Curley Julian Parrish (brother of Henry's later longtime bandmate, Avery Parrish), and brought home thirty-five cents. Soon after that, Sam "High C" Foster recruited him for a parade the Tuggle Institute band was marching in in Mulga, a tiny mining outpost north of town. "We marched for about thirty-five minutes to an hour and when we finished he gave me eighteen dollars. I made thirty-five cents the first gig and then eighteen dollars [the second]." Haywood came home, threw the cash on the bed, and announced to his mother, "I'm rich!" "That," he said, "had some bearing on me wanting to play music."[21]

Other incidents helped seal the deal. On another occasion, Haywood and a friend, drummer Snooky Davenport, got a gig with Snooky's aunt, a pianist, playing the birthday party of a white boy about their own age. "We played two or three numbers and the guy's mother told us, 'Let the lady play and you all come on and join the party.' We sat down and started eating ice cream and having a good time." It was the first time he had been "around white kids," and if racial mores prevented Haywood and Snooky from joining in the dancing, they did everything else those white kids did. "The games they had, we played them, then we would go back and play a couple of numbers and come back and have food." The experience opened up a sort of possibility Haywood had never imagined. "That was a kind of turning point in my life. I said to myself, 'If you can do something you are somebody.' That eliminated that bit of prejudice that I had seen so prevalent in Alabama, especially in Birmingham. If you could do something people accept you as something special."[22]

With that, Henry said, "I really went to work trying to learn that clarinet." With schoolmates Marcellus Green and Cornelius Aiken he started his own band, the Moonlight Serenaders, and soon, he bragged, "[we] got so good we were a threat to Fess Whatley's band." The Serenaders had more "spirit," and they were not locked into the score: while "the professor was strictly what's on the paper," Haywood and friends played how they chose. Whether they knew it or not, it was just what Whatley wanted: outside his watch, in their own homes and at the homes of their friends, students could rebel against the confines of his training—even as they drew from the skills learned in his classroom, even as they talked about the man constantly. On their own, they could cut up and improvise, let loose their youthful energy, and indulge the experimental potentials of the music. Even for those players who rebelled against his formalities—even for a "bad boy" like Haywood—Fess Whatley was the measuring stick. If they could call themselves a "threat," they knew they were going someplace. And, after all, why not?[23]

They were from Smithfield.

FOURTH AVENUE STOMP

In the summer of 1927, the Gennett record label arrived in Birmingham from Richmond, Indiana, bringing a load of equipment and a team of engineers. "Southern Artists to Make Records," announced the headline in the *Birmingham News*. "Making of Phonographic Discs Is Birmingham's Latest Industrial Effort." Gennett had announced plans to set up a temporary studio in the city, and it hoped to attract talent from across the South.[1]

A spokesman for the label addressed the press in grand terms. "The nation looks to the South," he said, "for its Dixie melodies, its jazz orchestras, its 'hot' music. Our initial reception here in Birmingham has been beyond our expectations." Gennett would "make a specialty of Alabama negro folk songs," a trade magazine reported, but Birmingham also seemed an ideal location for accessing a range of southern music styles, Black and white. Ambitions were high. The *Birmingham News* imagined the city becoming "a musical center for the south," and all through July and August a long procession of musicians trudged with their instruments up the stairs over the Starr Piano showroom on Third Avenue North, ready to set their sounds to wax.[2]

Despite the buzz, the results neither revolutionized the local economy nor jump-started any careers, but the recordings did preserve a time capsule of the city's diverse musical cultures. There were old-time fiddlers and banjo pickers, gospel quartets, Sacred Harp singers, white dance orchestras, and rustic blues players. The Reverend J. F. Forest, a Baptist preacher, delivered eight fiery sermons, a small congregation crammed around him in the studio, moaning, singing, and shouting "Amen." Luther Patrick, a white lawyer, country humorist, and future congressman, recited homespun verses, backed by a string band. Jaybird Coleman of Bessemer blew spirituals and blues through a harmonica. George Tremer, a Black pianist, recorded the bouncy "Spirt of '49 Rag," interspersed with kazoo and vocal sound effects. One of the area's many gospel quartets, the Dunham Jubilee Singers, rebranded themselves the Dunham *Jazz* Singers to cut a pair of decidedly secular numbers. "You Can Hear Those Darkies Singing" was a "plantation melody" dating to 1880 and the minstrel tradition, its lyrics full of old folks, ringing banjos, and moonlight. The flipside, "Honey Turn Your Damper Down"—its own lyrics packed with "jelly roll" and double entendre—was labeled a "Mamma Blues" after the bluesy "red hot mamas" of the day. The group's ability to straddle past and present, from minstrelsy's antebellum stereotypes on one side to syncopated vocals and hip, risqué slang on the other—and to do it all under the banner of "jazz"—suggests the broad, still evolving use of that term by 1927.[3]

The Gennett sessions also captured the sounds of three hot bands of Black Alabama musicians: Montgomery's Black Birds of Paradise, the Triangle Harmony Boys, and Frank Bunch and His Fuzzy Wuzzies, a team of young Whatley-trained musicians. One of the Wuzzies' tunes was an anthem to the scene that shaped them, an instrumental ode to the downtown district that was the heart of Black social life in the city. The record opens with a pair of lopsided *plink-plonks* from bandleader Bunch's piano, evoking a tipsy, stumbling gaiety. A blustery saxophone comes in next, then a clarinet sails over the sound, and suddenly the whole band is off, piano and banjo chunking out a rhythm while brass and reed players trade off solos. For three minutes the record moves with whimsical swagger, a breezy stroll on a good-time Saturday night, a lively and thriving scene come to life. They called it the "Fourth Avenue Stomp."

In the first decade of the twentieth century, the new culture of segregation relegated Black business in Birmingham to its own tiny strip of the city, a four-block stretch of Fourth Avenue North, beginning at Eighteenth Street and running west to Fifteenth. The goal may have been to keep Black people, very literally, in their "place," but the result was a vibrant, concentrated community of commerce, leadership, and leisure, a vital social hub that by the 1920s was packed with restaurants, theaters, barbershops, beauty parlors, funeral parlors, shoeshine stands, poolrooms, hotels, and the offices of Birmingham's most elite Black professionals: doctors, dentists, newspapermen, attorneys, accountants. Nightlife abounded. On Friday and Saturday nights, the streets swelled with a cross section of the Black community, from the most prominent civic leaders to the masses of working-class laborers. Steel-workers and miners came into town—from Pratt City, Bessemer, Fairfield, Dolomite, Ensley, and other surrounding communities—to celebrate the freedom and release of the weekend. Many of them worked the late shifts and then hurried home to cast aside their sweat-soaked and soot-stained clothes, reinventing themselves in fresh suits and tuxes. The women, many of whom worked all day as domestics, decked themselves out in their own finest dresses. They might hit Fourth well after midnight and stay past daybreak.

The scene flourished for more than half a century. Only with the arrival of integration—once Black business was no longer confined to a single, narrow space—did the avenue's reign diminish. Jessie Nelson ran the Nelson Broth-ers Café for decades in the district, selling millions of his signature bean pies. "They called us Little Harlem down here," he remembered, years after the avenue faded. "It was just full all the time. It was going *on* here." "See," Frank Adams agreed, "this *was* the town. Fourth Avenue was just the heart of ev-erything." Marcel Hopson, editor of the *Birmingham World* newspaper, put it this way: "If you ever see a lot of ants close together, or insects—almost bump shoulder to shoulder—that's the way the streets were." The crowds lasted all weekend long. "Beginning Friday night you hardly had elbow room, going or coming, up either sidewalk."[4]

Tuskegee-born Nathan B. Young Jr.—a Black lawyer, writer, visual artist, and classically trained musician—moved to Birmingham after his gradua-tion from Yale University Law School in 1918. His essay "Eighteenth Street (Birmingham): An Anthology in Color" opened with a survey of the varied sounds that pervaded the district at night. The streets themselves were full of grassroots musical expressions more ragged than the polished per-formances emanating from the dance halls and theaters. Visitors might encounter a vocal group like the Kitchen Mechanics Quartet (so called "be-cause they cook, wait table, and chauffeur for the rich 'white folks' on the Highlands") or a "strolling string band" composed of fiddle, guitar, and "a three string weather-beaten" bass. Especially common were "the blind beggars with guitars or accordions," guided through the streets by "half-naked" children rattling tin cups for tips. A boy observed by Young drew his own crowd with a bamboo flute, blowing "When the Saints Go Marching In," W. C. Handy's "Yellow Dog Blues," and other popular tunes. When one bystander called for the "Star-Spangled Banner," another, a veteran of the First World War, demanded, "What for? . . . I done heard too much of that tune in camps and over in France. An' what good we get from fighting in the war?" The vet told the boy to "play 'Sweet Mama'" instead.[5]

Nathan Young shared the veteran's disillusionment, finding the promise of America contradicted daily by life in Birmingham. As an organizer for the local branch of the NAACP, Young received frequent racist threats and, in an interview years later, recalled another memory of Eighteenth Street, "looking out of my little office window . . . and see[ing] the Ku Klux Klan in full regalia, led by the Birmingham police in parade." Since that moment, Young said, "I have known that the bottom of the totem pole for American democracy was in Alabama, Birmingham." After six years on Eighteenth Street, Nathan Young left the Magic City for good.[6]

Class distinctions were evident in the Fourth Avenue district, where Young's blind beggars shared the same limited space with the most prestigious community leaders. Birmingham's Black elite asserted a powerful presence in the district, pursuing an agenda of racial uplift that depended, in large part, on symbolism and the influence of example. Central to the Fourth Avenue scene was a host of Black fraternal orders, sister societies, and civic clubs whose endless calendars of meetings, luncheons, and gala dances reflected the political and social aspirations of Birmingham's Black middle class. Since the late nineteenth century, fraternal organizations like the Colored Knights of Pythias, Masons, Odd Fellows, and Elks had helped shape and empower Black communities across the country. The Masons, in particular, could even trace their roots back to the colonial era; their founding father, Prince Hall, became a Mason in 1775. Running parallel to the white orders with whom they shared their names—but from which their own members were barred inclusion—Black fraternal orders served the unique needs of their own communities, creating for their members a sense of social status, financial security, mutual cooperation, and racial pride. With their elaborate initiation rituals and ceremonial regalia, their frequent parades and dances, their local meetings, national conventions, and annual elections, these organizations offered an alternative, autonomous society, civic-minded and self-governing. Weekly membership dues helped fund innumerable services: burial insurance for members, financial aid for the needy, and educational scholarships for the young. Participation in the societies' elections allowed Black Americans, disenfranchised by their larger society, opportunities to cast ballots and hold office. The groups sponsored a range of charitable causes, spoke out on the subject of racial unity, and promoted a model of citizenship rooted in principles of character, cooperation, and friendship. While middle-class and white-collar professionals held the leadership roles, most members were working-class laborers; some paid their dues in produce if they were short on cash. Oscar Adams was Grand Chancellor of the

Knights of Pythias but insisted his son Frank, who worked the office as elevator and errand boy, shake hands with one of the members, a farmer named Mr. Huckabee: he wanted his son to feel the man's calluses and respect the grueling work that had put them there. Frank Adams never forgot the feel of Mr. Huckabee's hands, and he never forgot what they stood for.[7]

Symbolism mattered. The fraternal lodges themselves were imposing structures that represented in physical form the loftiest ambitions of the community's leaders, deliberate testaments to the potential of the race. The six-story Grand Lodge of the Knights of Pythias sat on Eighteenth Street, and members conducted their rituals and meetings on the top floor. Oscar Adams kept two offices in the building, one for fraternal business and the other for his newspaper. The temple also housed the offices of Wallace Rayfield, the Black architect who designed not only that building but over a hundred others in Birmingham—and others, still, all over the country and even in Africa, selling the designs by mail order from his office.[8]

Even more grand was the newer and bigger Masonic Temple on Fourth, a seven-story structure that housed the offices of numerous Black professionals, in addition to providing a business and social headquarters for the Prince Hall Masons. Anticipating its opening in 1924, the Masons announced in the pages of the *Birmingham Reporter* that the temple would boast "73 office rooms, 6 stores on the ground floor, 2 passenger elevators and 1 freight elevator," plus "several lodge halls and a rest room for the ladies." The grand second-story ballroom comfortably fit 1,500. On the first floor, Peterson's Pharmacy functioned as a favorite social hangout, and the Booker T. Washington Library served as the first lending library for Black patrons in Birmingham. For years, the NAACP kept its regional office on the sixth floor, rent free, while Birmingham's own local chapter operated out of the seventh. Well before the modern civil rights movement came to Birmingham, its foundations were laid by decades of political meetings and discussions that took place in the building. The meaning of the structure itself was deliberate: "The work of the fraternity," the Masons declared, "is a revelation to the entire public and shows what can be done among Negro people when they co-operate. . . . If [the temple] does no more than offer inspiration for the young men and women of the race, it has served a wonderful mission."[9]

The fraternities were not alone in their work. There was a universe of groups, small and large, in Birmingham, each devoted to some branch of political, charitable, literary, artistic, intellectual, or purely social pursuit. Meetings were constant, and membership in multiple clubs brought a certain prestige. Women's clubs espoused platforms of civic engagement,

Top: Prince Hall Masons gather in the second-story auditorium of Fourth Avenue's new Masonic Temple, 1924. Courtesy the Most Worshipful Prince Hall Grand Lodge, F. & A. M. of Alabama. *Bottom:* Members of the Knights of Pythias gather on Eighteenth Street, directly across from their own Grand Lodge. Courtesy Birmingham, Ala. Public Library Archives. These fraternal organizations and others like them presented powerful, sophisticated images of Black manhood, contrasting the portrayals of Black life prevalent in the dominant white society (as in the best-selling caricatures of Octavus Roy Cohen). The lodges were also consistent supporters of the city's jazz culture: young musicians gained their first public performance experience marching in the regular fraternal parades, and the Masonic ballroom seen here hosted a steady stream of live music, performed both by local bands like Fess Whatley's and by major touring acts.

Christian values, and philanthropic giving. The Order of Calanthe, sister society to the Knights of Pythias, was headed by Carrie Ann Tuggle and acted as financial backbone to her Tuggle Institute. Black-owned newspapers like the *Reporter* chronicled an endless whirl of events in their society columns, while local correspondents sent their social reports to the national pages of the *Pittsburgh Courier* and *Chicago Defender*, offering detailed accounts of the city's elite social set: who served dinner for whom; who was traveling or hosting out-of-town guests; which clubs were holding a luncheon, a meeting, a whist tournament, a reading, a scholarly discussion, a visiting speaker, a dance.

The clubs were essential supporters of the developing jazz culture, and not only in Birmingham: leading jazz artists across the country—Fats Waller, Duke Ellington, Cab Calloway, Count Basie—were Masons, and that organization's activities provided work and inspiration to countless musicians. In Birmingham, there was always a dance, and the society columns distilled each one into a few short sentences:

> The attractive young members of the L'Etude and D'Art club
> entertained with a Christmas soiree Wednesday evening at the
> Masonic temple celebrating their third anniversary. Christmas
> decorations were used profusely in the ballroom, where Whatley's
> Saxo Society orchestra rendered snappy dance numbers for the
> merry dancers. . . . Lovely creations were worn by the club members
> who danced the club special at 11:30 p.m. and later gave out pretty
> noise makers.

> The Highland Social club held its third annual dance at the Masonic
> temple Thursday evening. About 200 attended. The ladies presented
> a lovely picture in some of the season's prettiest models. At midnight
> favors of miniature music boxes, novelty whistles and coin purses
> were distributed. . . . Whatley's Society orchestra furnished music.

> The Climbers club held its annual dance Friday night at the Elks
> Rest. Some 200 of the society elite responded. Whatley's orchestra
> furnished music.

The affairs were genteel gatherings and emphasized what was called "polite" music (in the language of the social columns, music was a *furnishing*, like the curtains, streamers, and gilded decorations). Bands stuck mostly to formal dance fare derived from European traditions—waltzes, polkas, schottisches, and quadrilles ("qua-drooles," drummer Jo Jones called them, derisively)—but for all their studied gentility the dances gave crucial training and employment to the city's budding jazzmen. If Whatley ruled the scene, the sheer number of clubs created opportunities for other bands to pick up whatever engagements he left behind. Even the city's youngest musicians made music for the clubs: a small circle of ladies might hire one or two grade-school players to provide soundtrack for their afternoon teas. Meanwhile, all-day fraternal parades enlisted the Tuggle, Lincoln, and Industrial bands, whose players marched the streets, all over the city—and broke out, at day's end, in impromptu battles of the bands, one school attempting to out-blow the other.[10]

For participating students, the parades offered an eye-opening introduction to Black political and social power, a temporary, physical reordering of Birmingham's racial landscape. In Black communities across the South, parades served the same function: historian Tyina Steptoe observes that "through their public performance of jazz, young people of color from diverse backgrounds staked claims to local space" in Houston. In New Orleans, author Thomas Brothers notes, "parades offered disenfranchised Negroes a chance to assertively move their culture through the city's public spaces, the very spaces where African Americans were expected to confirm social inferiority," forced by custom and law to sit in the backs of streetcars and relinquish the sidewalks to white passersby. In Birmingham, Black fraternal members and student musicians could reclaim the same streets where, on other occasions, they watched police and Klansmen march in unified displays of strength. In the city's Fourth of July and Armistice Day parades, Black student bands were required to bring up the rear, marching behind not only their white counterparts but also the horses whose trails of manure they learned to sidestep. (In the 1930s, Lincoln School's W. W. Handy withdrew his band from the annual Armistice Day celebration, protesting this arrangement. "Our parents understood and appreciated Mr. Handy's decision," recalled his student, Frank Adams. "He said that that was an insult.") In the parades of the Pythians, Odd Fellows, Masons, and Elks, Black marchers could assert their own strength, with no such indignities spoiling the moment.[11]

The ornate and colorful Masonic Temple ballroom provided additional thrills, through the performances not only of local bands but of major national touring acts. Children, said J. L. Lowe, "would climb the walls from the street" to reach the ballroom windows and catch a glimpse of Cab Calloway, Duke Ellington, Earl Hines, or Lucky Millinder; to see the bands' golden horns and hear their golden tones; to watch the grown-ups, decked out in their tuxes and gowns, gliding and bouncing all over the floor. Among the children who "used to sit up and climb the window to try to get in there" —both at the Masonic Temple and the Elks Rest a few blocks away—was future bandleader Erskine Hawkins, still too young to get inside but sneaking any peeks he could and imagining himself in a band onstage. There was nothing more glamorous, he thought, nothing more magical. Certainly, in this regard, the temples were fulfilling their mission, even in their music: they offered inspiration to the youth, extending the promise of possibility unbridled.[12]

The lodges were not the only places where music mattered. Fourth Avenue was home, too, to an active theater district, a row of vaudeville houses and movie houses, all of which gave inspiration, training, and employment to local musicians. The Savoy, New Pastime, and Jefferson Theaters opened in the 1910s, all in the space of a few blocks. The Famous, Frolic, Hippodrome, Dixie, and Gay emerged in the 1920s. The Carver followed in 1930.

Just a block from these venues was that other theater district, the white theater district, with its own spectacular temples to the stage. Black patrons could attend shows in these spaces, too, but had to enter alleyway side doors and sit in balconies designated "Colored"; advertisements promised state-of-the-art "elevators for colored patrons," disguising insult as luxury. Segregation was pervasive, its conventions complex and its logic often absurd. "I like to tell the joke," said singer Evelyn Starks Hardy of Birmingham's Gospel Harmonettes, "that when a movie was comical, the white audience always laughed first," while the balcony sat quiet. Finally, "the ushers would ring a bell and then we were allowed to laugh." Beneath the joke's hyperbole was plenty of truth. Black patrons were reminded at all times that they were just visitors to a world that belonged to whites. It was important they watch themselves.[13]

On Fourth Avenue, however, things were different: patrons could visit any theater on their own terms, could sit where they liked, could laugh and clap and cheer when and how they wanted. There was plenty to take in, as all-Black touring companies presented sold-out stage shows multiple times a day. The New Pastime Theatre—"the Best Equipped Colored Vaudeville Theatre in America," ads said—featured two shows a night plus daily matinees, "especially for ladies and children who," as social custom dictated, "are unable to attend at night." Like other vaudeville stages, the New Pastime offered a diverse fare of musicians, comedians, and chorus girls ("MOSTLY PRETTY GIRLS," one ad proclaimed, with surprising ambivalence) and promised entertainment that was "CLEAN—REFINED—HIGH CLASS" and "MORAL."[14]

By the mid-1920s, Fourth Avenue's Frolic Theater had become the district's premiere vaudeville spot, boasting its own outstanding house band and bringing in touring acts from the TOBA circuit. TOBA was the Theater Owners' Booking Association, the nation's leading network of Black vaudeville theaters, a circuit that covered most of the East Coast and stretched as far west as Kansas City and Dallas. A well-known joke held that the acronym really stood for "Tough on Black Asses," a critique of the grueling travel schedules, the shoddy conditions of most accommodations, and the paltry salaries offered all but the most beloved acts; despite those complaints, the circuit ruled the world of the Black stage show. TOBA presented musical-comedy duos, boogie-woogie pianists, comedians, tap dancers, and a world of chorus girls, but the biggest stars were those sensational divas whose acts blended down-home blues with extravagant costumes and shimmering jazz band arrangements. When Ma Rainey played the Frolic in 1925, she began by belting out her "Moonshine Blues" from inside what appeared to be an enormous phonograph record player in the center of the stage. A member of her band described the scene: "She would open the door [of the phonograph] and step out into the spotlight with her glittering gown that weighed twenty pounds and wearing a necklace of five, ten and twenty dollar gold pieces. The house went wild. . . . Her diamonds flashed like sparks of fire falling from her fingers."[15]

Spectacles like this made the Frolic a favorite spot, particularly for men. Sammy and J. L. Lowe accompanied their father to the Frolic's shows when they were just boys, and Sammy remembered especially a performance by singer Ethel Waters. If her own act was less dramatic than Rainey's, Waters used what she had to bring the crowd to its feet. "The whole audience, especially Papa, screamed with delight," Sammy recalled. Waters "would sing a song, and then she would stand there while the band continued playing, and just shake her derriere. It was just like a vibrator was making her go 'round and 'round; and the audience gave her encore after encore."[16]

A greater sensation still was Bessie Smith, "Empress of the Blues" and TOBA's most popular star. Smith had a long history with Birmingham, booking local residencies as early as 1911, well before the dawn of her celebrated recording career. By 1912, she had launched a partnership with the Birmingham-born novelty dancer Wayne Burton, touring as "The Boy with the Insane Feet" and "The Girl with the Ragtime Voice"—or, simply, "That Boy and That Girl." "Bessie Smith stops the show nightly," papers cheered when the singer headlined the New Queen Theater, four years later. "Miss Smith is Birmingham's favorite when it comes to the 'Blues.'" By 1923, her performances at the Frolic left "streets blocked" and "hundreds and hundreds unable to gain entrance," her act bringing "the house to a riot of applause." She launched her 1924 touring season from the Frolic's stage, backed by pianist Fred Longshaw's popular house band, a seven-piece stable of Birmingham players. All were fixtures of the local scene, all products of Industrial High and Fess Whatley.[17]

Each night, whatever the main act, the band opened with a rousing overture. Alex Nabors, wrote Sammy Lowe, was "the first drummer I ever saw that tossed his sticks around his head, down on the floor, transferred them from his hands to his mouth, back to his hands, all without missing a beat." Saxophonist Murray Harper could improvise a wicked string of notes and then "pause to give a toothy smile"; then suddenly he would be "off again," blaring red-hot jazz from his horn, "his right foot . . . going like a piston." After warming up the crowd, the band filled in as needed throughout the show, holding its own with the day's biggest stars.[18]

Certainly, the musicians clicked with Smith, who played two weeks at the Frolic and then commuted for two weeks more to performances in Bessemer, the Longshaw band in tow; she then took the group on the road as her touring band. In the words of one Texas paper, Smith's ensemble "is composed of young fellows formerly of the Birmingham (Ala.) Industrial High School," and despite the players' youth—most were *barely* out of high school—"their music is equal to that of many older bands." "The special orchestra of seven musicians," wrote a Kansas City, Missouri, reporter, "was the real sensation of the unit. . . . These boys had the floor literally strewn with instruments and gave . . . fans one of the best musical programs they have heard in many a day."[19]

Longshaw stayed with Smith after she returned to New York, working for three more years as her music director and chief accompanist. He contributed multiple compositions to her repertoire (his anthem to holiday debauchery, "At the Christmas Ball," remains a minor classic). For a while, he was also her lover. The affair was full of jealousies, explosions, and tentative patch-ups, but it resulted in a legacy of historic recordings, most notably Smith's 1925 take on the "St. Louis Blues," a landmark performance that paired the singer with another music icon-in-the-making, the young Louis Armstrong. Historians ever since have lauded the two stars' work on that record, but the contributions of the Birmingham pianist, the session's third performer, also provided an essential element in the record's distinctive, unusual sound: beneath Smith's moans and Armstrong's instrumental asides, you can hear Fred Longshaw's harmonium, a small pump organ more typical of a backcountry church than any blues record or vaudeville stage. It is a sound later critics have again and again described as "wheezing":

Fred. H. Longshaw's Orchestra
with
Bessie Smith
"The Empress of Blues"

**The Fred Longshaw Orchestra, house band of Fourth Avenue's Frolic Theater
and backing band for Bessie Smith, c. 1924.** *Left to right:* **Murray Harper, Teddy
Hill, Fred Longshaw, Carl Bunch, Alex Nabors, Joseph Britton, Shelton Hemphill.
Courtesy Birmingham, Ala. Public Library Archives.**

the instrument creaks, almost breathes, throughout the tune, moving the
rhythm along in slow and steady church-house lurches, at once novel and
archaic.

"St. Louis Blues" became a signature for Smith. Armstrong, all his life,
counted the record as a favorite in a long and storied career. Longshaw, for
his own part, would disappear into the enormous shadow of his more famous
collaborators, rendered anonymous and invisible in one of the century's
most famous recordings. It is the sort of thing that would happen again and
again in the history of jazz: at key moments in the music—just outside the
spotlight's glare, on the sidelines or behind the scenes, writing or arranging
or directing the bands, setting the stage or providing support—there would
be a piece of Birmingham, an echo of Fourth Avenue and Industrial High.

If you only knew how to listen, you could hear the Magic City breathing in the grooves.

After the tour with Smith, the rest of the original Frolic band dispersed. Trumpeter Shelton "Scad" Hemphill, still in his teens, stayed on briefly in New York, recording a pair of tunes with Longshaw and Smith before enrolling at Ohio's Wilberforce College and joining the popular Wilberforce Collegians. By the close of the 1920s he was back in New York, performing in the Benny Carter and Chick Webb orchestras and establishing himself as a dependable sideman: he spent six years in the Mills Blue Rhythm Band, nine with Louis Armstrong, five with Duke Ellington. The rest of the Longshaw crew headed back to Birmingham—for the time being, at least—and when Gennett Records arrived in the summer of 1927, a few of them jumped on the chance to record. Murray Harper, the piston-footed saxophonist, cut three sides—"Sweet Patootie," "Canned Heat Blues," and "Chicken Supper Strut"—with the Triangle Harmony Boys, a group whose personnel has been otherwise lost to history; saxophonist Teddy Hill, trombonist Joe Britton, and banjo player Carl Bunch joined Carl's brother Frank to form the Fuzzy Wuzzies, creators of the "Fourth Avenue Stomp" and two other sides. But the records failed to make any of them stars; the musicians never received royalties or even held copies of the discs. Even more insulting, Gennett leased the recordings to other labels, which in turn slapped the performers with arbitrary pseudonyms: on some pressings, the Fuzzy Wuzzies became the New Orleans Strutters or Little Joe Jackson and His Boys, losing in the process both their names (there was no Joe Jackson in the band) and their unique regional identity.[20]

They would have to make their marks in other ways. A few remained in the pit at the Frolic, but for others the wider world beckoned. Joe Britton settled in New York and over the course of a long career demonstrated his ability to adapt to a range of settings, backing everyone from New Orleans giant Jelly Roll Morton to modern pioneer Dizzy Gillespie, from gospel guitar icon Rosetta Tharpe to the raunchy R&B shouter Wynonie Harris. Teddy Hill, one of the youngest of the bunch, in time would help remake the very culture of jazz; in 1927, seventeen and baby-faced, he set out on the road.[21]

As for Alabama's most famous bandleader: Fess Whatley showed no interest in making records, for Gennett or anyone else. He was understandably indifferent to the business of recording. However much collectors and historians would come to fetishize scratchy old 78s, a bandleader as busy as Whatley, and a businessman as shrewd, knew a handful of discs was irrelevant to success. On Fourth Avenue, a world unto itself, he was undisputed king; and in his classroom—day after day, year after year—he was building a more lasting contribution. By the mid-1920s his products, molded in the school and tested on the strip, were already making their way out into the world. Longshaw and Hemphill and Britton and Hill were only the beginning. Soon the floodgates would open.

FAMOUS RHYTHM

Even more than the vaudeville houses, young Sammy Lowe adored his trips to Fourth Avenue's movie houses. It was the era of the silent cowboy star—Tom Mix, Fred Thompson, Hoot Gibson—and for the Lowe brothers, the theaters made for endless entertainment. "We would go early in the morning and stay all day," Sammy recalled, "looking at the movies and listening to the drummer that sat in the pit." The theaters had something for everyone, were really more than just *movie* houses: they hosted Community Sings, club parties, religious revivals, fraternal meetings, and lectures. In 1924, a visiting minister, Reverend W. H. Hunt, gave a series of talks at the Famous, addressing the growing trend of the Black migration north and offering insights from his own travels. Be careful trading a "certainty" for a "non-certainty," the preacher urged his crowds: if you stayed where you were, where you knew what you had, you could do greater good "in the long run for our people."[1]

For many visitors, the greatest draw of these theaters was not the movies but their music. Before recorded sound crept into the pictures—the Famous and Champion screened their first talkies in 1929—live musicians provided the soundtrack. The drummer was the star, and in Birmingham the greatest of them all was Wilson Driver, the Famous house percussionist and one of Fess Whatley's original Jazz Demons. Outside Birmingham, Driver was a player whose influence outweighed his fame. Drummer Jo Jones, one of his direct protégés and a lifelong friend, would become one of the most celebrated and imitated percussionists in the history of jazz, an innovator whose work in the Count Basie band redefined the very nature of swing. Driver's daughter Sonia Sanchez (born Wilsonia Driver in 1934) would become a leading American poet, a central figure in the Black Arts Movement of the 1960s. Driver himself lived to be ninety-six and as mentor and storyteller helped preserve the roots of the music, spinning stories from the beginnings of jazz. One friend, drummer and writer Chip Stern, found "something Homeric" in his voice. "My father," Sonia Sanchez agreed, "was a great griot." He was famous, too, for his raunchy jokes.[2]

Born in 1904, Driver was drawn early into the art, and the showmanship, of keeping a beat. "When I was a boy," he told Stern, "I saw this guy by the name of George Earl cakewalking along in a street parade. He'd throw that stick up into the air, catch it with his right hand, keep the beat going with his left—Damn! And I thought, 'My God, I want to play drums.'" He took one of his mother's tin tubs, cut a hole in it, strung a rope through it, "slung that around my neck, and started beating on it," singing along to his own banged-out rhythm. His mother declared her tubs off limits, so he got a pair of cheap drumsticks, but those did not last, either. Strictly religious and aghast at her son's syncopation of a sacred tune, his mother confiscated the sticks, snapped them in two, and threw them into the fire. "See," Driver said, "you didn't play or listen to no blues or jazz music—that was for the riff-raff. My Mother thought all that was evil. I mean, she never saw a motion picture in her whole life."[3]

For Driver, though, music—and, indeed, motion pictures—held an un-avoidable allure. At Industrial High School, he struggled to keep rhythm on the big bass drum, so Whatley tied a string to his foot and yanked it in time, until finally the boy absorbed his own sense of the beat. After graduation, he became Whatley's first professional drummer and a ubiquitous presence on the social scene: in addition to his work on the bandstand, his gifts as a comedian and talker made him natural emcee for formal parties and balls. Like other Whatley musicians, he made his living as a teacher.[4]

Driver was playing the Famous even before he got out of high school, landing the drumming gig behind his parents' backs. New movie reels came to the theater with stock charts sketching out the instrumental parts and providing occasional song lyrics (the drummers were expected to double as singers); when there were no stocks, players improvised in response to whatever they saw on the screen. Usually Driver and a pianist provided all the music. "Sometimes, if it was Gloria Swanson, or one of them other la-dee-da pictures, we'd add a violin, clarinet and a trumpet. But mainly it was just the piano and drums."[5]

Driver became an institution in the Famous pit. Younger musicians headed to the theater just for the sake of the drums, indifferent to the cowboys who flickered in silence on-screen. One teenager, in particular, showed up every day for months, his eyes fixed on Driver's hands.[6]

His name was Jonathan Samuel Jones.

Jo Jones, as he later came to be called, left an impression on everyone he met. As an adult, he was strikingly handsome—he had "matinee idol" looks, producer John Hammond said—and as he aged, a gleaming bullet of a bald head only added to the power of his presence. He flashed a huge smile, confident and gleaming. Like his mentor Wilson Driver, he was a man gifted in his talk, legendary as a raconteur, his speech shot through with its own shimmering rhythm and swing. Jones spoke a perpetual jive that was hip, hilarious, and eloquent, aggressive and opinionated, his guttural voice spitting each word with gruff precision. An oral autobiography, published posthumously in 2011, captured Jones's voice in a series of interviews with author Albert Murray. Even a quick sample suggests the drummer's spoken style, full of riffing and irreverent free associations that spun their own logic, syntax, and style: "I sleep with my door unlocked, me and my Bible," Jones says in the book's opening pages. "My friend comes in, she locks the door. I've never locked my door in fifty-six years. Everybody understands how I play: I play free. I'm not afraid of a living person. I fear *God*. I got four hundred religions and five hundred cults. There are two people that give me strength: Billie Holiday and Lester Young."[7]

Everything with Jones was movement. Not only his drumming hands but his whole body, even his conversational style, seemed fueled by a constant frenetic energy. "Man," Ralph Ellison wrote, upon meeting Jones in 1955, "they tell a lot of wild stories about boppers but this stud is truly apt to take off like a jet anytime he takes the notion." For the young Sonia Sanchez, a visit from Jones was always exciting:

> When he opened the door my sister and I *ran* to get away from him because he'd come up to us, grab us one at a time, pitch us up in the air, hold a conversation with my father—right?—then turn at the last second and catch us. Which showed the amazing beat that he had—I mean, just that *rhythm*. I'm very serious, I kid you not: he would grab me, pick me up, throw me up in the air . . .
>
> He would also—every time he was seated, his leg was moving. It never stopped. It was a constant movement. I remember my sister and I used to look at it. He also chewed gum constantly. The leg would be moving, his foot would be moving, patting, and he'd be

chewing gum and talking at the same time; when we got ready to eat dinner at the house he took the gum out and stuck it underneath the table, and my sister and I would look at each other and frown, and go *oo-ooo*! But he was brilliance galore, seeing him play.[8]

In his work with the Basie band, Jones refigured the very role of the drummer. "You don't beat the drum," he said, "you play the drum," and his ability to engage the full musicality of the instrument was unmatched; his work on the hi-hat cymbals, at once propulsive and graceful, was legendary, as was the sheer variety in his approach to his drum set, his facility with the full resources of the instrument. He became, with years, a statesman of the music, a living repository of jazz lore and technique, an inspiration to the up-and-coming players he nicknamed "Young Talent." But he could be volatile and erratic, his temper as sudden as his wit. In his later years, he might conclude a concert abruptly, shouting at band members who did not perform to his standards and storming from the stage. Drummer Shelton Gary—another Birmingham transplant to New York and one of Jones's many followers—remembered him this way: "Jo said what he believed. If he thought you were wrong, or that you had behaved badly, if he felt you were a terrible person, he'd say so right out in the open."[9]

There was, most famously, that mythic moment at a Kansas City jam session, 1936, when a teenage, still-unknown Charlie Parker fumbled through an awkward, interminable solo. Exasperated, Jones tossed a cymbal at Parker's feet with a crash, sending the kid offstage amid the laughter of the crowd. It is a pivotal moment in the legend of Charlie Parker, one that has been retold and embellished for decades: he left the Reno Club humiliated but vowed to friends he would be back and then went home, holed up in his room, and practiced compulsively. The next time he showed up at the Reno, he was another performer altogether: he was, the story goes, *Charlie Parker*.[10]

Jo Jones himself seemed to enter the scene fully formed, sprang up out of nowhere. "As far as much of the music community is concerned," writes jazz historian Burt Korall, "Jo Jones was born when he joined Count Basie." In truth, Jones and his music had by then been years in the making, shaped by a rich early life on the road, by childhood tragedy, by a wide range of influence—and by the city of Birmingham, where the drummer first studied his craft. Unlike so many of his peers, however, Jones grew his music not out of the classroom and its teachings but by a rejection of that training and direct immersion, instead, in the city's professional musical culture.[11]

Born in Chicago in 1911, Jones spent the earliest days of his life, perhaps prophetically, on the move. His father—an electrician, carpenter, boat builder, and jack-of-all-trades—took the family wherever work led, finally landing in Birmingham. Two accidents in Jones's childhood would have profound effects on his development. First—"I was four, five, or six, I don't quite remember"—his entire body was burned badly in a fire. "I wanted," he said, "to copy one of my uncles who lit his cigar with a piece of newspaper." The trick ended disastrously, the paper flaming out of control and leaving Jones an invalid for more than a year. The doctors could offer little help; for relief, the boy slept in a tub full of ice water.[12]

The experience forced Jones into a different sort of childhood. During his slow recuperation he became an avid reader. He grew contemplative and uncommonly mature. And, he later recalled, "I'll never forget one thing. My father brought me silver dollars and a ukulele." It was his father, also, who suggested the field of entertainment as a way to make a living.[13]

Jones was still recovering from the accident when an aunt took him to witness P. G. Lowery's Ringling Brothers show, and the spectacle and its sounds changed him. "I heard—*I felt*—this bass drum," he said, attributing the revelation to "Mr. Emil Helmicke, the greatest bass drum player that ever lived. . . . Just playing the bass drum, he could get eight different notes out of it. He was one of a kind. I remember that bass drum hit my stomach and I never relinquished that feeling. That was my indoctrination to music. I couldn't keep still. My Aunt Mattie held me in her arms. That's when she bought me a snare drum."[14]

Gradually Jones recovered from his injuries. But, when he was ten years old, in 1922, a second accident devastated the family. "Some college students in Tuscaloosa didn't know how to fix a large piece of machinery," and Jones's father tried to help. "The machine—it was like a plow—failed, came apart, and a piece of steel struck him in the back, cutting him from the neck down to the base of the spine." Jones's father was instantly killed, and the boy was forced into early adulthood. "You could say I wasn't born no child," he would later proclaim, reflecting on the traumas of his youth. "I was born a man. Not a baby. Not a boy. A man, in capital letters. No questions, no semicolons, no parentheses, no commas. Period. A man!"[15]

Jones distinguished himself in grade school as both a musician and an athlete. "He was an excellent boxer," remembered Haywood Henry, a lifelong friend, and he became a minor legend at pool checkers, the intricate and ultrafast checkers game steeped in southern Black tradition ("He'd take his front line off the board, and still beat us," Henry marveled). Henry and Jones shared the same fierce sense of competition and the same love for a fight. "In gym class, I never knew if I could beat him or he could beat me," Jones later said of Henry, "and we too old to try it now."[16]

"Jo was also very wise for his age," Henry added. "He was way ahead. He had his life planned. Often he discussed what he was going to do, how he would become a famous drummer." First, though, Jones worked his way through every instrument he could get his hands around: trumpet, sax, piano, timpani, chimes, vibes. He danced. He sang. He knew he would make his life in music, yes, and there was no doubt that he would be famous, but it was not so clear, from the start, which instrument he would make his own. "I was playing all these instruments," he said; it took some time to realize "I was playing drums on all of them," mining each for its rhythmic, percussive, time-keeping potential. By his own account, Jones gave up trumpet when he first heard Louis Armstrong, saxophone when he heard Coleman Hawkins, and piano when he heard Art Tatum, each time realizing he had nothing else to offer the instrument. On the drums, he thought, there was still room for uncharted improvisation: what Armstrong had done for the trumpet, Hawkins the sax, and Tatum the piano, someone could still do for the drums, reshaping the role that instrument played in the music.[17]

Jo Jones thought himself just the man to do it.

First, he had more to learn.

It was hard not to notice Jo Jones in his seat at the Famous. "He'd be there every day in the second row," Wilson Driver said, "staring at me the same way a rattlesnake does at his victim." Finally, "one afternoon I was playing along with a Tom Mix movie, imitating the guys shooting with rim shots and all, and doing the horse's hooves on my wood-blocks. And when I looked up, there was Jo Jones."

"I'm a drummer, too," Jones introduced himself. "Let me show you."[18]

Jones already moved with a swagger of unreserved bravado. "It wasn't that he was such a sassy rascal," Driver said; "it's just that he always wanted to assert himself." Jones took Driver's sticks and showed what he could do: "he did a roll, but he wasn't using his wrists right. It was all arms and fingers, and he was sort of pushing down the sticks on the skin, not lifting up." Driver offered some encouragement and advice and suggested Jones come around for lessons, but Jones refused the offer, preferring just to watch Driver work—"Because," he spat, "you can't play no how." "He was aloof," Driver said; "he wouldn't let me show him anything at all." If Driver offered a tip, Jones barked back, "Wait until I ask!" Once, fed up, Driver told Jones he had worn out his welcome, but the kid just smiled—"I'll be back when I need something else"—and, soon enough, there he was, back for more, like nothing ever happened.[19]

Musically, their biggest difference was what Driver called "the reading thing." Jones would *have* to learn to read music, Driver maintained, but his would-be pupil balked. "I don't need notes for nothin'," he insisted, just instinct and an ear. The disagreement lasted all their lives. Reading, Jones contended, meant nothing to a musician on the road. "You could go to school and get your three or four college degrees," he said, "but when you get out here in the nitty-gritty, you can't be reading out of the textbook." The only education that mattered was experience, and those early days at the Famous proved a training more effective than any classroom could offer.[20]

Years later, Jones would elaborate on the many tricks and effects he had picked up at the theater: "You had to play for the sound of the lion's roar, you had to play for the horses' hoofs, you had to play also crickets, you had to play baby cries, bird whistles, and so forth." To accommodate all those sounds, the theater's drum kit was outfitted with an array of gadgets: wood blocks, whistles, cowbells, and a device called the "slapstick," a couple of wooden slats that, slapped together, made a comical whack. "When you came home late at night," Jones said, enumerating the clichés of the silent screen, "and you was wrong and you was drunk, what did your wife do? She slapped you across the head with a rolling pin!" This is when the slapstick would come into play—giving, Jones said, a whole school of comedy its name. However gimmicky, the movie-house conventions proved an important foundation: Jones remained ever fascinated by the range of sounds that could be manufactured from the raw materials of the instrument. Long after he had been established as a legend, he might still wow his crowds by abandoning his sticks altogether and with his bare hands unleashing a universe of sound.[21]

Jones may have been a difficult student, but he showed quick progress, single-minded discipline, and innate ability—"a born drummer," Driver called him—and he remained loyal, all his life, to the early mentor, only seven years his senior, whom he refused to call anything but "Mr. Driver." Asked if Driver had been his teacher, Jones responded with a growling self-deprecation: "I wasn't intelligent enough to study with him—he had only intelligent students. When I first met Mr. Driver, he had a trumpet, a tuba, an alto horn, a clarinet, a xylophone and a set of drums, and he could read on all of them, and knew all his music theory, too."[22]

"We were like brothers," Driver reflected, "but oh my God, he was a hard nut to crack. . . . Same way he was as a man, was the way he was as a boy. You couldn't tell him a damn thing. But you see, Jo wasn't mean, he just spoke out of turn. If he'd had the class in real life that he had on the drums, there would have been no stopping him." And even so: "Our relationship lasted through his life. I loved and respected him."[23]

Jones stuck with Driver at the Famous for only about six months—"several hours a day, every day." When Driver took a break, he let Jones cover for him: "but he was playing so much drums it just wore out my piano player." So Driver sent Jones down the street to the Frolic, where the boy played backup and ran errands for Butterbeans and Susie, TOBA's musical-comedy stars, who were booked often in town. Soon, Jones left Birmingham, but first he made a characteristic promise to Driver: "When I get back," he announced, "I'll be better than you."[24]

"We'll see," said Driver—but, he later confessed, "his prediction came true. He outdistanced me in almost every way. The roles reversed. He became the teacher." Driver did not hear anything from Jones for a few years, until one night he happened to catch a broadcast from Cincinnati: "And it was Count Basie and his band, and they announced that they had one of the best rhythm sections in the business." The announcer identified a "Jo Jones" on drums, and on the next number, Driver said, "the drummer raised hell."[25]

Driver was tuned in to the broadcast with some friends back in Birmingham. "Damn," one of them said. "You reckon that's the Jo Jones that you know?"

"Hell no!" Driver replied. "He can play, but he can't play *that* good."[26]

A CITY APART

"Birmingham's Harlem Is [a] City Apart," a headline blared in the *Birmingham News*. A writer for the white newspaper surveyed the commercial district that began on Eighteenth Street and ran down Fourth Avenue, heading west to Fifteenth. "Many white men have seen Eighteenth Street," the report began. "Only a few know it. No white man understands it."[1]

Jim Crow had created a gulf between white and Black Birmingham. "Just a stone's throw from City Hall," the *News* explained, was a place "where the Frolic Theater's bright lights twinkle and the Harlem Café beckons," where "lanky cotton hands from the Black Belt" came to "gape" as "dark skinned and dapper city boys strut their stuff." Fourth Avenue was a "paradise of barbecue stands and poolrooms, of soft drink parlors and barber shops," "the Mecca for cooks and chauffeurs on Thursday night, a heaven for miners and mill workers on Saturday night." And, to the paper's white readers, it was a territory altogether foreign.[2]

Some tried, unsuccessfully, to bridge the divide. Just before Christmas 1924, the Frolic announced its first-ever "MIDNIGHT REVIEW FOR WHITE PEOPLE," a seven-act "all-colored" vaudeville lineup headlined by blues sensation Ida Cox. "This Will Give the White People Their First Chance to See a Real Colored Vaudeville Review," ads announced: "We Promise This to Be the Treat of Your Life." Across the country, "Midnight Reviews" had become popular late-night attractions, inviting white visitors into Black spaces, and the Magic City jumped on the trend. Not even a downpour could spoil the turnout; a crowd of 1,200 spectators, all white, braved the rains to pay the sold-out show's one-dollar admission. The *Birmingham News* proclaimed the evening "an unqualified success," with "jazz, comedy, and

79

dancing . . . offered in full profusion." The crowd expressed delight not only over the performances themselves (the great Frolic house band "supplied the snappiest of airs") but also over the unexpected "spotlessness, comfort and appurtenances" of the facility; the sharp, fur-coated footman; and the "20 colored ushers in shining full dress," all "trained to the acme of courtesy." Two weeks later, a second sold-out revue—billed as a "riot of mirth and jazz"—introduced white Birmingham to Butterbeans and Susie, comedian Dookey Singleton, a contortionist, and plenty of music and dancing, all met with "encore after encore." The Frolic announced plans to make the events a biweekly feature.[3]

Not everyone was so enthused. D. E. McLendon, president of the Birmingham City Commission, declared the shows a "menace." (From 1911 to 1963, Birmingham voters elected a governing city commission, whose president functioned essentially as mayor.) McLendon admitted he had not seen either show, but he knew they could not be "good for the morals of the community. . . . I am of the opinion," he offered, "that the shows are objectionable from the standpoint of health, morals, and the intermingling of the races." Despite the Frolic's attempts to uphold the rules of segregation, McLendon insisted the white shows opened too soon after the Black shows finished, that white patrons were entering even as Black guests made their exits, that there was too much chance of contact for the public good. "It also seems objectionable to have numbers of white persons visit a negro section at that time of night," he added, expressing special concern for the safety of white children. To prevent future revues, he threatened an ordinance that would outlaw *all* live entertainment after midnight, but in the end he did not have to go that far. After a private meeting with McLendon and an attorney, the Frolic's manager gave in: there would be no more Midnight Reviews. For all their popularity, the events had not survived their first month.[4]

If white people in Birmingham wanted to access the city's "Harlem," they would have to turn, of all places, to the national pages of the *Saturday Evening Post* and its popular, long-running "Darktown Birmingham" column. There, the white writer Octavus Roy Cohen entertained readers across the country with his mythic recreation of the Fourth Avenue scene. Born in South Carolina, trained first as a journalist and lawyer, Cohen had settled in Birmingham in the 1910s and built a career from his "local color" fictional caricatures of African American life. The city's leading literary dean, he taught English at Birmingham-Southern College, a private white institution perched on the hill above Smithfield, and he founded the Loafers' Club, a circle of writers who met each Wednesday to workshop their stories at Cohen's home in the wealthy Highland neighborhood. Meanwhile, he built a career on his stories for the *Post*, which he anthologized in a series of books and expanded into numerous "Darktown" novels—helping disseminate, in the process, a range of gross racial stereotypes, all centered in a fictionalized Birmingham. So popular were his creations that many white citizens of Birmingham came to call the *real* Fourth Avenue "Cohen Town," renaming the city's most essential Black space for the white man who lampooned it.

The titles alone of Cohen's fifty-something books—*Polished Ebony*, *Highly Colored*, *Assorted Chocolates*, *Dark Days and Black Knights*, *Six Seconds of Darkness*, *Bigger and Blacker*—suggest something of their author's sensibility. Characters spoke in a thick dialect intended for laughs, and Cohen took special aim at what he considered the pretentions of Black Birmingham's social elite—the "Highly Colored"—whose dances, orchestras, top hats, and tuxes were refigured into crass comedy. Recurring characters included bandleader "Perfessor" Aleck Champagne, his Jazzphony Orchestra "blaring saxophoniously" from fraternal bandstands. Roscoe Griggs, a rival bandleader—"I is prob'ly an' undoubtlessly the greatest culud cornet player in the world," he bragged—was fatuous, scheming, and talentless. On the dance floor, a typical conversation might go like this exchange between protagonist Florian Slappey and Miss Eva Mapes, a "bear" of a woman in "an evening gown of corn-colored satin":

> "Miss Mapes, you suttinly looks swelligant tonight."
> "You seems kinder O.K. yo'se'f, Brother Slappey."
> "You slings a pretty wicked toe, Miss Mapes."
> "Us just nachelly belongs together dancin'."[5]

J. L. Lowe grew up, during the height of Cohen's popularity, in the very district the writer mined and distorted for his fictions. "Cohen wrote about Fourth Avenue," said Lowe, "and there were several mythical characters that he created for this area, and they were humorous and in some respects ridiculous in that they were stereotypes like Amos 'n' Andy." (Cohen would later, in fact, write for that radio series.) The Darktown stories led to four movie shorts, produced in 1929 and starring Spencer Williams, the Black actor, screenwriter, and director most famous for his own later work on the *Amos 'n' Andy* TV show. Ironically, the Darktown films provided rare early opportunities for Black artists—the Darktown short *Melancholy Dame* was the first talkie with an all-Black cast—and even if the films were riddled with stereotypes, they were among the only films in which Black moviegoers could see actors who looked anything like themselves on screen. These milestones, though significant, offered limited consolation because, Lowe continued, "that was what people who were seriously trying to get

information about Fourth Avenue were confronted with: they were confronted with the laziness of Blacks and their inability to speak the English
language." The truth was something else altogether. "Fourth Avenue was
able, in terms of our money, to rival any section in Birmingham. [We had]
tailoring shops, had a dry goods store, had several theaters, a record shop,
a peanut shop"—plus hotels, newspapers, a library, doctors, dentists, entrepreneurs, and philanthropists.[6]

Still, none of those achievements sold magazines to white America. What
sold, instead, was the toe-slinging Miss Mapes, the charlatan Roscoe Griggs,
and the "saxophonious" Perfessor Champagne.

Given the city's racial divide, it is no wonder that Black and white musicians heard and saw little of each other. But in the 1920s, jazz became a
national sensation—F. Scott Fitzgerald announced the "Jazz Age" as early as
1922—and white musicians and dancers were fixing their ears and moving
their feet to the sound. Across the country, white dance orchestras incorporated hot sounds and soloists into their performances, and in Birmingham
as elsewhere, white bandleaders catered to the trend, incorporating hot
music into a larger, crowd-pleasing repertoire that included love songs,
foxtrots, and the latest Tin Pan Alley and Broadway hits. Much as Octavus
Roy Cohen translated Black life into his own brand of cartoonish comedy,
white bandleaders found in Black music a usable resource for their own
forms of expression. On both sides of town, jazz belonged to the world of
elite society dances, as even the band names made clear: while Fourth Avenue boasted its Sax-o-Society Orchestra and Society Troubadours, white
dancers moved, just a few blocks away, to the strains of Jack Linx and His
Society Serenaders. In both Black Birmingham and white, "society" was the
thing—there were simply two societies.

As always, the balance was fundamentally uneven. Fess Whatley played
a steady stream of white dances, bringing his music into country clubs and
private homes, but the exchange did not go both ways: Black musicians had
no opportunities to watch their white counterparts perform. There were
occasional interactions behind the scenes—Fess Whatley and his student
Amos Gordon sometimes wrote arrangements for white bands to perform—
but the musicians never played together, even informally. Such gatherings
were not just socially unthinkable: under Alabama law, they were illegal. As
a teenager, Frank Adams wondered what Whatley's arrangements might
have sounded like when performed by white musicians. Did they sound like
us, he thought, or like something else entirely? There was simply no way to

know. Jim Crow stoked plenty of curiosity but left most questions about the other world unanswered.[7]

Black musicians might know the names of some of the bands, if not their sounds. There were, among others, the Bill Nappi Orchestra, Earl Simpson's Rhythm Kings, DeWitt Shaw's Vagabonds, Curtis Major and His Joy Boys, and Pierre Dale's Air-Dales (so called, the *Birmingham News* observed, "because they are a bunch of jazz-hounds"). The groups played in the city's most lavish venues: at the Tutwiler Hotel's gilded, Louis XIV–style "Gold Room"; in the ballroom of the Club Florentine, surrounded by Italian-inspired architecture; at the Cascade Plunge resort and pavilion, just outside town. A few of the groups made records; from 1924 to 1927, Jack Linx and his band trekked back and forth to Atlanta to record more than twenty sides for the Okeh label. That group's singer and banjo player, Maurice Sigler, cut four tunes of his own with a smaller combo before launching a successful career as a Tin Pan Alley lyricist. And when Gennett Records arrived in the summer of 1927, four white Birmingham bands ventured into the studio to save their sounds for posterity. The records that resulted were peppy, polished, and danceable but lacked the bluesier swagger and ragged edges that characterized Gennett's recordings of the Fuzzy Wuzzies and other Black Alabama bands. Like Birmingham's other Gennett recordings, these sides essentially disappeared, bringing neither fame nor fortune to the artists.

Radio did provide Black listeners their one point of access to local white bands. Not even Jim Crow could section off the airwaves, keeping white broadcasts out of Black homes or Black broadcasts out of white homes. Radio offered glimpses, however incomplete, into the other world. Growing up, Haywood Henry listened to two white Birmingham bands on the radio, but he had never seen the groups in person or talked, as a fellow musician, to their players. In the 1950s, he happened to meet Jack Linx in person—on Forty-Eighth Street in Manhattan, where Linx, long retired from playing, ran a music shop. Brought together by Linx's selection of woodwinds, the men discovered they had both moved to New York from Birmingham some years before. "I said that when I was a little boy I used to hear a wonderful orchestra on the air in Birmingham, and I told him the theme song. He said that it was his orchestra. The funny thing about it was that he told me that he had a Black woman singing in his orchestra, in Birmingham. This," Henry remarked, "was in the twenties," when such collaborations were unheard of, not only in the South but all over the country. Benny Goodman's much-touted efforts to integrate his own band did not begin until 1935—but a decade earlier, in Birmingham, Jack Linx's broadcasts were integrating the airwaves already, if invisibly and unnoticed. Regrettably, if Linx told Henry the name of that singer, Henry failed to record the detail.[8]

For most of white Birmingham, interest in jazz fizzled early. The music offered happy access to a national fad, but there was no greater sense of community, urgency, or local pride to propel a meaningful and lasting tradition. White musicians in Birmingham lacked the system of jazz apprenticeship that the Black community developed, early on, in its schools; there was in white Birmingham no equivalent of Fess Whatley, no sense of a jazz lineage being passed from one generation to the next, no widespread notion of the music as a vital means of economic survival and social prestige.

Cultural reservations also proved a barrier. In 1924, the white-owned *Birmingham Age-Herald* summarized a new study beneath the alarming headline "Jazz and Suicide." "Of the fifteen thousand suicides in the United States during the last year," the paper reported, "a large majority may be attributed to the jazz spirit." For many white Americans, "the jazz spirit" suggested, more than music, a culture of decadence, the soundtrack and inspiration to all manner of depravity: a world of bobbed hair and bootleg gin, of fast cars and loose morals. To some, the music's rise suggested also the dangerous intermingling of Black and white. As for suicide, "nobody doubts that the jazz spirit arises largely from the wish to get a kick out of life," but "those who have been lifted by jazz to the pinnacle of gayety naturally later fall into the dumps," a "morbid" mood wherein "the vital forces are low and the wish to live is relatively weak." The upshot was simple: jazz could be deadly.[9]

In 1930, Jack Linx retired his bandleader's baton, handing his orchestra over to a reed player named Coleman Sachs, who expanded the group into a larger, schmaltzier unit. A British researcher wrote to Linx at his Manhattan music store in 1961, seeking some information on the old records and the band that made them; Linx wrote back with a hazy memory of those days and with little interest. "It has been so long since I have had my own band," he confessed, "that I had to think a lot to remember some of the recordings." He owned only "one or two of those old recordings" anymore, and anyway, he added, "believe me they sound corny now."[10]

Black musicians may have been teachers, role models, even celebrities in their own communities, but, J. L. Lowe pointed out, as far as white Birmingham was concerned, "we were the hired help." To reach a second- or third-story ballroom, musicians had to ride the freight elevator, and to use the restroom "you had to find the one that said 'colored.'" If there was *no* colored restroom—which was often the case in the private homes where Black musicians played—they did not use the restroom at all.[11]

Travel presented other challenges. For a couple of Cadillacs full of Black men, the road could be dangerous, especially after dark. Fifty miles north of Birmingham was the town of Cullman, a center of Ku Klux Klan activity and one of the South's most notorious "sundown towns," so called for the threats such towns issued to Black visitors who lingered after dark. Despite the warnings, Fess Whatley and his band were regulars in Cullman, where local dances advertised "Professor Whatley and His Harlem Rhythm Boys" or "Fess Whatley and His Dark Town Dance Orchestra," assigning to the band whatever name promoters saw fit. Lowe recalled the year Whatley played Cullman's Roosevelt Ball, an annual celebration in honor of the president's birthday, but insisted on—and, remarkably, received—a police escort, both going and coming. "Even with the police," said Lowe, "we were all waiting for some kind of disturbance." The tensest moment of the night came when a trumpeter dropped his mute, "and one of the white girls ran up and handed it to him." The band waited for repercussions for this blatant social transgression, but nothing happened, and the show went on. Maybe, Lowe thought, the town did not deserve its reputation.[12]

Maybe. But Whatley continued to take precautions, for years, when his band traveled to and from Cullman. By the mid-1940s, he no longer required a police escort, but as protection he wore a chauffeur's cap for the drive; if he was pulled over, he would claim to be no more than a white man's driver, hired to ferry the "boys" to some rich white folks' function. As a bandleader and independent professional with his own fleet of new-model Cadillacs, Whatley knew the threat he posed to rural authorities, and he knew the threat they posed to him. The chauffeur's cap and subservient pose were his disguise. And they worked.[13]

Years later, stories of those Cadillacs and the Cullman County cops were common among Whatley's old students.[14] The anecdotes were almost always told for laughs—"A funny thing happened on the way home to Birmingham," Sammy Lowe began—but unmistakable beneath the surface were deadly serious subtexts. "Where the hell are you boys going so fast?" sneered the cop in Sammy Lowe's story.

"Mr. Officer," Fess replied, "we are musicians and we are playing for Mr. John T. Whatley, and Mr. Whatley will be angry if we are late."

"The policeman paused," Lowe continued, "scratched his head, and said, 'Y'all go ahead, but tell Mr. Whatley that I said *I'll* be mad if y'all keep driving so fast!" The caravan continued on its way, another controversy avoided, another story added to the repertoire. Hearing a white man with a badge utter the words "Mr. Whatley," however clueless he may have been to their meaning, was icing on the cake. Whatley's act may have given white authorities

Fess Whatley poses with one of his signature Cadillacs, late 1950s.
Courtesy Birmingham, Ala. Public Library Archives.

what they wanted, but it left them the butt of a joke they did not even know
had been played.

Fess walked a dangerous, delicate line. He was a powerful Black man in
the heart of the white supremacist South, a place whose social structure
depended on denying Black men power. Every musician knew the threats.
On the Bessemer highway, just west of Birmingham, traffic on some nights
slowed to a crawl, while hooded Klansmen burned crosses on the roadside
and drivers gawked from their cars. Whatley's players kept their heads down
and kept moving. The Cadillacs themselves, meanwhile, were powerful symbols that openly resisted the prevailing social order. Few drivers, Black or
white, owned Cadillacs in the early 1920s, when Fess first developed a taste
for the car; for decades the Cadillac remained a bold statement of independence, achievement, and assertion for a Black driver, especially in the South.
As late as 1949, *Ebony* magazine would declare "the Cadillac . . . an instrument of aggression, a solid and substantial symbol for many a Negro that
he is as good as any white man." These meanings were not lost on Whatley.[15]

If Fess always monitored his musicians for propriety on the bandstand, the
stakes were higher and the scene more heavily charged anytime the group

played for a white audience. The more fun white dancers had—the more freely they drank and moved to the music—the more trouble it might mean for the band. By the second set of the night, any room of white socialites would get looser and rowdier, the dancing more risqué, the tempers more volatile. J. L. Lowe recalled a typical night at a party in Mountain Brook, Birmingham's most elite white suburb, when the women's moves became racier and racier as the night wore on. "The type of dancing," Lowe explained, with classic Whatley-esque euphemism, "was not in the best interest of culture, and Fess told us to keep our eyes on the music, not to notice how they were dancing." The printed score, so central to Whatley's training, served yet another practical purpose: it doubled as a shield.[16]

Whatley may have carefully crafted an air of respectability and refinement in his band, but white dancers still saw and heard the stereotypes they sought. Hot jazz performed by Black musicians—"jungle music," it was sometimes called—provided just the excuse for members of white Birmingham's most elite families to indulge their fantasies of primitive blackness, throwing off their own mannerly decorum, dancing and drinking unrestrained, and embracing an exaggerated sensuality their social status typically held off limits.

A Christmas dance in the "lily-white" Highland neighborhood demonstrated the deeply charged dynamic.[17] "Fess had briefed the band," said Sammy Lowe, "telling us to be careful, be pleasant, and if spoken to by any of the white guests we were to say Yes sir, Yes ma'am, No sir, and No ma'am, and to never look any white lady straight in the eye. And if we were asked to play Dixie, we were to play it with a smile." The gig went well until intermission, when the band retreated to the kitchen for dinner. A white partygoer, twenty years old and stumbling drunk, lurched into the room, complimented the band's playing, and spoke directly to Fess: "When you boys go back, I want you all to get hot and play some jungle music." Fess agreed and smiled. "As for me," said Lowe, still a student but sitting in with Whatley's professional band of teachers, "I had often been called 'boy' by whites; after all, I was a boy in age. But here this young man calling the fellows in the band 'boy,' upset me [to] no end. I think it hurt me more so because of my admiration for Fess. Here was this man, in the true sense of the word, an outstanding member of the Black community, highly respected, outstanding in spiritual and material achievement—who had to take this belittlement of his manhood."

Fess voiced no complaint, evinced no humiliation or hurt, just went back out, the picture of poise, and played. He swung the band into a series of up-tempo numbers, calling his key soloists forward one by one. "We went into Congo Rock," Lowe continued, "an original of mine featuring [Wilson] Driver playing tom-toms. That did it. I guess this was what they called jungle music, and evidently what they had been waiting for. . . . Pretty soon the ladies were shaking their hips, trying to outdo each other."

And here came the next problem for Fess: he could not stop a room full of rich, inebriated white women from lifting and swishing their skirts and grinding their hips—and he could not let his men be caught seeing what was right in front of their faces. "Directly in front of the band, a lady in a flower-colored evening gown was shaking like mad. Fess said to the band, 'Eyes left, gentlemen!' but to the left of the band another lady was trying to outdo the one in the front by pulling her dress up to her knees and swinging her hips." Fess issued a new order: "Eyes right, gentlemen."

"But Fess," Wilson Driver protested, "they're dancin' all over the place!"

So Fess Whatley breathed out a final command: *Close your eyes, gentlemen!*

Racial and sexual mores followed Whatley's band well beyond the South; so did the band's reputation for its adherence to the day's most conservative conventions of conduct. Wilson Driver remembered, from the 1934 tour, a stop in Kenosha, Wisconsin, where "this white man come up to Fess" and gushed with appreciation for the band. "You know," he said, "Kenosha is just a stone's throw from Chicago, and we could have gotten a band from there, but when we heard about you fellows, and that you were all teachers in the city system, we figured we didn't have to worry about you and our women. One time the Black musicians from Chicago came over here and took advantage of our women, who had no better sense. So we just stopped having Black bands until you came along.'"[18]

Fess assured the man there was no cause for worry; all the fellows in his band were schoolteachers and married, and he had personally promised their wives he would "keep them straight." He had also briefed the band: "Even though we were up north," Sammy Lowe said, "we were still not to look at white women." In 1930s America, an unwanted, even an altogether unintended, look could get a Black man killed.[19]

There were other, more subtly charged interactions to navigate. On the same tour, one of the band's hosts offered the group some watermelon for dessert, but Fess declined on his musicians' behalf. "Unfortunately," he politely explained, "none of us like watermelon." "I know why Fess made that statement," Sammy Lowe said, years later. "Every sign we'd see along the highway of a happy Negro boy eating watermelon always upset Fess. However, as I looked at those beautiful red slices of watermelon, I wanted to say, 'Fess, just this one time . . . ?'" Lowe knew, though, to keep his mouth shut, knew that for Whatley a watermelon was more than a watermelon, just as a Cadillac was more than a Cadillac and—for better or worse—a band, always, was more than a band.[20]

"My father tells this amazing story," Sonia Sanchez said; but, she had to admit, "when I heard it, I didn't pay a lot of attention."[21] Sanchez had learned to tune out the tale her father, Wilson Driver, often repeated from his days on the road with Whatley—until one day she heard him tell it, this time to her own children, and she heard it with new ears.

> They were in this little Southern town. I don't remember where, if it was Alabama, Mississippi, whatever—and it seems that all these white women came down and were hanging around the stage, flirting with the musicians; and it got to be really dicey, right? And some guy pulled out a gun and said, "Okay"—it was going to be a rough scene there—"You guys play 'Dixie.'" These were schoolteachers, mind you, and they knew that they were being disrespected. They were packing up at the time, and Fess Whatley was getting them together, saying, "Let's get out of here; this is getting really messy." These guys were not flirting with the women at all, but the women were flirting with them.

By the time the "trouble" started, all the instruments had been packed but the drums. So Wilson Driver picked up his sticks, beat out a snatch of "Dixie," and bowed. "That was it and they left. He did what this drunken guy wanted him to do, and then they got out of Dodge."

All her life, Sanchez—the activist daughter, steeped in the politics of Black Power and protest—had winced at the story, embarrassed at what she had dismissed as her father's submissive gesture, rapping out "Dixie" with a docile bow for a crowd of racist drunks, an episode he now relayed as if it were a joke. "I think he might have said that he did a little dance, too, you know? And I said, oh, gosh, my *father* doing that!" But years later, standing in the kitchen, overhearing the old man repeat the story to his grandchildren, something inside her shifted.

"And I came out of the kitchen when I was cooking Sunday dinner, and I said, 'What an amazingly brave thing to have done, Daddy.' I remember he looked up at me. And I said, 'Because it wasn't what the guy wanted, but you gave him *something* of what he wanted,' right? And that was a brave thing to do. I remember being older, with my own children—that was a different interpretation, years later." What Sanchez heard now was the story of a man who "was able to put a cap on something that could have been very explosive and negative and dangerous," to put an end to the "ranting and raving and anger" of a drunken antagonist and get out of town in one piece—without, in the end, really playing more than a nod to "Dixie" at all. It was like other stories of the Whatley band, stories of the subtlest subversion in the face of white prejudice and power. Read this way, Wilson Driver emerged not as victim or pawn or shuffling clown but as hero, a man of bravery who met danger with creativity and calm.

Sonia Sanchez had spent her life embarrassed by the story. Now she began telling it herself.

THE GREAT WIDE WORLD

Birmingham had built for itself a thriving music community, a training ground and homegrown professional network for its players. But the place remained, essentially, a small town, and aspiring musicians fixed their gazes and tuned their ears northward for promises of something greater than Fourth Avenue could offer. While a core of players stayed home (often juggling their music with full-time teaching jobs), many others looked elsewhere, taking inspiration from the growing ranks of local-trained jazzmen already making it big in the country's most glamorous cities.

Jazz has always blended themes of rootedness and mobility, its distinctly local traditions engaging the world outside in a steady back-and-forth. For all its specific sense of place, the Birmingham tradition had movement at its core, was shaped by—and helped shape—the larger Great Migration. Often remembered as a movement out of the South, that historic shift first brought massive movement *within* the South, as Black families left the countryside for the nearest urban centers. Indeed, the first pioneers of Birmingham jazz arrived in the city from more rural outposts: Pops Williams and Fess Whatley from Tuscaloosa County; W. C. Handy from Florence; High C Foster from Cuthbert, Georgia. Their followers—the Birmingham players who would shape the sounds of the 1920s, '30s and '40s—tended to be first-generation children of the city, their parents transplants from any number of smaller Alabama towns: Livingston, Selma, Talladega, Gulfcrest, Demopolis. Those original migrants came not only for work but for the sake of their children's educations. Industrial High School was once again key, a beacon for families across Alabama, its promise fueling migration and remaking the cultural landscape of the city and the region. Its band room was not only ground zero for the burgeoning jazz culture but a space in which parents' dreams for their children could be made real. The next wave of migration followed: for many graduates of that Industrial band room, the music provided a way out of the South.

By the start of the 1930s, Birmingham's jazz diaspora already stretched across the country. Crip Miller was blowing a horn in Chicago, George Hudson in St. Louis. Frank Bunch had left his Fuzzy Wuzzies for Dayton, Ohio, where he started his own society dance orchestra; trumpeter Rushton Miller had done the same in Nashville. Herman Grimes, one of Whatley's original Jazz Demons, toured the South as leader of the Sunset Minstrels and then worked his way to Kansas City and later to Seattle, where he established himself as one of the Pacific Northwest's leading trumpeters. Brothers Cass and Ted McCord, clarinet and saxophone players, started with Ohio's Wilberforce Collegians, performing alongside fellow Birmingham exports Scad Hemphill and Henry Hicks; all four later made their way east, playing (often together) in one hot outfit after the next. As the first generation of jazz musicians took the new music overseas, Birmingham players were among its ambassadors. Trombonist Robert Horton spent the better part of 1927 in South America, touring Uruguay, Argentina, and Brazil in the Leon Abbey Orchestra; in 1930, trumpeter Leon Scott joined Chicago's Earl Moss Orchestra for a tour of France, Belgium, and Luxembourg. Cass McCord would traverse the globe for much of the thirties, playing Hungary, France, the Netherlands, Egypt, and India. He wrote his old maestro from the pyramids—"Hello Fess, I am still going strong"—and encouraged his teacher to write him in Bombay: "I'll be there next week for six months, and then to China, Java, etc. Regards to the boys."[1]

Back in the classroom, "the boys" listened enraptured as Whatley recounted his old pupils' adventures, holding up their latest postcards as proof. The underlying message was clear: stick to your studies, and one day it will be you out there on the road. "We would dream of the time people would be talking about *us* playing some place," said Sammy Lowe.[2]

In the early 1930s, no son of Birmingham was more celebrated back home than the young bandleader Teddy Hill. He was a national sensation on the rise, a recording artist and radio star, a bona fide celebrity whose picture hung on Whatley's classroom wall, an alum whose name Fess intoned often to his students. Hill was everything students could hope to be, and he was more than just a musician—he was the peak of hip sophistication, handsome and dapper and possessing a charming, disarming smile. He wore his hair in a conk and his mustache pencil-thin; he dressed extravagantly, in

Teddy Hill was among the first of Fess Whatley's musicians to find national success. Like other Whatley protégés, he sent back home to his mentor cards, letters, and signed publicity shots like this one. Courtesy Birmingham, Ala. Public Library Archives.

a fur coat or a white tuxedo, a flower pinned to his lapel. He was stylish, good-natured, and cool, the embodiment of the rising swing culture.

He was, for all that, fundamentally *nice* besides—"one of the sweetest leaders I ever worked for," trombonist Dicky Wells recalled (Wells's other employers would include Count Basie, Fletcher Henderson, Benny Carter, and Ray Charles). As bandleader, Hill set the example for his men. "He didn't do anything he didn't want you to do," Wells said. "He never drank too much on the job, and he was a gentleman. . . . Male and female, everybody respected him." Black entertainment columns not only held him up as a showman but lauded his skills as a businessman. Like his mentor in Birmingham, he was "a stickler for time," ultraprofessional and always punctual. He was confident but humble, remembered where he came from, and wrote home anytime he could.[3]

At Industrial High School, Hill had first enrolled in auto mechanic courses—but, wrote columnist Roi Ottley, "one day one of the motors fell on his foot and prevented further study. His enforced idleness made him study drums." He moved on, under Whatley, to trumpet and finally ("because of a broken tooth") to reeds. He joined the Frolic house band as saxophonist and was only fifteen when that group hit the road with Bessie Smith. Returning to Birmingham, he played with Frank Bunch's Fuzzy Wuzzies, and in 1927 he struck out on his own, landing first in Chicago and then in New York. He joined the George Howe Orchestra, which soon regrouped under pianist Luis Russell to become one of New York's earliest and most exciting swing bands. On occasion the Russell outfit backed Louis Armstrong onstage or in the studio; Hill appears with the band on two classic Armstrong sides from 1929, "Mahogany Hall Stomp" and "I Can't Give You Anything but Love."[4]

Next to the best of that band's players, Hill did not stand out as a soloist; but, as he would throughout his career, he distinguished himself in other ways behind the scenes. "He was a good team man," drummer Paul Barbarin said, noting an affable and upbeat devotion to the group, a trait that would color all of Hill's efforts. He was a natural organizer and administrator. Russell entrusted to him a variety of managerial duties, including one for which the fashion-plate Hill was perfectly suited: the selection of the band's wardrobe. Every chance he got, Hill outfitted the band with a new set of uniforms, the cost of which would be deducted later from each player's salary. The saxophonist's enthusiasm for the job sometimes strained the camaraderie of Russell's typically easygoing band. "I got mad," one player said, "getting this small salary and Teddy was talking about buying yet another uniform." They had come to make music, not collect suits—but the guys *did* look good, and Teddy was hard not to like. He stayed with Russell until 1931 and then launched his own band.[5]

The Teddy Hill Orchestra took off, fast. An eight-month residency at Harlem's Ubangi Club led to a stay at the Roseland Ballroom and then to a long-running relationship with the illustrious Savoy Ballroom. "The fellows in the band considered Teddy a good business man, because he kept us working," remembered saxophonist Howard Johnson. Hill projected a charismatic, confident presence onstage: "He was a good looking fellow, and he used to get up there and wave a long stick." At first he played alto with the band, "but after a while he put [the instrument] down and just waved the stick." Hill's earliest musicians stamped their leader with a nickname that surely made him feel good: they started calling him "Fess."[6]

Hill was becoming a force in New York's Black music scene, offstage as well as on. He was an active member of the city's musicians' union, Local 802, and he informally assisted owner Bert Hall at the Rhythm Club, the 132nd Street hangout at the heart of New York's jazz community. Hall had opened the club in 1929 as a space where Black musicians could gather, talk shop, shoot pool, eat, drink, jam, and pick up jobs; bandleaders knew they could check in at the Rhythm Club, day or night, to fill any openings in their rosters. When Hall died suddenly in the spring of 1932, Henry Minton, another prominent union leader, became the club's owner, and Hill served as one of three cooperative managers. "Business has increased under the new regime," the *New York Age* reported that summer, "and several loose screws tightened to place the venture on sound business principles." Hill—already cementing his reputation as promoter of new talent and as advocate for the fair and equal treatment of Black musicians—embraced the club's role as benefactor for unemployed musicians. In March 1933, he was elected the organization's president and in his expanded role established a formal booking office for club members and an assistance program for out-of-work players. "Getting work for the unemployed musicians is a difficult task, but one that is enjoyed by the new president," the *Chicago Defender* reported. "Teddy has become very popular with all club members because of his desire to do the right thing at the right time." This, too, would be part of Hill's reputation for years to come.[7]

If examples like Hill's made Whatley students thrill with possibility, an equal thrill was the arrival of celebrated visitors from the outside, men who not only had visited the North but were fundamentally part of it, whose lives smacked with the prestige, mystery, and dazzle of far-off worlds.

Occasionally one of these outsiders would leave a profound stamp on the local music scene, helping shape the ways Birmingham musicians understood and pursued their craft. In the dawn of the swing era, two touring acts made especially powerful impressions, mesmerizing audiences with their musical prowess and unforgettable showmanship.

Reverend George Wilson Becton of the Gospel Feast Party was a Harlem celebrity and force of nature, controversial and colorful and, for many years, a favorite recurring visitor to Black Birmingham. In January 1928, Becton kicked off a monthlong revival at the Sixteenth Street Baptist Church. "We are going to shake old Birmingham as she has never shaken before," he predicted, and, sure enough, Birmingham shook. "Becton Is Sweeping Birmingham," a front-page headline ran in the *Birmingham Reporter*; "Thousands Flock to Meeting—They Try to Explain His Power but Can't." One of the revival's central attractions—along with Becton's flamboyant preaching and showmanship—was what the paper labeled "Music Sublime," performed by a band of swinging prodigies. "If one did not see the faces of the Gospel Feast Party," the paper gushed, "it could be easily construed that they were angels and the music was played from instruments consecrated in Glory. They are young and active, full of fire [and] expression in song and music." Another report detailed the reverend's enormous entourage: "The World's Gospel Feast Party consists of thirteen young men who have consecrated their services to the Lord to do His work. The party is composed of two trumpeters, one violinist, organist, pianist, personal attendant to the evangelist, chauffeur, gospel singer, journalist, utility man, secretary and two managers." The reverend's wife, Josephine, performed triple duty as singer, pianist, and preacher.[8]

Becton's local following was large and eager enough that the *Birmingham Reporter* traced the party's movements across the country in blaring front-page headlines: "Dr. G. Wilson Becton, Dramatic Evangelist, Sweeping Philadelphia Like a Tidal Wave"; "Spectacular Becton Wages Great Campaign against Sin"; "Gospel Feast Party Invades New York"; "Dr. Becton Grips Harlem"; "People Crying for More." The crew was back in Birmingham in the summer of 1928 for another Gospel Feast, leaving dozens of converts in its wake. "89 Baptized," the *Reporter* declared; "Thousands Turned Away; Mrs. Becton Charms Great Crowds in Song."[9]

For all this enthusiasm, plenty of skeptics voiced their disdain for the flashy preacher and his "Consecrated Dime," a venture wherein Becton collected daily ten-cent contributions from his followers, promising thousand-fold returns. Poet Langston Hughes reviled the "Big Black Saint Becton" as a flagrant con man and in his memoir *The Big Sea* offered a biting portrait

of the preacher. Hughes visited Becton in his lavish home, where the reverend lived in evangelical opulence with his musicians and entourage. "There
were luxurious drapes at the windows," Hughes wrote, "with the sign of the
cross woven in them. There was a private chapel where Dr. Becton prayed
at dawn before a lighted cross. And he slept in a specially built bed with two
transparent crystal crosses in the bed-panels at head and foot—crosses that
gave out a soft glow as he slept, lighted, he said, by God." Becton, Hughes
concluded, "was a charlatan if there ever was one, but he filled the huge
church—because he gave a good show. He had a small jazz band with him,
playing church music in syncopated time, and they would begin to play early
in the evening so that the congregation would be in a good mood by the
time the Reverend Dr. Becton arrived." Hughes thought Becton "a very bad
preacher, running back and forth across the platform, mouthing inanities
and whistling for God, but he could make people shout, nevertheless. And
the stirring rhythms of his excellent gospel swing band would cause many
to rise and dance in the aisle for joy."[10]

No description of Becton overlooked that band, those swinging disciples who each night translated the Word of God into dance-hall rhythms
and sounds. Becton's musicians were in large part youths the evangelist
picked up and unofficially adopted on his travels through the South; the
band also kept tabs on the promising young players who sat in for this or
that revival, and months after sitting in, a musician might receive an invite
from Becton, along with train fare for the trip north. When they were not
on the road, band members lived with Becton in Harlem, where he enrolled
them in school and provided food, lodging, and a wealth of performance
experience. Parents swept up with Becton's message and charisma—and
hopeful for the opportunities such a move would afford their children—gave
the reverend their blessing as he took the young musicians under his wing.
Several Birmingham players, notably Haywood Henry and trumpeter Joe
Guy, would find their first tickets out of the South as members of the Becton
band. The job proved valuable training: while the schools emphasized strict
interpretation of the score, Becton balanced against more formal concerns
an appreciation for "head" arrangements, on-the-spot improvisation, and
the ability to move with the spirit, to channel and stir the emotion of the
crowd.[11]

Musicians did not have to join the show to feel Becton's influence. For
young Sammy Lowe, the revivals offered a model of showmanship equal to
any jazz band. "What I liked about Rev. Becton, though I didn't know it at
the time, was that through him I was initiated into seeing show business
at its best. Years later, I was to realize that what he was doing was like a

Broadway musical or a terrific arrangement of music." First, the band would get the crowd worked up, until finally Becton would make a dramatic entrance (he once held a revival in Birmingham every night for three months and each night emerged in a different overcoat). Then the preaching began: "Rev. Becton would build his sermon up and up and up until you'd think you couldn't take it anymore, then he'd bring it to an abrupt halt and stand there, ofttimes perspiring and you could hear a murmur go through the crowd as they thought about the things he had said." Sammy's brother, J. L., joined the church during Becton's revival and remained a member all his life. Though Sammy did not follow, Becton's showmanship and performance left another kind of impact on him—if not on his spiritual leanings, then on his music. "Rev. Becton influenced me to the extent that to this day when I make an arrangement I try to have contrast as far as the build-up goes," starting out soft, as Becton did in his sermons, and building to a crescendo.[12]

For Becton himself, the Party would soon be over—and his exit would be just as dramatic, just as sensational and controversial, as the legend he had created in life. In May 1933, in the city of Philadelphia, two white men kidnapped the preacher in his own car and filled his body with bullet holes. The car was found with Becton inside, still breathing but in critical condition. He died in the hospital, four days later.

The circumstances of Becton's murder were shrouded in mystery, the killers never found. A titillated public debated the possibilities: the evangelist ("Saint or Charlatan?" the papers asked) had run afoul of the mob, of real estate racketeers, of jealous husbands or rival ministers. On the day of the funeral, 12,000 mourners jockeyed for space at Harlem's Salem Methodist Episcopal Church. A riot erupted in the street, as the late Reverend Becton moved his followers for the last time into a frenzy.[13]

Just a few months after the death of Becton, another legend of Harlem made his own first appearance in Birmingham. While Reverend Becton had forged a long-running relationship with the city, Duke Ellington in a single visit would leave an impression every bit as acute.

Ellington had vowed he would never tour the South, citing the injustice of segregation and the threats of violence that had met other touring Black bands. In 1933, however, he changed his tune: encouraged by a recent run of successes—including his first, much-lauded tour of Europe—Ellington acquired a string of Pullman train cars, and his band headed South in security and style. Strategically, the cars allowed the band to circumvent the demands of segregated lodging while keeping the musicians insulated from potential violence; their sides emblazoned with Ellington's name, the cars became part of the band's exotic and elegant allure. From their mode of transportation down to their uniforms, members of Ellington's band commanded attention. Once they started playing, the effect only multiplied.[14]

Ellington's first southern tour electrified the imaginations of young Black musicians. Author Ralph Ellison witnessed the band's stop in Oklahoma City that fall and later captured the power of the players' appearances: "And then Ellington and the great orchestra came to town," he wrote, "came with their uniforms, their sophistication, their skills; their golden horns, their flights of controlled and disciplined fantasy; came with their art, their special sound; came with Ivy Anderson and Ethel Waters singing and dazzling the eye with their high-brown beauty and with the richness and bright feminine flair of their costumes, their promising manners. They were news from the great wide world, an example and a goal." A few years later, in college at Alabama's Tuskegee Institute, Ellison encountered Ellington again and this time got to shake his hand. "Those of us who talked with him were renewed in our determination to make our names in music," he wrote. (An aspiring trumpeter, Ellison in the end made his name in literature instead, but the music of Ellington and other pioneers was embedded in the sound and structure of his prose—including the jazz-drenched epic *Invisible Man*.)[15]

It is impossible to gauge how many young men drew inspiration and determination from Ellington's example as his train blew its smoke through the South. In Birmingham, the effect was profound. "We hadn't seen anything like that before," explained Frank Adams; he was barely old enough to hold a horn, but his father brought him anyway to witness the spectacle of Duke's arrival at the Masonic Temple. "The first thing I saw—I remember, I had seen a black tuxedo before, but I hadn't seen a tartan *plaid* one! He had a *tartan plaid tuxedo*, and—I always think about this—he looked, to me, like a *giant* of a man. . . . We were just in awe." The performance itself was nothing short of extraordinary.

The first number they played was "Ring Dem Bells." People were just frantic because they hadn't heard a band play like that. And they didn't have any space in time for anything but that music: as soon as they got through with one piece, [drummer Sonny Greer would] hit the gong—*bam!*—they're out there again, and off—*bam!* If you were out there dancing, it looked like he was *punishing* you, because he got through one fast number—*bam!*—another one—*bam!*—another one, right after the other one—there were some sweet numbers, too, but this was a *dance*. They didn't take any prisoners. I mean, they swung. They just swung the folks to *death*—I guess he figured that we wanted to dance down here. And he gave them enough that after about an hour they were soaked. They had no air-conditioning— they'd throw the windows up and they were perspiring. Men were putting their shirts back in their britches and women were pulling their dresses up. When they found out that the music didn't take any breaks, they just stayed out there as long as they could.[16]

Also in the audience was the teenage Sammy Lowe. "Believe me," he would later insist, "there is no comparison between just hearing a band and hearing plus seeing a band. We were able to enjoy the music and observe the way each individual moved, and his showmanship." The experience was enough to set the course Lowe would follow for the rest of his life. "Where up to this point I had been undecided as to what I was going to do in life, Duke Ellington and his band made up my mind to definitely be a musician: Duke in one night probably encouraged every Black musician in town to practice harder, for his band showed that artistic and economic success could be attained in music.

"People," Lowe said, "talked for days about that night."[17]

Some talked about it for decades.

Sammy Lowe remembered another kind of music, too, from his youth. The Lowes lived right by the L&N train tracks, and Sammy, J. L., and Leatha followed their path on foot to get to school or downtown. It was a fine line, financially, that separated Black middle-class families like theirs from the laborers of the mines and mills; but there were cultural distinctions that set the groups apart, and children of the Black middle class encountered on the tracks a different culture from the one they found in the social circles of their parents. For one thing, the tracks were a home for the blues: "The most authentic blues I ever heard, I heard on this railroad. Black men coming from work downtown would sing; some also played guitars; and in the quiet of the late hours you'd hear the blues, blues that were wailed pathetically, in the still of the night." Lowe was grateful later to have grown up by the tracks, grateful both for the romantic symbolism of the trains themselves and for the appeal of the tracks' music. "The L&N instilled in me a desire to travel," he explained, "and the music I heard gave me a true love for Black music." His work with the Erskine Hawkins band would always retain a rootedness in those southern blues of his youth, a sound that came not so much from the ballrooms and lodges of elite society as from the open air of the train tracks at night.[18]

Haywood Henry also remembered the daybreak sounds of those men who walked the tracks—"the most soulful thing you ever heard in your life"—but the train itself is what captivated him most: "I used to sit there and watch the trains pass and daydream about going to places." Asked near the end of his life to name a highlight of his career, Henry answered easily, telling the story of the daydreaming boy who sat and watched the trains. His greatest success was making that boy's dreams come true. Haywood Henry had gone places.[19]

Lionel Hampton went places, too. The future vibraphonist and band-leader spent his first years in Birmingham, raised largely by his grandparents; though he relocated with his family to Chicago around the age of ten, life in the Magic City had already provided important inspiration. His grandmother was a Church of God in Christ evangelist, and the percussive music of her church—a music much less staid than that of the Smithfield Baptists and Methodists—launched Hampton down a lifelong path. He recalled the sister who beat "the big bass drum" each week: "She'd start dancing and her eyes would roll up into the back of her head. . . . When her eyeballs disappeared," Hampton imagined, "her soul left her body and was on its way up to God." One Sunday the sister, enraptured, dropped her mallet and Hampton picked it up: "From then on, I was a drummer. I drummed on pots, pans, chair seats, the front porch railing, the front porch steps. The rest of the family complained," but Hampton's evangelist grandmother "looked forward to me playing in the church band one day. Maybe even being famous."[20]

If Hampton's grandmother's church proved one inspiration, his grandfather's train proved another. "In the South at that time the trains were a major form of entertainment for people, especially Black people," Hampton wrote, echoing Henry and Lowe. "Since we didn't go anywhere, the trains let us dream about faraway places. . . . The greatest show was the Special, which left Birmingham every evening about six o'clock. Hundreds of people came every day to stand just outside the station and cheer the spectacle. . . . The engineer, who was always white, blew the whistle. The fireman, who was always Black, rang the bell." The show held particular magic for Hampton because the fireman happened to be his grandfather. "When that train came through the Black part of Birmingham, . . . that's when my grandfather went into his act," shoveling the coal and ringing the bell like mad. "When he spotted my grandmother and me in the cheering crowd, he'd salute like a soldier."[21]

Even on that train, "the different duties of white and black"—the engineer with his whistle, Hampton's grandfather-fireman with his bell—"were clearly defined" by race. But—as it had since slavery and the spirituals, since the "gospel train a-coming" and the train "bound for glory," since the early metaphor of the Underground Railroad—the train offered a symbol for a world beyond, a means of deliverance to another, better place, real or imagined. The music of the 6:00 Special, the glamour of Ellington's string of private cars, the late-night blues wailed in the dark by the tracks, the promise embodied in a ticket from Becton—again and again the train connected Birmingham dreamers to a world of storybook romance and seemingly infinite possibility. It promised "faraway places" and a better life. The train was escape, freedom, and fantasy; it was movement, and all that movement entailed.

The train was entry to another world, and its whistle was nothing but music.[22]

ERSKINE

In 1938, Erskine Ramsay—Birmingham industrialist, inventor, and philanthropist—received a letter from New York City: 158 West 142nd Street, Apt. 22. It was signed Erskine Ramsay *Hawkins* and began, "Dear Sir: I know you are wandering [*sic*] who I am. I shall make it short and tell you now."[1]

This kind of letter was nothing new to Ramsay; he often received notes like it from the men and boys who bore his name. The son of Scottish immigrants, Ramsay had come from Pennsylvania to Birmingham in 1887 to work for TCI, the Tennessee Coal, Iron and Railroad Company. He rose through the ranks of the business and did not stop there: he patented dozens of innovations for the mining industry, built a fortune in investments, and cofounded his own coal company. He ran against, and lost to, Hugo Black for a seat in the US Senate. A champion of learning, he served nineteen years as president of Birmingham's board of education, pledging to improve the city's Black schools—a focus that won him support from Black families and threats from the Ku Klux Klan. A well-known eccentric and a proud Scot who turned southern heads by dressing in a kilt, he threw himself extravagant birthday parties, hiring Fess Whatley's Sax-o-Society Orchestra as entertainment and broadcasting the events on the radio, an announcer introducing each guest on arrival. Ramsay never married or had children of his own, but he took an active, paternal interest in Birmingham's youth, contributing to the quality of their education through his work with the schools—and keeping an eye out, in particular, for the many young people, Black and white, who had been named in his honor.[2]

By 1920, numerous Birmingham parents had named their newborns for Ramsay, who opened a bank account and deposited $100 for each infant so named—inspiring, as word spread, a local explosion of Erskines. The money could not be accessed until the child's twenty-first birthday, and Ramsay encouraged parents to add what they could in the meantime. The purpose of the gift was to inspire the "savings habit" and to contribute to the child's education; to access the gift, each new Erskine would have to demonstrate ambition and industry, completing a questionnaire that asked, "What is your aim in life?" Soon, more than 100 Birmingham families, Black and white, had brought their own Erskine Ramsays screaming into the world. Rumor had it the man was *paying* people outright to name their children for him, and expectant letters from new parents multiplied. After two years, Ramsay decided it impractical to continue with the bank accounts and hundred-dollar gifts, but he did send the latest Erskines engraved cups as mementos, and he kept correspondence with the many who wrote, each year, to introduce themselves. Ramsay responded with interest in their activities and offered fatherly encouragements, hoping his own success might inspire those boys to whom he had been linked in name.[3]

And so it was that Erskine Hawkins wrote from New York's Harlem, offering a short account of his life so far. His mother worked in the kitchen at Ramsay High School—another of the philanthropist's namesakes—and, Hawkins explained, "she thinks you're swell"; "so when I was born she named me after you. I've tryed so hard," Hawkins added, "to live up to that name. I am living now in New York and is the leader of an Orchestra named 'Erskine Ramsay Hawkins and his Orchestra.'" The band broadcast across the country three nights a week, and Hawkins offered to play any request Ramsay might want to hear. Meanwhile, he would dedicate the next Tuesday night's broadcast to Ramsay: "I am going to try and get them to announce your name but if they can not all the boys know and I want you to know it's for you." Hawkins's mother, the letter concluded, was visiting from home, and she was "working trying to make enough money to send my sister" to Alabama State Teachers College, Hawkins's own alma mater. "I am sending you a picture of me."[4]

Ramsay picked up his pen. "My dear Erskine: I am glad to see you are getting along in such a satisfactory way." To his regret, the local broadcast of a baseball game interfered with the radio signal, and he had been unable to hear Tuesday's show. He would "endeavor again" to hear the program and, as for requests, any of the band's regular repertoire would be fine—but if they could "mix a little Scotch with it," Ramsay would be delighted. He sent Hawkins's mother his warm regards, concluding with the sort of encouragement that characterized all his correspondence with the youth: "I hope that your further efforts will bring you increasing praise-worthy recognition."[5]

Hawkins's reasons for writing are not entirely clear. Like a lot of Ramsay's correspondents, he might have been hoping for some form of patronage: there is that reference to the family's financial needs, plus a great deal of flattery and the occasional exaggeration (in truth, Hawkins was billed without his middle name). Then again, the bandleader may have just wanted to show that he had made good, that he was building a life worthy of his namesake. For many young men, Ramsay was a kind of father figure, even if they had never met him, and Hawkins had been fatherless since the First World War.

Whatever his motivations, Hawkins was characteristically modest in his correspondence, downplaying the level of success he had already begun to experience. Just that year, his band had signed with a major jazz promoter, secured a recording contract with RCA, and become a standing sensation at Harlem's Savoy Ballroom. The musicians were rising stars in Black America, whose entertainment columnists had already dubbed Hawkins the "Twentieth Century Gabriel," some even declaring him "the hottest trumpet player in the world." White America, though, had not yet taken notice. Back in Birmingham, Erskine Ramsay would have had no reason to have heard of this particular Erskine or of his band.[6]

The photo Hawkins enclosed was an early publicity shot whose image countered the modesty of the written correspondence. In it, the tuxedoed young Hawkins is a portrait of uptown sophistication and self-confident ambition: his hair conked, a carnation in his lapel, handkerchief tucked into his breast pocket, he holds the trumpet to his lips with one hand, his head tilted and body leaned back into his best Gabriel pose, trumpet pointing skyward as if reaching for heaven's highest notes. Erskine's free hand extends a finger, also pointing up, his eyes fixed on that same skyward trajectory. There's no limit, the photo suggests, to the heights this man and his horn might climb.

No musicians better symbolize the spirit of Birmingham jazz than Erskine Hawkins and the members of his orchestra. The sense of community and brotherhood; the unshakable pride of place; the foundations of formal education and informal collaboration, of professional aspiration and personal style; the ecstatic embrace, back home, by family and fans—the Hawkins band united all these threads, personified vividly the dreams and values of the scene that shaped them. There are tragic chapters in the band's long history—one player's genius destroyed in an act of random barroom violence, another's life lost, victim to the dangers that plagued Black bands

Erskine Hawkins in an early publicity photo, mailed in 1938 to his namesake, Birmingham industrialist Erskine Ramsay. Courtesy Birmingham, Ala. Public Library Archives.

on the road—but above all, the group's story is one of gleeful ascension, a story that swings like the music at its core.

The musicians' shared roots stretched back into childhood. Most met in the Lincoln grade school band room and continued through Fess Whatley's orchestra at Industrial High; others attended Tuggle Institute, trained like Whatley by High C Foster. Their music congealed at Alabama State in Montgomery and soon, as the Bama State Collegians, they were taking the South, and then the country, by storm. For all their popularity, they occupy a modest space in most histories of jazz: they never aspired to the ambitious musical complexities of an Ellington, and for sheer, shimmering swing they did not match Count Basie and his band. Their crossover appeal to white America was limited, even as their greatest hits ("Tuxedo Junction" and the bluesy "After Hours") became anthems of an era. In their own day, their reputation rested largely on their role as a dance band, one of the country's finest and longest running. This, after all, was the chief ambition of the Hawkins men: to send dancers across the floor, even through the air, to create pure and sparkling soundtracks to endless good times. In these efforts, the Hawkins band was unsurpassed.

The group's longevity also made it unique: the band outlasted most swing-era ensembles and, in all its years, its lineup remained uncommonly consistent. In most bands, musician turnover was high; only Duke Ellington, with his familiar company of celebrity musicians, featured so many of the same players for so many years. But even Duke's players, for all their loyalty, were famous for not getting along. That kind of friction was not a problem for Hawkins, whose musicians cited their shared histories as the source of their cohesiveness, endurance, and abiding, infectious good nature.

"We were like a family," Hawkins explained. "That's the reason, I guess, I stayed in the business so long." It is a constant refrain in recollections by the Hawkins bandsmen: "We were a family"; "We were like brothers." They traveled together, created together, lived together, shared beds on the road, celebrated one another's birthdays on long, whiskey-drunk bus rides, swapped the same old stories about the folks back home. "Everything we'd do," Hawkins said, "we'd come to each other." About his old bandmates he insisted, many years down the road, "I can't forget those fellows."[7]

Hawkins was born on July 26, 1914, two days before war broke out in Europe. When America entered the fray, nearly three years later, his father, a butcher, joined the American Expeditionary Forces and was sent to the front lines in France. He did not return. Hawkins, his four siblings, and his mother moved into the home of his grandfather in Enon Ridge, a prestigious Black enclave adjoining Smithfield. Tuggle Institute was right across the street from their home, and the place became entwined with Erskine's life. All the men on his mother's side of the family were carpenters ("They thought I was going to be a carpenter," too) and had literally helped build the school; when a fire destroyed the original facility, they built its replacement. Founder Carrie Ann Tuggle was a family friend. But all Erskine cared about was the band.[8]

Every afternoon, that band marched a mini-parade in front of the school, and Erskine joined in from his grandfather's front yard, beating on tin cans or "playing" the family's picket fence with a stick. Eventually Granny Tuggle herself caught sight of him and was moved. "So she told my mother: 'I'll take that boy and put him in the school.'"[9]

"I think I must have been about six years old," Hawkins said. "I was about the youngest man in the band. They put me in the rhythm section with a triangle. . . . I was too small to carry a snare drum or anything else." High C Foster took particular interest in the boy: "He used to come over my house like 5:00 in the morning and knock on the window. My mother would wake me up and say, 'Professor Foster's out there waiting for you.'" Before the sun came up, Hawkins would be in the band room, sole audience to Foster's daily warm-up. "I was so small, he used to sit me up there on a shelf so I could hear him practicing." The high notes especially captured his imagination, as Foster unleashed his namesake sound, hitting not only the high C itself but climbing a full octave above that. In later years, Hawkins would make those same feats the trademark of his own performances.[10]

He started as a percussionist, moving from fence rails and tin cans to the triangle and, at last, to the drums. By the time he left Tuggle for college, he had worked his way through every instrument in the band room, switching from drums to reeds and then to strings ("I didn't want to leave anything out"), learning basic chords on the banjo and guitar and—before declaring his fingers too fat for the strings—fooling around with a violin. A cousin gave him a cornet, and with Foster as his model—"I used to try and copy everything he did"—he inevitably started reaching for the high notes. He befriended other young Tuggle musicians—trombonists Edward "Cap" Sims and Bob Range, trumpeter Jack Dozier—who would remain his bandmates for years and friends for life. Dozier was Granny Tuggle's actual grandson and Erskine one of her pets. The beloved lady died when he was fourteen, and for her memorial service he played taps at her grave.[11]

Hawkins's family supported the music, but with reservation. Erskine's mother played piano "sort of socially"; his brother James played a little trumpet; an older cousin, Johnny Richardson, played the best string bass for miles. But anything approaching jazz was forbidden in the home. "My family was *deep* in religion," Hawkins explained. "I couldn't play my horn in the house . . . especially as long as my grandfather was living." The church did, however, provide an outlet, as it did for so many young musicians: Erskine's mother, uncles, and aunts all sang in the choir, and around the age of nine he and his cornet were recruited for the service of the Lord. The music at Enon Ridge Methodist was stately and sedate—no sanctified singing and shouting, no "getting happy" in the aisles, *certainly* no syncopated sounds—but "every now and then, they'd let me have a few bars, as long as I didn't jazz it up." When the pastor himself praised Hawkins's horn, the boy's domineering grandfather relented. "From then on, he was really wonderful to me."[12]

Music in the church was one thing; the life of a professional musician was another. "My family didn't know anything *about* musicians," Hawkins said, "except that they were generally hungry." Before he had gotten to high school, Hawkins was picking up odd jobs with the theaters, "ballyhooing" on the sidewalks, drumming up customers to see the show inside. Sometimes he and other young players were hired to "tailgate," loading up in the bed of a truck and riding through residential neighborhoods, band blaring, to advertise an upcoming event. "Sometimes it was tough for my mother—like the time when she walked downtown and found me standing outside a theater with a bunch of musicians; I was blowing my brains out on a trombone. We had been hired to advertise the show inside. Mother just sort of looked at me—and walked on."[13]

His mother may not have known what to make of him, but friends and fellow musicians were impressed, and for the tempests he blew through his horn they gave him a nickname that stuck with him through college.

They called him "Iron Lungs."

Hawkins must have been ten or twelve when he discovered the music he came to know as jazz. On school nights, he lay in his bed in the dark, tuned quietly to the radio. On weekends he joined the kids outside the fraternal ballrooms, climbing walls and peeking through the windows. But what hooked him, more than anything, was that spot out in Ensley, where each weekend and all summer long the bands swung the latest sounds.[14]

The community of Ensley was built in the shadow of steel. TCI opened four huge blast furnaces and a steel plant there in the 1880s, and in 1899 the surrounding area—a swath of scrubby, uninhabited land—was divided into residential lots for workers. Developers dubbed the new community Tuxedo Park, likely inspired by the New York village of that name. Central to this development was TCI executive Erskine Ramsay; a towering office building in Ensley's downtown, like so many Birmingham babies, bore his name.

Just east of that downtown was Tuxedo Junction, a cluster of shops and clubs that grew up around the intersection of two streetcar lines. By 1905 the crossing had become the hub of a vibrant social and commercial scene, for both the neighboring Italian and African American communities who set up businesses there. The "Junction" referred to the streetcar crossing, and "Tuxedo" presumably borrowed from the already established Tuxedo Park, but the name soon came to reflect the proliferation of formal wear that characterized the spot at night. A shop on the corner rented tuxes to the steel men who left their own clothes at the counter as deposits, stepping out into the night remade in their fresh, borrowed finery. The American Woodmen, a Black benevolent society, ran a second-story dance hall over the tux shop, and bands played into the night.

Just around the corner from the Junction was an actual park—also called Tuxedo Park, later Tuxedo Junction Park, and finally Erskine Hawkins Park—an amusement and entertainment center for the Black community, bursting with lavish and varied offerings: a swimming pool and bathhouse, shooting gallery, skating rink, Ferris wheel, picnic grounds, dance pavilion, and bandstand. An advertisement in the *Birmingham Reporter* declared it "A NICE PARK—FOR NICE COLORED PEOPLE," the finest of its kind in the country. "They had all kinds of entertainment," said Hawkins, who went there every chance he got—especially in the summer, when the open-air pavilion hosted dancing every night. He played his first public gigs there, for private parties and for marathon all-day events, performing alongside seasoned older players: Pops Williams, drummer George Earl, and a bluesy trumpeter called "Shorty." Earl would pick up the apprentice musician at home—the man owned his own car, Erskine marveled—promising his mother he would be in responsible, respectable hands. Hawkins absorbed all he could, learning from the older guys, watching the dancers, honing his ear. He was just an upstart musician, awed by the scene and entranced by its sounds.[15]

He could never have guessed that one day—along with his friends from Tuggle and Industrial and Alabama State—he would make the Junction famous.

COLLEGIANS

In Montgomery, some 100 miles from Birmingham, H. Councill Trenholm struggled at the Great Depression's dawn to keep a college afloat. For southern states, the Depression arrived early and lasted long; for Black southerners, relegated already to society's lowest rungs, the financial wounds cut especially deep. Trenholm had succeeded his late father as president of the State Normal School for Colored Students in 1925; only twenty-five years old when he took the job, he proved an ambitious and visionary leader, directing the institution for thirty-seven years, expanding its curricula, facilities, and reputation. He remade what had been a junior college into Alabama State Teachers College for Negroes, an accredited four-year institution for the training of Black educators; he developed a laboratory high school on campus, where teachers in training could practice their craft; he added graduate programs and branch campuses. But as the Depression grew, the whole enterprise seemed impossible. The state cut the school's funding by more than half, prioritizing Alabama's white schools for public education dollars. Faculty members were forced to work for half their salaries, sometimes less, sometimes even to go without pay, and still Trenholm could barely keep the most basic utilities running. The school, as one student put it, "was on the brink of extinction." It might not have survived had it not been for jazz.[1]

Birmingham saxophonist Paul Bascomb arrived on campus in the fall of 1928. The timing was serendipitous: the school, under its new name of Alabama State, launched its four-year program that semester. Bascomb joined the first class of four-year students, just as President Trenholm worried over how to make ends meet.

One of ten siblings, Bascomb had come from one of Smithfield's many music-rich families. His father had played the bass drum in the Tuskegee Institute band; his mother taught piano at the Alabama School for the Negro Deaf and Blind in Talladega. An older brother, Arthur "Bubba" Bascomb, was a formidable blues and boogie-woogie pianist, and he taught his younger brothers to play in the gritty "alley" style many Smithfield homes might have discouraged. "By the time I was eight or nine years old," Paul recalled, "I was playing a saxophone my mother had bought me and was scuffling around Birmingham" with a couple of other boys: a drummer they called "Redd Foxx" (no relation to the later comedian) and a tap dancer called "Ground-hog." They would set up on the street and pick up change where they could, Groundhog fixing metal bottlecaps to the bottoms of his shoes in place of store-bought taps. Bascomb found work ballyhooing for a carnival sideshow on Seventeenth Street. "They had an elderly man playing saxophone, but he was a whiskey-head and they wanted me to take his place, which I did until my parents found out and made me leave."[2]

At twelve, Bascomb ran away from home, joining the Seals and Mitchell carnival show. "I was the youngest in the band but the star performer was Paul Semeo—he was half-Indian—who played piano and guitar. He used to put up a sign outside the place we were playing which read, 'Whosoever Will, Let Him Come—Piano Playing Contest.' Semeo had a terrific left-hand and nobody could beat him. We traveled all over the country: Mississippi, Georgia, Alabama, Tennessee, and Texas. We had our own chartered train and we would sleep on there after the show in the city, buy our own food and the chorus girls would cook it for us." Bascomb stayed with the outfit until one night in Shreveport when he accidentally shot himself in the leg—the gun he carried in his pants watch-pocket slipped during a dice game and fired—after which the show sent him back to Birmingham. He enrolled at Industrial, started his own band, and, still in high school, developed his first following of fans.[3]

Bascomb had no dreams of becoming a teacher, but Alabama State offered a good education and prospects for a future. He arrived that fall, tenor sax in tow, and quickly assembled the first jazz band on campus, a five-piece combo made up mostly of other arrivals from Birmingham: trombonist Cap Sims, saxophonist Wilbur Hollins, and, on alto sax and vocals, J. B. Sims. On piano they enlisted a Montgomery high schooler named Andrew Curtis Fair, a classical student with no interest in jazz but a knack for writing arrangements. In performance, the young pianist renamed himself *Percy* Fair, an alias he hoped would keep his family reputation unsullied; for all his propriety, his bandmates called him "Little Lord Fauntleroy." But Paul and the others coached him on the basics of syncopation and swing, and soon enough the group had a solid book of arrangements.[4]

The band was a campus sensation with Bascomb its star, his musician-ship and stage presence irresistible. To the girls he was a heartthrob (the yearbook declared him "Most Handsome Boy" of 1929); for other musicians, he set the bar. Even H. Councill Trenholm could not miss the stir Bascomb created, and he summoned the student to his office. The school needed fund-ing, he explained, and Paul's band was part of the solution. From now on, the student musicians would tour the South and beyond as ambassadors for Alabama State: their concerts and dances would recruit new students and spread the school's brand wherever they played. Most important, their earn-ings would buy food for the cafeteria and coal for the furnace and help pay teachers' salaries and maintain basic operations. In return, Alabama State would provide them tuition, transportation, uniforms, and management— as well as a world of professional experience.[5]

Trenholm already had in mind the perfect faculty sponsor and man-ager for the band: one of the school's newest hires, an energetic, ambitious musician and scholar by the name of Willis Laurence James. James was a violinist and tenor vocalist with an interest in both classical and vernacular music traditions; he was also a folklorist who collected traditional southern Black songs and encouraged his students to do the same, helping preserve the oral traditions of their families and their region. Trenholm had hired him to direct the school's music programs and to manage its vocal groups and marching band. Now he added Bascomb's group to the roster of James's responsibilities.[6]

Expanded to eleven pieces and dubbed the Bama State Collegians, the band played dances and went on tours, performed for the Masons and Odd Fellows and Pythians and Elks, provided the after-parties for Black colle-giate football games, and duked it out in jazz battles with the region's hot-test ensembles. Once a week, Bascomb and company broadcast over the airwaves from Montgomery station WAPI. Whatever money they made, they gave to the college, and the college, in turn, gave to them: whenever they toured, they made a dollar a day. Twice a week came another dollar for laundry. For every meal on the road, the school gave each man a quar-ter and a dime, more than enough to keep the band fed. At Ma Woodard's Place in Montgomery, they could grab a potato pie and a pig-ear sandwich for five cents apiece, a "belly washer," or ice-cold drink, for another nickel. Twice a year, each musician received a new, tailor-made suit. And their education—as much education as their schedule allowed—was paid for in full.[7]

The expanded group was something to behold. Bascomb may have been the star—fans dubbed him "Peerless Paul"—but J. B. Sims relished his own role as the group's wild-man emcee and singer, an entertainer in the Cab Calloway mold, singing loud into a megaphone, jumping and spinning and shouting onstage, tuxedo coattails flying and processed hair flapping. The band's arrangements had become more complex, and the musicians' versatility allowed for surprising variety: trombonist H. O. Thompson was especially inventive, scoring five-part harmonies for a full section of trombones.[8]

The Collegians continued their service to the school through the summers, and the summer of 1930 proved a milestone. On August 21 they opened a major tour with a dance in Louisville, Kentucky; on the twenty-second they played for the Masons in Evanston, Illinois; and for the month to follow they bounced from city to city: a national Baptist convention in Chicago on the twenty-third; an Elks convention in Detroit on the twenty-fifth; Pontiac, Michigan, on the twenty-sixth; Kalamazoo on the twenty-seventh; Pittsburgh on the twenty-eighth; New York City on the thirtieth. Labor Day kicked off a three-week engagement in Philadelphia, with side trips through Pennsylvania and New Jersey scattered throughout. Finally, on September 22, they rolled back into Montgomery, barely in time for the start of classes.[9]

In Detroit, the Collegians were joined by a full entourage from Alabama State, including the school's vocal quartet and marching band, which had been slated to lead the Alabama delegation in the Elks parade. Seizing the opportunity that spotlight afforded his school, Trenholm had written Fess Whatley to request a fresh infusion of Birmingham talent, and Whatley delivered, recruiting Erskine Hawkins and trombonist Bob Range from Tuggle and sending from his own student band Haywood Henry, J. L. Lowe, and trumpeter Wilbur "Dud" Bascomb, Paul's younger brother. By every account, the expanded band hit huge in Detroit, taking second place in the parade competition, bested only by a much larger unit of seasoned adults from Chicago. The whole thing was a triumph. "We were nothing but teenagers," Henry said—their ages ranged from fourteen to eighteen—but those teenagers were bursting with energy and armed with a repertoire that set them apart. "We decided that we would play *jazz*": instead of "Stars and Stripes Forever" and "all the marches we knew from high school," the band broke into big, thirty-piece arrangements of "Dinah" and the "St. Louis Blues," and as the musicians marched through the streets of Detroit, the crowds that lined their path broke out dancing. "I imagine that we were the first [marching] band to play jazz."[10]

After the trip, Trenholm offered scholarships to Henry, Hawkins, Range, and Lowe. Dud Bascomb—the youngest in the bunch but already one of the best—enrolled in the laboratory high school. Now the Collegians had competition: a new campus act, the Midnight Revelers, challenged the established band in a showdown at Alabama State's Tullibody Hall—"a titanic struggle," recalled J. L. Lowe, which pitted "the arrogant, vibrant Revelers" against the "confident Collegians." The older group kicked off the battle in style: "Peerless Paul played flawlessly," wrote Lowe, and J. B. Sims sang and spun at his manic best. But when the Revelers took the stage, multi-instrumentalist Haywood Henry established himself as Paul's possible peer; Jimmy Mitchell—a Birmingham saxophonist and crooner, who had just quit a vaudeville road show to join his friends at the school—opened his mouth and "launched his long reign as an idol of females"; and trumpeters Erskine and Dud brought down the house, "pouring it on . . . in chorus after chorus."[11]

Dud Bascomb, in many ways, was his brother's opposite. Paul was suave, assertive, and sometimes hotheaded; Dud was physically small, shy, and eternally agreeable, preferring to assert himself through his careful, complex solos and then to step back into the sidelines. As budding trumpeters, both Erskine and Dud idolized Louis Armstrong and recreated his every solo, note for note, from the records. But Dud developed a knack for thoughtful, subtle solos that in time would point toward modern jazz. Erskine was the showier performer, turning his boyhood bandmaster's hallmark into his own calling card. He drove the crowds wild with his rendition of Armstrong's "Shine," stepping to the front of the stage to unleash a barrage of high C's—more than a hundred at a time, one after the next, relentlessly, impossibly—while the rest of the band, hysterical behind him, counted off each note aloud as it came.[12]

President Trenholm wasted no time. He rebranded the new group the *Bama State* Revelers, enlisting them to the service of the school and placing them, too, under the management of Willis Laurence James. Now the groups would canvas the state together, traveling as a team but waging war onstage. Some nights, one group would drop off the other for a gig and then head down the road for another show in another town, doubling the reach, reputation, and revenue for Alabama State. Back in Montgomery, they held late-night jam sessions, trading riffs among themselves and with local players. The dormitories bolted their doors each night at eleven, and the musicians crept back onto campus hours later, slipping through an open window in the dorm—until, Hawkins said, "the dean got tired of us coming up the fire escape . . . so he just left the door open for us." The administration was willing to look the other way, so long as they kept bringing good money to the school.

"We raised quite a bit," Hawkins said. So "the school kept going on, and we kept eating."[13]

With its Revelers and Collegians, Alabama State developed a kind of JV/varsity system that would serve the college for years: as students in the top-tier Collegians graduated or turned professional, there were seasoned Revelers ready to take their spaces, in turn opening up new seats in the JV band. A pipeline of Birmingham talent helped ensure no vacancies went unfilled.

In 1931, Collegians H. O. Thompson, Wilbur Hollins, and J. B. Sims all graduated, moved back to Birmingham, became teachers, and started their own bands on the side. Paul Bascomb left school for a job with C. S. Belton's Society Syncopaters, one of the best of the southern territory bands; nicknamed the "Duke Ellington of the South," Belton was a major regional bandleader with an unbeatable stable of sidemen, and for Bascomb the job was a dream come true. Meanwhile, the first generation of Revelers rose to become the next wave of Collegians, making that band more formidable than ever.[14]

The pace of travel was unrelenting. "I can't remember after the first year ever going to school for more than two weeks straight," Haywood Henry said. "We didn't have sleep," added Hawkins. To help keep up with their schoolwork, Trenholm assigned them tutors for the road. Demand grew, not only in Black spaces. "We were probably the first Black band to play the white universities all over the South," Henry guessed. Some white schools held sumptuous banquets, and the musicians relished the meals, even if it meant enduring the absurdities and insults of segregation. "They just put up a screen around us" for the duration of the meal; "when we would finish eating, they would take it down," and the band would resume its playing.[15]

In 1933, according to a report in the *Atlanta Daily World*, the Collegians played 233 engagements, the Revelers 213—numbers that did not even include their many gigs on campus. A third group, the Bama State Cavaliers, was added in October, and by New Year's Eve that group had picked up 45 dates of its own. The three ensembles constituted an impressive little army, an "aggregate of 42 students including traveling student managers and student bus drivers." They had played in eighteen states that year, everywhere "within a radius of 800 miles of Montgomery," and they were "making new friends each week." They were huge hits in Chicago, a city full of southern Black migrants, including a wealth of Bama State alums; the *Chicago Defender* reported that one night in that city, "4,000 patrons from every section of the Southeast" came out to soak in their "distinctive rhythms" and feel that much closer to home. Newspapers declared the Collegians "America's greatest collegiate band" and the South's hottest band, period. Other schools knew they had nothing on Bama State. Birmingham saxophonist Newman Terrell enrolled at Tuskegee Institute, forty miles east of Montgomery, but the music there was not the same. "'Skegee' had a good military band," he said, "but all the young fellows wanted to join a swinging band and Alabama State had *three*."[16]

When Willis Laurence James left for Spelman College in 1933, Hawkins picked up some of his teaching duties. President Trenholm himself assumed the duty of managing three separate bands, responding to a mountain of correspondence, booking dances, juggling schedules, negotiating terms, issuing contracts, and facilitating promotion—all, incredibly, while running a college.[17]

The southern Black press celebrated the Collegians' rise, outlining the players' strengths with the linguistic exuberance that characterized the entertainment columns of the day. In the *Atlanta Daily World*, columnist Lucius Jones bemoaned the impossibility of singling out any one Collegian over the others. Curtis Fair (he had scrapped the "Percy" by now) "rambles all over the sharps and flats like a man slipping on a banana peel lying on an ice coated surface while free-wheeling on roller skates"—the comparison was intended as a compliment—while "Jimmy Mitchell toots that sax and sings and wails and moans like a man possessed!" Erskine sounded just like Louis Armstrong, Jones raved, and just as one soloist got hotter, the next would "open up" more and more, in response—"and [this] is where the pyrotechnics start shooting off."[18]

A major victory came in May 1934. "Belton Bows to Ala. Collegians," a headline read in the *Pittsburgh Courier*, and in one winding sentence the paper announced the news: "While the Bama State Revelers were making a triumphal entry into Thomasville, Ga., under the auspices of the popular Rex Club, and the Bama State Cavaliers were opening up the Harrogate Springs summer resort near Wetumpka, [Alabama,] the nationally-famous Bama State Collegians, senior dance orchestra at Alabama State Teachers College, dolled up their home auditorium, received the widely-publicized Belton's Society Syncopaters in a torrid jazz battle, and sent them away acknowledging and good-naturedly accepting the superior caliber of the Collegians." All night the Collegians held their own, and once those in the Belton crew had exhausted their strengths, the younger band kept pulling out new tricks, new energy, new solos. After the Syncopaters offered a take on the "St. Louis Blues," the Collegians struck back with their own, higher energy treatment of the same tune, and at midnight Erskine Hawkins—"with his

130 high 'C's' in 'Shine'"—signaled "a clear-cut victory" for his team. Surely Paul Bascomb—who, papers noted, had traded in his Bama State gear for "the flashy uniform of the Belton clan"—must have felt, even in defeat, some sense of pride.[19]

Another symbolic win came the next summer. "Fess Whatley Loses," exclaimed the *Atlanta Daily World*. "The Bama State Collegians again displayed their superior musical ability at the Masonic Temple in Birmingham when they trounced 'Fess' Whatley and the Saxo-Society unmercifully in his own 'hometown' before 1,000 enthusiastic dance lovers."[20]

First Belton and Bascomb, now Fess. They had outplayed their peers and the professionals, outplayed their own idols, even outplayed their own famous mentor.

The Bama State Collegians were ready, now, for anything.

Haywood Henry was the first to leave the South. His ticket out was a telegram that arrived, unexpectedly, from Reverend Becton of the "Consecrated Dime": "Would you like to come to New York," the message read, "and join a gospel party?" Haywood had played with Becton's band during one of its previous stints in Birmingham, and apparently he had left an impression; now the preacher tracked him down to Montgomery.[21]

Haywood was hungry for a change, sick of the racist barriers he had come to expect in the South. As well as a musician, he was a star athlete who had clocked 9.5 seconds in the hundred-yard dash, missing the world record by one-tenth of a second; the color of his skin barred him from participating in state championships, excluding him from competition or acclaim off campus. Already searching for an exit, he jumped on the invite from Becton. "They sent me twenty-five dollars. I put a ticket in my pocket of my suit, and somebody stole the suit. . . . I wrote to them that somebody stole the ticket and the suit, so they sent me another ticket and twenty-five more." He had never seen that kind of money tossed around so freely. He went downtown, bought a bag, packed "two pair of underwear, two pair of socks, two handkerchiefs, two of everything that I had, and left all the rest of the junk right in my room." He got on the train and was gone.[22]

The rest of the band was not far behind. By now, they were "Collegians" in little more than concept and commitment: they were rarely in the classroom, and their studies only served as distraction from the touring that amounted almost to a full-time job. The school took good care of them and provided for their every need; they were celebrities on campus and at dance halls across the South—but one thought began to nag: for all their success, they were still exclusive property of the college. If they really started going for themselves, what might they accomplish?

The band by now had glimpsed the lives of professional musicians up close, sharing double bills with any of the major touring bands that played Alabama State. One of Erskine's particular heroes was pianist-bandleader Earl Hines, whose broadcasts and records Hawkins studied obsessively. When Hines played Montgomery in 1934, the Collegians faced his band at three battles in a single day: at a local theater, at a white country club, and on the Bama State campus. Hines was impressed. ("I never heard so many high notes before in my life," he later remembered. "They were hitting them all over the ceiling!") Back in Chicago, he urged his manager, the influential Joe Glaser, to check out this young group from Alabama, and Glaser extended an invitation to audition, sending about $100 for the trip to Chicago. The musicians sat on the money—it was a risky move, and Glaser's invitation included no promises—but the encouragement from Hines and the cash from Glaser were major confidence boosters, confirmations that the band was ready for something beyond their native South. Erskine had an aunt in Newark, New Jersey, who suggested the group skip Chicago and come to New York instead. She was close enough and could "look out" for the band; besides, Haywood was writing his old bandmates prolifically from Harlem, doing his best to entice them with descriptions of the city and its music.[23]

Once before, on a 1931 tour, the Collegians had played some shows on Long Island, their first glimpse of New York. But that trip had been a bust: they felt invisible there, in over their heads and unready for the big time. Three years later, they were a better band, and the timing felt right. Hawkins wrote back to Glaser, expressing his thanks but explaining the band's other plans: if you could ever use us on the East Coast, he wrote, please get in touch. The Bama State Collegians had made up their minds.[24]

They were going to New York.

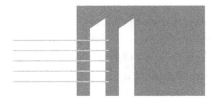

EFFLORESCENCE

Back in Birmingham, the music scene only grew. The decade of the thirties saw an explosion in homegrown music, what Jothan Callins would dub the "Efflorescence Period of Birmingham Jazz." New bands proliferated, friendly rivalries erupted, fresh collaborations emerged. Each year, new players came out of the schools, eager to make themselves heard.[1]

There were more and more places to hear the music, too. Just north of Birmingham, in Pratt City, the Grand Terrace (named for the famous Chicago ballroom) hosted bands, dances, and club meetings in its glamorous Rainbow Room. In Woodlawn, just east of the city, there was the Owls Club, nicknamed the "Little Masonic," where trumpeter Leo Hines led the house band and hosted the city's most explosive jazz battles. But Fourth Avenue remained the beating heart of everything. One of that district's dominant personalities, and a principal architect of the growing jazz scene, was a blind entertainment booker named Monroe Kennedy. More, perhaps, than anyone, Kennedy expanded Birmingham's jazz horizons, bringing national acts to the Masonic Temple stage through his booking company, the Temple Amusement Syndicate. For the Elks he produced an annual "Minstrel," a widely attended evening of classical music, comedy, and popular song; even the local white order of Elks hired him to organize its own most elaborate entertainments. Local columnist Katherine Kent Lambert presented the jovial, joking Kennedy as "one of the most interesting persons in the city": "He enjoys shows, baseball games, knows all the players and their records, plays chess, expert solitaire; likes motor driving and horseback riding. . . . He is an expert in sound and can recognize a friend through his voice, who he has not seen for twenty years." Kennedy was "always cheerful" and "the best dressed man in the city"; he wore bright, colorful shirts, suits, and ties, always impeccably matched; he appeared often in the social columns and counted among his friends a slew of prominent entertainers around the country. Fiercely undeterred by his blindness, he was known to move through dances at the Masonic, gently bumping into and speaking to the patrons—"I haven't seen you in a while," he would joke, slapping backs and shaking hands—and calculating in the process the evening's precise attendance.[2]

Kennedy opened his own venue in 1936—the Cotton Club Casino, he called it, after the Harlem nightspot—and it became an instant favorite, registering more than a thousand reservations for its first night in business. The national Black press praised the club's physical design, its entertainment offerings, and its potential for Birmingham. "To those seeking privacy where the mischievous ought be committed," one writer coyly observed, "private booths are the shields." Indeed, the space was partitioned to allow multiple walks of life to exist side by side, oblivious of others' presence: "Elderly persons and children may attend the dances and at the same time remain obscure by sitting in the balcony overlooking the dance floor. Private parties are sure to have their day at this modern casino and 'the good and the bad' can both attend and 'never the twain shall meet.'"[3]

The real social centerpiece of the district was the Little Savoy Café—or Bob's Savoy—owned by Bob Williams, another of Fourth Avenue's best-liked and most influential personas. Characteristically dressed in a tuxedo and Shriner's fez, a cigar clamped in his mouth, Williams was a tireless promoter of Birmingham's Black businesses and fraternal societies, a champion of local sports, and an advocate for civil rights, hosting political strategy sessions in his café and devoting himself to Black opportunity and community. Bob's Savoy stayed open late, offering dining, drinks, a pool hall, private banquets, club meeting spaces, and music. It served as headquarters to the Birmingham Black Barons, the Negro League baseball team, and it became hangout, too, for the celebrity athletes who passed through town, from Joe Louis to Jackie Robinson. Renowned entertainers also gravitated to the spot, sometimes playing impromptu late-night shows after their Masonic gigs, just across the street.[4]

If these venues welcomed all classes, within their walls social distinctions were delineated nonetheless: as the paper said of Kennedy's Cotton Club crowd, "the good and the bad" could share the space but never need meet. In the words of one historian of the era, Bob's Savoy was "in every way an exact replica of the caste system that existed within Birmingham's Black populace." Steel workers and coal miners crowded the first floor, while visiting celebrities, athletes, and white-collar professionals gathered upstairs amid more upscale accommodations. Fourth Avenue was gathering spot for all of Black Birmingham, but the community was no monolith, and diverse groups claimed their own corners of the shared space. For special occasions, venues even began to open their doors to white visitors: sometimes a Black band performed upstairs at Bob's Savoy for an exclusively white crowd, and for the evening all Black drinkers and diners came together downstairs.[5]

The Magic City pulsed with entertainment. A reporter from the *Chicago Defender* spent one New Year's Eve in Birmingham and recounted the details of an exhausting night on the town. He had stayed at Bob's Savoy through midnight, then headed to a dance hosted by the Esquire Club, then moved to the Elks Rest, whose Omega Ball only *started* at 3 a.m.; next he moved to Woodlawn and the Owls Club, where still other decked-out dancers moved ecstatic and unrestrained past daybreak.[6]

Fess Whatley, of course, remained king of the dance scene. Monroe Kennedy even complained that Fess had built what amounted to a monopoly of the best-paying and highest-profile jobs; only Whatley, Kennedy said, had the resources to book the lodges and dance halls a full year, even two years, in advance, effectively shutting out the competition. Fess was unfazed by the criticism: as more venues cropped up, there was enough work to go around.[7]

Many of Whatley's own products had begun local bands of their own. Whatley's stiffest competition came from Howard "Bubber" Funderburg's orchestra, which boasted the powerful pianist John L. Bell, a trio of sensational trumpeters, and Birmingham's "Queen of Swing," singer Bernice Bates. Former Bama State Collegians J. B. Sims and H. O. Thompson were broadcasting with their own band on local radio and touring the Deep South with their raucous theme song, "Muck the Muck." Curley Julian Parrish, hailed from childhood as a prodigy on violin and piano, directed the Personality Entertainers, and his soft-spoken younger brother, Avery, had his own radio broadcast as a solo pianist. Twin brothers Frank and Fred Greer led the Black and Tan Syncopators, and Fred Averytt directed the Society Troubadours, a group of high schoolers sponsored by Whatley. Sammy Lowe, himself still in high school, remembered jealously how the Troubadours scored a plum gig, playing one of the weeks-long marathon dances that the Depression had made a national craze. The events were broadcast over the airwaves but were best witnessed in person: crowds turned out nightly to gawk at the sweaty, spent bodies of competing couples, the dancers propped against their partners and swaying just enough to stay in the running for a hefty cash prize. For up-and-coming musicians, the marathons offered a shot at local stardom. Trumpeter Johnny Grimes performed with the Troubadours and, Lowe said, "featured 'Stardust' with a half-closed plunger one night. . . . The next day the word spread like fire that he was the greatest trumpet player in the world." Further fueling the magic of it all, Grimes was dating the band's singer, Hannah Mitchell. "It was just like a Hollywood movie."[8]

Lowe himself was making music with the Black and Tan Syncopators as well as with Paul Bascomb's latest band. Between tours with C. S. Belton's orchestra, Paul set up shop in Birmingham; Dud Bascomb, returning from Montgomery, reenrolled at Industrial High in order to make music with his brother. Paul by now was a full-blown hometown celebrity, but he was a more effective soloist than bandleader or businessman, and earnings were slim. After a packed-out dance, the musicians would gather around a table with the night's cash piled in the center. First Paul took out the "ducks," then he would push the dimes to each player, one at a time, "until the dimes ran out." Next came the nickels and then the pennies—"until," Sammy said, "all the money ran out." It was a slow, disheartening process, and most nights each band member made only thirty or thirty-five cents in all; but, Lowe told himself, "the point was at least I was working with a big band and I enjoyed what I was doing."[9]

For high school musicians like Sammy and Dud, the summers brought opportunities to tour with professional bands, thrilling introductions to show business and "the road." In the summer of 1933, singer-bandleader Jean Calloway passed through town in need of musicians; Paul assembled a band for her summer tour, recruiting both Sammy and Dud. Calloway drew crowds mainly on the strength of her last name: she was no relation to the popular Cab, but she nonetheless milked the association for all its worth, billing herself "Cab's Sister" and making a signature of "Minnie the Moocher," its vocals belted out by a drummer named Mutt. Marquees blared "CALLOWAY" in enormous letters ("You had to get up close to see 'Jean,'" Sammy said), and you could hear Mutt's "hi-de-ho" from three blocks away.[10]

The experience left its mark on Sammy, who kept an extensive diary of the tour and still relished the memories, decades later. Besides the "hi-de-ho" and the crowds, he remembered the long bus rides and the conversations that accompanied them: discussions always sooner or later returned to "politics, President Roosevelt, the NRA, WPA, and the Depression itself. These talks I never joined in," said Lowe, fifteen years old at the time, "because I felt—which was very stupid of me"—that African Americans had no place in politics. (A telling exception was John T. "Fess" Whatley, the "one Negro at that time that I knew had ever voted." Whatley, no doubt, had made sure his students knew he was a voter.) Still, the experience introduced Sammy to both the expansive world beyond Birmingham and the tightly constricted, richly concentrated world of the tour bus itself, a space he would come to value as site for group bonding, discourse, and debate.[11]

The road itself bestowed on young players an essential prestige. After the tour, Sammy and Dud returned to school, eager to act the part of big shots. "Dud and I put on our new style suits, one-button rope shouldered coats, with bell-bottom trousers, and went to see Professors George Hudson and J. T. Whatley, arriving at recess time. We strutted like two proud peacocks around the school grounds, saying hello to our friends. They all wanted to know 'How was it up north?' We happily told them, exaggerating quite a bit about how great it was in Chicago, Kansas City, and St. Louis. We didn't tell them that half the trip was in the South." Their musical mentors, meanwhile, offered "contrasting" reactions to their tour. "Mr. Hudson wanted to know about the musicians we had met, and the places we had played, the bands we had heard, and about road life in general." For Fess—"always the businessman"—there were just two questions, stiff and practical: "Did we make any money, and did we save any?"[12]

Back in the classroom, Lowe was maturing into a talented arranger, a development he largely credited to Hudson. His reputation eternally, inevitably overshadowed by Whatley's, Hudson was nonetheless a "very progressive band conductor" who constantly pushed his students' limits, introducing new ideas and even allowing for occasional improvisation. One rainy day, Hudson halted practice to write on the blackboard, explaining to the class "what a chord is all about"—"how to form major and minor chords and augmented chords, the sevenths, and he went as far as the ninths." For Lowe, "it was like a new world opened up." That afternoon, he rushed home from school, spread the family's stock charts across his bed, analyzing the interplay between each part—and after that, "I went arranging crazy." Hudson invited him to write arrangements for the school band, and Fess gave him a spot with the adults in the Sax-o-Society Orchestra, paying him twenty-five cents for each new arrangement. In 1935, Lowe composed a jazz-tinged march for his graduating class. To hear his own compositions and arrangements brought to life by a band, to witness the resulting acclaim of the crowd—these were experiences that changed Sammy Lowe forever, shaping his professional identity for decades to come.[13]

For all this activity, the jazz scene remained a world of men. Opportunities for women and girls, when they existed at all, were tightly restricted, typically limited—as was common across the country—to the roles of singer or pianist. While bands like Bubber Funderburg's or the Society Troubadours might feature a female vocalist—Bernice Bates, Hannah Mitchell, and Dolly Brown were favorites—most of these singers disappeared from the scene after a few years at most. A promising vocalist typically left the bandstand once she married, a custom that abruptly ended numerous careers, and not only in music: female schoolteachers were likewise required to retire from the classroom after marriage.[14]

One of the few women to find a place in the local jazz scene was pianist and teacher Mary Alice Clarke, the only sister in one of Birmingham's most prominent musical families. Her brothers—Pete, Richard, Chuck, and Arthur ("Babe," or "Bay-boy") Clarke—would work, between the four of them, with just about everyone: Chick Webb, Duke Ellington, Louis Armstrong, Teddy Wilson, Benny Carter, Billie Holiday, Cootie Williams, Johnny Hodges, Lionel Hampton, Jimmy Smith. Mary Alice, for her part, accumulated a host of degrees—from Birmingham's Miles College, New York City's Sherwood Music School, Atlanta University, and Chicago's DePaul University—before returning permanently to Birmingham, where she served for years as organist and music director at the prestigious Sixteenth Street Baptist Church (her mother had earlier held that position, and so for nearly a century the two Clarke women, along with Haywood Henry's sister, Mabel Barker, shaped the music of the landmark church). She was also a stalwart in Whatley's band, not only the exception to his ban on female players but one of the group's longest-running and most versatile members, juggling vocals, piano, accordion, and vibraphone, the instrument that gave Whatley's Vibra-Cathedral Orchestra its distinctive sound and name. Mary Alice knew how to swing, but—proper lady that she was—she kept the "jazz" label at arm's length: in the 1980s, she declined her nomination to the Alabama Jazz Hall of Fame, insisting she was an *orchestral musician*, not a jazz player.[15]

While Mary Alice Clarke stayed close to Birmingham, singer and schoolteacher Ethel Harper was determined to make her name in the larger world outside. Harper's parents, both teachers, died when she was nine, and she had come to Birmingham from her hometown of Selma to live with an adult brother and his wife. In a self-published memoir she remembered that, before she arrived, the "big city with bright lights and big crowds" weighed in her imagination with a kind of mythological power, thrilling and terrible: she had heard that the train as it pulled into town would pass right over the giant Sloss Furnace, and the idea haunted her. "If the furnace was open and the passengers could see the fire," she thought, "all would be destroyed," the train itself melted down, its passengers consumed in molten steel and flame.[16]

Mary Alice Clarke, a pioneering woman in Birmingham's male-dominated jazz scene, played in Fess Whatley's band for years but preferred to be remembered as an orchestral, not a jazz, musician. The longtime music director of the prestigious Sixteenth Street Baptist Church, she also taught generations of girls to play piano. Courtesy Birmingham, Ala. Public Library Archives.

As a student at Industrial, Harper joined the Dramatic Club, directed by Principal Parker himself; after the group performed at the upscale Jefferson Theater downtown, Harper determined to spend her future onstage. All her life, she would attempt to juggle her passion for performance with an equal passion for the classroom; but while society applauded men like Whatley for their dual roles as teacher-bandleaders, Harper discovered that, as a woman, she would be expected to choose.[17]

In 1919, a decade before Paul Bascomb launched that campus's Collegians, Harper enrolled at Alabama State. She graduated at seventeen (top students in southern Black schools often skipped a grade level or more in their schooling, accelerating their paths to graduation) and landed her first job at a school in Northport, Alabama. Her salary was $62.50 a month—"a small fortune"—and, in addition to her classroom duties, she directed the student choir and earned extra income teaching private music lessons. Soon she was back in Birmingham and teaching at Industrial, where she directed students in her own original plays and organized the annual Girls' Minstrel, a musical and theatrical showcase that was one of the school year's most reliably popular events (there was a Boys' Minstrel, too, and competition for the best show was high). Outside of school, Harper was a mainstay of the women's organizations, president of both the Progressive Thirteen and the City Federation of Colored Women's Clubs; she was an active social hostess and was frequently presented as vocal soloist at club meetings and events. She hosted and participated in regular "Negro History" programs, in which members presented on Black history or performed literary excerpts and musical selections. She acted and sang in local theatrical productions, including a 1932 staging of the landmark Black drama *Heaven Bound*. The same year, the Periclean Club hosted a Negro Authors Book Week, featuring an opening lecture by Langston Hughes and a presentation on Black folk songs by Alabama State's Willis Laurence James. Harper created and directed the week's much-praised closing pageant, "The Awakening," a "story of aspiration" starring Industrial students and featuring a musical backdrop of Negro spirituals, "sung with fervor and religious ecstasy."[18]

She also started her own dance orchestra. "Permission was given me by the principal of the high school," she wrote, "to form an orchestra with some of the boys from the band department." Ethel Harper's Rhythm Boys, for which she served as singer, director, and emcee, "made quite a name for themselves, playing for social affairs through the state" and competing successfully in local jazz battles. In 1935, Harper spent her summer break bouncing between New York City and Chicago, staying with friends, making the social columns, and performing on the radio and in nightclubs. "Miss

Harper, who divides her time between teaching high school and leading a band, will try her hand at night club entertaining," wrote a columnist for the *New York Age*; she appeared at that city's Poosepahtuck Club, where manager Fats Savage reportedly "went and rigged himself out in a brand new linen suit" to impress the new singer. At summer's end she returned to Birmingham, Industrial, and the Rhythm Boys. She relished her role as bandleader, but, she wrote (with characteristic reserve), "it was with regret that finally the Board of Education felt I must relinquish this activity because it was too strenuous along with my teaching chores." Harper's ambitions, anyway, lay elsewhere. In June of 1936, she abandoned those chores and returned to New York.[19]

The Rhythm Boys kept going without her. "Some of them," she wrote in 1970, "went on to become top musicians and today are members of some of our leading name bands." Her memoir gets no more specific than that, but one of those musicians would develop one of the century's most visionary—and unconventional—ensembles. Before Ethel Harper left town, she passed leadership of her Rhythm Boys to a precocious, inventive pianist and composer from Industrial High, a bookish and sensitive young musician everyone called "Sonny."[20]

The opportunity would mark Sun Ra's emergence as a bandleader.

THE MAGIC CITIZEN

Sun Ra never exactly claimed Birmingham as his hometown. Instead he cited outer-space origins and spoke of his "arrival" on this planet; conventional notions of a "birthplace" or "birth date" were beside the point.

"I arrived from a distant solar system," he said, "and combusted in the Magic City—Birmingham, Alabama." In interviews, he refused to be tied to reporters' preoccupations with the trivial details of calendar dates, "time zones," and geographic coordinates.[1]

"You were born in Alabama?" one writer asked.

"That's where I arrived," came Sun Ra's characteristic answer: "Birmingham, Alabama. I grew up in the Tabernacle Baptist Church. But I truly was an alien. And my father—I really believe my father was not a man. . . . He was another kind of spirit, a dark one. I was a baby in his arms."[2]

Some interviewers kept pushing for a more traditional sort of biography. "You were raised by your mother and your grandmother?"

"I was really raised by the creator of the universe who guided me step by step."[3]

Sun Ra was like his music, he explained: neither was *born* in the traditional sense. Instead, the man and his music just happened—combusted, appeared, landed, or arrived—and their essence was eternal. "JUST SAY," he wrote, that "I ARRIVED ON THIS PLANET SOME OTHER WHEN AT SOME SEEMING-POINT OF THEN ON POSSIBLY THE LEFT SIDE OF NOW. TRUE MUSIC IS NOT BORN . . . IT BE: IT IS OF COSMO-BEING GIFT-MAGNIFICENCE." In Sun Ra's conception, the true musician, like any true music, existed beyond time.[4]

After he left Birmingham, Sun Ra would become a musical icon and a hero of the avant-garde; one of jazz music's most creative, far-reaching, and outrageous personalities; a prolific composer, bandleader, and poet-philosopher whose true home, he maintained, was the cosmos, his music the expression of an urgent, interplanetary mission. Sun Ra merged his music with inward philosophy and outward spectacle, performing anthemic "space chants" and free-jazz explosions alongside loving excursions into the long history of blues and swing. He sought through his music to expand the narrow consciousness of mankind, tuning his listeners in to interplanetary visions and opening them up to greater harmonies—with themselves, with each other, and with the larger universe. It was a weighty ambition, and Sun Ra never found sustained acceptance within the mainstream; but from the musical and cultural margins he would build an influence and map a legacy that would attract followers for decades to come—indeed, he predicted (and time will tell), for *centuries*.

If in the mythic scheme of Sun Ra's mission, Birmingham was no more than "some seeming-point of then"—an arbitrary point in time and space, irrelevant to his true identity—the city in fact shaped his music and sense of self to a much greater degree than most fans and followers have realized. For all the otherworldliness that marked his career, for all the evasiveness with which he addressed his origins, and despite a long, self-imposed exile from his earthly hometown, Sun Ra and his music were always rooted in the place of his youth, the city from which he first looked up and saw the stars. And, one way or another, Sun Ra would always return to Birmingham.

Herman Poole Blount grew up just across the street from Birmingham's Terminal Station, the enormous, cathedral-like train depot in downtown Birmingham. He was still a boy when the city erected a sign there, one he saw every day from home, pronouncing Birmingham the "Magic City." It was a phrase that would stick forever with the man who would become Sun Ra; in later years he would riff in his compositions and his poetry on the over-lapping themes of magic and magi, imagination and majesty, and he would reclaim the "Magic City" name as a metaphor for his own transcendent utopian visions. A year before his death he would tell a reporter—almost inaudibly, barely capable of speech—that he had grown up "where the sign was," referencing a landmark by then decades gone.[5]

The boy was marked, himself, for a kind of magic. He was named for Black Herman, a Black itinerant magician famous for staging, among other feats, his own burials and resurrections. Nicknamed "Sonny" in his youth, in 1952 he would formally change the name to Le Sony'r Ra, or Sun Ra, the "true" name he said predated his arrival on earth, connecting him also to ancient mythology with its echoes of the Egyptian sun god, Ra. Friends, old and new, continued to call him "Sonny" (or "Sunny") all his life. As for "Blount," he explained, "It wasn't no good name for me." As he pointed out, "It didn't have no rhythm."[6]

Well before he left Birmingham, Sonny was already building around him an air of mystery. Frank Adams, fourteen years Sonny's junior, joined his band when Adams was a teenager, and the older musician was a wonderfully head-scratching cipher. "You just couldn't figure him out. Did he have a mother, or did he have a brother? Everything was a mystery about him." In fact, Sonny did have an older sister, Mary, and a half-brother, Robert; his parents separated when he was young, and he was raised by his grandmother and a beloved great-aunt, Ida. Some years later, Mary Blount Jenkins would smart at her brother's refusal to acknowledge home or family, and she bluntly dismissed the myth and mystery in which Sonny wrapped his origins. "He was born at my mother's aunt's house," she told the *Birmingham News* in 1992, "over there by the train station. I know, 'cause I got on my knees and peeped through the keyhole.

"He's not," she said, "from no Mars."[7]

Sun Ra, though, preferred to speak of outer space. In a 1978 interview for *Cadence* magazine, critic Bob Rusch suggested "a vagueness" about the musician's early career and proposed, hopefully, "Perhaps we could go back to your earliest memories."

"Well," Sun Ra answered,

> actually the vagueness comes from the fact I never been part of the planet, I've been isolated from a child and away from it. Right in the midst of everything and not being a part of it. . . . It was as if I was somewhere else that imprinted this purity on my mind, another kind of world. . . . It's like someone from another planet trying to find out what to do. That's the kind of mind or spirit I have, it's not programmed—from the family, from the church, from the schools, from the government. I don't have a programmed mind.

If at times Sun Ra described his outer-space identity as literal fact, insisting "I am not a man," in moments like this his language emphasized the metaphoric nature of those claims ("It was *as if* . . ."; "It's *like* . . ."; "That's *the kind of* . . ."). Whatever his origins, Sun Ra from his earliest memories had felt himself secluded from his surroundings; lonely as a child, he was fundamentally, somehow, *different*, and his difference from those around him gave him a lifelong distance, eccentricity, and originality of perspective.[8]

Years later, Frank Adams would defend Sun Ra against critics who called him a fake or a clown, accused him of gimmickry, or even questioned his sanity. Sun Ra, Adams insisted, was wholeheartedly genuine: "He was that way," said Adams, "because *he was that way*. He didn't conceive of himself as being a part of the world. So his evaluations *of* the world were not the evaluations we have." Sun Ra, Adams argued, "had never seen anyone who was like him." The metaphor of outer space and faraway planets offered a meaningful vocabulary and symbolism for a being who always understood himself a stranger in a strange land.[9]

Sonny Blount's first instrument, he later said, "was a kazoo, or maybe it was blowing through a comb," sometime around the age of six. A few years later, his mother gave him a piano—"an *arrival*-day present"—and, he claimed, he could play it by ear, immediately and instinctively. Sonny's sister, Mary, already played piano and gave her brother some of his first lessons. As Sun Ra would tell it, Mary resented the fact that the piano was Sonny's, not hers: she was the one who had already been taking lessons, and Sonny had never expressed an interest in playing. Their grandmother had resisted the idea of giving the boy a piano, too—musicians, she warned, always died young—but (like many another Birmingham grandparent or parent) she did make an exception for church music, so Sonny worked up a repertoire of hymns. Very quickly the whole family, Mary included, regarded the boy a "genius."[10]

Sonny was also exposed to music from more secular sources. The family owned a collection of blues and jazz records—Bessie Smith, Mamie Smith, Fletcher Henderson, Ida Cox—and from an early age Sonny encountered many of the musicians firsthand. "I saw the whole Black panorama of pure Black culture," he would say with pride; "even as a baby in the cradle" he encountered legendary performers, both in person and on record. Banned from white-owned hotels, touring Black artists slept in Black-owned board-inghouses or private homes; there was one such home next door to the Blounts, and Sonny saw all sorts of entertainers come and go. He took in every act he could, accompanying his great-aunt Ida to the Fourth Avenue theaters or taking the streetcar to Bessemer or Ensley. For all its way-out and future-leaning experimentation, Sun Ra's later music would always return to these early pioneers, building on their legacies as the crafters of a unique Black identity and culture.[11]

At Industrial, Fess Whatley championed the young pianist (and class valedictorian) as one of his star performers. But Sonny came to deride the school's emphasis on polite music, marching tunes, classical arias, and genteel popular sounds. "Educated people," he complained, favored sweet bandleaders like the schmaltzy Guy Lombardo; at assemblies and other school functions "they didn't play no jazz." The irony was obvious and underscored the school's complicated relationship to the music: "I wouldn't have known nothing about jazz, and I was going to an all-Black school. They considered jazz as being indecent, I suppose."[12]

Nonetheless, Sun Ra credited his broad musical training to Whatley's professional band, in which he performed. "During my years in High School," he wrote, "I played and studied all forms of music and the theory of the same." The wide-ranging repertoire and stylistic diversity of Whatley's Sax-o-Society Orchestra laid important groundwork for Sun Ra's own all-encompassing tastes. "He had a huge repertoire," he later recalled of Fess; "that's the reason I know about standards, because he had everything all the way back to the stomp, Dixieland. We played everything." Throughout his own career as bandleader, Sun Ra's performances would bring together the entire history of jazz, incorporating blues, swing, and standards alongside the wildly experimental, linking the past to the future in an expression of what he considered a kind of musical infinity. This catholicity of tastes was, in part, a product of his Birmingham roots.[13]

Indeed, the Birmingham years established numerous themes that would run through Sun Ra's career: the sheer size of the bands; the diversity of the repertoires; the Whatley insistence on discipline; the camaraderie and communal, musical journey of the late-night rehearsal ("That's more than likely why I liked big bands. Staying up all night, sometimes rehearsing with other bands of people my same age in school")—all of these hallmarks of Sun Ra's later career found their roots in the Magic City. As unconventional a musician as Sun Ra would become, he made a home, early on, in the relatively staid and stiff scene in which Whatley ruled. "They only played for exclusive people," he remembered of Fess's band. "Mostly only played for white people in exclusive places and social clubs where the Black people at. Black society and white society." Compared to other music towns, Birmingham "was sort of like an aristocratic center; it was really *society*. In fact," he added,

> while I was there, I never did play in what you call a tavern. I played
> for social clubs—black ones who had their social clubs, and they'd be
> together and they'd rent a place, and every week you had a social thing.
> . . . That's what it was, it was another kind of society. It wasn't the white
> world, but it was some people that was together, and they were very
> beautiful. But when I came to other cities, it wasn't like that—they didn't
> have what Birmingham had, they had taverns and all like that, night
> clubs, and I wasn't used to that. I was used to playing for society things.[14]

The society world shaped Sonny's imagination in other ways as well. From about ten years old into his teens, he belonged to the American Woodmen Junior Division, which met weekly at Eighteenth Street's Pythian Temple, where he observed a fascinating system of secret handshakes, mystic rituals, and exotic regalia. Members of groups like the Woodmen, Pythians, and Odd Fellows marched through the city with ceremonial helmets, swords, and shields; decorated their meeting spaces with esoteric symbols, suggesting access to arcane knowledge and hidden histories; and packed their lodge closets with colorful ritual gowns. Of his time with the Woodmen, Sonny explained that "I learned all about secret orders, discipline, and how to be a leader"—all key themes of Sun Ra's later career.[15]

The dazzling visual of those early bands would also serve as inspiration. As longtime Arkestra member Danny Ray Thompson would reflect, "If you just look at what happened to all the bands that came before Sun Ra, that came out of the South, first and foremost it was a show. . . . You could play anything as long as you had a show. And Sun Ra believed in that. And the more outrageous the show was the more people liked it." Sun Ra himself put it this way: "When jazz first started, musicians were fashion-plates, really. Louis Armstrong had almost a thousand suits. And you could see musicians back there; they *dressed* . . . they were wearing things that put another image out there, and they were successful."[16]

Not only through their music but through their dress and demeanor, the bands—like the fraternities—offered an alternate mode of existence. If Sun Ra ultimately abandoned the bow ties and tuxes for more outrageous attire, he was building all the same on the jazz tradition of the *show*, a full-fledged event loaded with pageantry and spectacle. Like his own early idols, he could "put another image out there"—one full of music, movement, costumes, and symbols—providing a glimpse of new possibilities and unexplored realities.

The music Sonny came to love, like Sonny himself, never seemed to fit in society—certainly not in the "mainstream" society constructed and constricted by whites—but it revealed to him the beauty of Blackness, and he hungrily consumed it. "While in high school I never missed a band," he wrote, "whether a known or an unknown unit. . . . Some of the bands I heard never got popular and never made hit records, but they were truly natural Black beauty. . . . The music they played was a natural happiness of love, so rare I cannot explain it. It was fresh and courageous; daring, sincere, unfettered. It was unmanufactured avant garde, and still is, because there was no place for it in the world; so the world neglected something of value and did not understand." "Unmanufactured" may seem an odd description for a music so carefully crafted, but for Sun Ra, music so pure, so sincere, so free from outside interference simply and naturally *was* (again, "it be"). And since society made no place for it, the music remained always "avant garde," eternally on the cutting edge—providing a deep reserve of timeless forms and ideas from which the bandleader could draw.[17]

A final lesson Sun Ra absorbed early on was the sense of unity that those bands made possible. The big bands provided a different, community-driven, and ultimately empowering sort of existence that stood in contrast to the corrupt and destructive societies Sun Ra had seen on the earth, in the South. "The Black people were very oppressed," he explained, "and were made to feel like they weren't anything, so the only thing they had was the big bands. Unity showed that the Black man could join together and dress nicely, do something nice, and that was all they had. . . . So it was important for us to hear big bands."[18]

Or, as he put it on another occasion: "A band can demonstrate unity among men more than anything else in the world."[19]

By high school, Sonny was throwing himself completely into Black Birmingham's world of music. He performed with Paul Bascomb's band and the Society Troubadours student group; led his own Nighthawks of Harmony, playing for dances and over radio station WAPI; and accompanied tap dancer Prince Wallace and gospel singer J. William Blevins. With his close friend Avery Parrish (the Bama State Collegians' future star pianist), he traded musical ideas, practiced piano duets, and experimented with compositions, the two friends encouraging and inspiring each other to write their first tunes. Around 1933, he ambitiously sent one of these pieces to the New York songwriter and publisher Clarence Williams, a prominent Black entrepreneur with a catalog of hits to his name but a reputation, too, for unscrupulous business practices. Williams recorded the piece with his own band, apparently without giving compensation or credit to its young composer. Sonny would not make this mistake again: in later years, he would circumvent the corruptions and control of the music industry by releasing his prolific output on his own label, El Saturn, a pioneer in independent, artist-centered music production and a true do-it-yourself operation (Sun Ra and the members of his Arkestra often designed album covers and labels by hand, writing and drawing directly on the individual products). Even if Sonny saw no reward for his first stab at song publishing, the Clarence Williams Orchestra's 1933 record serves as an important historical marker, the first documentation of Sun Ra's efforts at composition and a unique window into his early musical world. Presumably, the tune—like the Fuzzy Wuzzies' "Stomp," six years before—took its inspiration from Birmingham's

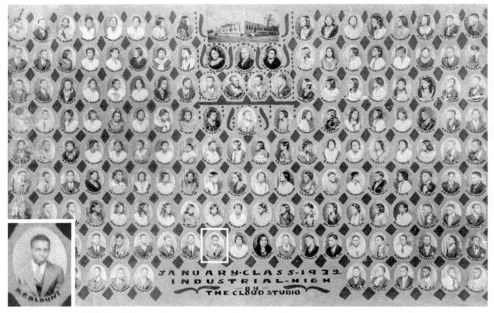

Industrial High School, Class of 1932. Herman Poole Blount—class valedictorian and the future Sun Ra—is pictured just above the word "January," at bottom. Other notable musicians pictured here include Amos Gordon, Newman Terrell, and Melvin Caswell. Courtesy Birmingham, Ala. Public Library Archives.

own Fourth Avenue, where "natural Black beauty" reigned: Sonny called the piece "Chocolate Avenue."[20]

In the meantime, Sonny was also emerging as a leader in Ethel Harper's Rhythm Boys. In his version of the story, the real reason Harper gave up the band was a bit more sensational than Harper herself let on: the school's leadership simply was not comfortable with a female teacher—young and glamorous, dressed in an evening gown and crooning love songs—fronting a stageful of teenage boys. It was one thing for Whatley to do it, but Harper was a woman, and the whole thing pushed the bounds of propriety. "Everybody talked about fifteen or sixteen fellows being up there under a woman," Sun Ra explained. "They talked about her because she was a schoolteacher . . . and it was a big scandal." In fact, Harper was "very dignified"—a prominent women's clubber and nothing ever but pure professionalism—but "a lot of people were jealous of her." Gossip spread, and "the fellows in the band got worried . . . so some kind of way, they voted to give me the band. And the next thing I know I saw my name out there—and I didn't ask for it, they just said I was the person that should be the leader of a band. So my destiny in music was determined by other people—not me."[21]

Fess Whatley was also encouraging Sonny's leadership. In the fall of 1934, just back from his own tour of the country, Whatley sponsored the Sonny Blount Orchestra on the same circuit. Fess "bought the bus and everything," Sun Ra said. In Kingsport, Tennessee, newspapers announced:

"FESS" WHATLEY
Birmingham's King of Jazz
Presents His Hottest Band
SONNY BLOUNT
and His Orchestra
The South's Greatest Swinging Band
Radio—Dance—Vaudeville Sensation
At
FLORAL CASINO
9 to 2
Saturday Night, October 12

The same paper praised the group as "one of the south's greatest bands with several novelty attractions and dancers." When the band appeared in Asheville, North Carolina, papers noted its makeup of "thirteen young college men," including one "Joseph Sanford, former member of the 'Bama [State] Collegians." In December, the *Pittsburgh Courier* reported that Blount's orchestra had "created quite a sensation" before "a capacity crowd" in Danville, Illinois. "All graduates of Industrial High," the paper added of the musicians, "they are also former pupils of J. C. [*sic*] Whatley better known as 'Fess.'" Anticipating a repeat performance in Louisville, Kentucky, the *Chicago Defender* urged locals to catch the unique act: "The orchestra will feature its red hot rhythm, its melodic crooner and unusual tap dancer."[22]

In the year ahead, Sonny's band became a repeat favorite at Atlanta's Sunset Casino, and columnist Lucius Jones dizzily chronicled the group's rise in the pages of the *Atlanta Daily World*. "Sonny Blount and his torrid 14-piece jazz orchestra will seek new worlds tonight," Jones announced in February 1935, declaring the group "one of the sweetest and most versatile jazz bands to play the local populace." (The reference to the band seeking "new worlds" seems now a prophetic turn of phrase, hinting at Sonny's pursuit, even then, of musical unknowns; it is also hard, in retrospect, to ignore the press's frequent descriptions of Sonny's act as "unusual"—an intriguing but painfully vague choice of words.) At intermission, Sonny stood on the bandstand and announced that "his band could whip the Troubadours"—the Sunset's regular act—"in their own premises." When he returned a month later—"Set for

War," the headline announced—"the whole city [was] all worked up about this unusual attraction."[23]

Certainly, Jones had done his part to stoke the tension, devoting his column for days to the coming showdown, weighing the strengths of each band. "Sonny Blount and his men are given credit generally for having the best reed section among the bands performing in this circuit," he wrote, "while there is little doubt as to the all-round excellence of the Troubadours. . . . Sonny Blount is a pianist of unusual capabilities, but [the Troubadours'] Jay Gholston . . . is certainly one of the flashiest young orchestral pianists and arrangers in the band game." With characteristic exuberance, Jones anticipated the "staccato of piano notes . . . the vibration of tenor banjo and bass viol strings . . . the purr of the orchestral drums . . . the wailing of saxophones . . . the sobbing of trumpets and trombones . . . and the resonance of dancing feet," as the Troubadours "combat the invading band of Sonny Blount." In the "tussle" that ensued, Sonny's "red-hot jazz orchestra" capably "extended those Troubadours to the breaking point" before an estimated crowd of 800 fans. Until their recent departure for New York, the Bama State Collegians had been "dixie's best young band," but Sonny, who knew those Bama Staters well, now believed his own group heir to their title—and Jones himself could not dispute the claim. When the Blount aggregation returned to Atlanta that summer, Jones advised readers that "Sonny Blount and his men . . . have some of the hottest and most distinctive jazz in Dixieland and it'll be a grand and colossal mistake not to hear them."[24]

Even as his reputation grew, Sonny struggled against the pull of his destiny. Echoing his grandmother's reservations about the lives of musicians, Sun Ra would later claim he had hoped to avoid the kind of fate that hounded all sorts of artists and visionaries. "I had read about poets and writers and wise men all having a difficult time as human beings," he said, "so I didn't intend to get into that."[25]

Instead, in the fall of 1935, he enrolled in college.

"I decided that I didn't want to be a leader on this planet, in any capacity. So I left the band and I went to college, 'cause I had a scholarship: A&M College in Huntsville, Alabama. . . . That college, you didn't fool around; you had to get your lessons, because they wanted to keep their A rating." He enrolled in teacher training courses and told his Birmingham bandmates he was giving up music. "And then," he said, "here comes the band—everybody in the band came to the college." Sonny attempted to shake them off, but they told him, "'Wherever you go, we're going.' . . . They moved into the dormitories, got their beds and everything." In the end, the college president "got in on it," offering each musician a scholarship. "So," Sonny said, "I wound up still being a leader."[26]

One should always take Sun Ra's stories with many grains of salt, but this description is not so far-fetched as it might appear. Sonny's friends at Alabama State had by now set the model for all southern Black colleges to follow, the bands were proven moneymakers, and Sonny was already a respected regional bandleader. So A&M "bought a bus, streamlined bus . . . they gave them uniforms, they bought books—and there I was, stuck with a band again." At last, he gave in: that fall, Sonny Blount and his A&M Collegians began appearing at both white and Black dances in the area. "Ever since, I knew that my destiny is to be a composer and to be the leader of a band. So it wasn't determined by me, you see. Something wanted me to be in the position I am."[27]

Sonny did not stay at A&M for long, but his experience there would prove transformative. When he was not rehearsing or performing with the band, he buried himself in the library, studying ancient history and religion and trying to get at the deepest, most elusive meanings of the Bible. And it was at A&M, he would explain in years to come, that he had his first encounter with the "spaceways."

Sun Ra told the story many times: he was contacted by spacemen who brought him onto their ship and, he said, to "a planet that I identified as Saturn." The aliens told him to stop his teacher training and instructed him in their own discipline, conveying to him a fuller vision of his destiny. "They would teach me some things that when it looked like the world was going into complete chaos, when there was no hope for nothing, then I could speak, but not until then. I would speak, and the world would listen. That's what they told me."[28]

Soon he was back on the planet and, when his freshman year finished, back in Birmingham: leading bands, making headlines, and speaking over the course of late-night rehearsals new and unusual truths he had brought back from the cosmos.

At last, he had stopped arguing with destiny.

• • •

The Birmingham jazz tradition grew from a complex well of influences. The schools provided the tools—and offered, through the examples of both teachers and alums, crucial models for success. But the schools were only one piece of a broader musical ecosystem: also essential were the circus, the church, and the vaudeville stage, with its comedy, costumes, music, and dance. Then, too, were the fraternal dances and women's teas, teenage talent shows, carnival tent shows, and a rich a cappella harmony tradition rooted in the spirituals and in Black cultural pride. Musicians were steeped in a universe of Community Sings, ladies' private music schools, and a vital culture of public street parades; they found inspiration in moving-picture accompanists, low-down pianists, local and national radio broadcasts, collegiate dance bands, and major touring "name" bands. For many, the world expanded in the summers, as they set out, wide-eyed, with their first traveling shows. All these streams of influence were shaped by conventions of class and gender and region, by the culture of racial segregation, by conversations about the meaning and importance of community, by theories and strategies of racial unity and uplift. When Birmingham players hit the road, they took it all with them, inside them, growing from these foundations not only their own futures but the future of America's music. And if—as Sonny Blount increasingly believed—music could even change the world, no one was better equipped than these Birmingham musicians to do it.

PART II

ARRIVAL

By the time his old bandmates arrived from Alabama State, in the summer of 1934, Haywood Henry had made himself at home in New York. After three months with Reverend Becton, he had left the Gospel Feast for his first big-time gig, a series of engagements with the Kaiser Marshall Orchestra at Fifty-First Street and Broadway's Empire Ballroom. The setup with Becton had been more than comfortable: the whole band lived together in the reverend's lavish, three-story apartment, their every need paid for. "We had maid service, free laundry, and a cook who did delicious food. I worked about an hour and a half a night and they paid me thirty dollars a week, which was wonderful in those days. . . . I was very well off financially," he said, but still, something was missing. He started hanging around the Rhythm Club, about a block away from Becton's church, and catching the name bands that played the Savoy Ballroom. Henry was enthralled not just by the music but by the way the players dressed, the cool they exuded from even their looks alone. He decided he would have to improve his own look, shedding his all-too-obvious "Alabama style" for a more modern, uptown appearance. Above all, he would have to start playing *jazz* with real jazz musicians, not just swinging gospel for the sanctified set. He hooked up with brothers Pete and Dick Clarke of Birmingham, both already well-connected on the scene; they introduced him to the crowd at the Woodside Hotel, a hub for Harlem's jazz community, and got him onstage for a set at the Savoy. Another Birmingham musician, Leon Englund, invited him to sit in one night with Marshall, and Marshall invited him to stay for the Empire gig. Haywood gave his notice to Becton: at the Empire he would make only twenty-eight dollars a week and would have to cover his own living expenses. "But," he said, "I was doing what I really wanted, playing jazz."[1]

All the while, he kept up his correspondence with the Collegians, encouraging them to come see what New York had to offer. By the time the band did arrive, Henry had assumed a chic urban posture: "I had gotten New Yorkish by then, and I had on gray suits and Florsheim shoes and a pocket full of money, fingernails all manicured, hair conked." When the Collegians showed up one afternoon at the Rhythm Club, he was embarrassed, almost incredulous, to see in them how "country" he must have looked, himself, just a few months ago. In addition to his new wardrobe and the requisite conk—the chemically straightened hairstyle that in those days symbolized hip urbanity among Black male musicians—Henry had upgraded to a gold saxophone, a gift from Becton; here now came all his old bandmates with their battered and beaten silver horns (musicians from "down South" always carried silver instruments, often dinged, dented, and out of tune). The rest of the band would not lose much time before acquiring conks, new suits and shoes, and golden horns of their own.[2]

Country or not, the band was a hit with northern audiences, and Henry as host relished their success, showing them off at jam sessions and observing their shows from the sidelines. He found them a place to stay—"Just two rooms, because they weren't going to sleep there anyways." (In those days, he said, "I didn't know what sleeping at night *was*.") The Collegians had not booked any gigs in New York City itself; their scheduled tour culminated in a date at Asbury Park, New Jersey. But word about the band traveled, and at Asbury Park they played to a large and enthusiastic crowd, which included key members of New York City's jazz elite. "It was the talk of the town," Erskine Hawkins said. "This young boy comes from the South—and they were talking about *me*—hitting all those high notes." Bandleader Benny Carter and promoter John Hammond both came away impressed. Frank Schiffman, co-owner of both the Harlem Opera House and the Apollo Theater, was in the audience, too, and he booked the band for a weeklong engagement at the Opera House, promising each man forty dollars.[3]

The Collegians wowed their first New York crowds with the same high-energy act that had made them a sensation back home. Hawkins belted out his signature stream of high Cs, a hundred in a row, the band counting off each note as it came, and "then I'd hit an F above it, to end it up. I was doing that like five or six shows a day for a whole week." "I stood in the back," Haywood Henry recalled, "and I never felt so proud of those guys in my life."[4]

A weekend gig at the Apollo followed. By now, Haywood had rejoined the Collegians full-time. Headlining comedian Jackie Mabley (later famous as

"Moms" Mabley) worked the group into her act, riffing on their fresh faces, good looks, and wide-eyed innocence. "Look at them," Mabley announced, suggestively. "Young fellows all twenty years old. . . . Girls," she advised, "you better get them now—because give them six months and they're gonna be *hip!*"

"And," Haywood said: "that was the truth. It didn't take long."[5]

The Collegians never returned to Alabama State. New York was too full of opportunity, the band's momentum there too strong. If they ever hoped to go professional, this was their moment. They sent word to Montgomery: they weren't coming back.

President Trenholm, at first, was furious: a major income stream had just walked out on him, had even absconded in the process with one of the school's buses, the "Collegians" name still emblazoned on its sides. (Eventually they sent the bus back, empty, with a driver, though they held on to the name, performing as the Bama State Collegians into 1937, long after they'd arrived in New York.) Even as a bunch of defectors, however, the band's reputation could bring only good press to the college. The players were no longer sending home their earnings, but Trenholm—staking his own claim to the now-famous name—enlisted in their absence a new group of student Collegians, with Amos Gordon, a Whatley-trained saxophonist, at the helm. Shifting incarnations of Bama State Collegians, Revelers, and Cavaliers would remain a core piece of the school's identity into the 1950s, and the bands would continue to incubate talent. A subsequent lineup of Collegians would become the nucleus of the dynamic R&B outfit the Treniers, a group that in the late 1940s and '50s would help bridge the sounds of swing and rock and roll. The original group would eventually be forgiven its transgression of leaving, would be hailed indeed as the start of it all; the college would award Erskine Hawkins an honorary doctorate in 1947.[6]

For now, though, the band needed work. They found a manager named Hyman "Feets" Edson, a fast-talking entrepreneur with a hundred ideas and a dubious record as businessman, con man, and ubiquitous Broadway character. Feets was a creature of Manhattan and a type of personality the Collegians had never seen back home. He walked on crutches but struck an imposing presence, physically strong, heavily built, and well known for a history of gangsterism; he smoked giant cigars ("the biggest cigars known to science," one observer put it); he talked big and laughed hard and clapped friends and strangers loud on the back. He had sold bootleg gin during Prohibition, had operated speakeasies and worked for the mob, had developed a reputation as an ace getaway driver, and had been, some said, a ready and dependable hired gun. He had never gotten rich—all the money he made never seemed to last—but through the 1920s and '30s he had tried dozens of money-making schemes, some on the level and others decidedly not: had "dabbled," one reporter wrote, "in the boxing game, the horses, the night clubs, the real estate gag . . . and several thousand other pursuits." After Prohibition he ran a series of clip joints, seedy liquor houses where he made a business of fleecing each night some portion of that limitless populace that he perceived as suckers: out-of-towners, drifters, drunks, and the gullible rich, all waiting and deserving to be duped. He rolled crooked dice and scammed customers with "phony champagne," diluted beers and doctored checks, slipped them Mickeys and occasionally subjected them to blackmail. The source of his nickname was a matter of some debate: he simply had bad feet (hence the crutches), or (despite the crutches) feet so strong he would use them, like third and fourth fists, for fighting. Once, maybe more than once, he had been ordered dead and was picked up by hitmen (this was the most-often-repeated story about Feets, but here again the details varied from telling to telling: maybe he had left a lost bet unpaid; maybe he had ripped off gangster Owney Madden's own *mother*), but his gift for talk and irresistible charisma had saved his life. Not only did he convince his would-be assassins to let him go; he also talked them out of twenty dollars.[7]

Now Feets was drawing on his nightclub connections to act as agent for up-and-coming talent, and the Collegians seemed a good bet: a novel act with an upward trajectory but no representation and few connections. He introduced himself to the players, and they immediately hit it off. From other sources they heard rumors of Feets's gangster activities, stories at once outrageous, hilarious, romantic, and mysterious. It was hard to know what was real and what was embroidered by gossip, magnified by Feets's outsize personality. Certainly, he was friendly and funny and full of worldly knowledge. He shook their hands and patted their backs, bought them drinks and talked of the future. They liked him.[8]

The group that settled in New York included Erskine and Marcellus Green on trumpets; Jimmy Mitchell and Robert Sanford, saxophones; Bob Range and Cap Sims, trombones; Avery Parrish, piano; Big Jack Morrison, drums; LeMeyer "Leemie" Stanfield, bass; and William McLemore, guitar. Soon they sent back to Birmingham for J. B. Sims and the Bascomb brothers. One night at a club, Haywood ran into Julian Dash, a tenor player from South Carolina who had enrolled at Bama State on a music scholarship and played with the guys back home; he had since made his own way to New York, and the group welcomed him in. The press and the crowds ate up the band's unique story: college boys, southerners, and friends since childhood, there was nothing else like them on the scene. Observers cited the players' youthful exuberance and endless reserves of energy as keys to their appeal. The group's elders, Paul and J. B., were still shy of twenty-five; Dud, the youngest, was "just going on eighteen." Sammy Lowe, who would join them soon, was two years younger than Dud.

One rule that Fess Whatley had always impressed on his students: as soon as they arrived anyplace new, they checked in, first thing, with the union. New York's Local 802 was technically integrated, unlike the locals back home, but in 1934 it was still notorious for rejecting Black applicants. J. B. Sims held it a lifelong point of pride that he successfully arranged memberships for the entire band, even as other musicians were turned away. They rented a few rooms at the Woodside Hotel. Feets bought them pawnshop overcoats for the coming New York winter and hustled around town to find them work.[9]

After a few weeks of odd jobs, the group scored a steady, prestigious gig at one of Harlem's wildest, most colorful nightspots, the Ubangi Club, backing Gladys Bentley's uproarious floor show. Raucous, raunchy, and defiantly over-the-top, Bentley wore a white tuxedo, top hat, and tails and fronted a forty-member ensemble of musicians, dancers, and female impersonators. ("They had a line of chorus girls and a line of gays," marveled Haywood, "and the gays were as pretty as the chorus girls.") Dancing, singing waiters moved through the room, and the cast onstage performed comic musical skits with titles like "Reefer Smokers Ball" and "Nudist." Admission was free. With its gleeful embrace of sexuality and a diverse audience—including Black, white, gay, and straight—the Ubangi cultivated an atmosphere that was unrestrained and open-armed. Outspoken about her own lesbian identity, Bentley—who had married a woman, and a white woman at that, in a civil ceremony in New Jersey—was famous for her dirty parodies of popular songs, her lyrics so explicit the Ubangi was repeatedly raided and shuttered for its purveyance of smut. Each time the club reopened, Bentley renewed the act with vigor, undeterred.[10]

Young and explosive, the Collegians synched perfectly with the Ubangi's energy and irreverence. They kicked off their act with a medley of hammy imitations, mimicking the theme songs of Duke Ellington, Cab Calloway, and other stars. Then they broke into their own novelty arrangement of "St. Louis Blues"—"and we would play it," said Henry, "and play it. At the end, Erskine would walk in from one wing, and 'Dud' would walk in from the other wing, and they would start battling one another," each one-upping the other's best solos. Then "Jimmy Mitchell and I would wrap our saxophones around one another and start dancing. And the bass player would get over

Erskine Hawkins and the Bama State Collegians in a photo postcard from New York's groundbreaking Ubangi Club. Courtesy Alabama State University Archives.

the bass, whipping it like riding a horse." A photo postcard from the club provides a glimpse of this promiscuous clowning: two pairs of embracing musicians flank the stage, bodies and horns intertwined, while at center three more straddle the bass, a white-suited J. B. Sims sandwiched in the middle, arms outstretched, handkerchief waving.[11]

Shows started at 6:30 p.m. and continued until five in the morning. They were making fifty-four dollars a week, per man, and eating for free at the club. Haywood and Dud shared a room at the Woodside, "and we had suits hanging all around the walls. Twenty-five dollars would buy a suit every other week." They were living lavish and large; said Henry, "[We] changed clothes three times a day."[12]

"Alabama State Collegians to Go on Dance Tour Shortly," announced an October 1935 headline in the *Pittsburgh Courier*; "Demands Coming In from Every Part of Country." The story burst with exclamatory prose, proclaiming,

"Erskine Hawkins and his Bama State Collegians have succumbed to the lure of the wide open highways! . . . The band, a strict collegiate band, has written pages in musical history which sound like romantic fiction! Two years ago they were a bunch of college boys from down Montgomery way . . . with nothing but burning ambition and the will to do or die to spur them on." Now they were Ubangi Club sensations, and they were just getting started. "The band swings out in a manner typically their own," the *Courier* continued: "They blow 'hot' and they blow 'sweet.' Headed by Erskine Hawkins, who is destined to take his place as one of the really great trumpet players of the race, they've been going places and doing things. . . . And now, in order to satisfy the demands of a greedy public, they're hitting the road."[13]

"[We] went back South," Erskine explained, "so people could see us—let them know how we were getting along." The tour stretched as far south as Florida, but the natural highlight was Birmingham: they played their hometown twice, going and coming, eager to show off their slick transformations, and the Magic City embraced them. In Atlanta the band's return was also met with great anticipation, the Sunset Casino's management "positively guaranteeing" the group to be "the one and only original 'Bama Staters," distinguishing this group of Collegians from the newer acts sent out by the college—and from any number of unauthorized imitators. "Yowsah," exclaimed the *Daily World*'s Lucius Jones in advance of the show, "the stuff will be here in just one week from today."[14]

The acclaim was a thrill, but the expenses of travel ate through the band's earnings. It was an unusually cold winter in Florida, and crowds there were small. "When we were coming out of Mobile," said Henry, "we didn't have enough money to cross a long toll-bridge, so we had to hock a baritone sax." Next, Henry hocked his watch. On the return trip through Birmingham, he borrowed twenty dollars from his schoolteacher sister; before the bus got back to New York, he had lost it all shooting dice.[15]

The South was always home—and it always provided the band's most enthusiastic crowds—but New York became a special kind of heaven. The place pulsed with life, its unceasing energy intoxicating. When the musicians finished their gigs, they would go out and find someplace to jam, trading solos with players from other bands—and increasingly trailed by a tail of admirers.[16]

The band became regulars at the Savoy Ballroom, a place that would become central to the group's identity. The Savoy billed itself, without too much hyperbole, the "World's Finest Ballroom"; singer Lena Horne called it the "Home of Happy Feet" after its beautiful frenzy of stylized dancers.

Certainly, there were other dance halls, but there was nothing like the Savoy. Located on Lenox Avenue between 140th and 141st Streets, the ballroom occupied a full city block, offering half an acre of music, glitz, drinking, and dancing. Admission was cheap, allowing for large and diverse crowds, but the scene was luxurious: the Savoy boasted a giant polished hardwood floor, mirrored walls, two bandstands, colored stage lights, and a room that teemed with voguish dressers and dancers. Like the Ubangi, it distinguished itself by rejecting segregation outright; Black and white shared the floor space with a mix of old and young, the working classes and the social elite. "At the Savoy Ballroom," observed a writer for the *New York Amsterdam News*, "social, racial, and economic problems fade away to nothingness."[17]

The music never stopped. Both the Savoy's bandstands supported a dozen musicians or more, and each night two bands played alternating forty-minute sets, one act jumping in as the other played off. There was no time lost as musicians set up or broke down or lingered at the bar, just an endless barrage of music from some of the country's greatest bands. Especially exhilarating were the Savoy's much-touted jazz battles. The Collegians had excelled at these sorts of contests back home, even besting Fess Whatley on his own turf; at the Savoy, the competitions were waged on a higher scale, presented as epic clashes of musical titans. No winner was formally announced, but audiences—and the next day's entertainment columns—made their opinions clear, and the players had no doubt whether they had won or lost. The battles were waged in fun and reflected the mutual admiration of the competing bands, but winning was a source of tremendous pride, the rivalries were real, and losses could hurt: the Collegians sometimes found themselves exhausted, even in tears, in the wake of battle.[18]

It was the dancing, as much as the music, that made the Savoy famous— and the more the bands pushed each other to the brink, the better that dancing became. The floor comfortably fit some 2,000 bodies, but big nights could draw twice that number. In later years, musicians recounted how the whole floor moved up and down in one pulsating rhythm with the dancers (it was widely reported that the floor had to be replaced every three years to hold up against the Savoy's relentless stomping). The competitive energy of the bandstand—its emphasis on individual expression, artistry, and one-upmanship—extended to the floor, where heroes (and professional dancing careers) were made. Many patrons came just to watch; buses loaded with tourists poured their gawking crowds into the ballroom for the sheer sake of the spectacle. Hollywood stars and visitors from across the globe came in to celebrate the dizzying buzz of the scene.[19]

The Collegians made the place their home.

New York may have boasted some of the best musicians in the world, but for Hawkins and the band Birmingham remained, for years, the most dependable source of talent: anytime they needed a new player, there was no question where to look. "I understood that when you got to New York," Erskine explained, "you didn't want to put a member in the band that [you] didn't know too much . . . about." What you wanted was a known quantity, someone who would not "get in there and disrupt the band," someone who knew how to play, how to work, and how to get along. So "when I needed an extra man, I sent back to Birmingham and got somebody that we knew."[20]

It was the Bascomb brothers who suggested they send for Sammy Lowe. Lowe had graduated in 1935 from Industrial High and enrolled, at the suggestion of Birmingham's Fred and Frank Greer, at Tennessee A&I College in Nashville. The Tennessee State Collegians, that school's up-and-coming band, was full of Birmingham talent: in addition to the Greers and Lowe, there was trumpeter Nathaniel Atkins, drummer Melvin Caswell, and a sensational one-armed pianist and arranger named Dan Michael. But "the spark of the band," said Sammy, was a Tennessean, bassist Jimmy "Kid" Blanton, who in a few years would pioneer a new role for the bass in his work with Duke Ellington. It was a top-notch band—but, ironically, the success of the Bama State Collegians proved detrimental to Lowe's tenure in the group. A&I's president, William Jasper Hale, had been comparing notes with Alabama State's H. Councill Trenholm and found he was missing an opportunity. At the start of Lowe's second semester, Hale told the musicians they would have to start giving the school all earnings from their extracurricular gigs, income they had previously been able to keep for themselves. They would also have to start doing more to earn their keep, working between their gigs and their classes on the campus farm. Immediately, the players began looking for their exits.[21]

For Sammy, the telegram from Paul Bascomb came just in time. The band wired fourteen dollars for transportation, and Sammy's parents sent another ten, enough to get him to New York and leave a little extra in his pocket. Sammy was still playing a shoddy old trumpet, so Frank Greer gave him his own, "still practically new," and late one night, after a campus dinner and dance, Jimmy Blanton walked him to the bus station. The whole ride north, Sammy kept the telegram from Bascomb in his hands: "Come right to New York," he read, and read again, "to join Bama State."[22]

Never had so few words contained so much magic.

UP FROM DOWN SOUTH

"In New York City," Frank Adams said, "you could go and stand on the corner. If you were there about fifteen minutes, you would see somebody from Birmingham, a musician, come up, and they'd say, 'Where are you staying, man?' and take you somewhere to stay." Birmingham players migrated to Chicago, Cleveland, Cincinnati, Detroit, anyplace there was music and work, but New York had a special draw. Many made it their new home, at least for a time, planting themselves in the heart of jazz culture, etching themselves into the always-evolving sound.[1]

One night in January 1936, the Bama State Collegians were playing the Savoy Ballroom when they spotted an old friend in the crowd. The Count Basie Orchestra had just arrived in town for a residence at the Roseland Ballroom, a gig that marked the band's much-touted New York debut. Like everyone, the Collegians had heard the buzz about the band, its distinctive rhythm section, and its knockout drummer. Birmingham's Jo Jones, for his own part, was eager to see how the old Bama Staters were making out at the swanky Savoy. "He came down to the club to check us out," Haywood Henry said.

> I had been hearing so much about him, so the reunion was exciting.
> . . . We reminisced about Birmingham and talked music. Then he sat
> in with us and really was swinging.
>
> After that, we got together at band battles at the Savoy
> ballroom—Basie against the Erskine Hawkins band.

Never mind who won or lost: onstage, in competing bands, these grade-school friends pushed each other as hard as they could, Jones driving the

Basie group with the propulsive shimmer of his drums, the Hawkins men responding with their fiercest swing. Haywood could not help but swell with pride as he witnessed his old friend's rise as the most widely imitated drummer in the business.[2]

Jones had traveled widely since leaving Wilson Driver at Birmingham's Famous Theater. Like Sonny Blount, he enrolled briefly at Huntsville's Alabama A&M, where he studied with celebrated cornetist James H. Wilson. He toured with vaudeville and medicine shows, "little girlie shows" and circuses, and he played the Chautauqua circuit of educational lectures and entertainments. In later years, he would bemoan the lack of diversity—and the critical lack of travel—in the training of most musicians. "They never saw the people," he complained of younger players; "they weren't on the circuses and carnivals, they didn't hit the forty-eight states—villages and hamlets, you know. After World War II it got so they could get in an aeroplane and they never see nothing." The music suffered as a result.[3]

Jones, on the other hand, learned directly from the disparate group of older, itinerant entertainers he met on the road, many of whom had what he called "foreign intrigue." "These people—Hungarians, Lithuanians, trapeze artists, and what have you—they taught me how to eat, how to think; they taught personal hygiene, moral and civil discipline. . . . They didn't lecture us, but they showed [us] youngsters the way."[4]

Work was unpredictable, but something always turned up. A band might run out of money and break up, mid-tour, leaving musicians stranded—in "Chattanooga, Louisville, Paducah or whatever"—but another show would always come through, needing players. "Sometimes they didn't even have a set of drums. I'd borrow a snare and a bass drum, and use a coat hanger for a cymbal holder." Jones's versatility was an asset: besides drums, he played piano and vibraphone, sang, and danced. Once he did settle on drums, his work on that instrument was informed by every corner of the music and entertainment worlds that reared him, from his silent movie days through the world of tent shows. His greatest influences were the dancers, whose routines he observed and absorbed, and his own dancing skills shaped his approach to the drums. "When one least expected it," writes jazz historian Burt Korall, "he would offer his vision, in a solo or fill, of a dancer from long ago, or one he heard the night before," translating their remembered footwork into the rhythm of his sticks.[5]

Jones worked his way west, settling for a while in Omaha and playing with several of the territory bands that covered the Midwest. In St. Louis, he joined the popular Jeter-Pillars Club Plantation Orchestra, reuniting with one of his old Birmingham mentors, trumpeter George Hudson. (Not to be confused with the longtime Birmingham music teacher of the same name, *this* George Hudson had established himself in the Midwest early on and emerged as a mainstay on the St. Louis jazz scene: first as sideman, then as leader of his own influential orchestra—Miles Davis, Ahmad Jamal, and Clark Terry would all pass through his band—and finally as a high school bandmaster.) Jones played briefly with the Bennie Moten Orchestra, the group that set the standard for Kansas City swing; musicians from that ensemble would soon form the nucleus of the Count Basie band.

Jones often told the story of how he came to work with Basie. He arrived in Kansas City in early 1934 and was hired for a Valentine's gig with the pianist's new, still-unknown ensemble. Jones played well enough that Basie offered him a permanent spot, but the drummer demurred. The Basie group played at another level than he did; besides, he still had not even settled exclusively on the drums. "Up to that time," Basie remembered, "he had thought of himself as being a piano player who could also sing and dance."[6]

Jones himself put it simply. "Shit," he said, "I wasn't good enough to work with Basie's band. What the hell would I be doing up there?" But Basie liked his style and, in the summer of 1935, hired him for a standing gig at the Reno Club, a cramped and dingy Kansas City nightclub that catered to ranchers, drifters, gamblers, prostitutes, and musicians. Drinks were cheap—beer a nickel a glass, whiskey a dime—and marijuana passed openly from hand to hand; a lunch wagon set up just outside, "horse-drawn and stacked high," one regular recalled, "with liver, pig snoots and ears, hog maws, fish, chicken and pork tenderloins." There was an elevated oyster-shell bandstand barely big enough to accommodate the musicians; when a tune required bassist Walter Page to pick up the tuba, he left the instrument onstage, went outside, and leaned through the window to play. It may have been a dive, but the music was thrilling. Basie invited musicians to participate in wide-open jam sessions beginning at four on Monday mornings and continuing well into day. Radio station W9XBY aired late-night broadcasts from the club, and on clear nights the signal's reach covered much of the country and stretched into Canada. Refining his sound, bit by bit, Basie worked with a handful of drummers before he sent for Jones. "And that's," he said, "when that band really started swinging."[7]

Kansas City drummer Cliff Leeman had seen the Reno act a few times with other drummers on the stand; when Jones joined the group, the transformation was remarkable. "I walked in one night," he said. "I'll never forget it. Jo was sitting up there above the band, smiling and cooking. The band was on fire. Basie had found the recipe and Jo was a key part of it." All of a sudden, "the band became unbelievable." Sitting in his car outside a Chicago jazz club one night, impresario John Hammond was scanning the radio dial and picked up one of the Reno's broadcasts. He began writing Basie, eager to meet, but the bandleader never responded; so, after two months of unanswered letters, Hammond showed up in Kansas City to check out the band in person. "The first thing I saw," he recalled, "was the high bandstand, at the top of which sat Jo Jones surrounded by his drums." Hammond had never seen anything like it: the subtle inventions of Jones's brushstrokes, his agility with the sticks, the range of effects he coaxed from his cymbals, the "extraordinary wit" of his playing. Then there was his tap-dancer's foot: Hammond positioned himself where he could watch it all night, moving furiously at the base of the drumkit, unleashing its own rhythmic commentary on the music. "I never was so completely overwhelmed by a drummer before or since as I was that first night at the Reno. . . . His concept of drumming was completely different—so natural and flowing." If Jones had earlier been intimidated by the Basie players, he had come by now to relish his role in their midst. "Jo was always smiling," Hammond said. "What he did *worked*. He lifted the band and he knew it!"[8]

Basie's group developed a freer, looser sound than the leading big bands played. Unlike their contemporaries out east—and unlike Jones's Birmingham peers—many of Basie's men barely sight-read music if they read it at all; they preferred to work from head arrangements, playing by memory and ear, creating a music steeped in blues riffs and brimming with infectious, easygoing energy. The heart of the band was its rhythm section: on percussion, Jones abandoned the bass drum for the hi-hat, keeping time with a steady, open swing, while Walter Page laid down a distinctive walking bass line, the two men playing on all four beats, rather than the more common two-beat approach. While Jones and Page established the band's forward momentum, Basie on piano offered accents, vamping, interjection, exclamation, and commentary, contributing to a sound both laid-back and joyful. The rhythm section also freed up a creative space for the soloists—notably tenor saxophonist Lester "Pres" Young and trumpeter Hot Lips Page—to explore new forms of expression. When Haywood Henry finally heard the band in New York, he was astounded by the soloists' ability to explore their voices onstage; in most bands, certainly in the Collegians, the whole orchestra would be playing so loud—drums banging, brass blaring—that soloists had to pour their full force into their horns just to be heard. Every time he stepped up for solo, Haywood said, "it was like in a battle royal." In the Basie band, there was room for a new kind of nuance, a freedom that other orchestras envied—and quickly did their best to imitate.[9]

As far as John Hammond was concerned, this band was the future of swing. Hammond devoted himself to the group: he sang the musicians' praises in the press and connected them with a New York management agency, which in turn arranged their first major tour. The jump to the big time, though, was not entirely smooth. Basie hastily expanded from nine pieces to fourteen, but with no arrangements and not enough practice for a band that size, the group was forced to clumsily improvise. An engagement at Chicago's Grand Terrace was a major step up in the world, but the musicians were caught off guard by the demands of the venue's elaborate floor shows. Hammond himself was "astonished" that the band was not fired on the spot, but he cited Jones as the group's saving grace. "The chorus girls loved the band, because it was so easy to dance to. Jo Jones, a dancer himself, knew how to play for dancers." The band survived the gig.[10]

Before Basie and company left Chicago, Hammond arranged an impromptu recording session for a stripped down, five-piece version of the group (a sixth man, Jimmy Rushing, provided vocals on two of the tunes). Basie had just signed with the Decca label but had not yet recorded; for the Chicago sessions, the group wriggled around its contract by recording as Jones-Smith, Inc., hiding behind the generic-seeming surnames of drummer Jo and trumpeter Carl. Space was tight—there was room only for Jones's snare drum and hi-hat—but the band was born in cramped environs, and Jones excelled at creating complex worlds of sound from even the most limited palette. The four resulting sides—"Shoeshine Boy," "Evenin'," "Lady Be Good," and "Boogie Woogie"—distilled the band's essence, highlighting the seamless interplay of Jones, Basie, and Page and setting the stage for Smith and (in particular) Young to elaborate on and embellish the theme. If it was possible to bottle and sell the magic of the Reno, this was how you did it.[11]

The fuller band was still working through its growing pains as the players made their way to New York. The Christmas Eve Roseland debut fell short of expectations—critics complained the band was out of tune—but within a few weeks, the group had hit its stride. Before the engagement was over, guitarist Freddie Green was added to the rhythm section, completing its signature sound, and the full ensemble synched into a unified whole. After the end of their run at the Roseland, Count Basie and His Orchestra headed to the Decca studio, and the results confirmed their power. For years to come, the Basie band would represent the pinnacle of swing.

But Jones, at first, had doubts about New York. Any vision of that city as a racial utopia was burst when, on that first Christmas Eve, a hot dog vendor down the street from the Roseland flatly refused him service. An argument erupted, Jones drew his gun (he always packed a weapon, a holdover from his tent show days and standard Kansas City practice), and a passing policeman intervened. Somehow in the end Jones still got his dinner, but he was "torn up" by the insult of it all. He told the band he was leaving New York as soon as he could. "I don't like the hot dogs," he spat. But in the end, he stayed.[12]

Sammy Lowe was enchanted, as he pulled into New York, by the bright neon lights—but was put off by the blistering snow that met him when he stepped off the bus. He was embarrassed to be spotted for a southerner, right off the bat, just from the way he spoke or from the food he ordered at a diner, was heartbroken to be treated like a rube by wisecracking uptown slicks. "Pay no attention to those people," Haywood Henry reassured him, when he got to the Woodside Hotel. "Everybody you'll meet in New York is somewhere up from Down South." They just did not want you to know it.[13]

For a while, the Collegians struggled to find management adequate to their ambition. Feets Edson was, at best, an inconsistent advocate for his clients, and his gangster mystique had finally worn off. Rumor circulated that Feets had been hired by a promoter to persuade two star members of the Teddy Hill Orchestra from taking a competing gig across town; Feets allegedly threatened to shoot off the players' fingers. Simply put, he was not the kind of man to whom you wanted to hitch your livelihood.[14]

Work for Black bands, the Collegians discovered, was controlled by a handful of white businessmen, booking agents, and club owners, many of them tied to the mob and few with their clients' best interests at heart. This had not been the case back home, where Black bookers, managers, and promoters like Monroe Kennedy, J. B. Barker, J. Earle Hensley, and Fess Whatley himself had created their own infrastructure, supporting the bands from within their own community. While Birmingham's segregated system had resulted in an insulated, self-sufficient entertainment ecosystem, musicians discovered another model entirely once they left the South.

"We tried to go Black," Haywood Henry said, describing the band's search for new management, "and they blackballed us for a year." Leon Englund of Birmingham briefly managed the group, without success. Next they hired Henry Minton, an established supporter of the Black music scene—he had previously run the Rhythm Club, with help from Teddy Hill—but as manager even Minton lacked connections to the best dance spots or broadcasting opportunities. Jobs trickled in, maybe two nights a week: it was enough to keep them eating, but it made for a life spent mostly waiting. With regret, they parted ways with Minton. Then they met Moe Gale.[15]

A striking counterpoint to Feets, Gale was businesslike and unassuming, a fan, himself, more of opera than jazz but nonetheless one of swing music's most powerful promoters. A former luggage salesman and loan lender, he had never aspired to work in the glitzier world of entertainment; "all I ever wanted to be when I was a young man," he said, "was an accountant," and he had started at NYU with that career in mind. But a few turns and a chance business partnership made him co-owner, and then owner outright, of the Savoy Ballroom, and soon he was managing some of the day's most popular acts: Chick Webb and Ella Fitzgerald, Rosetta Tharpe, Benny Carter, the Ink Spots, Teddy Hill.[16]

If "going Black" was not a viable option in New York, the Collegians decided to go for the best the city could offer, and with Gale they found not only the immediate boost they needed but a fruitful, decades-long partnership. Gale proved critical in shaping the band's successes, transforming the act from the nation's premier collegiate (or ex-collegiate) band into a name orchestra on par with other headlining acts. He pointed out, for starters, that the players were "getting too old to be Collegians"; besides, they were long unenrolled and, back in Montgomery, a new crop of students was using the same name. The musicians had always seen themselves as a collective in which every member was an equal, but they conceded the need for a leader whose name could be blasted out front. With his show-stopping high notes, Erskine Hawkins was the band's biggest star; but, soft-spoken and not especially eloquent—his thick accent and rough diction gave away his deep southern roots—he was reluctant to take the job of leader. "We'll *teach* you to talk," his bandmates insisted, and the trumpeter relented. "We had to damned near force Erskine to assume the leadership," said Haywood Henry, but by the fall of 1938, the Bama State Collegians had become Erskine Hawkins and His Orchestra.[17]

Hawkins himself was rebranded along the way. A radio announcer ad-libbed the new title during a broadcast from the Savoy, Gale latched on immediately, and the entertainment columns followed suit. Back South, Erskine had borne the grittier nickname "Iron Lungs"—he had been a steel-town prodigy, after all—but in Harlem, city of dreams and wonders, the earthy old name gave way to one more fittingly transcendent, a name both modern and mystical, forward-looking and mythical.[18]

For the rest of his life, Erskine Hawkins was the "Twentieth Century Gabriel."

In later years, Ethel Harper would describe a certain "bulldog tenacity" as her most distinguishing trait. Whatever the ups and downs of the entertainment industry, she was not one to give in easily—or, indeed, to give in at all. She was hellbent on carving a space for herself in the world.[19]

In the summer of 1936, after twelve years in the classroom, Harper arrived in New York. She brought with her two of her students, Albert Phillips and Williams Keys, both dancers, promising their parents she would help get them started in show business. She planned to spend the summer hustling gigs for all three of them; in the fall she would continue her own education in the graduate program at Columbia University. Her goal, still, was to balance her love for performance with her calling to teach.[20]

To find work, Harper—like countless other new arrivals—drew on her connections from home. She received encouragement and advice from saxophonist Eddie Brown, a former Industrial teacher who had recently jumped from the classroom to the stage, landing a seat with the Jimmie Lunceford Orchestra. Brown took Harper to the Apollo Theater, where she auditioned for and earned a spot on the venue's popular Amateur Hour. Her performance of "Without a Word of Warning" won her a weeklong engagement at the theater. Billed the "Singing School Teacher from Alabama," she was backed by yet another Birmingham export, bandleader Teddy Hill.[21]

As they often did of Birmingham acts, promoters and the press made much of Harper's background in the classroom. "Bama School 'Marm' Wins Amateur Hour," reported the *New York Amsterdam News*: "Miss Harper teaches English in Industrial High School, but in her leisure she dances and sings torch songs for the fun of it and within the walls of her own home." "The piece de resistance of the night," the *New York Age* reported of her Apollo debut, "was the big timey singing of Miss Ethel Harper, a reformed school teacher from Alabama." That paper, though, qualified its praise: "If she's smart she'll stick to her pedagogy as the existence of singers is for [the] most part precarious. . . . That night club songstress can sing but so do oodles of other people whom I know. No she isn't likely to set the world on fire."[22]

That writer's assessment echoed a widespread dismissiveness toward female singers, a condescension and indifference that prevailed among critics, club owners, and even bandleaders, for whom "girl singers"—commonly labeled "canaries," "chirpers," or "warblers"—were often deemed interchangeable. Even so, for Harper, the Apollo gig represented a greater financial success than any classroom might offer. For a week's performances she netted $125; "by comparison with my teaching salary of seventy-five dollars per month, one can readily see how I could be lured away from the world's most honored profession." Harper was quick to add, all her life, that "my love for children exceeded my love for the theatre"—but the opportunity and temptation of the stage proved strong. By the summer's end, she had called off her plans with Columbia.[23]

Fresh from her Apollo debut, Harper toured for four months with an ensemble stage show, *Connie's Hot Chocolates of '37*. She was cast as a member of a trio, the Melody Maids, and discovered a love for the kind of close harmony singing that would define the next decade of her career. After the show closed, the Melody Maids tried and failed to land independent gigs of their own. The group disbanded, but Harper was convinced a similar act could make it.[24]

She worked every angle she could. In 1937 alone she organized, trained, and performed with six vocal harmony groups, all with limited success. She hired an agent, and when he proved too slow, she "walked the Broadway beat" herself, knocking on doors and booking her own gigs. She studied for five months with a vocal coach, and she worked a continual string of side jobs: as domestic, waitress, hotel clerk, and switchboard operator. She subsisted largely on hot dogs.[25]

Harper's next break came with another stage show, this time on Broadway. Produced by the white stage impresario Michael Todd, *The Hot Mikado* was a swing reworking of the Gilbert and Sullivan operetta, featuring dancer Bill "Bojangles" Robinson and an all-Black cast of outrageously costumed singers and dancers. The show opened in March 1939 to enthusiastic reviews, and Harper prepared herself for a long run on Broadway. But Todd had other ideas.[26]

On April 30, 1939, the New York World's Fair opened on what had previously been a sprawling ash heap in Queens, transformed now into the "World of Tomorrow": a city within a city, full of exhibitions and pavilions, a celebration of present wonders designed to offer giddy previews of the future. After eighty-five acclaimed Broadway performances, *The Hot Mikado* made a new home in the fair's $250,000 Hall of Music, and for Harper and the rest of the cast, the glamour of the production fizzled right away. On Broadway, they had been performing eight shows a week; for the fair, producer Todd expected twenty-one shows a week, with no raise in salary. The theatrical union protested, the performers refused to go on, and finally Todd relented, begrudgingly upping their pay to meet the union minimum. The act may have been a hit, but resentments lingered; at the fair's close in September, Todd fired the whole cast and then took the show on the road with a new slate of performers. "We were all terribly hurt," wrote Harper, "that we, who had started a man on the road to great success as a producer, could have been treated in such a fashion."[27]

Soon, though, Harper was back on Broadway, again with high hopes. The new show borrowed *The Hot Mikado*'s model: *Swingin' the Dream* crammed the stage with 150 performers for a jazz-fueled adaptation of *A Midsummer Night's Dream*. It was an ambitious project with a remarkable cast, one that included singer Maxine Sullivan as Titania, Louis Armstrong as Bottom, Butterfly McQueen as Puck, and Jackie "Moms" Mabley as Peter Quince. Benny Goodman wrote the music and performed with his sextet, a racially integrated lineup that also included Lionel Hampton, Fletcher Henderson, and Charlie Christian. It must have been, one historian has written, "one of the most fascinating bombs of all time": the play was uniformly trounced by critics (it was, several quipped, more "nightmare" than dream) and closed thirteen days after it opened.[28]

"Work in the theatre is indeed uncertain and at times disillusioning," Harper mused; "but when it gets in the blood, you just keep looking ahead and hoping for the best."[29]

Thank God for that bulldog tenacity.

BLUE RHYTHM FANTASY

By the mid-1930s, Birmingham's Teddy Hill was well established as one of Harlem's top personalities, not only as a bandleader but as a provocative voice in the music business and a champion of Black talent. The *New York Amsterdam News* praised his cross-country broadcasts from Radio City Music Hall for providing a platform to other Black artists, deliberately spotlighting works by Black composers and hosting Black musical guests. Fan mail—from as far north as Toronto and Montreal and as far south as Miami—poured into NBC's studios. "The hometown folks down in Birmingham sent a deluge of letters," reported the *Chicago Defender*—a fact that "made the young maestro feel mighty good."[1]

Back home, indeed, Hill remained a hero. On a trip to New York, Industrial High principal A. H. Parker made a public presentation to the notable alum, describing to New Yorkers the bandleader's celebrated status at his alma mater. The *New York Age* reported that "John Whatley has set Teddy up before the students as a model young man who has achieved the kind of success other Industrial High graduates should go after." That item, reported in August 1935, was not the day's only news about Hill; a column on the same page of the *Age* described a meeting of New York Local 802, in which Black bandleaders convened "to discuss the unfavorable conditions in Harlem among colored musicians as relative to prices, etc." Hill—for now, at least—defended his manager, Moe Gale, whose Savoy Ballroom, he said, offered fair wages; but he complained about his treatment by the Apollo, whose most recent offer for a week's engagement, though admittedly above union scale, failed to reflect the Hill band's true worth. "The job was refused," the *Age* reported, "because Teddy felt that he and his band were entitled to yet higher pay."[2]

The Teddy Hill Orchestra, seen here with Hill at front, embodied Harlem sophistication and style—and helped launched the careers of several notable soloists. Courtesy Birmingham, Ala. Public Library Archives.

Hill may have developed a reputation as "one of the nicest musicians in New York," but he was no pushover: he became known, too, as a man who stood his ground, who knew his worth and expected to be treated accordingly. In the fall of 1935, there was talk that he might join forces with Louis Armstrong, merging his bandleading talents and his stable of musicians with Armstrong's established celebrity and skill as a front man. But by October, papers reported, "the expected merger . . . collapsed." The explanation: "Teddy says that he has worked for years to bring his organization to the heights it commands today and he would be recreant to himself if he allowed his name to be submerged to another individual"—even if that individual *was* Louis Armstrong. "No satisfactory billing to Teddy could be reached," the report concluded, "and he refused to sign a contract."[3]

The news reflected more than Hill's business sense. It also sent a message that would often be repeated: Teddy Hill was no man's but his own.

The immense popularity of the Teddy Hill Orchestra has largely been for-gotten today, overshadowed by the later achievements of its members—and drowned out, in public memory, by the recordings of Hill's more prolific rivals. The Hill group's limited and uneven recorded output—barely two dozen tunes, waxed from 1935 to 1937—only hint at the true prowess and popularity of the band, whose dances and broadcasts embodied the heyday of Harlem swing. One observer described a typical Savoy Ballroom scene, in which that venue's famous dancers could do nothing but stand and listen: "When Teddy Hill's men begin swinging the last choruses of the specialty number 'Christopher Columbus,'" wrote the critic Otis Ferguson, "the danc-ers forget dancing and flock around the stand ten deep, to register the time merely with their bones and muscles, standing there in one place with their heads back and letting it flow over them like water. . . . The floor shakes and the place is a dynamo room, with the smoky air pushing up in steady waves. . . . It's a music deaf men could hear."[4]

As a musician, Hill was a solid section player but no star soloist. His great-est gift—first as a bandleader and later as manager of one of the country's most legendary nightspots—seemed to be his ability to identify, surround himself with, and nourish great and innovative players. His orchestra's re-cords are most significant, today, as historical markers: two of the century's most influential and innovative trumpeters, Roy Eldridge and Dizzy Gilles-pie, both made their recording debuts with Hill, Eldridge at the group's first session and Gillespie at its last. For Gillespie, playing with Hill was—very literally—a dream come true. He was a teenaged, novice musician gigging around his hometown of Cheraw, South Carolina, when he first encountered Hill's band on a neighbor's radio, broadcasting live from the Savoy. "The whole band gassed me," he recalled. "I didn't even know their names, but, man, they used to pop it. Now I know my heroes in that band were Roy Eldridge, trumpet; Chu Berry, tenor saxophone; and Dicky Wells, trombone." All he knew that night, though, was that "they were terrific, and I went home with my head so full of music that I dreamed I had sat in with them." For now it was only a dream, but soon he would do more than sit in: by the spring of 1937, Gillespie had come to New York and talked himself into a spot in the band, even filling in Eldridge's old chair in the trumpet section. At a recording session that May, the nineteen-year-old Dizzy recorded solos on four Teddy Hill sides, including the group's radio theme, "Blue Rhythm Fantasy," and the staple "King Porter Stomp," revealing himself a rising talent to watch.[5]

But Gillespie proved an immediately divisive addition to the group. Older band members took a quick disliking to him, declaring him too wild, too un-learned, and unpredictable, both in his playing and in his overall demeanor.

He had been hired, some gossiped, more as a babysitter for Hill's young daughter than on the merit of his music (Gillespie vehemently denied that claim). "Some of the fellows resented Dizzy," Hill told jazz writer Leonard Feather a decade later. "When the possibility of a European tour came up, there was some talk of getting a man with more of a reputation. Some of the men even threatened to leave if Dizzy was kept in the band. I thought Diz had possibilities, so I called their bluff and told them to go ahead and leave. They stayed."[6]

For that European tour, the band would appear as part of the Cotton Club Revue, a sixty-person stage show that also included singers, comedians, chorus girls, a team of professional Lindy Hoppers, and a clowning "Tramp Band," whose members dressed in patchwork suits and performed with washboard and kazoos. The group set sail for Europe, but the trouble began before the musicians even stepped off the ship. It became clear that not only was Dizzy inexperienced; he also *sounded* different, and as the band rehearsed en route to Paris, he refused to get serious. When he played, he thrust his jaw forward and puffed his cheeks into undignified balloons. During another musician's solo, he goofed off, danced around, or pretended, with impish exaggeration, to play his own horn. Nonetheless, the tour was a success. "Teddy's band is undoubtedly one of the four or five best bands in the world," wrote French promoter and critic Hugues Panassié. "Beside Duke Ellington's orchestra, this is the best band which ever came to France." In Paris, Django Reinhardt caught the act nightly and then jammed with the musicians until morning. The entourage played the Moulin Rouge for six weeks, the London Palladium for a month ("Hi, Fess," Hill wrote to Birmingham from London; "Having a fine time here"), and entertained King George VI. Since 1935, no American band had played the UK—to preserve opportunities for native-born bands, the Ministry of Labour had discontinued work permits for foreign musicians—but an exception was made for the Hill group, since it appeared as part of a larger theatrical revue. Still, government restrictions cramped the group's typically exuberant style: rather than play in the more spacious pit, musicians had to share a stage crowded already with dancers, and they were forbidden to call attention to themselves by any extra movements. Even with the stipulations, the band attracted good press and gave crowds a rare glimpse of a real American jazz band. After London came a week in Dublin, where between shows Hill and his players rowdily celebrated Joe Louis's defeat of British boxer Tommy Farr. There was a final week in Manchester, and then they sailed for home.[7]

The very idea of the band's international acclaim only added to its clout in the States. The Hill orchestra had never been bigger, and it seemed poised for still greater heights. But the group's simmering offstage tensions, along with a growing disenchantment with the music business, foreshadowed changes that would soon break up the band and shake the whole world of jazz.

"Pardon me," a columnist for the *Pittsburgh Courier* began, in the fall of 1937, "while I PRAISE Teddy Hill (whose band is one of the very best you will ever hear), for flatly refusing to fill [another] Apollo Theater date in Harlem, because of too little pay! You see, Teddy Hill has just returned from abroad where he was not only paid well, but was also treated like a grown-up gentleman." Hill's return to the States foreshadowed, in this regard, the experience of many Black servicemen who would come back from the Second World War unwilling to tolerate any more second-class citizenship at home. The *Courier* columnist applauded Hill as a new kind of role model. "Yep, Teddy, modern Negro leadership must come from modern Negroes": a persistent hindrance to progress, the writer continued, were the many "Uncle Toms," inside the music industry and out, who led their lives according to terms set by whites. Hill simply refused to cooperate. He had already built a reputation for speaking his mind, especially where the treatment of musicians or matters of race were concerned; he continued now to hone his knack for saying *no* to any job that might compromise his musicians' manhood or his own. The same resolve shaped his touring policy, which pointedly rejected dates in the South. Music had provided Hill a ticket out of Jim Crow's heartland, and he did not mean to subject his band to the racial insults of his youth.[8]

Like any good son, however, he did head South *without* the band, skipping his latest Apollo date to spend time, instead, with his mother in Birmingham. When he returned to New York, a reporter asked if he would play Washington, DC's celebrated Howard Theatre: "I will not play any of these theatres," he answered, "unless they stop trying to make all the money themselves and give us poor performers a chance to make a living wage." With that, the reporter concluded, "The youthful musician who had all Europe at his musical feet, plucked a dollar bill from a huge roll, gave it to a beggar and was off at top speed in his new '37" Lincoln Zephyr.[9]

Teddy and his band were modern in more ways than one. On the sidelines of the bandstand an increasing spirit of experimentation was percolating, and shifting sensibilities raised important questions about the future of popular music. Hill's group had always been a balancing act: his men made their names by perfecting the swing sound of the early thirties, but they leaned forward also into more modern territory, as key soloists sought to push the conventions of rhythm and melody. In Europe, there had been clashes between the group's more conservative players and the new ideas and brash persona of Dizzy Gillespie; but at the end of the tour, some of the older guys who had opposed the presence of "the frantic one" left for other jobs, making room for more progressive musicians. Gillespie himself went on a brief hiatus as he worked out some complications with the musicians' union; when he returned a few months later, he found a more hospitable environment. The Teddy Hill Orchestra seemed to have caught up with him.[10]

The trumpet section became decidedly more hip. Hill hired two new players, Al Killian and Joe Guy, both young and innovative, and both out of Birmingham. Killian had trained under Fess Whatley and played in Sonny Blount's band back home; Guy had come to New York with Reverend Becton and worked with several major acts before joining Hill. Another new addition was trumpeter Carl "Bama" Warwick; a native of Brookside, Alabama, he too first studied music in Birmingham schools before moving north, as a teenager, with his family. And Hill added to the band one more "find" from his hometown, seventeen-year-old singer Melba Smith, the "Cyclone of Rhythm," a Miles College student whose vocals in Howard Funderburg's Jazz Masters had made her a Birmingham favorite.

A 1943 article suggests that Smith shared Hill's disdain for the power brokers of the music industry: "Managers and agents told her what to sing and she became disgusted with the show world and called it quits," the *Norfolk New Journal and Guide* reported. She would come back, though, as Bonnie Davis, adopting the alias to sidestep the American Federation of Musicians' recording ban of 1942–44—and reached number one on the Harlem Hit Parade with "Don't Stop Now." She continued to perform and record as Bonnie Davis into the 1970s. She would also, in 1945, have an affair— and a child—with Hill, but the couple did not last, and Teddy (despite his portrayal as "family man" in the press) took no part in the parenting. The daughter—Tony award–winning singer and actress Melba Moore—would have no relationship with her father.[11]

The usual story of the Hill band maintains that its modern soloists did not jibe with the needs of the dance floor, but the truth, as always, is more nuanced. In fact, the Savoy dancers relished the innovations on the bandstand and responded with innovations of their own, a creative back-and-forth that held true to swing tradition. "Dizzy Gillespie was featured in the brass section of Teddy Hill's screaming band," one dancer remembered. "A lot of people had him pegged as a clown, but we loved him. Every time he played a crazy lick, we cut a crazy step to go with it. And he dug us and blew even crazier stuff to see if we could dance to it, a kind of game, with the musicians and dancers challenging each other."[12]

Another of the band's most cutting-edge creators, drummer Kenny Clarke, joined the group in 1939. Born in Philadelphia, Clarke had apprenticed in bands across the Midwest and East Coast; by the time he joined Hill, he had become bored by the dominant sound in swing. "I'd gotten tired of playing like Jo Jones," he said; since Basie's explosion on the scene, every band had been doing its best to replicate that drummer's style, and Clarke was ready for a change. He moved the beat to the top cymbal, where he experimented with timbre and pitch; then he used the other resources of the drum kit, including the bass drum and snare, to punctuate the rhythm in unexpected places, adding offbeat accents, kicks, and asides. The musicians called it "dropping bombs," and the technique jolted some of the players. "Man," said Hill, imitating the sound of Clarke's bombs with a couple of nonsense syllables, "every time I turn around, he's going 'klook-mop' 'klook-mop . . . !'" Hill's onomatopoeic invention stuck: Kenny Clarke was known, forever forward, as "Klook-mop," or just "Klook." Hill would label a whole new movement in music *klook-mop*, after his drummer's sound. "Later on," he said, "we called it Be-bop."[13]

In some ways, Clarke's bombs were born of necessity, a defensive response to the band's sound: Hill pushed his players to such furious tempos, the drummer had to invent a new way of keeping up. With sparse but well-timed bombs, he could underscore the rhythm and help propel the soloists further, all while maintaining the energy and momentum of the band. "We started getting into the new style of playing when Kenny Clarke came into Teddy Hill's band," Gillespie would say, with pride—a fact that made Teddy's next move a surprise.[14]

He fired Kenny Clarke.

Dizzy's modern licks were one thing, but for some musicians and dancers Klook's experiments were a step too far. Hill again was caught in the middle, fielding complaints of band members who groaned they could not follow the drummer. But Clarke and Hill split ways amicably—"You're playing some hip things," the bandleader said—and soon enough he would call on Klook again.[15]

Hill's band, anyway, would not survive 1939. As Clarke saw it, the demise of the Hill orchestra reflected bigger problems in the world of swing, and those problems had little to do with music. The big band era was done in, Clarke maintained, by greedy white businessmen, agents, and club owners who held the livelihoods of Black bands in their hands, exploiting the musicians for too little pay—the very problems Hill had been protesting for years. "By the late thirties," said Clarke, "it was over. That's why fine people like Teddy Hill quit playing music. Teddy quit as a bandleader because Moe Gale . . . and all those people wanted to tell him who to have in his band, where he was going to work and why he was going to work. He had nothing more to say, so he quit."[16]

Indeed, Hill's relationship with Gale had become particularly frayed. Gale's top star, bandleader Chick Webb, had suffered severe health ailments since childhood and died in June 1939, still in his early thirties; Webb's orchestra had been the Savoy's house band, and now Gale debated which of the ballroom's other most popular acts—the Hill band or the Erskine Hawkins band—should take that spot. Of the two Birmingham bandleaders, Gale chose Hawkins, throwing the biggest weight of his resources behind that group's success. (Certainly Hawkins, who would always consider Gale "like a father," was the less confrontational option.)

He hired Hill, meanwhile, to play a running exhibition at the New York World's Fair, the same World's Fair that burned Ethel Harper that summer. Like *The Hot Mikado*, "The Evolution of Negro Dance"—in which the Savoy's best Lindy Hoppers presented the "dances of the future" to the backing of the Hill band—made for a stunning attraction. But, again like *The Hot Mikado*, it promised backbreaking, exploitative work for the performers, both musicians and dancers. ("I was working there for one day," one dancer complained, "but it was so grueling that I stopped. They were doing ten or twelve shows a day, plus ballyhoo for ten minutes before [each] show.") Conflict flared between Hill, Gale, and the union, and Hill's relationship with his manager ruptured. His band was cut from the fair and now could land only irregular gigs at the Savoy, previously his best and most consistent gig. With work getting scarce, Hill encouraged his players to take whatever jobs they could. By the end of the year, he had given up the band.[17]

"It was a damned shame that band had to break up," said Dizzy Gillespie, "because we were just beginning to get into something new." But, it seemed, the band had run its course. "Teddy got out of the business."[18]

When he returned—just a few months later, this time off the bandstand—he would play the business his way and, in the process, help launch a new era in music.

DANCE THE NIGHT AWAY

Moe Gale's prize act, the Erskine Hawkins Orchestra, was meanwhile building an unstoppable momentum. Everywhere the band went, it drew crowds and acclaim. "They made me feel good," Hawkins said of his fans, "because they came out in droves." The band knew how to entertain. There was nothing fancy, nothing highfalutin or overcomplex in the Hawkins show: the players prided themselves on a music that was immensely danceable and wholly accessible. "I wasn't no Duke Ellington for musical variety," Erskine said, "because we didn't have those type arrangements. We had a good, simple arrangement where people could hum and they could feel rhythm and dance to it." "Ninety per cent of the time," Haywood Henry concurred, "we were playing for dancers, so we didn't go in for tricky arrangements." The object was to fill the room with bodies and with sound, and the band's essential ingredients—straightforward melodies and arrangements, fast tempos, big volume, and a down-home style steeped in the blues—won the musicians fans across the country, especially back in the southern states. "Other bands drew in the South," Dud Bascomb explained, "but we played simpler music. We could even draw the coalminers, because they could understand what we were playing."[1]

Onstage, the band continued to play off of its members' much-publicized youth, putting on shows full of variety, humor, and drive. Hawkins may not have been much for public speaking, but he grew into his role as showman. "I'm gonna really kill you this show," he would tell the crowd, and the musicians would swing into "Sweet Georgia Brown," a showcase for Paul Bascomb since their days at Bama State—then, as Paul tore through the final chorus, Erskine would come to the foot of the stage and break into an old-fashioned country buck dance ("I wasn't no dancer," he would admit, "but I had my style"). He loved the hokum of it all: he might grab another band member and dance across the stage like they had done at the Ubangi, and the audience ate it up. "We did a little clowning," he said, "while other bands just sat there and played straight." Hawkins, perhaps, was too modest—and a little too awkward—to take himself too seriously; more often than not he made himself the target of his own self-deprecating quips, and between tunes he kept his bandmates cracking up behind him.[2]

Hawkins also demonstrated his virtuosity by working his way around each instrument on the stage, sliding in behind the drum kit or grabbing and blowing one of his bandmates' horns. Some nights he would tell a musician to go have fun, then he would take over that player's instrument for the rest of the set. It was an extra bit of theater that kept things festive and unpredictable onstage. But Hawkins was only a piece of the band's appeal. He was the first to admit he was not the group's best musician, was not even its best trumpeter (that was Dud). But Erskine did not mind being upstaged on his own instrument in his own band. "I liked to share," he said, with characteristic equanimity. "People go in to see everybody that can be seen." His job, as he saw it, was to share his spotlight freely.[3]

The model worked: the best of the band's music sparkled with a special kind of affection and camaraderie, a spirit of warmth and fun steeped in shared childhood and college years. The Hawkins men reveled in each other's success. "There was no jealousy in the band," Sammy Lowe insisted; "we all felt the better each individual was known meant our position as a top band was solidified." Each soloist had his own following. Dud and pianist Avery Parrish were particular stars, and singer Jimmy Mitchell—with his good looks and big, crooning voice—brought a seductive, romantic sensibility to the group. (For an extra touch of class, Mitchell also added an *e* to his last name, becoming Jimmy *Mitchelle*.) Haywood Henry, like Erskine, could play anything with a mouthpiece but offered his most distinctive solos on clarinet and baritone sax, giving the latter instrument a more prominent role than it had in most bands. Sammy Lowe, for his contributions behind the scenes, drew his own little clique of "young, would-be arrangers." In fact, as it had since college, the band boasted several talented arrangers—notably Parrish and Lowe—who could churn out "three or four arrangements a week." Some pieces, reflecting the band's roots as a cooperative unit, were true group arrangements, each soloist pitching in ideas.[4]

On tenor sax, Paul Bascomb was a favorite for his powerhouse solos, helping pioneer the wild "honking" tenor sax that would soon become a fixture of rhythm and blues. His perceived rivalry with fellow tenor saxman Julian Dash highlighted the dynamic that made the band work. "Whenever we played," said Sammy, "we'd see a bunch of admirers in front of Julian and another bunch in front of Paul, and they would applaud every time 'their' man took a solo"—often breaking into arguments over which was best. "Erskine got so he would call their numbers back to back, and the crowd loved it." Indeed, Hawkins's ability to read the room—to call the right tune, the right tempo, the right solo at the right time—was one of the gifts, further honed with each tour, that made him an ideal leader. For the sake of the show he could milk the crowd's combative spirit, all while reinforcing the cohesion of his players.[5]

For nearly twenty years, the band made the Savoy its base of operations, and in that ballroom's famous battles, the musicians developed a distinct homefield advantage: they knew the crowd's tastes and rhythms and the room's acoustics inside out, knew how to play the scene for maximum effect. "If a band came in with better arrangements," said Haywood, "we'd beat them with showmanship." If the competition played fast, they played faster. "Sometimes the crowd up there wanted exhibitions," showy solos demanding attention, "but more often they just wanted to swing all night long"—and swinging all night was what this band did best.[6]

The band's famous family dynamic extended to the whole Savoy crowd. "Everyone [in the audience] knew everyone in the band," Haywood said, "because we all stayed together so many years. . . . I know some nights at the Savoy I knew ninety percent of the people there. It was a very warm thing." The double-bill setup allowed musicians plenty of time to mingle: "You were off the stand 40 minutes in an hour, so you were socializing with your friends, people who knew you by name." Even with crowds in the thousands, a spirit of intimacy ruled.[7]

Still, the band was subject to its share of criticism, most of it aimed squarely at the leader. Early critics, praising Hawkins's trumpet, made a running joke of his unrefined speech. "Erskine Hawkins can take deserved bows for his blistering trumpeting," one reviewer announced but added, "For Gawd sakes, stop trying to be an announcing M.C." In a list of "[Things] We'd Like to See in 1937," another writer expressed hope that Hawkins would pay "a lot more attention to his diction and enunciation while acting as an 'M.C.'" but nonetheless conceded, "He's otherwise brilliant." As late as 1940—six years after the band's initial Harlem success—a reporter for *Variety* offered the familiar backhanded compliment: "Hawkins can now proximate the top colored bands for musicianship . . . although the maestro will have to acquire just a bit more polish. For instance, that bad diction."[8]

Some critics, white critics in particular, lambasted Hawkins for his "showboating" style, a too-heavy reliance on those frenzies of high notes, gaudy displays that smacked more of gimmickry than musicianship. Detractors dubbed Erskine "Irksome," perhaps forgetting it was his pyrotechnics that first drew in the crowd, just as when he had ballyhooed for the tent shows as a boy. Critics, Sammy Lowe complained, "were always down on [Erskine]. They didn't realize that the reason the band was in New York in the first place was because of his high notes, which excited the public."[9]

For all its success onstage, it took the group some time to successfully translate its sound to wax. The band's first venture into a studio, in the summer of 1936, had made for an inauspicious debut. "We just didn't know how to record," confessed Haywood Henry. "We knew how to play in person, but on records, everyone in the sax section had a different vibrato. We weren't too much in tune, either." The results were a rude awakening, a comedown from the thrill of their live shows. Hearing those first sides, Dud Bascomb was horrified and humbled: "How bad," he said, "could we get?"[10]

Gradually the musicians warmed up to the studio. By the time Moe Gale signed them, in 1938, to Victor Records and its Bluebird subsidiary, the band had found its groove, and its strongest records—swinging, up-tempo numbers like "Raid the Joint" and "No Soap"—captured some of the energy and exuberance of the group's dances. Other blues-soaked tunes like "Weddin' Blues" and "Bear Mash Blues" reflected the players' distinctly southern roots. Still, the band's first major hit took the musicians themselves by surprise.

"Tuxedo Junction" began, inconspicuously, as a head arrangement—an unwritten piece worked out by ear and performed from memory—designed as throwaway backdrop to a comedy routine and recorded as an afterthought. For the rest of their lives, band members recounted the piecemeal manner in which they had cobbled together the tune. It had started on the road, at a gig at Baltimore's Royal Theater, where comedians Pigmeat Markham and George Wiltshire needed some background music for their act. Julian Dash threw out a string of opening notes; others—Erskine, Haywood, Sammy, Dud, and relative newcomer Bill Johnson—added their own riffs, and over the course of their week at the Royal a loose arrangement congealed. It was not much more than a piece of rhythmic filler, but it began to figure increasingly into the band's live shows, providing a vamping transition between sets. It did have an infectious, hummable hook, and, said Sammy, "It always seemed to strike a good groove with the dancers."[11]

In July 1939, near the end of a Victor recording session, the guys found themselves one song short. "They wanted to know what my sixth tune was gonna be," Hawkins remembered; "I said give me a half hour." Someone in the group proposed that bluesy riff, really just the suggestion of a tune, that they had been using on the road. They sketched out a three-minute arrangement, anchored by trumpet work from Dud and a soaring clarinet solo from Haywood; then they set it to wax. The tune needed a name, and the band's valet, an old friend since Birmingham, suggested "Tuxedo Junction" in homage to the scene back in Ensley.[12]

"Nobody," Sammy confessed, "ever dreamed it would get air play—let alone become a hit." Almost arbitrarily, they listed just three of the contributors' names as composers, "Hawkins—Dash—Johnson": a decision that, Haywood Henry later moaned, cost him and the others half a lifetime of royalties.[13]

Back in Birmingham, Ivory "Pops" Williams, now sixty, told his own emphatic origin story for the tune. For years he would swear that "Tuxedo Junction" borrowed not only its name but its melody from the Ensley hub. The central riff, he said, was straight from "Shorty's Blues," an old Junction favorite, a tune Hawkins had often heard as a boy. According to Pops, the tune belonged to the trumpeter known as "Shorty," one of the players in Williams's band.

"I'd recognize it anywhere," he said, and his eyes smiled: "Where did those boys get that?"[14]

"Erskine Hawkins always remembered Birmingham," Frank Adams said. "He put it in his songs, like 'Tuxedo Junction,' and 'Bear Mash Blues.'"

A lot of people don't know this, unless they were from Birmingham: *Bear mash* was a terrible drink that came out in the late thirties, and it was prevalent when Erskine Hawkins was growing up. It was made out of a fermented alcohol with some vegetables—and a little piece of shoe polish, they tell me, was in it—and they mixed it and let it ferment. They make it in prisons now. And the alcoholic contents were violent: you would be sick, but it was habitual. Once you drank it, it was like a narcotic: you'd call your employer, "I can't come in, I won't be back Monday"—you won't *ever* be back with that bear mash, because it changed your lips, it did everything.

There was a place on the south side of town, the alley, where they sold bear mash. When Erskine Hawkins got to be coming into his own, he would make these songs up and they would name it out of places they knew when they were young. Like there's one called "Nona." Now, Nona's was a house of prostitution that they would visit when they were in college down there in Montgomery. So they did "Nona" and they did "Bear Mash," and they did "Dolomite," because there's a little city right outside of Birmingham called Dolomite, Alabama. This was sort of like a code: if you lived out in California, you wouldn't know what in the world *bear mash* is. And if you lived in New York you wouldn't know where Dolomite was. That was a little code that endeared Erskine to his home.

"Man, he's got one called 'Dolomite'—*Dolomite*, man!"

"The fool's done gone and put '*Bear Mash*' down there!"

You knew about it, and it was a hit.[15]

The band's members did not know they were sitting on something big, that "Tuxedo Junction" would resonate with listeners, whether they were in on the code or not. The record's A-side, "Gin Mill Special," was supposed to be the hit—but, Erskine said, "people started turning the record over. And that's how it started moving." At a show in Galveston, Texas, they started into "Tuxedo Junction," and the crowd went wild. The tune had never gotten that kind of response, so they shrugged it off as a fluke. But the same week in Atlanta, those opening notes drew the same unlikely response. It was no coincidence: in town after town, crowds were waiting for the tune. That tour, said Sammy, was "the turning point of the Erskine Hawkins band": the former Collegians were no longer just a popular dance orchestra; they were hit recording artists. By the time they got back to New York, they knew that they were stars.[16]

The centerpiece of the record was Dud Bascomb's trumpet solo, which he recreated each night on stage, exactly as he had played it on the record—and which a generation of trumpeters learned to reproduce faithfully, themselves. When Bascomb launched into that solo at the Savoy, the whole room sang along, belting out each note in unison, mimicking the trumpet's sound in a string of wordless syllables. For all his unassuming demeanor, Dud was carving out a fresh space within the swing tradition that looked forward to the harmonic and melodic complexities of bebop. Erskine may have been the front man and the showman, blasting out an impossible string of high notes, and most record buyers and jukebox dancers assumed they were hearing the bandleader's trumpet on "Junction"—it was his name, after all, on the label—but listeners in the know recognized Dud as the real trumpet hero, capable of immense creativity, sophistication, and range. Bebop pioneer Fats Navarro made a name for himself, early on, playing Dud's "Tuxedo" solo note for note, night after night, with Andy Kirk's Clouds of Joy. In St. Louis the young trumpeters Miles Davis and Idrees Sulieman bonded over their common ground: they had both memorized all of Dud's solos off the Hawkins sides. Dizzy Gillespie was a lifelong admirer of Bascomb, whom he considered perhaps "the most underrated trumpeter" in the business. "He was playing stuff in Erskine Hawkins' band back in 1939 that was way ahead of its time," Dizzy said, insisting that "guys like Dud Bascomb laid the foundation" for modern trumpeters to come. Yet another of those trumpeters, Clark Terry, remarked that Bascomb "would pick beautiful notes out of the chord that the average person wouldn't even think of settling on. He would play flatted fifths, flatted ninths even back then in the early forties." According to saxophonist Von Freeman, "Every trumpet player had to know" Dud's iconic "Junction" solo; for that matter, "all the horn players," regardless of instrument, learned to play it. In a 2000 interview with the Smithsonian's Jazz Oral History Program, Freeman began to sing a bit of Dud's part, recorded more than sixty years before. "It was like a story," he said of the solo.[17]

Once white America discovered the tune, in a recording by Glenn Miller, "Tuxedo Junction" became unstoppable. One afternoon in the summer of 1939—just after Hawkins had cut the original, but before it was released— the two bandleaders shared a bill at the Savoy, and Miller was taken with the live performance of the tune. He asked Erskine if he could put out his own record of it, and Erskine was happy to oblige. Released the following February, Miller's version was an instant hit, selling 115,000 copies in just the first week, quickly eclipsing the original in sales, and shooting to Billboard's number one spot. Another white bandleader, Jan Savitt, issued a third version almost immediately. Suddenly "Tuxedo Junction" was everywhere.[18]

Not everyone was thrilled. A headline in *DownBeat* asked, "Are Colored Bands Doomed as Money Makers?" and writer R. L. Larkin argued that white bands like Miller's and Savitt's played "nothing but Negroid music," often "hiring Negroid arrangers" to develop their sound—but with access to the most prominent venues and best radio airtimes, those bands were reaching ears and drawing cash that Black bands could not access. "Thus the colored bands are no longer distinctive as they once were. The whites are sufficiently stealing their stuff." Black bands, all the while, were forced to maintain grueling tour schedules just to make ends meet. "Many a Negro musician's health cracks. And the pay isn't high."[19]

The article ignited vigorous debate in the jazz world. Many of Larkin's points would be echoed by musicians and critics for years to come, as artists like Elvis and the Rolling Stones catapulted to success while the Black artists who inspired them struggled to survive. But not all Black writers and musicians endorsed Larkin's critique. Bandleader Lucky Millinder published a rebuttal in the *New York Amsterdam News*—"Negro Bands Are Not Doomed," his headline assured; "Colored Orks Still Tops"—and he turned to Hawkins's "ork" as a case study. "Hawk, who has had his band of the same musicians from the same college in the same small town for the last 12 years, has gone far with Moe Gale. Far enough to play every major white theater in the country and repeat his engagements during the same year." The band was doing much more than getting by, Millinder contended, and if Miller, Savitt, or anyone else cared to take a crack at the tune, there was no need to hold back.[20]

For the *Pittsburgh Courier*, the "Battle of 'Tuxedo Junction'" was just the latest in the jazz battle tradition, and under big and boldfaced headlines—

Savitt vs. Miller vs. Hawkins!
Swingsters Wage "Wax" War over Year's Best Tune

—the paper reveled, from the sidelines, in the competition. It was not so much a matter of race and appropriation, the *Courier* contended, as a kind of sparring on record, an extension of the competitive spirit that fueled jazz culture at its best, from staged cutting contests to the readers' polls that each year ranked the country's top soloists and bands. Even as Glenn Miller's "Tuxedo Junction" was surpassing the Hawkins record, Hawkins had begun broadcasting his own "far superior version of 'Indian Summer,'" one of Miller's own signature tunes. If Savitt was the next contender to corner "a goodly share of the cash register gravy"—blending Miller's smoother delivery with the quicker tempo and cool, swinging style of the Hawkins original—then the battle had just become that much more compelling for the record-buying masses.[21]

"A lot of people thought that Glenn Miller had taken my number, stolen it," said Hawkins. "But there was not truth in that." Not only had Miller personally sought Hawkins's blessings, but his cover gave the original a much welcome boost. "Every six months I hear from 'Tuxedo Junction,'" Hawkins laughed, decades later: "I get a [royalties] statement." He would record his own subsequent versions of the tune, sometimes with lyrics, and it would be widely covered by artists ranging from Ella Fitzgerald to Bob Wills and His Texas Playboys, from Chet Atkins to Tito Puente. In the 1970s, the vocal group the Manhattan Transfer made it a signature song, reviving its popularity for a new generation. Hawkins embraced it all. As his band toured the country, he announced a nationwide competition: nominate your own small town and we may write a tune for *it* next.[22]

The longer the band was away from home, the more homesick this, their greatest hit, made the musicians feel. "We made the recording with RCA in New York City," Hawkins told a reporter, "but our hearts, souls, spirit and anything else you can think of were in Birmingham. We were proud of it and we said so in 'Tux.'"[23]

They may have "said so" in the abstract, but singable words would make that connection complete. Also scrambling to get some of the "Tuxedo Junction" gravy, multiple publishers pitched lyric ideas to the band, and Buddy Fyene, a Brill Building lyricist, landed the coveted gig. Working from Erskine's description, he created a tribute to the Junction back home and what it meant to the players. "Feelin' low," the new words began,

> Rockin' slow
> I want to go
> right back
> where I
> belong

The lyrics made explicit the song's connections to home, expressing a yearning the musicians, for all their growing success, could not help but feel. New York City had its thrills, but Tuxedo Junction had something else entirely.

> Way down South
> in Birmingham
> I mean, South
> in Alabam'
> there's a place
> where people go
> to dance
> the night
> away
>
> They all drive
> or walk for miles
> to get jive
> that southern style
> an old jive
> that makes you want
> to dance
> 'til break
> of day

At the original Junction in Ensley, the tune became inescapable, both in the area's neighboring Black and Italian communities. "They work to its beat out there," the *Birmingham Post* reported, describing the song's constant play on area jukeboxes. "A shoemaker down the street drives his nails all day long to the swing of the music. Waiters in a café on the other corner do their jobs to its beat. Even the dishes seem to catch the rhythm of the piece. A barber up the street cuts hair to it. And even passersby seem to slow to meet its cadence." The tune was "reaping [a] nickel harvest" for local business owners—even as some shopkeepers had grown sick of the craze. In a photo, an aproned teenager named Benny Guzzetta, his lips puckered into a whistle, leaned against the entrance to his boss Joe Giovino's shoe shop. "All he does now," Giovino complained, "is stand in the doorway all day long whistling 'Tuxedo Junction.' He's gone crazy with the tune like everybody else, and I still got to listen to it."[24]

For the Birmingham area's Black communities, the song became a source of deep and lasting pride. Bands at the real Tuxedo Junction's American Woodmen hall inevitably made it their theme song. School bandmasters adapted it for their students to perform. (Sammy Lowe sent his own handwritten arrangement for Fess Whatley's students to play.) A writer for the *Birmingham World* launched a successful campaign to have the song adopted as official theme of the first annual Steel Bowl, the Black college football championship to be held New Year's Day, 1941, at the city's Legion Field. "The mob will sing it and swing it at half time," one journalist predicted— and, sure enough, another reported, the Parker and Rosedale High bands, "both gloriously garbed, strutted grandly" as they blasted the tune. Two weeks later, the song lingered in the air: "They're still singing Erskine Hawkins's 'Tuxedo Junction' in this big, sprawling town of 127,000 Negroes," the *Atlanta Daily World* reported. "Somehow the song . . . sounds keener and endlessly more pertinent in the Birmingham atmosphere. The beat of the bass fiddle, the blare of the trumpets and trombones, [the] sonorous howl of the reeds and the 'Junction' time seems to swoon one to sleep."[25]

By now, everyone in America knew the tune—but Black people in Birmingham knew it belonged to *them*.

THE ROAD

Increasingly, each appearance by the Hawkins band in Birmingham was cause for celebration. "You all know him," one local Black weekly proclaimed, referring to the bandleader. "He belongs to us. We shout for joy every time he comes this way." "Whenever they came to Birmingham," said Frank Adams, remembering the band's Masonic Temple dances, "there would be so many people in there that you could walk off the stage on *heads*—they were packed in there like that, you could just walk off and go on out the door." Before its main show the band would sometimes play a free concert at the high school, and Adams never forgot the time one band member was unavailable and Fess Whatley provided a student musician to fill the vacant spot. "I wished it had been me up there," Adams said, "but I played the wrong instrument." He made sure that if his turn ever did come up, he would not be found wanting: before the band's next appearance in Birmingham, he had learned to play every one of its hits—just in case he was needed.[1]

Between their long stretches at the Savoy, Hawkins and his players toured relentlessly. They played for Black crowds and white crowds, crowds where the races mixed freely on the dance floor, and crowds where a rope drawn across the floor segregated white and Black into halves, two groups dancing side by side but officially separate, in accordance with local custom. They played for the social elite and for the working class, for the debutantes and the steelworkers. There were occasional theater jobs, but they played most of all dances: in schools and auditoriums and huge warehouses converted to temporary dance halls, the only spaces big enough in some towns to accommodate the crowds. Especially in the South, small-town one-nighters were huge sellers for the band, events planned and anticipated for weeks, even months, by little communities for whom big-name entertainments were rare and thrilling events.[2]

The pace was demanding; occasionally the "jumps" from one gig to the next would be furious cross-country hauls. On the bus there was plenty of time for conversation, much of it serious and impassioned. Always there was talk of race and of racism: of the Jim Crow indignities of the South; the nuances of prejudice from one town to the next; the hypocrisies and contradictions, manners and mores, that shaped the country's obsession with color. They discussed Hitler and impending war and, then, the impending draft. They talked about women: the wives many of them left in New York, the girlfriends they had accumulated around the country. They talked especially of other musicians. They may have become celebrities themselves, but back on the bus they gushed over their favorite players, the inspirations and idols whose examples kept their own egos in check.[3]

Every town had its own personality and its own distinct culture. Miami was a great town for dancers, and the musicians learned how to work the city's floors, swinging hard with a full set of their liveliest numbers; then, just before intermission, they would switch into their lowest-down, most sensual blues. "On the slow numbers," Sammy said, "they would stand with their partners in one spot, their clothes wet with sweat, with their bodies quivering all over. . . . We'd take intermission with them hollering for more." Another favorite spot was San Antonio, where racial mores were looser, Black and white and Mexican dancers all mingling on the floor with refreshing freedom. In much of California the three groups similarly coexisted, but in Bakersfield and Pasadena racial prejudice loomed even larger and uglier than it did back home. In Los Angeles, Black musicians could always find white women ready for a night's romance, an alluring taboo their celebrity made possible far from the South; but all through the Pacific Northwest there were no women, white or Black, to be found, and there was, said Sammy Lowe, "very low morale" on the bus.[4]

Sometimes there was violence. Once, during the war, a scuffle broke out on the floor and, quick on his feet, Hawkins swung the group into "The Star-Spangled Banner." The appeal to wartime feeling worked: drunken brawlers unclenched their fists and stood at attention, and the dance proceeded without incident. A fight at the Two Spot Ballroom in Jacksonville, Florida, ended more dramatically. When one patron grew violent, the bouncer shot him coolly in the head; dancers gasped and screamed, but the promoter waved for the band to keep playing, and the show went on, the fresh corpse on the floor for the rest of the night. Couples, said Sammy, "would dance over to the motionless body, they would take a look, and dance away so that others could dance by and look. The dance continued, and I'm sure it was the Hawkins band's worst performance." After all, "how can you concentrate on playing your instrument with a dead body six feet away?"[5]

Even in Birmingham, crowds could become unruly. Once the band played the City Auditorium, whose capacity ran to 6,000, and the players were proud to see the place full. "We were embarrassed however," wrote Lowe, "that the biggest fight of the entire trip among the dancers occurred that night. When the many policemen hired to maintain order came in with arm-fuls of nightsticks, we should have known fights were a common thing in Birmingham. Besides, my brother J. L. had told me that practically every boy and—get this—every girl, carried a knife" or straight razor and danced with their weapons open in hand. At intermission a fight finally erupted, and "it was a lulu," at least a hundred dancers joining in the brawl. The scene also revealed the brutality of the white law in Birmingham: "The police moved in, swinging their nightsticks, cracking heads right and left. The Birming-ham police department was lily white at the time, and it gave us a feeling of indignation to see them whacking Negroes on their heads." The dance was cut twenty minutes short.[6]

The whole thing disappointed and embarrassed the band. "Some of our folks," said trombonist Cap Sims, "ain't ready yet," but Sammy was not hav-ing it: "Maybe *your* folks ain't ready," he answered, "but my folks are ready!" "Mother Dear," J. L., and Leatha Lowe, embodiments always of respectable decorum, all "sat quietly in the mezzanine."[7]

As far as the band was concerned, the *South* was anyplace outside of New York: "Well, folks," someone would announce, each time the bus crossed into Jersey, "we are now Down South." Conditions only intensified the farther south you went.[8]

The first, most constant hurdle was simply finding lodgings and restau-rants that opened their doors to Black customers. Basic human needs proved complicated: the musicians made their bathrooms behind gas stations, in ditches, or in the woods. On the road their celebrity disappeared, leaving them as unwelcome and anonymous as any other Black travelers. Often there would be one or two white men on the bus—a bus driver or road manager, assigned by the Gale Agency—and that little bit of whiteness could sometimes help the group avoid conflict. At whites-only restaurants, band members waited on the bus while their white emissary went inside for the food (in Black neighborhoods, the musicians picked up the food while the manager or driver waited). "When you're hungry," Sammy Lowe recalled, "you shrug your shoulders and say, 'What the hell.'" Born and bred in Birmingham, they knew how to stay out of what was then called "trouble," and they preferred to avoid conflict. Sometimes, though, "trouble"—the widespread southern euphemism for racial conflict—found them.[9]

The threat of violence was ever present. At the start of 1940, the city of Greenville, South Carolina, was embroiled in a violent upsurge of Ku Klux Klan activity, and direct threats from the Klan caused promoters to cancel an upcoming Hawkins dance. Black newspapers across the country chronicled a rising tide of anti-Black violence; recapping a single week in the summer of 1947, the *Pittsburgh Courier* reported that "seething unrest continued to sweep the Nation as the wave of terror throughout the South struck fear into millions of Negroes." A series of short, numbered bullet points rattled off the latest recorded acts of both vigilante terrorism and police brutality: "Negro homes in Atlanta were bombed. . . . Knoxville detectives began investigating a new KKK outbreak. . . . Relatives of the alleged slayer of a white man near La Grange, Ga., were missing. . . . Chief of Police in Norlina, N.C., shot and killed an unarmed Negro." Back in Greenville, one "lynch-mad" local, freshly acquitted from his involvement in a much-publicized lynching, had gone "on a rampage . . . and poured bullets into a carload of Negroes." Item number six in that week's list of terrors: "Three 'drunken' officers in Tuskegee, Ala., dragged a member of Erskine Hawkins' band from a bus, took him to a lonely road and beat him."[10]

Other descriptions of this incident, either in the press or in the musicians' recorded reminiscences, have not surfaced. The band's tour schedule places the group in the Tuskegee area at the time, but less clear is the identity of the beaten musician or whether he was taken from the tour bus itself or from local public transit while in town. What is clear is the pervasive threat of harassment and brutality that faced band members in their native region. Both Sammy Lowe and Dud Bascomb described a similar incident, in the early 1940s, when the bus broke down somewhere in the middle of Georgia. The band waited for help, but the police arrived instead, threatening to have the whole group arrested for what they deemed suspicious activity. "We had a driver with us," said Dud, "who had never been down south before, a big fellow, six-foot tall, 220 pounds"; when the officer accosted the group, that driver, who was Black, cursed back. The officer struck him in the head, "the blood flew like an oil well, and he fell over in the ditch." Only the band's road manager—only, that is, the presence of a white man—was able to calm the officer down, preventing further violence. (Even then, Sammy wondered what might have happened if the officer knew the manager was a Jew.)[11]

On another occasion, the bus was parked by a restaurant when a couple of white men began hurling racial slurs at the musicians. One of the men stuck out his foot and tripped trumpeter Marcellus Green, who spat back profanity. An argument flared and the white men stormed off—but in minutes they returned, Sammy said, with "ten or twelve white guys running towards us."[12]

Chaos followed. "We all got into the bus. Fast! They were armed with sticks and clubs and started banging on the bus," demanding the band hand over Marcellus. The road manager, Teddy Wilde, stepped out to try smoothing things over, but to the band's surprise—surely those rednecks wouldn't hit another *white* man—the group punched him and slammed him into a wall. On the bus, the musicians got ready for a fight. "The only 'weapons' we had were our trumpets, saxophones, and trombones," but each man rummaged through his case to find whatever he could, "a mouthpiece or the instrument itself": anything that might be converted into a weapon. One of the valets positioned himself at the door of the bus with a fire ax—but just as Teddy managed to squeeze back onto the bus, the police arrived, half-heartedly attempting to settle things down. "I guess it was the sheriff who jumped out, came over to the bus, and said, 'I'm sorry about this, fellows, but I won't be able to hold them back.'" So the bus took off, the white assailants still banging on its side. "For fully twenty miles or so," said Lowe, "nobody said a word."[13]

By nature of their profession, band members considered themselves unique experts on the cultural geography of American prejudice. That prejudice took many forms. In Charleston, South Carolina—a frequent stop for the band, the hometown of saxophonist Julian Dash, and a community with its own distinct, long-standing jazz culture—strict divisions of complexion and class defined local Black society. More than once, the Hawkins orchestra headlined an elegant Charleston soiree—only, after the dancing was done, for the evening's light-skinned host or hostess to turn away a band member or his date on the simple grounds of skin tone. ("He hasn't done anything," one hostess said of Dud, politely explaining why he was not welcome in her home. "He's a perfect gentleman. It's just that he's too dark.")[14]

Occasionally the music itself proved useful in breaking down the walls of prejudice. Fueled by swing, even the conventions of segregation might—temporarily—crumble, right before the bandstand. Once night the group played a Durham, North Carolina, schoolhouse, white spectators on the upper level, Black spectators below, both levels full to capacity. As the music got hot, the whites up top started finding their way down the stairs—until, Hawkins said, "wouldn't you know it: everybody was down on that floor dancing together." At a warehouse dance in Rocky Mount, North Carolina—"Big place," said Erskine, "10,000 people"—a single rope divided the room in two, a typical setup for makeshift southern dance floors. But early in the evening, dancers tore down the line and kept right on dancing, undivided and unrestrained. "I'll never forget it," Erskine remembered. "And the funny thing, they never tried to put the line up no more." For the duration at least of that night's entertainment, the dividing lines of law, color, and custom simply ceased to matter.

"They just forgot all about it."[15]

Since they had settled in Harlem, several members of the Hawkins band had married. Pianist Avery Parrish married Velma Middleton, a singer with whom the band sometimes appeared (later, she would become Louis Armstrong's longtime vocalist). Erskine and others brought up and married girlfriends from Birmingham, setting up house in their New York apartments. There was talk, for a while, of building a kind of compound for all their families, buying up a row of homes in Long Island, but the idea faded with the disruption of the Second World War.[16]

Band wives shared their own kind of bond, watching their husbands set off for weeks, sometimes months, at a time. Their official role was to "wait," holding down the home front and—according at least to the entertainment columns—"pining for their hubbies." Often they joined the men for the southernmost leg of a tour, staying with family and friends in Birmingham while the band worked its way through the region; on all other tours, they remained in New York. The women knew their husbands cheated on them on the road, but as long as the men were faithful at home, they tended to abide the infidelities in silence.[17]

The Hawkins band was unabashedly a boys' club, but over the years a series of female vocalists passed through its ranks. In the summer of 1938, Lynette Dobbins—a Birmingham schoolteacher, a graduate of Alabama State, and the daughter of Professor T. M. Dobbins, a beloved Birmingham principal—won a local "Miss Glamour" contest, an honor that scored her a monthlong trip to New York and auditions with several talent scouts. The *Chicago Defender* reported that Dobbins was "in line for a hook-up with Erskine Hawkins and his famous band," but a deal never materialized, and Dobbins disappeared from the entertainment scene. (She would make headlines nearly three decades later for another reason entirely. In the 1960s, her husband, Hobart Taylor Jr., serving as associate special counsel to President Lyndon Johnson, became one of the highest-ranking Black men in the US government; Lynette Dobbins Taylor earned the unique distinction of being the first Black woman to dance with a president at his inaugural ball.)[18]

As 1938's fall tour approached, the Hawkins band announced the first full-fledged quest for a "girl singer," an elaborate stunt no doubt cooked up by Moe Gale. At each stop, the band would host an amateur contest for local vocalists; the top ten from across the country would be invited to New York to compete for a long-term contract with the band. The gimmick generated plenty of buzz, but in the end the spot went to Ida James, who at only eighteen was already an established name: known for her "baby talk" singing style, James had been performing on radio and stage since she was twelve and had spent two years already with the Earl Hines Orchestra. After six months with Hawkins, she left to pursue independent projects. Dolores Brown, a singer in the Duke Ellington Orchestra, filled her spot, but Brown's own tenure in the band ended when she married one of its trumpeters, Marcellus Green—and, papers reported, promptly "left the band to assume housekeeping duties." As in other aspects of American society, the role of wife trumped professional ambition—and the culture of the tour bus, while allowing the addition of a "chirper," left little room for spouses. Dolores Brown, now Dolores Green, joined the other wives at home.[19]

Much of Sammy Lowe's unpublished memoir is concerned with life on the road: the late-night bus ride conversations and whiskey-fueled birthday rituals, the headaches of interstate travel, the complications of race in America. The group comes off as a freewheeling band of fun-loving brothers, and Lowe matter-of-factly describes the frequent sexual encounters that took place on the road, even lays out each musician's preferred style of picking up women. For all this attention to detail, there is one significant absence: the band's succession of female vocalists barely appear in Lowe's account, leaving readers to wonder about this sole female presence on the bus full of boys. The women are also absent from the extensive interviews other band members gave through the years, and—far less likely to be interviewed than their male counterparts—they left behind few testimonies of their own. Relegated to a marginal space on the sidelines, their purpose was to add a touch of romance, sex appeal, and glamour to the stage, appearing in lush gowns and singing soft, poppy love ballads. Occasionally a girl singer broke out as an acclaimed and respected artist—an Ella Fitzgerald, Helen Humes, or Billie Holiday—but most (like Birmingham's Ethel Harper) struggled to get noticed, and the press often devoted more ink to their looks than their talent. A typical reviewer, saying little of her voice, complained that singer Ida James was "encased in a long, flowing gown" for one Hawkins show and moaned that "a pair of legs would have helped more than you'll ever know."[20]

For Birmingham's Laura Washington, the gowns were skimpy enough as it was. Washington was only thirteen when J. L. Lowe first heard her sing and prevailed on Fess Whatley to break his ban against females and feature her in his Sax-o-Society Orchestra; after Washington graduated high school, Lowe recommended her to his brother, Sammy, and in 1946 she joined the Hawkins band, promoted as the "Girl with the Bedroom Voice" and landing the band one of its last real hits, the ballad "I've Got a Right to Cry." Washington was awestruck by the glamour of New York, but, she said, "we also played in some rough spots, like tobacco warehouses in North Carolina. Inside, it was so cold the musicians wore overcoats while they played. Out on the dance floor there were big empty oil drums which burned wood to try and heat the place. I'd be singing in a flimsy evening gown and be *freezing*. A few songs then I'd run back into the bus to try and stay warm."[21]

Another rare female perspective comes from the singer and actress Della Reese, who joined the band in its waning days—in the early 1950s, during the last gasps of the swing years—but at the start of her own successful career. Even then, the band was going strong at the Savoy, and, Reese remembered, "it was a ball every night. From the bandstand, watching the ballroom dancers gliding across the floor—doing fast jitterbugs or slow beautiful waltzes—was such a pleasure."[22]

But, she added, "the downside was that I was given three songs to sing and three songs only"—so for "nine months solid" she rehashed those three songs night after mind-numbing night. Even worse, behind the scenes Reese was treated like the band's silly kid sister. (By then, the men were all nearing forty, but as they grew older their "girl singers" always remained ingenues, barely twenty.) When they toured with Nat King Cole—"my idol," Reese wrote, "my angel of inspiration, my biggest and most important influence"—the band teased her relentlessly for her obvious crush, right in front of Cole, right in front of their entire audience. The experience was humiliating. At the end of the tour, Reese quit, striking out on her on as a singer. Still, there was one "upside" to the Hawkins experience: "I was forced to invent a multitude of different ways to sing the three songs—articulating the words differently, changing my phrasing, adapting my interpretations, whatever it took so that I could keep them fresh for myself and sing with meaning and feeling." It was an accident of the band's built-in chauvinism that Della Reese emerged a stronger, more inventive and nuanced singer.[23]

In the winter of 1941, the Hawkins crew embarked on a lucrative twenty-one-week tour with the Ink Spots, another of Moe Gale's biggest acts. Geared specifically to a white urban, northern market, the tour covered a circuit of the nation's top theaters and never dipped below the Mason-Dixon Line, granting the band a welcome reprieve from the stresses, insults, and dangers of its southern tours. Each night followed the same routine. First, the band warmed up the crowd with one of its hardest-swinging, high-energy "flag wavers." A dance and comedy act, Moke and Poke, followed, one tumbling while the other tapped in fantastic rhythm, both of them spouting fast-paced rhymes ("We're Moke and Poke / It ain't no joke / That's all she wrote / The pencil broke!"). Next, Avery Parrish performed the instrumental "Three Little Words," wearing a pair of white gloves that became illuminated in the dark: on the final chorus the stage went black, leaving visible only his bright-glowing hands, a spectacle that never failed to bring down the house. Before the applause died out, the band launched into "Tuxedo Junction," and the musicians continued swinging softly while Red and Curley, another comedy-dance act—also from Birmingham—took the stage. Finally, the Ink Spots appeared, concluding the show with a set of their silky-soft harmonies.[24]

Parrish was always a star, a highlight of any set, with or without the glowing gloves. "I don't like to throw the word 'genius' around," Haywood Henry said, "but of all the musicians I've been around, I think Avery was one who deserved it." Other bandmates shared Henry's assessment, citing Parrish's effortless knack for crafting thoughtful, original arrangements. "He could sit down and write" an arrangement, Henry said, "like he was writing a letter. He could compose on the spot, too. . . . Any type of thing you wanted he could do it." Much like Dud Bascomb, Parrish was unassuming and never overtly ambitious, preferring to fade into the background. Sometimes the other guys would have to "bribe" him to write an arrangement: for a bottle of gin, he would sit in the back of the bus, quietly "fixing something" the band could use to open its next show. By the time they reached their destination, the players would have a brand-new number to try on the crowd.[25]

Parrish's landmark hit, "After Hours," was rooted in an old blues tune that Paul and Dud's brother Arthur Bascomb used to play back home (Arthur called it "Mississippi Blues"). Ironically, Parrish himself had no interest in being forever linked to the blues, a form too raw for his tastes, and his bandmates had to "force" him, sometimes, to play it. Initially he had adapted Arthur Bascomb's rolling blues riff into a lead-in to "Fine and Mellow," the tune popularized by Billie Holiday and performed in the Hawkins group by Dolores Brown. Onstage, Parrish would embellish the theme for several minutes, building a simmering, sensual groove until finally Brown leaned into the mic. The band recorded "Fine and Mellow" in the summer of 1940, but there was no room on the record for Parrish's prologue and flourishes,

The Erskine Hawkins Orchestra plays to a rapt hometown crowd at Birmingham's Masonic Temple. Hawkins takes the trumpet solo as pianist Avery Parrish smiles for the camera. Courtesy the Alabama Jazz Hall of Fame.

so he pared his intro to a single chorus. (Listen to it now, and you can hear the famous "After Hours" clearly foreshadowed.)

In a repeat of the "Tuxedo Junction" session a year before, the musicians found themselves again one tune short for the date. Hawkins suggested Parrish cobble something from the material he had just cut from Brown's vocal number, and within minutes they had a simple head arrangement. Leemie Stanfield's walking bass line lent a mellow backdrop to Parrish's steady-rolling fingers; Hawkins, switching places with drummer Big Jack Morrison, laid down a soft, ephemeral beat, while Morrison acted as conductor. In the record's last minute, a stripped-down horn section added a gentle swing. At the end of the session, everyone wrote down a name for the tune and put it in a hat. One of the engineers submitted "After Hours."[26]

The record would rival "Tuxedo Junction" as the Hawkins orchestra's most enduring hit, and it became an inescapable standard among blues, jazz, and pop pianists for years. A sensuous, twelve-bar blues, the piece perfectly evoked the late-night scene of its title and at live shows provided hypnotic showcase for Parrish's sensitive style, the pianist's hands moving from moments of emphatic force into a light, tinkling trill that commanded a room's attention. Even skeptical reviewers of the band—those turned off by the bandleader's "screeching" trumpet—consistently praised the genius of Parrish, and fans showered him with applause.

* * *

At the start of the 1940s, Birmingham's fingerprints were all over the culture and sound of swing. Both "After Hours" and "Tuxedo Junction" were on their way to becoming omnipresent anthems, tunes that would define a generation. Dud Bascomb's solos were cutting a path for ambitious young trumpeters to follow. The drumming of Jo Jones had shaped the sound of not just the popular Basie band; Jones's widely imitated style had remade every jazz drummer's approach to the instrument, had so much set the standard that younger drummers like "Klook-mop" Clarke would finally have to rebel against it if they hoped to make their own names. In the Teddy Hill band, musicians like Klook and Dizzy Gillespie were already pointing to a new kind of music; as bandleader, Hill himself helped bridge swing to the modern era, creating a space for fresh talent—and demonstrating, behind the scenes, a kind of modern leadership that stood up and spoke out for Black musicians, refusing to work on anyone else's terms. Underneath all these developments—inaudible to any but the most perceptive hometown ears—were Wilson Driver's movie-house drums and Arthur Bascomb's piano blues; the echoes of Tuxedo Junction dances with Pops Williams and Shorty; the strict professionalism, musical precision, and unbending personal pride of the Fess Whatley training.

For Birmingham musicians in Harlem, the Magic City was ingrained in their music and in their hearts. But New York had become another kind of home—"our utopia, our ultimate paradise," Sammy Lowe called it, a place that seemed as vibrant and free as their dreams. For all the city's glamour, there remained challenges: unethical and exploitative managers and venues, grueling work hours, racial prejudice and the threat of violence on the road. For women, the challenges were amplified: a woman's role was narrowly prescribed on the scene, work was fickle, success always somehow qualified. Even the stubborn optimism and untiring commitment of an Ethel Harper guaranteed little security or respect. And there were greater trials to come.[27]

One December morning in Detroit, two teenage sisters, Helen and Josephine Gentry, rode the streetcar downtown for a matinee theater appearance by the Hawkins orchestra.[28] They sat, starstruck, through the show, enthralled by Hawkins's horn and smitten by Jimmy Mitchell's vocals. At the show's climax, the spotlight fell on the piano and the room seemed to hold its breath; when Avery Parrish struck the opening notes of "After Hours," time stopped. Once the spell lifted, the girls had no choice: they had to witness Parrish play that song again. A movie ran between the band's performances, and the sisters waited, patient, in the dark until the band started up again.

The second show was no less magical, and "After Hours" again rendered them defenseless; their parents would be furious, but they had to hear it once more. They sat again through the movie, drank in a final show, and at last hurried home in a panic, dreading whatever consequences they might face for disappearing all day. As they rushed through the streets, however, a commotion jolted them from the day's reverie and eclipsed any fears of punishment. The adult world around them was consumed in a flurry of talk, the grown-ups repeating over and over the news.

Pearl Harbor had been bombed, and America was headed to war.

WAR

Five days after the bombs fell on Pearl Harbor, Birmingham's first Black draftees left for the fight. Twenty-four soon-to-be soldiers attended a fried chicken luncheon at the Masonic Temple, where both Black and white civic leaders spoke on themes of "Negro heroism and patriotism." From there, they marched to the train station as well-wishers cheered. The Parker High School band led the way, sending them off with "Stars and Stripes Forever" and that most local of anthems, "Tuxedo Junction."[1]

Musicians would scramble to find their places in the wartime landscape. For years, Fess Whatley had supplied fresh talent to national bandleaders and college presidents; now he served as unofficial talent scout for the directors of army, navy, and air force bands, sending his products to military bases all over the country. At Fort Benning, Georgia, drummer Alton "Snooky" Davenport, longtime fixture of Whatley's Sax-o-Society Orchestra, directed the 334th Armed Service Forces Band and led the camp's popular Reception Center Chorus. Bandleaders Howard Funderburg and Frank Greer, trumpeter Johnny Grimes, and brothers Chuck and Arthur "Babe" Clarke, both saxophonists, joined over 5,000 other Black musicians assigned to the "Great Lakes Experience" naval bands stationed across the country. Other Whatley musicians joined the 313th Army Air Force Band, stationed at the Tuskegee Army Air Base and billed as the "Army's Busiest Band": in just one month, that group played more than fifty engagements, covering thousands of miles, entertaining officers and servicemen, and raising more than a million dollars for the war effort. The best musicians in the 313th— including Birmingham's Amos Gordon, J. L. Lowe, Newman Terrell, and Dickie Harris—also belonged to the Imperial Wings of Rhythm, a swing

During the Second World War, Birmingham musicians filled the ranks of Armed Services bands across the country and overseas. Here, Private Alton Davenport, one of Fess Whatley's longtime drummers, rehearses the Fort Benning Reception Center Band, 1941. Courtesy National Archives, photo no. 111-SC-123950.

band known popularly as the "Imps"; the best of *those* musicians played in an even hotter combo called the Solid Seven. Such notable visiting acts as Louis Armstrong and Lena Horne performed with the Imps at the posh new service club on the Tuskegee base, and informal jam sessions followed.[2]

By the start of the war, big band swing had become entrenched as the country's most popular sound. For many Americans—Black and white, at home and abroad—the music had come to represent all the country stood for: its freedoms and its optimism, its distinctive and original popular culture. Work flourished for musicians; while some players served Uncle Sam from the relative safety of the military's bandstands, civilian orchestras also found a steady stream of wartime jobs, appearing at military bases, USO dances, and fundraisers for the effort. But the war also brought fresh challenges to Black musicians, and it served to highlight and intensify the country's deep-rooted culture of racial injustice. Some members of the country's top bands saw the draft as a threat to the lives they had worked so hard to create, and they avoided its summons as long as they could.³

The Count Basie band was setting up for a show one night at the Plantation Club in Watts, California, when a stranger approached the bandstand. "This young guy came out," remembered saxophonist Buddy Tate, "zoot suit on, big chain down to the knees like Cab Calloway. He introduced himself, and we thought he was a fan." All night, the stranger bought the band drinks. Finally, he flashed an FBI badge at Jo Jones and his good friend and bandmate, Lester "Pres" Young, and he handed them an address: if they did not report for induction at nine the next morning, they would be tracked down and arrested.⁴

Jones was offered a spot in a navy band, a cushy deal many musicians would eagerly have grabbed, but as long as he was not drumming for Basie, he had no desire to drum for the war. "I said no. Since I have to go in the army, I'm *really* going in the army. I'm a soldier. . . . I ain't gonna play 'Stars and Stripes Forever.'" A photo published in *DownBeat* pictured a smiling Jones and Young jamming together in uniform, but the shoot was just a gimmick—neither man was playing music in the service, and the carefree spirit suggested by the photo gave no hint of the anguish that would come. For Young, the military experience was emotionally, psychologically, and physically damaging, a trauma from which the saxophonist would never fully recover. Jones's own time in the army, if less traumatic, also took its toll. For basic training, both men reported to Fort McClellan, Alabama, some sixty miles from Birmingham; on Sundays, Jones left the base to visit his old mentor Wilson Driver, who was struck by the change he saw in the drummer. "Each time," Driver recalled, "he sat on the floor with my two young daughters—they must have been five and six at the time—and made puzzles. . . . That's all he did." The two friends would head downtown for a drink, and Jones would "just sit there, looking around and out into space, listening to music. He didn't have a terribly good time in the Army. And he fretted about Pres. I asked him to bring Pres with him. He said, 'I can't get him out of camp.'"⁵

For what it called a "difficult character," the army considered Young a disciplinary problem, and when drugs were discovered in his locker, he was placed under arrest—with his bandmate Jones initially assigned as his guard. Young went before a hearing that labeled him with psychopathic tendencies; he was dishonorably discharged, forced to forfeit his pay, and sentenced to a year of hard labor in a Georgia stockade. When finally he emerged from the ordeal, he was changed: withdrawn, bitter, and depressed. He kept all others at a distance, drank heavily, and grew increasingly dependent on the drugs for which the army had so vigorously punished him.[6]

Jones assured his friend that he would be out soon himself and—just like old times—they would both be back on the bandstand with Basie. Jones did rejoin the band in early 1946, and such recordings that year as "The King" and "Muttonleg" proved the drummer was still a phenomenon and right in step in the changing music scene. Somehow, though, things were never quite the same: Jones became convinced that, since he had entered the service, younger drummers had moved on from the innovations he had pioneered, newer talent was replacing him, and he had been left irrevocably behind. In time, he evolved into "Papa Jo," a revered icon, but the reverence he inspired was as papa-pioneer, no longer as a crucial, creative force in the music. He had bouts with illness and depression and, like Young, drank more and more. He grew increasingly bitter and volatile, his angry outbursts isolating him from the music community—even as his drumming continued to exhilarate and as fans continued to marvel.[7]

For Ethel Harper, the war years coincided with a pinnacle of professional activity. Since 1937, Harper had tried to launch a successful vocal harmony group, but none of her efforts seemed to stick. Finally, at the start of 1942, she answered a call for auditions in the offices of Moe Gale: "At least two hundred girls" tried out for a new vocal quartet, and Harper made the cut. They would be called the Four Ginger Snaps.[8]

"Qualifications were high" for membership in the "Snaps," Harper noted. Singing was key, but there were other factors: "facial beauty, ability to read music, proportionate figure sizes, weight, and height, with complexions blended as one." The singers debuted on Ed Sullivan's *Harlem Cavalcade*, a four-month revue at Broadway's Ritz Theatre; from there, they picked up engagements at Kelly's Stables and the Apollo. Then they hit the road, where wartime opportunity kept them in steady demand—so much so that "we had to beg for time off to rest our diaphragms." They played military benefits and appeared at the Hollywood Canteen, the star-studded LA nightspot where servicemen were treated to free entertainment while volunteering celebrities waited and bused their tables or washed dishes in the kitchen. They performed on *Jubilee*, the Armed Forces Radio Service program created specifically for Black troops stationed overseas, and they starred in three musical film shorts, two with patriotic themes: *When Johnny Comes Marching Home* and the bubbly *Keep Smiling*. In the latter, they mugged for the camera, sang about war stamps and bonds ("Give me six! . . . I'll take ten!"), mocked Mussolini and Hirohito, and generally cheered on the cause. "Crush the Japanese," they harmonized gaily, "hang the Führer, and everything will be *all root!!*"[9]

Offstage and off-screen, behind the harmonies and smiling, morale was much lower than the singers let on. In some ways, the Snaps gig was a dream come true, the very opportunity for which Harper had yearned. Crowds ate up the foursome's charm, and, in addition to the group pieces, each vocalist performed her own solo numbers, so all of them found their own ways to shine. The singers accumulated a growing wardrobe of stage gowns, which Harper adored. But there were conflicts from the outset. It started with the matter of complexion, one of the "qualifications" on which they had been hired. One of the singers, Virginia Robinson, was fairer-skinned than the others, and some promoters complained: "They liked our music," Harper wrote, "but they didn't like the picture presented by the group." The talent agency took the "imbalance" seriously; even the group's name was meant to suggest a certain light-brown complexion. Before their first year as an act was over, Robinson had been replaced, purely on the basis of skin tone.[10]

Charles Ford, her replacement, was a pianist, arranger, and vocalist whose addition brought some new energy into the group: as an artist he added a fresh versatility to the act, and the interplay between female and male seemed to connect with the crowds. Even so, the departure of a founding member, forced by factors completely unrelated to the music, foreshadowed tensions to come. However compelling their harmonies, and whatever the strengths of any individual member, the Snaps were designed as a product, crafted in a management office for musical, visual, and commercial effect. The result was a successful five-year run but one whose foundations were shot through with insecurities, competing ambitions, and creeping distrust. Singers worried they were replaceable cogs; they quibbled among themselves over money and picked at each other's faults, real or imagined. After the war, another reshuffling in the lineup signaled the end; Harper and two others performed briefly as the *Three* Ginger Snaps and then dissolved the group.[11]

Ethel Harper would not return to public performance for nearly a decade.

Already a best-selling hit, "Tuxedo Junction" became a ubiquitous anthem of the war years. For its creators, the song had always been about *home*, in the most specific sense, and even if most listeners knew nothing of that original Junction, the song's celebration of and nostalgia for hometown experience was something any wartime American might adopt. A mythic "Tuxedo Junction" became any American's home—"right back where I belong," the lyrics said—a direct counter, geographically and emotionally, to that other world "Over There."

Glenn Miller, the man who brought the tune to white America, became himself a symbol for the war. For a while, his popular Army Air Force Orchestra was stationed at Maxwell Air Force Base in Montgomery, just a few miles from Alabama State and a couple hours' drive from the real Tuxedo Junction. (If Miller made a pilgrimage to either spot, no one reported it.) Next, in an effort to counteract Hitler's propaganda machine, Miller—relocated to England—hosted a series of radio broadcasts for German audiences, turning "Tuxedo Junction" and other hits into advertisements for the American way, amiably addressing the enemy between tunes, both in English and a stumbling, drawly German. "America," Miller told the Germans, "means freedom. And there's no expression of freedom quite so sincere as music."[12]

Soon, Miller's music took on a new resonance. In December 1944, somewhere over the English Channel on its way to a performance for Allied troops in Paris, Miller's plane disappeared. Its remains were never found. For white Americans especially, the bandleader represented not just the spirit of their country but, now, the sacrifice and tragedy of the war. His records, one GI wrote, became "a tangible tie to what we are fighting to get back to"; songs like "Tuxedo Junction" were "tied up with individual memories, girls, hopes, schools." Miller himself had been eager to return to the American dream idealized in his songs: he had recently bought a house in suburban California, and he planned to settle down there, cut back his performance schedule and focus on family, play some golf, grow some oranges. During the war, he had traveled with a wooden replica of the new house, his personal vision of the *home* this war was about.[13]

He had named it "Tuxedo Junction."

For members of the Hawkins orchestra, the first challenge of the war years was not the looming draft—that challenge would come soon enough—but the impact of the war on travel. With gas and rubber shortages across the country, bus travel was in short supply; the band pleaded with Gale to arrange transportation by trains, but that option was expensive, and segregation laws complicated matters down South. Until the war was over, Gale announced, the band would travel by car; and so, in 1941, the "Hawkins Convoy"—three crowded cars and a trailer packed with instruments and equipment—hit the road, the musicians grumbling useless complaints. After some negotiation, the Gale agency at least agreed to supply professional drivers, sparing the players the extra duty of driving all day themselves. Still, the setup was rife with frustrations: there were breakdowns and flat tires; the drivers kept long, sleepless hours; and the cramped and irritable players rode zombielike from lack of rest.[14]

They were just outside Chattanooga early one Sunday, on the way to Nashville, when the life of the road caught up with them. The convoy's second car rounded a curve to see Haywood Henry on the side of the road, arms flailing: the lead car had veered off the road, hit a soft shoulder, and flipped onto its side in a ditch. The heavy equipment trailer prevented it from tumbling further, but the wreck was bad, and the cause was predictable. The overworked driver, behind the wheel through the night, had fallen asleep on the job.[15]

As Haywood recounted the accident to his bandmates, bassist LeMeyer Stanfield emerged from the ditch, trumpeter Marcellus Green in his arms. Everyone in the car had sustained minor injuries, but Green was hurt bad, his right leg crushed between the car and the ditch, his foot lacerated—"as if," Sammy Lowe described it, "someone had taken a knife and cut it into strips." Green remained calm—*serene*, Lowe said—as his bandmates maneuvered him into the second car and rushed him to Nashville for help. The foot, they feared, might need amputation; chances were good Green would spend the rest of his life on crutches.[16]

Haywood, Sammy, and Dud Bascomb stayed behind to fill in the members of the third car; then they flagged down a bus headed for Nashville. As they reached the city, Erskine's car happened to pull alongside their bus at a stoplight. They called out the window, "How's Green?" and were shocked by Erskine's reply: Marcellus Green had died, a result of internal injuries. "The passengers on the bus, most of them white, shared in our sorrow," Sammy later recalled, "and the last few miles to downtown Nashville the bus was quiet as a morgue."[17]

The musicians made it through that night's show with difficulty—they were aghast to find Green's chair already set up in its usual spot onstage, and his trumpet's silence echoed through each arrangement they played—and then they canceled all gigs for two weeks. A few nights before the wreck, the band had been in Birmingham, where the hometown crowd had packed the Masonic Temple as always; now they returned for a funeral at the Reverend John Goodgame's Sixth Avenue Baptist Church. At the request of Fess Whatley and George Hudson, Sammy and Dud spoke about the music profession to students in the Parker High School band—but this time, their remarks felt empty and awkward. The profession had lost some of its glamour.[18]

Widely reported in the Black press, the news of Marcellus Green's death was more than a tragedy: it was a call to arms. Discussions of the accident invariably turned to the conditions Black musicians were forced to contend with, and the Hawkins band again found itself a central exhibit in debates over the disparate realties faced by Black bands and their white counterparts. The *New York Amsterdam News* blamed the US Office of Defense Transportation for leaving Black bands in crisis; between the tire shortage and the obstacles of segregated travel, Black bands faced nothing short of extinction. "At the time of the accident," the paper reported, "the Erskine Hawkins band was on a three month road tour. As in the case of most Negro bands, the majority of their bookings are in the South. Yet because of Jim Crow restrictions and prohibitive costs, colored bands cannot travel through the South by rail." White bands, meanwhile, "travel as they wish in any section of the country because they are booked in the best hotels, night clubs, and radio station jobs. Such spots are closed to colored bands and as is apparent in the death of Marcellus Green, the risk incurred in traveling by private cars through the South threatens to force them out of business." These kinds of alarms had been sounded before—*DownBeats*'s predictions of "doom" for Black bands had raised the same points—but now the stakes were higher. "The Negro musicians, upon whose contributions modern American music has been founded should [not] be placed in a position where their lives are jeopardized."[19]

Moe Gale released a public statement in direct challenge to the government, outlining the conditions that plagued Black bands and led to Green's death. He traveled to Washington to discuss the issue in person with Joseph Eastman, director of the Office of Defense Transportation. Nothing came of their meeting.[20]

Gale did, at least, reverse his own transportation policy. Earlier, his agency had rejected the band's pleas for train travel, primarily on the basis of the expense. "Now that Green was dead," wrote Sammy Lowe, "and dead because of what the band had feared from the beginning—a sleepy driver and a highway accident—the office had changed its mind." Really, there were no other options—the musicians refused to play at all if they were forced to ride in any more cars—and so the Hawkins tour resumed by rail. Even so, along with the headaches of frequent delays, there were the indignities of Jim Crow to contend with, and the southern tour highlighted for the band the contradictions of an America at war. Everywhere they went, the "colored cars" were crowded past capacity with Black men in uniform. In Louisiana, musicians boarded a train that was also hauling German prisoners of war, and they were forced, as always, into the last two cars on the train, cars that were crammed already with Black servicemen. While America fought for freedom overseas, this was the state of things at home: a long train of sleeping cars crossed the country, its beds occupied by enemy soldiers, while American servicemen—and the originators of one of the war's essential anthems—rode in the rear, competing for room to sit down.[21]

The band did in the meantime pick a replacement for Green. In Birmingham for the funeral, they persuaded another hometown player, Alvin Robertson, to fill Marcellus's chair. Robertson was a good musician, an old friend, and a seamless fit for the group—but, a few weeks into the tour, in Oklahoma City, he bowed out. He was homesick, he apologized: he missed his wife and just was not cut out for the road. "This was unheard-of to us," Sammy said: "leave a job where he was making more money than he had ever made, playing in a name band, and leaving before going to *New York City*?! We just couldn't understand him." For Robertson, though, the stability of home trumped the thrill of the big time. He took the train back to Birmingham and stayed off the road, taught school, and raised a family. He was still in Birmingham two decades later when the city's growing racial strife reached its climax. On September 15, 1963, running a few minutes late, he dropped off his daughter Carole in front of the Sixteenth Street Baptist Church. When a bomb exploded in the building's basement later that morning, Carole Robertson was among the four girls who were killed. Grappling with the illogic of grief, Alvin Robertson would always place some of the blame on himself. "I often tell myself," he said, in the long aftermath of loss, "if I had stayed with the Hawkins band my daughter would probably be alive today."[22]

Fourteen years old at her death, Carole shared her father's love of music. A clarinetist, she had performed in Parker High School's marching band.

The draft brought its own dilemmas. "Hawkins Hit Hard," one headline announced, as the military siphoned players from the band. Eventually, inevitably, Erskine himself received his "papers," but the government granted him a deferment to finish his scheduled tour—then told him to await further notice, which never came. While he waited, Hawkins turned thirty, and he suspected he may have "aged out" just as the war was winding down. Maybe the government decided he was doing enough as it was, with all those USO dances and servicemen's shows. One way or another, Erskine Hawkins remained on the bandstand through the war.[23]

Sammy Lowe, for his part, was not about to risk his own future on the draft.[24] "The night before I was to take my physical for the army I smoked two reefers," he explained. The reputation of the Hawkins bandmates as clean-cut college types had followed them into adulthood, and the image was more or less true: all of them kept their distance from the drugs that pervaded so much of jazz culture. Still, if Sammy could convince the draft board that he was just another jazz addict, he knew they would not take him. The two reefers were his homework.

His act would have to be convincing. "As you go from one doctor to another, you hear the many guys claiming they can't see, or hear, or walk well, that they are allergic to this or that . . . all of their excuses being made, trying to stay out of the army." Lowe's own plan was foolproof: all he had to do was confirm the army's built-in biases, playing into his music's most popular stereotype. A psychiatrist asked directly if he smoked marijuana ("I do"), how it made him feel ("a little silly . . . but it certainly makes me feel good"), and if he was addicted ("Yes sir, I am; I just can't do without it"). He was rejected from service.

At the next rehearsal, Lowe regaled the band with the story of how he had beat the army—the reefer bit worked, he said—and the guys ate it up. As it happened, Lowe kept the real truth to himself. He had managed to glimpse a note on his file from the psychiatrist, who identified the addiction claims as a poorly acted ploy. What really saved him from service was a surprise unearthed in his physical: he had tested positive for syphilis. For better or worse, the disease—contracted on one of many late-night, anonymous hookups on the road—kept Sammy Lowe out of the war. It put an end, too, to those sexual exploits, which he had gleefully embraced as perks of the job. Soon, until its symptoms finally subsided, it would bring him bouts of miserable discomfort and intense mental anguish. But Sammy did his best not to let on, repeating the tale of his trickster heroics—how he conned the army by getting high and telling lies—and the story always left the room in stitches.

For the Hawkins crew, one of the greatest tragedies of the war years had no connection to the conflict overseas.

Avery Parrish, perhaps the band's most celebrated star, was the first of the group's core musicians to strike out on his own. Songwriter Hoagy Carmichael had opened his own nightclub in Los Angeles, and in 1943 he offered Parrish a permanent, high-paying gig there, an opportunity too good to resist. A few months later, Parrish was catching up with a friend in a Los Angeles dive when a stranger tried to pick a fight. Parrish told the man to leave them alone, but when he turned back to his drink, the man grabbed a barstool and came at him from behind, striking him in the head and knocking him unconscious. When Parrish came to, thirty hours later in an LA hospital, he was a broken reflection of his previous self, all but speechless and largely paralyzed. The papers reported on his condition from the hospital: "Among the few words he is capable of is 'yes' which he articulates in both the affirmative and the negative." Tragically, he "cannot use his famous hands. The musician occasionally laughs childishly and calls 'hey' for a nurse." A nerve specialist attempted an experiment, wheeling him to a piano and placing his fingers on the keys, but he "didn't seem to remember anything about the instrument."[25]

Over time, through a regimen of exercises, Parrish did regain some strength in his hands, and he even recorded a new version of "After Hours" with Paul and Dud Bascomb in 1946. He never, however, regained his full mental, physical, or musical capacities. He moved in with his mother in Harlem and took a string of menial jobs: "working in restaurants," Dud said, "washing dishes, and things like that." When he died in 1959, he was employed as a porter in a bottling company and had not recorded or performed in years. "He was still living with his mother," Dud continued, "when he went to a place on 127th one night. He was drinking, and he fell down a flight of stairs," the impact compounding the previous injury to his brain. He was found in a coma on the street and died five days later in a Harlem hospital. He was forty-two years old.[26]

"After Hours," however, thrived with a life of its own. By the mid-1940s it had become so widespread a standard in America's Black communities that it was nicknamed "the new Negro national anthem," "Lift Every Voice and Sing" notwithstanding. Innumerable couples slow-dragged to its groove, and every aspiring blues and jazz pianist did his or her best to master it. In New York, legendary bebop disc jockey Symphony Sid made it his radio theme. It was the nightly theme, too, for Nashville station WLAC's long-running late-night broadcast, also called *After Hours*, a show famous for introducing white teenagers to the Black rhythm and blues that begat rock and roll. In 1950s Detroit, a young Aretha Franklin, not yet in her teens, learned to play it; her father, the Reverend C. L. Franklin, sometimes dragged her out of bed at three or four in the morning to perform the tune for visiting friends. Even without the aid of lyrics, the tune communicated volumes to any listeners who recognized its unmistakable sound. At a house party in Clarksdale, Mississippi, one pianist reclaimed it in the 1960s as commentary on the local curfew. "They don't 'low me to stay up in Clarksdale after twelve o'clock," remarked Wallace "Pine Top" Johnson, as his fingers moved into Parrish's classic rolling blues: "I'm gonner give the police a little bit of this 'After Hours.'" An anthem to sensuality, a testament to Black cultural pride, a harbinger of rock and soul, a wordless expression of protest—Avery Parrish's most lasting creation was large enough to contain it all.[27]

Marcellus Green and Avery Parrish were lost from the band for good. Other musicians, taken by the draft, returned as their military commitments ended, and Erskine always saved their seats. When a drafted musician returned, the original player and his replacement were both welcome to stay, so by the end of the war the group had ballooned to its largest membership yet, as many as twenty-two pieces. It became a band even bigger than the "big band" sound required, but it provided a welcome home for a whole community of musicians. The Hawkins ensemble had always prided itself on being a family, and all its members, old and new, had a place.

The group survived the war, but the era's hardships signaled difficulties to come. For a while, even the band's steadiest gig disappeared. Acting in response to calls from the military, New York officials padlocked the doors to the Savoy Ballroom in the spring of 1943. The Savoy had become a favorite spot for servicemen, Black and white alike, and military authorities complained that it bred prostitutes and pimps, spreading venereal disease among the soldiers and sailors who came there to dance. According to a government report, in just ten months 164 servicemen had contracted VD from women they encountered there. The city shut the place down on charges of vice, but Harlemites were sure of the truth: it was a fear of "race-mixing"— of Black and white people dancing together and going home together— that closed the Savoy. The ballroom had been New York's most open, most racially inclusive venue, and city leaders had not liked it.[28]

Even in the "paradise" of Harlem, that adopted home of so many southern transplants, racial tensions had been mounting. Discriminatory housing practices in New York and abuses of Black servicemen nationwide stoked the frustration and anger, and the targeting of the Savoy was only the latest affront. Black leaders and journalists railed against the decision: not even New York, one writer declared, was immune from "the cult of Southernism." In the *People's Voice*, a Black leftist newspaper, poet and composer Andy Razaf published an ode to the ballroom, pronouncing it "guilty" of nothing but "national unity":

Of practicing real Democracy
By allowing the races, openly
To dance and mingle in harmony

By summer, tensions reached a boiling point, and riots erupted in Harlem. In the aftermath, Mayor Fiorello La Guardia agreed to reopen the ballroom.

The venue continued into the 1950s with the Hawkins group staying on as its long-running house band. But its heyday as the country's capital of swing was over.[29]

For that matter, swing itself was endangered. The big band sound that sustained the country through the war began, now, to lose its hold on the public and soon would seem a stodgy throwback. Throughout the war years, a new music had been percolating beneath the surface, a sound that relied not on big bands swollen with musicians but on small, informal combos honing their craft in all-night clubs and impromptu jam sessions. A new musical culture was emerging, a new spirit of experimentation and a whole new kind of cool.

Once again, Birmingham musicians would help usher in the change.

19

TEDDY'S HILL, BILLIE'S GUY

In the 1940s, Curley Julian Parrish—pianist, educator, and older brother to the celebrated Avery—moved north to Long Island and, in his "Bama on Broadway" column for the weekly *Alabama Voice*, began sending readers back home a stream of giddy dispatches. "Here comes the column with what the hometown and state boys and girls are doing on the magic strip known around the world as 'good ole' Broadway," his first report began; it was a great and glittering world, he beamed, one that brought "fortune to thousands" but "by the same token crushed the chance of stardom for millions."[1]

Parrish made no further mention of those crushed millions but instead reveled each week in the bustle and thrill of his state-mates' triumphs in a wide range of fields. There were doctors, scholars, comedians, writers, scientists, religious leaders, and sheer social steppers. But of special interest were the musicians, whose names he crowded into his columns. "SHELTON HEMPHILL of Birmingham will be one of the outstanding trumpet features at Carnegie Hall next month," he wrote, anticipating Hemphill's upcoming gig with the Duke Ellington band. And "now that JOHN GRIMES has gotten the military tunes of Uncle Sam's Navy outta his trumpet, he's clipping off Spots here and there along the main stem, faster than an 'A' Train will bring you up town." Also making waves that week were trumpeter Nelson Williams, dancers Red and Curley, Ethel Harper, Lionel Hampton, Dud Bascomb, and—from Montgomery—Nat King Cole. "These are the names you'll see blazing away in a million lights up Broadway tonight."[2]

Also appearing in the column (if not in those lights) was drummer Wilson Driver, recently relocated to Harlem and, for the most part, retired from music. In Birmingham, Driver had worked as a teacher and a musician, but teachers' pay in New York was too low to provide for his daughters, and work as a musician would keep him too often from home. Even so, Driver proved a key musical force: he became a kind of unofficial ambassador for Birmingham musicians in New York, his Lenox Avenue apartment an outpost for old friends and fresh arrivals from home. He also served as mentor to younger percussionists: through Jo Jones he befriended some of the bebop era's most legendary drummers, including Sid Catlett and Max Roach, both of whom revered the older man as an unsung pioneer. Catlett offered to secure him a job in a band but warned he would have to make a choice—"of being with your family or just having a family"—and Driver, a single father whose wife had died in childbirth, easily made that choice: he found a job with the Chock Full o' Nuts chain of cafés. Family came first.[3]

Still, he kept a hand in music. Jones and Catlett recommended him for side gigs around town, and Roach sent him young student drummers to train. "Sid set me up with this gig in the Village—I can't remember the name of the joint, Silver Slipper or something—that lasted four years," Driver said. "I was making more money as a part-time musician than I was working full-time during the day." All the while, his apartment brimmed with visitors, growing famous for its birthday and New Year's parties, always full of music. For daughter Sonia Sanchez, the whole scene added up to an extraordinary education. On Saturday nights, Driver would take her and her sister to one of the clubs on Fifty-Second Street, and if they could not get in, "he went inside, and he'd bring out some musicians to meet us. . . . Or [we would] go to the Apollo, and we could go backstage . . . and hear the music. We stood backstage and heard the great Billy Eckstine. And the great Sid Catlett would put me and my sister on his knee and talk to us and say how beautiful we were, and would kid my father about having such pretty children. I remember that: all these great musicians we met, and my father proudly presented us to them."[4]

Another musician Sanchez met through her father was the ex-bandleader Teddy Hill. There were new sounds and ideas percolating in the New York clubs, and Teddy from the beginning was at the heart of the change. The *New York Amsterdam News* announced Hill's latest venture at the start of 1941, reporting that his "old fans have not deserted him. . . . Established in his new job as host and managing director of Minton's Playhouse . . . Teddy is proving as big a drawing card as he was when he waved the baton behind the footlights." In the end, it was neither as musician nor as bandleader that Hill would make his greatest mark but in this latest and longest-lasting of roles: as manager of Minton's Playhouse, celebrated wellspring of a new kind of music. Under Hill's leadership, the spot developed a reputation that quickly grew to the stature of myth. It is hard to name another place that figures so prominently in the legends and lore of jazz than does Minton's. "What was happening at Minton's," wrote Ralph Ellison in a celebrated 1958 essay, "was a continuing symposium of jazz, a summation of all the styles, personal and traditional, of jazz. Here it was possible to hear its resources of techniques, ideas, harmonic structure, melodic phrasing and rhythmical possibilities explored more thoroughly than was ever possible before." Pianist Mary Lou Williams simply called it the "house that built bop."[5]

A famous photograph underscores the significance of the place. In 1947—less than a decade after the club's founding, but long after its landmark status had become entrenched—photographer William Gottlieb accompanied Thelonious Monk to Minton's for a *DownBeat* photo shoot. Teddy Hill showed up, along with trumpeters Roy Eldridge and Howard McGhee. Gottlieb's camera captured the four men in staged conversation beneath the club's signature awning, producing what historian Robin D. G. Kelley has called "one of the most widely circulated and iconic photographs in jazz history": a "Mount Rushmore of modern jazz."[6]

In fact, Minton's was not the only space in which the new music developed; Clarke Monroe's Uptown House, just down the street, played a parallel role. And while the legend of Minton's has cast each of the venue's jams as a who's who of modern jazz, one in which players self-consciously forged a revolution in sound, the revolution in truth was less dramatic. "Some of those histories and articles put what happened in ten years in one year," said Monk. "They put people all together in one time in this place. Over a period of time, I've seen practically everybody at Minton's, but they were just in there playing. They weren't giving any lectures."[7]

Minton was Monroe Henry ("M. H.") Minton, the same Minton who had earlier managed the Rhythm Club with help from Hill and who had briefly, unsuccessfully, managed the Bama State Collegians. Born in 1884 and known as "the old man" by the forties, he had been playing or promoting jazz since the music's earliest roots in ragtime and vaudeville; he had been the first Black delegate to the New York musicians' union and had long been a champion of working Black musicians. Minton opened his playhouse in 1938 in the basement of West 118th Street's Cecil Hotel, but the place had a slow, disappointing start. He hired a couple of managers, but they failed to attract a crowd. Then he hired Hill.

As manager, Teddy Hill drew on the same strengths that made him excel as bandleader: his affable, disarming personality; his sharp business sense; his ability to identify and nurture new talent; his devotion to Black musicians.

Bebop pioneers at Minton's, in an alternate take of William Gottlieb's iconic 1947 photo. *Left to right:* Thelonious Monk, Dizzy Gillespie, Howard McGhee, Teddy Hill. Courtesy the William P. Gottlieb / Ira and Leonore S. Gershwin Fund Collection, Music Division, Library of Congress.

Until it folded, just a few months earlier, Hill's band had been a launching pad for fresh musical voices, and his soloists had hinted at new directions for jazz. But in the band there was always that tension between old and new, complaints about Dizzy's antics or Klook-mop's bombs. At Minton's, new talent and ideas would be given room to flourish. "Hill turned the Playhouse into a musical dueling ground," Ellison wrote; under Teddy's supervision, "Minton's became the focal point for musicians all over the country."[8]

"When Teddy took over," explained Kenny Clarke, "Minton's changed its music policy. Teddy wanted to do something for the guys who had worked with him. He turned out to be a sort of benefactor since work was scarce at that time." Not long ago, Hill had fired Clarke for pushing the boundaries of the music too far; now, that kind of pushing was just what he wanted. Hill hired Clarke as house drummer. The invitation may have come as a surprise—but "after we talked a while," said Clarke, "I knew what he wanted."[9]

What Hill wanted was a place for free expression and exploration, a music venue built for the musicians themselves. "You can drop all the bombs, all the re-bop and the boom-bams you want," Hill told his old drummer. "You can do it here." At Minton's there were no dancers who had to be catered to, no commercial trends that had to be followed, no impresarios to impress. On Minton's stage, musicians were free to work out new ideas, to play whatever they wanted, however they wanted. "Teddy never tried to tell us how we play," Clarke said. "We just played as we felt." Loyal always to his ex-bandsmen, Hill recruited another of his former sidemen (and a fellow Birmingham export), trumpeter Joe Guy, along with bassist Nick Fenton. For house pianist, Hill tapped a newcomer from North Carolina, a visionary artist named Thelonious Monk.[10]

Under Hill's design, Monday nights—traditionally the deadest night of the week, and a night off for musicians—became the foundation for a whole new culture. Hill turned Monday into "Celebrity Night," inviting musicians for a down-home feast: fried chicken, sweet potatoes, ham hocks and greens, black-eyed peas, grits, biscuits, ribs. For musicians, food and drink were free; for many—displaced southerners like Hill himself—those Monday night spreads evoked the warmest comforts of home. Late into the evening, musicians would take the stage and jam. Other nights, the house band welcomed friends to sit in. Technically, Local 802 barred its members from participating in such sessions—in a jam, everyone but the house band played for free, and union and nonunion players mixed onstage, flouting union rules—but, thanks to Henry Minton's connections, officials looked the other way.

New things were afoot. Musicians experimented with harmony and time, developed complex chord progressions and variations, pushed tempos to their fastest extremes. Lesser talents and more conventional players could not keep up—could not keep the time, follow the changes, or compete with the demands for improvisational virtuosity. According to the oft-repeated story, the innovations of bop developed at least in part as an attempt to "scare off" what Dizzy Gillespie, another Minton's fixture, called the "no-talent guys." "That's how we came to write different chord progressions and the like," Clarke added. "We did that to discourage the sitters-in at night we didn't want. Monk, Joe Guy, Dizzy, and I would work them out. . . . As for those sitters-in that we didn't want, when we started playing these different changes we'd made up, they'd become discouraged after the first chorus and they'd slowly walk away and leave the professional musicians on [the] stand."[11]

The music did not have a name in those days—it was just "modern music" or "that music they're playing up at Minton's"—but, whatever it was, it was working significant changes to the culture of jazz. This was music that rewarded, perhaps demanded, close and careful listening, music created not by the marquee bandleaders but by their sidemen, turned loose to take center stage and forge their own unscripted paths. This, above all, was an insider's music: either you got it, or you didn't. The players were something other than entertainers; they were artists, their music insisted, and their work took on a new seriousness with the role. Minton's was neither the first nor the only after-hours jam spot, but it embodied and canonized, more than any other locale, the idea and the image of the modern jazz club.[12]

With Hill at the helm, Minton's remained a Harlem landmark for twenty-nine years, but the music that defined its reputation took off almost as soon as Hill arrived. Even before American troops headed to war, the new sound was underway; by the time Hill himself was drafted—he played in army bands in Europe and the Philippines—the Minton's legend was secured. Around 1940, a white Columbia University student named Jerry Newman began bringing an acetate recorder to the club, and his recordings, eventually released to the public, preserved a portrait of the music in its developmental stages. The titles assigned to some of the recorded improvisations—"One for Teddy," "Up on Teddy's Hill," "Down on Teddy's Hill"—paid affectionate tribute to Minton's host, the room's genial central presence, the beaming patron saint of bop.[13]

It is worth noting that Birmingham's most influential bebop personality made his contribution offstage, not as musician but as businessman. The classic Birmingham training—with its tradition of reading, sobriety, and devotion to the group—had been suited perfectly to the swinging big bands, collegiate dance bands, society orchestras, and military dance units. Bop was something else entirely, and, next to the legions of Magic City swingers, relatively few Birmingham exports made this new music their own. Joe Guy, Minton's original trumpeter, was an important exception.

In 1944, critic Herbie Nichols caught a performance at New York's Onyx Club by the Oscar Pettiford band, which that night included two Minton's stalwarts, Guy and Thelonious Monk. Nichols's review was the first published notice of the inventive, unorthodox Monk, and it praised the band as a whole for its "mélange of rich chords, rhythm and fire." As for the trumpeter: "Joe Guy is a brilliant consistent trumpeter. His liquid legato style on ballads is clear and rich. This fellow plays brilliant jazz in the same category as the master, 'Dizzy.'" Nichols was not alone in this opinion: Joe Guy was clearly a musician to watch, a player poised for still greater success.[14]

So it seemed, anyway, at the time. But while Dizzy's and Monk's would become household names, Joe Guy—his own name suggested a bland anonymity—would simply self-destruct, disappearing altogether from the scene. Guy appears in histories of jazz, when he appears at all, as little more than a footnote. Again and again he emerges, horn in hand, at key moments in the development of modern jazz; before he comes into focus, he's gone. He's there on the sidelines in all the histories of Minton's, there at the outset of the new bebop sound; he's there on the seminal records of Coleman Hawkins, providing background on "Body and Soul" and other classics, there in the first all-star lineup of *Jazz at the Philharmonic*. You can hear him, too—blowing "little dibs and dabs," in the words of Frank Adams, a friend and admirer—behind Billie Holiday on many of her mid-1940s records. ("He'd kill you with that muted trumpet," Adams said.) For a while, Guy and Holiday were husband and wife—that, at least, was how they introduced themselves, even if they lacked the papers to prove it—and his self-destruction was tangled up with hers.[15]

Guy had left Birmingham, young, with Reverend George Becton's Gospel Feast Party, entrusted by his own preacher father to the religious and musical training Becton's Party promised. He came of age in Becton's plush Harlem apartment, attending school in New York, honing his instrumental skills in nightly revivals—and, like Haywood Henry and many another protégé of the "Consecrated Dime," falling in love with "New Yorkish" ways, graduating into the secular temples of the city's nightlife. Whenever he came back through Birmingham, he exuded a new kind of cool that even the city's other homegrown successes could not touch. Erskine Hawkins's men, to be sure, were icons, successful and dapper and even heroic. But Guy— who stood aloof and wore shades inside and at night, who attacked his solos from unconventional angles—seemed another kind of breed. Frank Adams was a teenager in 1943 when he first saw Guy perform with the Lucky Millinder Orchestra, and in the trumpeter he recognized something both familiar (he was, after all, thought Adams, from *here*) and something altogether new, something exotic and alluring. "When he came to the Masonic Temple, he had on dark glasses—I hadn't seen dark glasses—and he had a camel's hair coat on, and everybody loved him because he was a *homeboy*. So every time he would play one of those obbligatos behind somebody, they would just cheer for Joe."[16]

Guy's early career mirrored in many ways that of Dizzy Gillespie, to whom he was often compared. Both men began their careers by emulating Roy Eldridge, and both would occupy Eldridge's old spot in the Hill band. Both would follow Hill to Minton's, Guy as a member of the band, Gillespie as a prominent recurring guest. In 1941, the white bandleader Charlie Barnet hired Guy at Dizzy's urging. Barnet was among the first to lead an integrated band; but, as the group's *only* Black musician, Gillespie got sick of being held up and questioned by security guards and other authorities, so he appealed to Barnet, arguing that another Black presence in the group might reduce the hassles and suspicion. The strategy seemed to work, and Gillespie "had a good time" once Guy joined the group.[17]

Like Dizzy, Guy helped bridge the swing and bop eras by importing ideas from Minton's into the mainstream of swing. Trumpeter Cootie Williams, veteran of the Duke Ellington and Benny Goodman Orchestras, launched his own band in 1942, and Guy introduced into that group's repertoire the distinctive compositions of his friend Thelonious Monk. With Kenny Clarke, Monk composed "Fly Right" (later known as "Iambic Pentameter" and finally "Epistrophy"), which became the opening and closing theme for Minton's house band; Guy brought the tune to Williams, who made it his own radio and dance theme and recorded it with his orchestra in 1942. Unreleased for years but regarded today as a classic, the recording provides access to the developing sound of modern jazz—and offers, through its central trumpet solo, a compelling portrait of Joe Guy in his prime.[18]

Somewhere along the way, Guy caught the ear, and eye, of Billie Holiday. She was only five years his senior, but the difference seemed greater: she was certainly more famous and was already wearier of the world. Joe Guy, for his part, was young and handsome and full of ideas, and his playing anticipated the future of jazz. He became Holiday's trumpeter, her bandleader, and her lover. He also supplied her drugs.[19]

Guy has fared poorly in the historical treatment of Holiday. In her biographies he is typically cast as villain, another bad man in a string of bad men, all more or less interchangeable. The 2001 Ken Burns documentary series *Jazz* narrates Holiday's downfall in crisp prose and portentous delivery, a series of terse declarations that suggest straightforward cause and effect. "In 1941," a heavy voice-over intones,

> she married a sometime marijuana dealer named Jimmy Monroe and began smoking opium.
> Then she moved in with a good-looking trumpet player named Joe Guy.
> He was addicted to heroin.
> Soon she would be using it, too.[20]

In fact, historians have quibbled over whose habit came first. Biographer Meg Greene depicts Guy as "the man who introduced her to heroin and was in part responsible for her addiction." Donald Clarke, author of *Billie Holiday: Wishing on the Moon*, may be more accurate on this point, as accurate anyway as anyone can know: "It would be pointless to blame Lady for his addiction, or him for hers; she had plenty of friends who had bad habits, and anyway a heroin plague was under way."[21]

"I'm grown-up," Holiday herself once said to *DownBeat* magazine. "I knew what I was doing. Joe may have done things he shouldn't, but I did them of my own accord, too. . . . Joe didn't make it any easier for me at times—but then I haven't been any easy gal either." One way or another, the couple got hooked, and their addictions took a toll. Guy's solos became increasingly imprecise, even erratic. He began missing recording dates and gigs. For a period in 1945, Holiday and Coleman Hawkins (Guy's boss at the time) were headlining nightly at Fifty-Second Street's Downbeat Club, but Billie and Joe repeatedly missed the engagement, holed up instead in their hotel room. A young Miles Davis was among Guy's enthusiastic admirers at Minton's, but he also recognized the opportunity that Guy's failings provided. Each night, Davis stopped by the Downbeat to see if Guy had showed. If he had not, Davis took his place.[22]

Many of Holiday's acquaintances came to dislike or distrust Guy, some seeing in him nothing more than a drug-running "errand boy," a leech who hustled up heroin for Holiday and hung around for any leftover fix. Bassist Al Lucas shared an apartment for a while with Guy and his brother Jimmy, a drummer who had also moved up from Birmingham. The brothers, Lucas reported, could barely take care of themselves. Between them, they owned one pair of good pants: "When one went out, the other couldn't go out. He'd have to wait for his brother to come back." Still, Lucas said, "Joe Guy was a nice, quiet guy, nice to be around until he got hooked. Then you couldn't trust him." Weighing in on the fruitless debate, Lucas added, "He got hooked when he met her."[23]

All the while, both Holiday and Guy were being trailed by the US government, whose growing antidrug campaign had made special target of Black musicians. Every day, narcotics agent Jimmy Fletcher discovered, Guy would obtain an ounce of heroin from a connection in the city and then deliver the drugs to Holiday. Fletcher had to admit his targets were creative, even recruiting into their service Holiday's beloved boxer Mister, a constant companion with whom the couple shared their beers and even their junk. Each day, Fletcher said, "Guy walked the dog from way down on Morningside Drive up to 125th on Eighth and told the dog to go ahead. The dog would walk right in the Braddock Hotel," where Holiday was staying. "The elevator operator was waiting for him." Mister would ride up to Holiday's floor, step off the elevator, and walk right to her door. Secured behind his collar was the day's ounce of heroin.[24]

In September 1945, Holiday and Guy set out on an ambitious professional partnership. "We decided I would have my own band and Joe would be the leader," Holiday wrote in her biography, *Lady Sings the Blues*. They got "a big beautiful white bus" with "Billie Holiday and her Band" painted on the side and planned a wide-ranging tour, with Joe as booker and bandleader. The press lauded the duo as an exciting new power couple. "As far back as the days when he appeared with Lucky Millinder Guy was an attraction," the *Chicago Defender* observed, "and with Billie working with him one may expect box office records." Holiday and Guy set their sights on greatness. "We sure went for the greasy pig when we started that one," she wrote.[25]

Holiday's mother, Sadie, invited the band to her place before they left New York, gave everyone sandwiches and drinks, and hung "a few fancy little curtains in the back of the bus to dress it up." But even that first afternoon might have warned the couple they were in over their heads. "It was the first time out for me and Joe as band leaders and we didn't know enough about it to keep a platoon of Boy Scouts together, let alone grown men." While Sadie worked on the curtains, "the cats began wandering off" for a drink or a fix. "I'd get everybody collected," Holiday explained, "count noses, and find one cat was missing. While I was finding him, two more would sneak away." Still, initial press for the tour was positive and Guy kept the team steadily booked; the war was on, and besides the dance halls and theaters, there were plenty of service clubs to hit.[26]

Soon, though, things began to unravel. Barely a month into the tour, word came that Sadie, Holiday's mother, had died. Billie was devastated. Singer Carmen McCrae, Holiday's friend and protégé, recalled that "coming back from her mother's funeral, Billie was telling Joe Guy . . . over and over again, 'Joe, I don't have anybody in the world now except you.'" But Guy, McCrae maintained, could have been anybody—his name, after all, was *Joe Guy*. "She needed someone to say that to. She felt completely alone."[27]

Then there was the question of the marriage itself. In the midst of the tour, Guy's first wife announced that she and her ex had never legally divorced, and the marriage to Holiday was a sham. Indeed, many in the couple's circle understood that Holiday and Guy had never made their union official with a license or ceremony. As best they could, the couple ignored the gossip, but their relationship was under strain, held together, it seemed, by little more than shared addiction and ambition. Meanwhile, the authorities were closing in: in the spring of 1947, agents raided the couple's New York hotel room, discovering sixteen capsules of heroin stashed in Holiday's stockings.[28]

At her trial that May, Holiday threw herself on the mercy of the court. At her manager's advice, she rejected the aid of a lawyer and pled guilty to the charges, hoping to receive treatment for her addiction. Instead, she was sentenced to a year and a day in the Federal Reformatory for Women in Alderson, West Virginia. From there, she sent letters to the Pennsylvania prison cell where Guy awaited his own trial. "I Wish to god I could do anything to help you," she wrote, "but as you know both My hands are tied." She promised to send a magazine photo of herself—"so you don't forget What I look like (smirk)"—and offered to have a friend send a photo of Mister ("so you Will be able to at least look at your family"). "I cant Write your Mother and Dad as I can only Write a few people," she added. "But tell them I love them." In closing, she urged him to have his brother Jimmy or their friend Bama Warwick send his picture to her.[29]

Guy's letters have not survived. But a few days later, Holiday wrote again, just before bed. "I am going to try so hard to dream of you," she wrote, then admonished, "Don't laugh. Sometimes I am lucky and can." The writing is full of heartache, suggesting a greater tenderness than Holiday's biographers have typically allowed the relationship. It is full, too, of hopeful, if naive, promises. "What ever happens at your trial sweetheart," her letter goes on, "keep your chin up don't let nothing get you down. It won't be long before were together agian. My lights has been out every since I last saw you. But they will go on for us all over the world. Write to me Joe as soon as you can. Ill always love you as ever your Lady Billie Holiday."[30]

In September, Holiday appeared before the US District Court in Philadelphia as witness in Guy's trial. Her testimony confounded the prosecution. At her own trial she had effectively blamed Joe for her habit; now, she explained that the drugs might have been his, but they might not have been.

Birmingham trumpeter Joe Guy and Billie Holiday, in a photo inscribed to Holiday ("my Darling wife") from Guy. Courtesy Kim and Gary Hatfield.

Either way, they were for her use, not his. The jury deliberated for less than an hour while Holiday, her testimony concluded, was hurried back onto a train for Alderson.[31]

"Billie Holiday's Mate Freed," the headline announced in the *New York Amsterdam News*. "Word from Blues Singer Would Have Landed Joe Guy in Pen." The jury had found Joseph Luke Guy not guilty; Billie had spared him. It was the end, all the same, of the couple's romance, and the end of Joe Guy's career. "The guys on the street," the paper reported, "intimated that [Holiday's] trumpet playing husband, Joe Guy, who was exonerated of dope charges, had recently taken an apartment in the 200 block of 129th St., but nobody could quite agree on the exact house." As far as Holiday's biographers are concerned, Guy's story ends there—with a kind of vanishing act, a loss no one seemed much to mourn. In the words of one writer, Guy "permanently dropped out of music" and "died in obscurity"; according to another, he "faded back down South where he was born." For most historians, Guy simply disappears from the stream of history, his brilliant future—widely predicted, less than a decade before—evaporated, his friendships broken, his "marriage" dissolved, his once-lauded talent shot through. By the time he left New York, the Minton's story, in which he had played a key role, had already attained the status of legend. In March 1947, just two months before Guy's arrest, Jerry Newman commercially issued a three-disc collection of the informal recordings he had made at Minton's, a 1941 session in which Guy and the rest of the house band jammed with guitar virtuoso Charlie Christian. Neither Guy nor the other musicians received any revenue from the release. In the meantime, modern jazz kept moving along without him. When people spoke of bop, Joe Guy's trumpet was seldom mentioned.[32]

Still shy of thirty years old, he had just one place left to go. He went back home, to Birmingham.

IF IT'S IN YOU

  If the beboppers introduced modern ideas into the mainstream of jazz, Sonny Blount in Birmingham was preparing to take the music still further. Sonny's experience at Alabama A&M—both his reluctant leadership of the collegiate band and his alleged encounter with the alien race—had nudged him in a new direction, into a new conception of himself. After a year in Huntsville, he briefly considered switching schools, even auditioned in Montgomery for the latest iteration of the Bama State Collegians, but by the start of the school year, in the fall of 1936, he was back in Birmingham, forging a path uniquely his own. At A&M he had enrolled in teacher training courses, pathway to a conventional middle-class existence; now he envisioned himself, instead, as another kind of leader, *"a world teacher,"* the first of his kind. He organized a band whose primary purpose was rehearsal for its own sake, a team of players he could work and push and polish, exploring his ideas in what seemed an endless stream of practice. His home became its own musical universe, with Sonny at the center: rehearsals might begin anytime, day or night, whenever he summoned his musicians, and they might last for hours. There was as much talk, sometimes, as music, as Sonny lectured his bandmates on a litany of overlapping subjects: music, history, religion, philosophy, and—strangest of all to his bandmates—outer space.[1]

  But Sonny also remained a prominent member of the city's established musical culture. His Sonny Blount Orchestra was a dance fixture and a headlining contender at events like the Negro Tuberculosis Association's T.B. Battle or Local 733's musicians' union showdown, contests that doubled as fundraisers for community causes. He rejoined the Society Troubadours, with whom he had played in high school, emerging—as he did in all his groups—as the star. In 1937, under the direction of bandleader Jimmy Luverte, that group recorded eight tunes for the Vocalion record label, half of which were issued, all of which disappeared into obscurity. Sonny did not likely appear on those records (he took Luverte's spot as leader around 1940), but he certainly occupied the same musical circles, and the records— sweet and peppy, fun-spirited if conventional—offer a glimpse into the entertainment world he inhabited.[2]

Promoting an upcoming broadcast on local station WSGN, a 1935 advertisement in the *Birmingham News* announced "SONNY BLOUNT and His Famous Recording Orchestra," but no evidence exists that Sonny recorded before he left Birmingham, over a decade later, and in his many interviews he never mentioned any recordings from the era. He did, however, register at least three of his early compositions for copyright with the Library of Congress. The first of these pieces—"Alone with Just a Memory of You," dated December 1936—credits Sonny Blount with the music and a Henry McCellons with the lyrics; 1940's "My Sweet" and 1941's "That's the Way I Feel Today" both identify Herman Poole Blount as sole composer. (On one of the scores, the middle name "Poole" appears in quotation marks, already suggesting Sonny's distance from his earthly, family name.) The compositions place Sonny comfortably in the poppy, sentimental songwriting trends of the day: "You're as sweet as a rose in the springtime / I dream of you night and day time," his 1940 lyrics forgettably declare. (Dreaming, a familiar cliché of Tin Pan Alley love songs, figures into two of the three Birmingham-era tunes and would remain a staple of Sun Ra's lyrics for the rest of his life.) In 1941, Sonny playfully complained of "the lonely blues, a dreary blues, a moanin' sighin' blue blues / A can't live without you blues," concluding, "That's the way I feel today." Since Clarence Williams had stolen his "Chocolate Avenue" in 1933, Sonny had become conscious of protecting his creative property; even if nothing further came of these compositions, he by now saw himself as a professional artist and creator with clear ambitions in the business of music.[3]

He was also performing with a vocal quartet, the Rhythm Four (or *Ripple Rhythm Four*, as a Ripple Tobacco sponsorship dictated). From 1939 to 1943, the group's daily fifteen-minute broadcasts over radio station WSGN appeared amid a diverse midday lineup that also included "hillbilly" string bands, white dance combos, kiddie shows, talk shows, classical pianists, preachers, comedians, and political commentators. The quartet entertained, too, at the usual Black society functions and appeared in variety shows at the leading white theaters. Both the city's Black and white newspapers

Sonny Blount (Sun Ra) in an early photo with his quartet, the Ripple Rhythm Four, October 1940. The original caption in the *Birmingham World* reads, "Birmingham boys who are making a name for themselves in the radio world. The Ripple Rhythm Four who broadcast over WSGN at 12:30, Mondays through Fridays. Reading from left to right they are: Morris Ridgl, Sonny Blount, Richard Cannon and Clarence Driskell." Courtesy Alabama State Department of Archives and History.

heralded the Rhythm Four as "Birmingham's favorite quartet," a bold statement in a town loaded with quartets. Birmingham's gospel tradition had grown up alongside the city's jazz culture; in addition to the vocal harmony training all students encountered at Industrial High, a handful of influential, independent quartet trainers helped develop a distinctive Jefferson County sound. By the 1930s many local acts—the Birmingham Jubilee Singers, the Famous Blue Jays, the Bessemer Sunset Four, and more—had found success as recording and touring artists and performed frequently across Birmingham, from church concerts to union meetings to radio broadcasts to baseball games. The members of Sonny's Rhythm Four were steeped in the same tradition, and at least some of them had direct ties to the gospel community: bass singer and guitarist Clarence Driskell also sang with an outfit called the Heavenly Four, and Jimmy Ricks, who performed briefly with the group, was a celebrated trainer of quartets and a veteran of the pioneering Birmingham Jubilee Singers.[4]

Despite these gospel roots, the Rhythm Four singers distinguished themselves by performing a mostly secular repertoire and—unlike the other a cappella quartets—incorporating Sonny's piano and two guitars. The group also provided a platform for Sonny's skills as an arranger. Advertisements and newspaper write-ups promised "Sparkling Rhythms!" and "Scintillating Harmonies!" or praised the foursome's "modern," "distinctively-styled" arrangements of popular ballads and folk songs." The Black-owned *Weekly Review* singled out Sonny as "a composer and arranger of no little talent," noting that "when he's not working with the Ripple Rhythm Four, Blount leads his own orchestra." The white *Birmingham News* introduced the group as "one of the finest singing organizations in the South" and added of the group's repertoire, "Their blended harmonies are applied to currently popular ballads and Negro spirituals." The same paper compared the singers favorably to the nationally popular Ink Spots, famous for their smooth, gentle harmonies.[5]

A 1940 item in the *Weekly Review* hints, again, at the possibility of an early Sonny Blount recording—if not a commercial release, then perhaps a kind of demo taken from one of the group's broadcasts. "They're so good," the *Review* reported of the four, "that an advertiser in New York"—presumably Ripple Tobacco—"heard one of their recordings and said: 'I must have them to advertise my product in Birmingham!'" Certainly, the act, like Sonny's other projects, distinguished itself from the competition. A later headline in the *Weekly Review* succinctly defined the singers' appeal: "They Do Jive Differently."[6]

"I never thought I would be a musician," recalled pianist and trumpeter Walter Miller. "It just happened that I used to hear the sounds far away; maybe a couple of blocks away." Miller, about thirteen years old, traced those sounds to the home of a classmate, saxophonist Huntington "Big Joe" Alexander. Big Joe already belonged to Sonny Blount's band, and Miller soon followed, launching a lifelong friendship with the bandleader. He went on to play with Lionel Hampton and spent years working for Ray Charles, but he always came back to Sonny and his band; a disciple for life and a direct link to Sun Ra's early years in Birmingham, he was the only musician whose collaboration with Sun Ra spanned half a century and all eras of the bandleader's career.[7]

"Sun Ra's always been out there," Miller said. "He's been speakin' about outer space ever since I met him, from a kid out of grade school." And it was not only space: "Sun Ra was the guy that always talked about electricity. Constantly, he told the musicians that there would come a time when all the musicians would be involved with electricity. They would have electric instruments. And this was in the *forties*"—years before such predictions came true.[8]

Sonny himself would be a pioneer in electrified music, which he introduced into Birmingham's most elite social spheres. "Tonight at eleven o'clock," the *Birmingham World* reported on January 3, 1941, "members of Birmingham's 'gilt-edge' social set will be converging at the Elks Rest where the Esquire Club, popular young men's organization, will be host at their annual dance. Music for the occasion will be furnished by the popular Society Troubadours' Orchestra [with] vocal sallies by lovely Dolly Brown. Sonny Blount, pianist with the aggregation[,] will introduce his new instrumental solo rage which has captured the fancy of dance-goers hearing the novelty in private dance sessions." On the same newspaper page, the "Society Slants" column dropped the same mysterious bait: "The orchestra has planned to introduce a new instrumental treat and you had better be on hand for . . . this 'gyration special.'"[9]

Sonny had first unveiled the new contraption at a Christmas night dance with the Rhythm Four; no one in Birmingham had seen or heard anything like it. As bandmate Frank Adams recalled, Sonny was always drawn to new technologies: transistor radios (with which he picked up the most modern sounds from New York), wire recorders (which he set up on the Masonic Temple stage when an act like Duke Ellington's came to town), and now this strange instrumental device, which he made a centerpiece of all his musical endeavors. Introduced by the Hammond Organ Company in 1939, the Solovox was a small amplified keyboard that could be attached to any piano to create moody, electronic vibes. Sonny adopted it immediately and by the end of 1940 was already producing with it electric sounds that would not enter the mainstream—of jazz, gospel, or any other genre—for another couple of decades. Fittingly, the eerie, unearthly hum of the thing anticipated also the sci-fi soundtracks of countless late-night flying-saucer movies, another trend well into the future.

The Solovox became a central feature of Sonny's act. "Tonight, 9 till 1, Sunset Casino will be jumping," the *Atlanta Daily World* predicted in the summer of 1941,

> as Sonny Blount and his famous swing band from Birmingham, Alabama, "sells jive" for Atlanta gay nightlifers and jitterbugs de luxe.

The famous Hammond organ will be worked overtime as Sonny, widely heralded for his lofty rank as an artist on the "solo-vax" [sic], will be a singular treat for the guests.[10]

A few months later, Sonny played the opening of Club Congo, a new venue on the Bessemer highway, and for the next year his "Solo Vox Band" led the floor show each Saturday and Sunday night. Club Congo offered entertainments more adventurous than dances with the Masons or Elks: here, Sonny's band was the central feature in a twice-weekly "Variety Show of Live Wire Entertainment," events whose casts also included "Ace Comedian" Jazzbo Williams, an "Exotic Shake Dancer" named Madame Sonja, and Chick, the "Prince of the Rug Cutters." The shows mimicked the glamorous, sometimes wild revues of venues like Chicago's Club DeLisa; they also offered Sonny a broader, freer canvas on which to develop his act. At the Congo, musicians provided more than backdrop to elite dances; they presented a full-blown spectacle, full of costumes and humor, synthesized Solovox vibes, and wide-open swing. In the pages of the *Weekly Review*, J. B. Sims—former Bama State Collegian and now Birmingham's most irrepressible social columnist—repeatedly extolled Sonny and his Solovox as the hottest act in town.[11]

For Sonny, nights at the Congo foreshadowed musical adventures to come. But all the while, and for all his band's acclaim, Sonny's sense of otherness and isolation only continued to grow. He may have won fans and attracted a core of musician-followers, but there was no one to whom he felt truly close. "Sonny was just one of those guys," said Wilson Driver, "who had a way about him—kept his own counsel." Part of his difference was physical: he suffered from a testicular hernia, which brought him tremendous periods of pain, left him uninterested in sex, and underscored for him a private sense of deformity. Increasingly, he found it difficult, even impossible, to relate to humanity—and as humanity edged toward another world war, sweeping him up in its storm, he suffered a trauma that would only alienate him further.[12]

Sonny's bandmates began leaving for the service as soon as the war broke out. Trumpeter Richard Johnson became a featured soloist in Snooky Davenport's Fort Benning Air Force Band; Richard Cannon, a member of the Rhythm Four, was also at Fort Benning, singing in its Reception Center Chorus. Sonny had no interest in working for the war, either on the battlefield or on the bandstand; he could not comprehend what he perceived as man's desire to destroy his fellow man, and he took interest in the work of the Southern Negro Youth Congress, a Birmingham-based civil rights organization whose leaders condemned the war, advocated nonviolence, and demanded, instead of another global conflict, a national commitment to racial justice at home. In October 1942, Sonny applied for and was granted classification as a conscientious objector. Assigned to nonmilitary service in a Civilian Public Service camp, he sought deferment on the basis of the physical condition that racked his body.[13]

In *Space Is the Place: The Lives and Times of Sun Ra*, biographer John Szwed first revealed the details of what for Sonny would be a traumatic, life-changing experience. Writing to the National Service Board for Religious Objectors, Sonny explained that his "whole left side from head to foot is burning and aching," noting that doctors had been unable to explain or treat his condition. "I don't see," he wrote, "how the government or anyone else could expect me to agree to being judged by the standards of a normal person." Sonny's heightened sense of difference, he wrote, drove him further into music as his only solace: "Music to me is the only worthwhile thing in the world, and I think of it as a full compensation for any handicaps I have." His letter emphasized his distance from and suspicion of the "normal" world and stressed, by contrast, the alternate universe granted him through music. "I am sure no one could begrudge me this one happiness. . . . Of a truth it is all I have in the world, being motherless, fatherless and friendless, too, for that matter. Unfortunately, I have learned not to trust people. I am a little afraid of normal people. Their greatest desire in life seems to be to maim and destroy either themselves or others."[14]

Sonny appealed next to the local draft board but was rejected outright by its all-white panel, whose members refused to even hear him make his case. When he failed to report to the CPS camp, he was arrested. "Negro Orchestra Leader Held under Draft Laws," the headline read in the *Birmingham News*: "Charged with failure to report for entrainment for a work camp at Kane, Pa., . . . Herman Poole Blount, 2508 Fourth Avenue, North, a Negro orchestra leader, was held for the Grand Jury." Sonny's bond was set at $1,000, and he was locked in a Jasper, Alabama, jail cell, forty miles northeast of Birmingham.[15]

His treatment, he knew, had everything to do with the color of his skin, was predetermined by the systematic oppression that defined his society. From the Jasper jail, he wrote again to the National Service Board, hoping to find a sympathetic ear. "Unfortunately, I am not living in a part of the U.S.," he explained, "but more a section which seems a member of the Axis and which is determined that no Negro will ever receive justice." He noted the flippant dismissal of the Birmingham draft board and observed that "there can never be any fairness" in any such organization "unless one Negro is involved in the deciding." Linking the ways of southern prejudice to the evils of the enemy overseas (the draft board "smacks of Hitlerism," he wrote), Sonny echoed the complaints of countless Black Americans: How could America fight fascism abroad while its own culture of oppression continued to thrive unchecked? Meanwhile, he was sinking into a profound despair, robbed of his music and reputation. He considered suicide but ultimately rejected "murder in any form" and resisted. "I dread tonight," his letter concluded, "and the days are so lonely, being musicless."[16]

After more than a month in jail, Sonny was put on a train to the Pennsylvania CPS camp, where he continued to argue he was unfit for work—but where he could at least enjoy the company of like-minded individuals, Black and white, discussing matters of morality, war, and nonviolence. He underwent psychiatric evaluation and was deemed both "a well-educated colored intellectual" and "a psychopathic personality": a diagnosis that paralleled the army's damning assessment of Lester Young and reflected, more than Sonny's own mental condition, the psychopathy of the society that judged him, a society in which Black intellectuals were considered by definition aberrations and dangerous. He was taken off work duty and allowed to focus exclusively on his music, providing entertainment for the other men in the camp. Finally, after nearly two months, he was discharged for his disability and returned to Birmingham. As Szwed explains in his biography, Sonny came home "changed," full of a rage his fellow musicians had never seen in him. He plunged himself back into music, filling his days and nights—compulsively, sleeplessly—with the only relief this world had afforded him.[17]

Frank Adams was a teenager when he joined the Sonny Blount band, not long after Sonny's return from the camp. Adams knew Sonny had a reputation as an eccentric—sometimes he walked around town, people said, in strange robes and sandals—but he was respected, too, as an innovative and exciting bandleader. Adams had been recruited to the band by upperclassmen Walter Miller and Big Joe Alexander, who were already making music unlike anyone else in the high school. Fess Whatley was one thing, Adams said, but, "man, Sun Ra: that was jazz."[18]

Sonny's players expressed in their music a sense of their own individualism and an openness to exploratory improvisation, qualities foreign to a band like Whatley's, with its rigid commitment to the score. Now Adams belonged, at once, to both Whatley's and Sonny's bands, and the two environments—and the trainings they offered a budding musician—could not have been more different. First there was the issue of experimentation.

In Whatley's band, "when they finished the music in front of them, that was the end of it. But Sun Ra went into this wild improvisation." Sonny extended tunes for chorus after chorus, and he sent his soloists to the edge of the stage for lengthy improvised excursions, pushing them to find something new to say. Both bandleaders made a byword of "discipline," but Sonny gave the word new meaning. For him, discipline entailed a kind of spiritual as well as technical precision, an all-consuming commitment to the practice and potential of music. Though he was always crafting new arrangements of increasing complexity, he rejected blind devotion to anything so mundane and predictable as the printed score. *His* brand of discipline, he explained, required musicians to tune themselves to something deeper, something higher, to listen for the demands of "the Creator" and for the voices within themselves.[19]

But Sun Ra by no means rejected the musical text. In later years he developed a series of numbered compositions known as "Disciplines," producing more than a hundred in all; Sun Ra's Disciplines required each musician to recreate a prescribed musical phrase over and over at length with unwavering precision, because, the bandleader warned, "the slightest variation would destroy the thing." In Birmingham, even onstage, he might stop a number mid-performance and work it over until the band got it right. At the same time, he encouraged musicians to have fun, to experiment, to stretch themselves and seek new forms of expression. He would put on a record and have his players study the soloist's message ("Listen at it," he would demand, "listen at what he's *saying*"), and he pushed them to find their own unique, inborn, and inevitable modes of communication. "If it's in you," he prophesied to Adams, "it will come out."[20]

Sonny gathered around himself a crew of musicians, most of them several years younger than himself, who were ready to try new things. "It was sort of like a family," Adams said, and Sonny's home—ramshackle but bursting with music and inspiration, its floor stacked with records and cramped with musicians—"was *heaven* when you got in there." In addition to Alexander, Miller, and Adams, the core of the group included alto saxophonists Teddy "'Velt" (for "Roosevelt") Smith and George "Jarhead" Woodruff; Warren Parham and "a player named Warfield" on tenor; trombonist Nathaniel Atkins; vocalist Fletcher "Hootie" Myatt; and bassist and arranger James Swine. Melvin Caswell, a fixture of the Whatley band and Industrial High School's tailoring teacher, played drums, and Whatley's bassist, Iva "Ike" Williams (not to be confused with Ivory "Pops" Williams), sometimes sat in. Another close associate of the group was Dan Michael, the one-armed pianist and (like Caswell and Atkins) former Tennessee State Collegian, now established as director of music at Rosedale Negro High School. Michael was a prolific composer of complex vocal and instrumental arrangements, which he taught to Rosedale students or pitched to local bands. His weekly radio program, *Sunday Down South*, featured his intricate piano renditions of the spirituals and provided "radio experience to outstanding Negro talent," promoting young performers—including vocal groups, jazz bands, and classical soloists—and highlighting the work of contemporary Black composers. With the help of a prosthetic hand, Michael also became well known for his note-perfect rendition of Avery Parrish's "After Hours"; in the late 1940s, he would move to New York to become a member of the Erskine Hawkins Orchestra, filling the seat once held by Parrish himself. Now he hung around the Blount band and churned out fresh arrangements for the group to perform.[21]

Sonny's group was a loose conglomerate of musicians, and he welcomed any player who showed up for a rehearsal or gig. "He wanted to know how you sounded and how *you* sounded," Frank Adams explained. "If two bass players showed up, they were both on the job: he'd have two. Some of the musicians might have complained, because they'd have to split the money more ways," but that did not matter to Sonny. He "wanted to hear what each one of them could do: how it all sounded together." All his life, Sun Ra would brag on those early Birmingham bandmates, their musical dedication, and their culture of discipline. "It was like a select group of musicians," he said, "who all was very nice, who didn't get drunk or use drugs or nothing, who was very interested in the band . . . and they really coordinated together: a true sort of, you might say, brotherhood. It was really a very wonderful band."[22]

"Sonny Blount always had himself a nice bunch of musicians," Wilson Driver said, "but even then his music was a little too far out for most people. . . . So Fess got all the good paying society jobs, and Sonny'd end up playing all these rough joints on the outskirts of town." Looking back, several of Sonny's contemporaries said the same, placing the bandleader outside the mainstream of the city's society dances. Sonny's manager, J. B. Barker, did loudly complain in the summer of 1944 that Whatley had unfairly snatched for himself Sonny's enviable standing Monday night dance gig at the Masonic Temple, bumping Barker's client to the less-popular Tuesday night spot. But Sonny continued, nonetheless, to play his share of "bow-tie jobs," and he remained a Fourth Avenue fixture, even as he expanded his horizons. Dancers at the Masonic enjoyed his new excursions in sound (whatever the night of the week), and in the pages of the *Weekly Review* J. B. Sims continued to praise his band as the best in town, promising dancers that Sonny "[will] 'knock you out' with his Solovox and his very latest instrument, the Celeste": another keyboard invention, similar to a glockenspiel, whose name derived from the angelic sound of its bell-like chimes. The *celestial* connotation no doubt appealed to Sonny.[23]

Even if he remained active on the society scene, Sonny likely felt more at home in other, less restrained venues. Frank Adams recalled how Sonny's band played, weekend after weekend, in the Smithfield Court housing project and at informal gatherings in Birmingham's poorer Black neighborhoods. "Those guys," Adams said of the band, "didn't wear tuxedos; they wore what they could. He didn't tell you certain things to wear, like all the other bands would, and as a consequence, they said he never got those jobs over at Mountain Brook Country Club—because his band would be in their BVDs or whatever. *Somebody* might have a tux on, but the next guy might have his T-shirt on. And Sun Ra wouldn't discuss that. It was all okay."[24]

These were different scenes than the glitzy fraternal dances downtown. "The common man," Adams continued, "they just wanted something to get hot and sweaty, and they didn't pay but about fifteen cents to get in." The musicians were not making much money, either. "We'd go after a gig to 'pick up our dust'—that was a musician's term. Your 'dust' was your little earnings." But the rewards were much deeper, and the environment was electric. "They would play this 'Hootie Blues' that would go fifteen minutes. Teddy Smith would be out there playing, playing, swaying from side to side; the people would be hot and sweaty and *perspiring*, and he'd go on and on and on." More than sixty years later, Adams still lived in Smithfield, still drove past the same housing project on his way to work, and "every time I pass by that place . . . I want to look in there, to see if we're still playing."[25]

Out on the Bessemer highway, Sonny had also resumed the kinds of exuberant floor shows he had played, before the war, at Club Congo. Sonny Blount's New Rhythm Style Band or Masters of Jazz played each weekend at Pratt City's Grand Terrace Café, appearing alongside the shake-dancing Madame Twannie; Lillian Harris, a "Mammy Blues Singer"; the "Fast Stepping Floorshow" of Mess Around Brown; and the sensational Chick, billed before the war as a mere "rug cutter," now reborn as a "famous female impersonator." Admission was fifty cents, and the band took requests. On Sundays, local law prohibited public dances, so dancing began at midnight—officially Monday—after the floor show. At least one visitor complained that there was no place to sit and watch the band, the floor was so crowded with jitterbugs.[26]

Working within existing structures and traditions, Sonny offered some of the city's most popular entertainments, even as he pushed at the norms.

"He always made things interesting," Walter Miller said. "He always knew what music to play of the day, along with his own thing that he was doin'." Sonny's "own thing," even then, was truly, entirely his own. "I used to be with him alone," Miller said, "and he would go into his Solovox, and his celeste. He played celeste *and* his piano [simultaneously], you know. He gets out on these things, and you don't *really* know what he's doin'. But you know it's *somethin'*. You begin to feel it. You listen at it long enough, you know it's somethin' there. But it was so far ahead of my time, and the rest of the people's time, until you could hardly *picture* a man doin' a thing this far ahead of time."[27]

Singer Fletcher Myatt recalled another advantage, made possible by Sonny's technologies. On his wire recorder, Sonny would "catch" broadcasts from the East and West Coasts and then transpose the performances from his recordings. "The next day we would practice all day . . . and play that particular number that night. So that made us ahead of the other bands that were in the city. That's the reason that Sun Ra, as you would call him—Sonny Blount as I would call him—had the best band in the city at that particular time: *modern*, or any *other* thing you want to call it."[28]

In his column for the *Weekly Review*, J. B. Sims did more than praise local bands (which he did, a lot); like other Black journalists all over the country, he chronicled the culture of racial injustice that plagued his community. Sims did not mince words: "We have no fear of what we write here," his column announced, even as he condemned a local police force notorious for its violence. One week he reported that an officer, "without the slightest provocation," unloaded his gun indiscriminately into a Black café, killing an unsuspecting patron (the officer later claimed that someone there had thrown a radio at him, to which Sims responded, "*Pht-t-t-t!*"). "The killing," Sims noted with scorn, "has gone down in the books as JUSTIFIABLE HOMICIDE, perpetrated by an Officer of THE LAW IN PERFORMANCE OF HIS DUTY." And "we've got another one for you yet": the same week, a group of policemen boarded a streetcar, ordered a group of Miles College students to move to the rear, "and in attempting to have the ORDERLY students move back, 'ACCIDENTALLY' hit quiet little Miss MARGARET GWIN over the head with a BLACKJACK twice." Recent research by a Jefferson County coroner has shed light on the historical pattern of fatal shootings of Black citizens by police officers in Birmingham, a long-standing tradition of "justifiable homicide" at the hands of local law enforcement. From 1909 to 1939, records reveal 217 police shooting deaths, with the trend increasing over time; of the 212 where the victim's race was identified, 85 percent were Black. The incidents went largely unreported in the white press, but J. B. Sims reported what every Black person already knew: Black lives in Birmingham were under assault.[29]

In August 1944, the Sonny Blount Orchestra played the grand opening of a new public swimming pool in Tuxedo Park, an event expressly designed to heal some of the city's racial wounds. The pool and its opening were loaded with significance. Just around the corner from the now-famous Junction, Tuxedo Park had boasted, years before, a privately operated pool for Black swimmers, but that facility had long since fallen into disrepair. Every one of the city's public pools, meanwhile, served white Birmingham exclusively.

A petition for a public pool had been started the previous summer by the Southern Negro Youth Congress, the same organization whose anti-war stance had earlier resonated with Sonny. Headquartered in Birmingham since 1939, the congress was an influential civil rights coalition founded to dismantle the culture of lynching, to resist segregation, and to enfranchise southern Black voters. The group united under a common cause a diverse array of the city's Black community: young and old, laborers and white-collar professionals, Communist organizers and more cautious civic leaders. It kept its offices in the Masonic Temple, where it also provided leadership classes, led voting drives, and hosted social events. Fess Whatley had helped fundraise for the organization, and Whatley's orchestra and Sonny Blount's Rhythm Four both played dances sponsored by the congress. The campaign for a pool garnered headlines when Erskine Hawkins himself, in town for a hometown gig, stood onstage, trumpet tucked under his arm, and ceremoniously placed the first signature on the petition.[30]

For local white leaders, the proposed pool presented a visible, tangible, quickly achievable antidote to the city's long-simmering racial tensions, an opportunity for racial diplomacy and good publicity. Even the *Birmingham News* observed the need for a "Negro pool": Black servicemen on leave from Fort McClellan came often, seeking leisure, only to find Alabama's largest city provided them no place to swim. "The situation tends to give the city a bad reputation," the *News* complained. "And it is not just." The City Commission appropriated $3,600 for the project, but the bulk of funds came from wealthy white donors who expressly adopted the pool as "symbol of [a] good race relationship" in Birmingham. Organizers politely rejected contributions from Black donors—including Parker High School, which offered $1,000—insisting the pool was a gift, the symbolism effective, only if the white community shouldered the full financial load.[31]

Most of that load was borne by two prominent philanthropists: businessman Louis Pizitz and industrialist Erskine Ramsay, namesake of Tuxedo

Junction's most famous son. At the pool's opening, Ramsay, a few days shy of his eightieth birthday, described the facility as his "happiest contribution" to the city. Pizitz frankly acknowledged in his own speech that Jimmie Jones, previous president of the City Commission (and thus, essentially, mayor), "was known to hold reservations on all projects of benefit to Negroes." Elected in 1925 with support from the Klan, Jones had held the position until his death in 1940; new leadership, Pizitz suggested, meant a step forward in race relations, and the pool was proof of good things to come.[32]

Both Black and white attendees considered the opening event a success. Two of the city's most prominent Black preachers, Reverend John Goodgame and Bishop Benjamin Garland Shaw, spoke words of invocation; members of the Negro Boy Scouts raised a flag; multiple city government representatives gave (for the most part, self-congratulating) speeches. Since Erskine Hawkins himself was not in town, Sonny Blount was hired to "pinch-hit." When his band "whipped up 'Tuxedo Junction,'" reported the *Weekly Review*, "the hearers went into a frenzy," and the pool was officially open.[33]

Despite this success, some Black observers bristled to see their community's donations refused in the planning; the gesture may have been well-intentioned, but it smacked of a too-familiar paternalism and hinted at bigger problems. The pool was only the start of "planned recreation for Negroes in Birmingham," a parks official proclaimed at the opening, but then he "warned" the crowd, "The way you receive and use this one will determine other appropriations for Negro recreation." In fact, the community's embrace of the pool determined nothing. Eight years later, Reverend Goodgame and A. G. Gaston, the Black millionaire, appealed to the parks department, expressing the need for a second pool. The Tuxedo Park facility, once promoted as the first of many projects to come, remained the only pool for "the more than 100,000 Negroes in Birmingham," and even it was too shallow for divers and lacked adequate restrooms or drinking fountains for the masses who used it. In less than a decade, the pool's role as symbol of racial communion had faded. The *Birmingham News* accused Goodgame and Gaston of "trying to stir up trouble." In 1961, when a court order required the integration of all public parks and pools, Eugene "Bull" Connor, the city's commissioner of public safety, insisted that Black and white would swim separately, or else they would not swim at all.[34]

He ordered the Tuxedo Park pool filled with concrete.

Sonny Blount was long gone from Birmingham by the time Bull Connor's concrete filled the pool. He was well-enough acquainted, as it was, with the city's racism. By the time he left, he had clashed several times with local white authorities, from the draft board to shopkeepers to the city's aggressive police force. Gentle by nature, Sonny seemed genuinely hurt and confused by the altercations. Walter Miller recalled Sonny's distress after an officer repeatedly blocked his path as he walked home one night ("What have I done to you?" Sonny pleaded, bewildered). Even before he joined Sonny's band, Frank Adams had absorbed the tales of police harassing Sonny for walking the streets in his unusual robes. According to one story, the police threatened to place him under arrest or strike him with a billy club, but Sonny softly announced they would be paralyzed if they tried because, he whispered, *"I'm from Mars."* The story may (or may not) have been apocryphal, but it reflected either way the mythology that trailed Sonny early on, and it captured Sonny's very real opposition to the society and authorities that surrounded him. "This was flower power before flower power was ever thought about," Adams said, linking Sonny to later countercultural and nonviolent traditions. "This was Dr. King before Dr. King."[35]

Local newspapers revealed further confrontations with white authority. J. B. Sims reported in the *Weekly Review* that Sonny had been kicked out of a Fourth Avenue shop—located in the heart of the Black business district but run by a white man—after voicing a "mild protest" that a hat he had taken there to be cleaned had come back damaged. ("Knowing Sonny," Sims pointed out, "'MILD' is the word for his protest. Sonny always conducts himself in a gentlemanly manner.") A few months after he played the pool opening, Sonny filed a formal complaint against Tom Briskey, the parks department's supervisor of Negro recreation, one of the very officials singled out as a cause of the pool's success. According to an item in the *Atlanta Daily World*, Sonny accused Briskey of using "unpleasant methods in halting a dance which Blount's orchestra was playing at Smithfield Court." Though the specific details were not recorded, Birmingham authorities were known for using excessive force in "keeping the peace" in the Black community—and Sonny, despite that well-known mildness of manner, did not mind speaking out against injustice, even if his protests came to nothing. A month after he issued his complaint, the city banned outright *all* dances at the Smithfield projects' auditorium.[36]

Sonny was mystified by the cruelty and illogic of racial prejudice. "They are my brothers," he told his dubious bandmates when conversation turned to the ways of Birmingham's white folks. "They are my brothers," he repeated, "but some of them don't know it yet."[37]

Since at least 1935, Sonny's bands had been entertaining Birmingham's white community, both in their local radio broadcasts (sometimes advertised in the pages of the *Birmingham News*) and in the ballrooms and dance pavilions of the Highland Park Country Club, the Hollywood Club, Queenstown Lake, and other elite spots. In the 1930s and '40s, some venues, both white and Black, began to flip their segregated seating arrangements for special one-night events, much as the Frolic Theater had earlier attempted in its short-lived series of "Midnight Reviews." Twice in 1945 the Masonic Temple held dances for white visitors, advertising in the *Birmingham News* the "New Swing Sensation: Sonny Blount and His Orchestra." In March, a "Nine o'Clock Barn Dance" and "All-Star Jitterbug Special" promised to be "the most exciting event of the season" and advised dancers to "come early, be patriotic, [and] obey the curfew": a nationwide mandate, briefly imposed during the war, which shut down all nightlife at midnight. By late September, the war was over, the curfew was lifted, and white readers of the *News* were invited back for a "Victory Jubilee Dance," again featuring Sonny and his band. Given Sonny's own experiences—with the war and with Birmingham's racial realities—one can only wonder what he thought, playing patriotic dances for the city's white community.[38]

He was conceiving, anyway, a music that transcended nationality and race, that considered war immoral and rendered it irrelevant. Sonny had no use for earthly conflict, whether between the world's powers, between Black and white, or between his own bandmates. "If you get to fussing and fighting, that's okay," he told his musicians; he would simply get on his spaceship and leave.[39]

In the meantime, instead, he got on a train. At the start of 1946, Sonny Blount left Birmingham for Chicago, intent on creating a new future, and a new past.

There were worlds within him, waiting to come out.

SWING ON TRIAL

As Sonny Blount worked his way to Chicago, the state of jazz was in flux nationwide. The war years had wrought major changes in the culture of the music, and the old titans of swing struggled to find their place. Bebop had made the big bands seem hopelessly square, and the smaller clubs—places like Minton's and the dimly lit, low-ceilinged basement venues on Manhattan's Fifty-Second Street—had helped drain the life from the sprawling ballrooms of the 1930s. Bebop was not the only threat to swing: high-energy combos like Louis Jordan and His Tympany Five proved that a small unit could move crowds at least as much as the larger (and more expensive) aggregations. In Birmingham, Fess Whatley railed that these changes were dismantling the music profession: "bobtail bands" like Jordan's—small combos "with their tails cut off," Fess said with scorn—were putting his musicians out of work. Rhythm and blues was replacing jazz altogether as a form of popular music, and by the rock and roll explosion of the 1950s, tuxedoed bands of more than a dozen pieces seemed decidedly dated. Many of Birmingham's best musicians, deeply rooted in the swing tradition, would be forced to recalibrate if they hoped to survive.[1]

A few found a home in the exuberant, small-combo R&B sound that prefigured the rise of rock and roll. The late 1940s brought a new breed of outrageous tenor sax "honkers," "wailers," and "screamers," ecstatic and blustery soloists who leaped with their horns from the stage, strutted up and down bar counters, and generally whipped their crowds to a frenzy. Big Joe Alexander of the Sonny Blount Orchestra moved from Birmingham to Detroit and then to Cleveland, where his ferocious tenor became a fixture on the local scene; his combo played nightly at Rip's Shangri La, a club whose owner posted a standing $500 reward for any challenger who could "outblow" Joe (none ever did).

With his own well-established powerhouse tenor, Paul Bascomb was a natural fit for the new era of screamers. He had long been the most restless of the Hawkins men, a star soloist (and, initially, the band's leader) unsatisfied with his supporting role. Before the war was over, he persuaded his brother Dud to join him in co-headlining their own bands, developing both a full dance orchestra and a smaller combo. (Dud was reluctant but agreed: the Erskine Hawkins Orchestra was like family, but Paul *was* family, and blood won out.) They got some good gigs and cut a handful of records but by the end of the decade went their separate ways. Paul worked a stint in Count Basie's band and Dud briefly joined Duke Ellington's orchestra, but he missed the easy camaraderie of the Hawkins band. ("I just didn't feel like fighting over [solos]," Dud said. "It wasn't a band like Erskine's, where a guy would turn round and say, 'No, man, I think you ought to have this solo.' In Duke's band, every man was fighting for himself.") By the close of the 1940s, both brothers were leading combos of their own. Paul settled in Chicago, becoming a familiar presence in that city's nightclub scene. Though he failed to score any hits, singles like "More Blues—More Beat" and "Pink Cadillac" demonstrated his ability to adapt with the times; several years before the genre had a name, his 1948 single "Rock and Roll" clearly articulated the sound and spirit of the new music to come.[2]

The Hawkins orchestra held on through the changing times with more success than most big bands. In 1945, the group scored a number one R&B hit with "Tippin' In," a riff on Ellington's "Don't Get Around Much Anymore," arranged by relative newcomer Bobby Smith; the addition of Birmingham's Laura Washington provided an additional boost the next year. Erskine did his best to keep the act fresh. In 1948, he publicly urged other bands to follow his lead in exploring "new forms of entertainment." "The public wants more than just dance music for their money," he explained. "There is no novelty and the public is currently hungry for novelties in music." Rather than break down his band, he broke convention by *expanding* the act into the Erskine Hawkins Dance Carnival, a variety show that presented driving swing for dancing, an intimate set by a stripped-down version of the band, a "squad of scintillating vocalists," and—in case all those other enticements fell short—free electronic prizes. The carnival played 110 towns in 120 nights, breaking attendance records in otherwise flagging venues and grossing almost half a million dollars—a formidable achievement in swing's heyday and, papers cheered, "a box-office miracle" in the current slump. Hawkins's embrace of novelty, though, went only so far: he was not about to give up his beloved big band sound. A few months after the carnival tour, he defended swing in a staged "trial" at the Apollo Theater. "The Twentieth Century Gabriel will act as the Clarence Darrow of Swing," the *Chicago Defender* reported, "present[ing] his case" in a "medley of fast-paced" hits. "On the basis of that medley of melodies audiences can judge whether the Hawk's favorite music style is here to stay or just another fad of yesteryear which will have to give way to bop." Hawkins admitted he had been nervous to see, in the first show's front row, "dozens of teenagers dressed in be-bop outfits right up to the berets and drooping bow ties"; but the crowd loudly approved his musical "defense," and the press reported that "a delegation of be-bop costumed youngsters" even came backstage, seeking his autograph.[3]

Even as similar groups called it quits, the band kept working through the 1950s. The jumps became longer—"You'd have to ride 500 to 1,000 miles now to get to your next engagement"—as favorite venues closed up across the country. Even Harlem could not keep it going forever: the Savoy Ballroom was razed in 1958 to make room for a housing project. Two years later, Hawkins shaved his band down to a combo. The most loyal of the old members, Haywood Henry and Sammy Lowe, turned to freelance gigs in New York; of the original Bama State crew, only bassist Leemie Stanfield remained.[4]

Sammy Lowe was stoic about the changes. The public's embrace of smaller bands like Louis Jordan's made sense, he admitted: "their music was simpler, more basic" than either the heavily arranged big band sound or the more esoteric, intellectual bebop. "The big bands had gotten bigger and bigger—we had five trumpets, four trombones, six saxophones, and four rhythm—and the arrangers were having a ball"; but, he confessed, "it was all getting too complicated. I'm glad some of the things I wrote then didn't get on records, because they were just over-arranged. I think it was a time for a change, anyway. It couldn't go on forever." Of all the old Hawkins crew, Lowe was most adept at reinventing his career, and in the 1950s he emerged as a sought-after arranger and music director for a host of popular acts. In the rock and soul era, Lowe distinguished himself on multiple counts: he could write a good arrangement, assemble and direct a top-notch band, and—unlike other jazz players, who wanted it known they found the new music beneath them—could be trusted not to (very literally) laugh in the faces of talent he was hired to support. In 1956, his ability to keep a straight face got him a job arranging for the Platters; their first record with Lowe, "My Prayer," hit number one on the pop charts, number two on the R&B charts, "sold over three million records," and kept on selling for decades.

Suddenly Lowe was in constant demand. In 1959, he hung up his trumpet to focus exclusively on work behind the scenes, arranging and conducting for Sam Cooke, Nina Simone, James Brown, and others. He had another number one hit in 1961, conducting the Tokens' "The Lion Sleeps Tonight"; in 1966, he arranged Brown's "It's a Man's, Man's, Man's World," which also went to the top of the charts.[5]

Lowe frequently brought his old friends to the recording studio; Dud Bascomb, Haywood Henry, and Birmingham trumpeter Johnny Grimes appeared together often in the James Brown band. Session work paid musicians' bills, but the rewards had their limits. Haywood's versatility assured him plenty of gigs: he was a master (and "monster") on any woodwind and could slide into all sorts of musical contexts, performing in the pits of Broadway shows, backing soul stars, touring Europe with aging swing heroes, and plugging into a revival of interest in New Orleans Dixieland. The work, though, left him unfulfilled. In the swing days, the best sidemen could stake out their own spaces in the spotlight, but in the studio or pit they became invisible, interchangeable, and anonymous. "You do the work, but you don't get the credit," he complained. "Even your relatives don't know you're on the record. You tell them you worked with James Brown or Frank Sinatra, and they look at you kind of funny and say, 'Well, what were you doing? Where? I can't hear you.'"[6]

By the 1960s, Dud Bascomb said, "everything was very confused. . . . Half the people wanted jazz and half wanted rock 'n' roll. When we played jazz, the agency [Bascomb's management, Universal Attractions] would get a bad report, so we had to turn around and play rock 'n' roll. A lot of kids would walk in, say, 'Oh, man, they're playing jazz,' and walk out." Dud's band did its best to accommodate the day's competing tastes, but each gig was a high-wire act, and venue owners could be unforgiving if the band misstepped. One New Jersey club hired Bascomb's quintet on the condition they stick to rock and roll. ("The owner of the joint said jazz brought in beer drinkers, and he wanted whiskey drinkers.") At one point in the night Dud stepped offstage to make a phone call, and his stomach sank as he heard the band slip into an old ballad from the 1930s. "That did it," he said: the owner told the band not to come back.[7]

Even Sammy, for all his success, took his paychecks where he could: a job, in the end, was a job. By the mid-1970s he found himself scoring "a porno picture" called *Patty*, an X-rated retelling of the Patty Hearst story. "I wrote two or three serious things" for the movie, he said, "and one of them was very good," but he found his efforts wasted. "It was supposed to be a love scene and I had beautiful music, but what they were doing wasn't so lovely."[8]

Erskine himself had no intention of playing someone else's music. Years before, the band had agreed, against his own protests, to put his name out front; now that name gave him a clout the others lacked, even if only as throwback for a certain nostalgic set. Since his midteens he had lived in perpetual motion, on the road for a long stretch of each year. Finally, though, "it was getting too much": the road was "a young man's business," and he was no longer young. A weeklong engagement in 1967 at a Borscht Belt resort became a more than twenty-year residence. "It's prolonged my life," he later said of the job. The music did not change, it only got smaller, stripped to a handful of players, and the Concord Hotel lounge became a cozy time capsule. "I didn't change my style of playing," he was proud to say. "I didn't like to go like bebop or rhythm-and-blues. . . . I don't got nothing against what young people are doing, but I figured: Why should I change my style to theirs?" And "why should we try to take theirs away from them?"⁹

Hawkins and his old bandmates still considered themselves a family, albeit now a scattered one, and in 1971 they reconvened for an album, *Erskine Hawkins and His Orchestra Reunion! Live at Club Soul Sound*. The record was nostalgic by design—its back cover included a sepia photo of a much younger band in its prime, and the liner notes paid tribute to those members who had died—but the music was fresh, warm, and fun. A small audience of wives, friends, and relatives cheered on the band between songs; Jimmy Mitchell crooned an old standby; and a new generation of players joined their fathers in the lineup, bringing a refreshing groove to familiar tunes and suggesting an unbroken stream of tradition. The notes provided brief bios of the new additions: Wilbur "Dud" Bascomb Jr., whose electric bass line fueled an extended, surprisingly funky "Tuxedo Junction," had recently graduated from NYU and "has already become busy on the recording scene." Sammy Lowe Jr., providing electric keys, would "study music at Wesleyan University in Connecticut this fall."¹⁰

Jo Jones continued to have moments of greatness, even off the bandstand. Witnesses credited him for sparking Duke Ellington's explosive 1956 "comeback" at the Newport Jazz Festival, a moment that returned Ellington and his band to the spotlight after years of creeping obsolescence. Jones had performed earlier the same night and now stood offstage, "shouting encouragement," in the words of manager George Avakian, "and swatting the edge of the stage" with "a rolled-up copy of the *Christian Science Monitor*." Jones did not need a single tom, cymbal, or stick to transform the scene: "The saxes began hollering back at Jo, then the rest of the band joined in, and by the time [tenor saxophonist Paul] Gonsalves had sprung the dancers loose it seemed that bassist Jimmy Woods and drummer Sam Woodyard were playing to Jo as much as to anyone else." Ellington himself considered Jones "the driving force behind our big success at Newport," declaring him

> the man with a blueprint for a bouncing, boiling bash, the man
> in the pit with the git-with-it git. Out of sight of the audience,
> in the pit in front of the grandstand, slapping a back beat with a
> newspaper, talking to us, he prodded us into a *Go, Baby!* drive that
> developed into the rhythmic groove of the century. . . . I don't know
> what would have happened if Jo Jones had taken over at the drums,
> but what he did, when he did it, and where he was doing it, must
> have been the most fitting position for him when that night caught
> fire.
>
> If we had had Count Basie at the piano, and Freddie Green on
> guitar . . . well, I don't know, maybe we would have scorched the
> moon.[11]

Maybe so, but Basie and Green were *not* onstage that night, and neither even was Jones: the audience was oblivious to the role he played from the sidelines. Musicians knew Jones was still capable of this transformative, driving energy, that he still knew how to elevate every instrumentalist around him. With the most limited of resources (even a battered *Christian Science Monitor*) he could still communicate volumes, still outplay anyone. But the spotlight, he knew, had abandoned him, and he stewed in bitterness. More and more, "Papa Jo" railed that his contributions went unrewarded while the younger drummers he had inspired got the best gigs and biggest accolades. "My father always tried to get him to calm down," Sonia Sanchez said, recalling the drummer's frequent visits to Wilson Driver's Lenox Avenue apartment, "but he didn't want to calm down—he felt like that was such an outrage against him as this great genius, really, and he thought that he wasn't appreciated at all." But, Sanchez wrote in one poem to Jones,

> we still hear yo fierce tides
> yo midnight caravans singing tongues into morning,

and she assured him:

> you been ahead so long
> can't many of us even now
> follow the scent you done left behind.[12]

The shift toward smaller acts on more intimate stages affected more than just the big bands. The stage spectacles that had launched Ethel Harper's career—shows like *Connie's Hot Chocolates*, *Harlem Cavalcade*, and *The Hot Mikado*—also dried up after the war. After the breakup of the Ginger Snaps, the singer opted for a lifestyle more stable, if less glamorous, taking a job as a waitress at a Fifty-Second Street restaurant. When her employer purchased the stately Outpost Inn in Ridgefield, Connecticut—"a fabulous spot . . . with sleeping facilities and a beautiful cocktail lounge"—Harper worked there, too; some nights, after wrapping up her waitressing, she would slip into one of the old gowns and sing for the guests. On a good weekend, between waiting tables and singing, she banked a hundred dollars. For a performer with ambition, it may have seemed a real comedown, but the work brought a sense of freedom and financial security Harper had never known. Since leaving Birmingham she had never lived alone or even maintained a steady address; now she rented her own apartment, on the corner of Fifty-Second and Broadway, setting up a comfortable home and hosting memorable musical parties. She also hired a vocal coach to keep herself in shape—just in case another shot at the spotlight did come her way.[13]

Nearly a decade passed before it did. Then, in the spring of 1955, a chance encounter with a producer landed her a starring role in *The Negro Follies*, a throwback to the ensemble shows of her early career. For six months, Harper toured Italy, reveling in the sights, the spotlight, and the bravas of the crowds—but finding herself at the mercy of unscrupulous, unreliable management. After months of shortchanged salaries and flimsy excuses, the cast disbanded, mid-tour. Harper picked up some gigs at a ritzy Palermo hotel but soon returned, disheartened, to New York. She was unsure where to turn when an unlikely solution presented itself.[14]

She would become the next Aunt Jemima.

For decades, the Quaker Oats Company had hired Black women to play the part of its pancake mix mascot. In 1893 Nancy Green, a former slave, debuted in the role at the Chicago World's Fair. Green and her successors traveled the country, making and selling pancakes, singing spirituals and pop tunes, giving presentations to children and housewives. They dressed in the mythic garb of the plantation mammy—red-and-white-checked hoopskirt, apron, and head rag—and announced their arrival, wherever they went, with Jemima's trademark catchphrase: "I's in town, honey!"[15]

Harper had been back in the States for just two days when she ran into Edith Wilson, a friend and mentor from the *Hot Chocolates* days. Wilson was a seasoned jazz and blues singer, vaudeville actress, recording artist, and radio star; she had cut her first records as early as 1921, had performed in Europe and on Broadway, and had appeared in television and film. Since 1948 she had been playing her last and longest-running role, as Quaker's most successful Jemima. When she bumped into Harper, fresh from her overseas disappointments and back on the beat for a job, Wilson was on her way to a pancake promotion in Connecticut and invited Harper along. The women had remained friends since the 1930s, and Wilson had more than once over the years urged Harper to consider the gig. Harper had always dismissed the pitch out of hand; but now, Harper wrote, "I was out of a job. This time I listened with an interested ear." Wilson outlined Jemima's duties for Harper, bought her some clothes, and introduced her to the Quaker management. Harper took the job.[16]

Certainly, she had her misgivings, beginning with the costume. Harper prided herself on a wardrobe that was stylish, expensive, and dignified. Jemima's image dripped with minstrel-show clichés, subservient poses, and romanticized Old South nostalgia. Civil rights groups blasted the character for the stereotypes it helped reinforce in the popular imagination; for decades already, critics had complained that Jemima was demeaning, degrading, and fundamentally unredeemable. With a new and urgent civil rights movement taking shape around the country—Black citizens in Montgomery would undertake their landmark bus boycott just as Harper set out on her first Jemima tour—those long-standing complaints were becoming louder and more widespread. In 1955's *Notes of a Native Son* James Baldwin announced a new era, proclaiming that "Aunt Jemima and Uncle Tom are dead"; but that very year Ethel Harper stepped for the first time into the hoopskirt and head rag, breathing her own life into the myth.[17]

It would take intellectual and emotional preparation, she reflected, "to give this job the necessary dignity and interpretation of which I first could be proud—and, hopefully—those members of my race who had qualms about anyone who played this character could also be proud." Like the other living Jemimas, Harper did see in the mascot potential for redemption; the role even offered a chance to subvert its own stereotypes, to sneak into the white world—through, of all things, the Jemima disguise—a positive new image of Black Americans. Indeed, it is impossible to imagine Harper, a strong-willed woman of regal bearing, playing the inarticulate, subservient stereotype. The "new" Jemima, as developed by both Wilson and Harper, scrapped the old dialect for the polished speech of a schoolteacher, and Harper strove to bring touches of glamour to the role, moving into a room or across a stage like a movie star. Her reconciliation to the act may have required some rationalization and mental acrobatics, but Harper came sincerely to find value and meaning in the work. The Jemimas, she

Two Ethel Harpers: in a 1937 publicity photo and as Aunt Jemima, 1950s. From the collections of the North Jersey History and Genealogy Center, the Morristown and Morris Township Library.

later maintained, did valuable work: they addressed service organizations and civic clubs and raised many thousands of charity dollars. Since leaving Birmingham, she had yearned for the classroom and a direct engagement with children; as Jemima, she felt a step closer to that old calling.[18]

For three years, Harper appeared on radio and television, at county fairs and in parades. She worked with the Lions, Kiwanis, and Rotary Clubs; spoke to schoolchildren about nutrition and manners; performed in homes for the elderly and for the developmentally disabled; and served on judges' panels in all manner of competitions. Everywhere she went, she sang, sometimes performing duets with a white actor who appeared as another grocery aisle icon, the Quaker Oats man. For illustrators who depicted Aunt Jemima on boxes of pancake mix and in advertisements, Harper served as model. To children—who had heard her voice on the radio and seen her face on their breakfast tables—Harper, or at least Harper's Jemima, was a celebrity. They wrote her letters, and she took pride in writing each child back by hand, including a glossy photo that she signed with her character's name.[19]

Harper also appeared a few times a year at large-scale, multiday promotional events, kicking off with a "Pancake Day" in which "Aunt Jemima would reign supreme." Her appearances were hyped in advance, her entrances dramatic affairs. Locals took part, before each event, in a contest to guess her precise mode of arrival: she might come in a helicopter or riding a fire engine; she might arrive by seaplane, train, or motor scooter. "The weirdest of all was being sealed in a cardboard box and carted by American Express," Harper recalled. "After arrival, there was a huge parade during which Aunt Jemima was welcomed by the Mayor and presented with the key to the city."[20]

One wonders how Harper maintained "the necessary dignity" while shipped in a box, in a head rag and apron; and all those city keys, it must be noted, were handed not to Ethel Harper herself but to the myth she embodied. But Harper never apologized for the role, which she kept until Quaker retired the living mascots altogether. Soon she would become a prominent community worker for civil rights and a passionate promoter of Black history in the schools. In her memoir, she took pains to defend her Jemima work, but in private she confessed to friends that she had taken the job out of "grim necessity," her best bet for financial survival when she knew no other place to turn. Despite her reservations, Harper had thrown herself into what she considered worthwhile service work, and her Jemima years marked her transition from the entertainment field to a career of devoted community service. In her life's final act she grew into a tireless and respected civic leader—no longer in the guise of Jemima but as the formidable Ethel Ernestine Harper herself, a "liberated Black woman," as one friend described her.[21]

Ethel Harper was far from finished.

Sonny Blount, in the meantime, was pursuing his own vision of Black liberation—and his own Black mythology—with an evolving musical philosophy at its center. As the heroes of the swing era struggled to stay relevant, Sun Ra became unlikely keeper of the big band flame: while other bandleaders were breaking down their units, he built and expanded his own community of players to create a music that honored the big band tradition while pushing it into uncharted territory.

Upon arriving in Chicago, Sonny immersed himself in the music scene. He played in the Fletcher Henderson Orchestra, writing arrangements and rehearsing the band for one of his longtime heroes, a bandleader now past his prime but one of the first undisputed architects of swing and an artist Sonny still viewed not as a man but an angel, altogether another order of being. He became a fixture at the Club DeLisa, crafting arrangements for all the major acts and absorbing all the theatrics—the costumes, dancing, and comedy—of the shows. He organized, wrote for, and produced records by jump blues combos, swing orchestras, and vocal harmony groups. And he developed his own orchestra, the Arkestra, which for the rest of his life would become the primary canvas for his ideas. As other scholars have noted, the band's name reflected Sonny's interest in both mythology and wordplay: the group doubled as an *ark*, offering (like Noah's) means of deliverance from a dying world, and the word's symmetry ("Arkestra" begins and ends with mirror images of "Ra") added further to its significance. But the band's name was also a play on Sonny's southern roots. In Alabama, most musicians Sonny knew pronounced "orchestra" *arkestra* anyway: regardless of spelling, in the mouths of Sonny's contemporaries, the last word in the Erskine Hawkins Orchestra, Fess Whatley's Vibra-Cathedral Orchestra, or Sun Ra's Astro-Infinity Arkestra always sounded the same.[22]

Sonny immersed himself, too, into reading and research, exploring a world of biblical prophecies, occult philosophies, ancient mythologies, and arcane texts. These interests had begun back in Birmingham, where he had processed the teachings of the church alongside the mysticism and rituals of the fraternal orders and had mined the Booker T. Washington Library, in the basement of the Masonic Temple, for its invaluable volumes on Black history. In Chicago he met a fellow seeker, Alton Abraham, who became his collaborator, business partner, and patron. Together they founded a loose collective of outsider-intellectuals devoted to the exploration of history's forgotten wells of knowledge. They championed, in the words of biographer Paul Youngquist, a "countercultural spirituality" that could offer a transcendent, alternative reality for Black people worldwide. Much of Sonny's inspiration came from ancient Egypt, whose history and mythology provided uniquely Black alternatives to American culture, Christian tradition, and Western philosophy. In Chicago's Washington Square, Sonny declaimed his evolving ideas on race, religion, history, and art and distributed typewritten broadsheets full of emphatic capitalization and sensational, oracular headings: "MESSAGE TO THE SPOOK"; "WHAT MUST NEGROES DO TO BE SAVED?"; "THE WISDOM OF RA"; "NEGROES ARE NOT MEN"; "UNITED STATES AT THE CROSSROADS"; "THE BIBLE WAS NOT WRITTEN FOR NEGROES!!!!!!" To an all-Black audience, he promoted the embrace of impossibility and immortality—not the immortality of the Christian afterlife but a transformation of the present moment. "WE MUST SET OUR MINDS TO ACHIEVE THE ABSOLUTE IMPOSSIBLE," he wrote. "WE MUST CONQUER DEATH. IT IS OF THE UTMOST IMPORTANCE THAT WE CONQUER DEATH HERE AND NOW. WE MUST TAKE THE FIRST STEP FORWARD BY MAKING LIFE REAL."[23]

Art offered one means to salvation, a pathway toward making life real. "THE LOVE OF BEAUTY IS THE BEGINNING OF WISDOM," he wrote, echoing his old mentor Fess Whatley, whose own Golden Dozen Traits of Character insisted on a "love of the beautiful." And like Fess—like, even, Birmingham segregationists, who had begun to decry new developments in music for their own racist reasons—Sonny did not consider all art equal. As the 1950s brought the rock and roll revolution, the South's most vicious segregationists denounced the music, fearing its suggestions of teenage rebellion, sexuality, and (above all) race mixing. Sonny may not have shared those particular concerns, but he did find the new trends in music to lack the necessary substance. "THE PEOPLE OF ALABAMA WERE RIGHT," he wrote, "WHEN THEY SAID THAT ROCK AND ROLL IS NOT THE BEST FORM OF MUSIC TO FEED TO THE YOUTH OF AMERICA." Sonny would develop a music on a higher plane, a music designed for spiritual nourishment and earthly deliverance.[24]

He transformed himself in the process. In October 1952, he legally changed his name to Le Sony'r Ra, leaving "Herman Poole Blount" behind him for good. Many have assumed that Sun Ra never looked back, that he broke emphatically from Birmingham, that by cloaking himself in a new name and mythology he rejected outright the place of his youth, only returning near the very end of his life—either in an act of reconciliation or because he had no place else to go. Certainly, there is some truth to this interpretation:

Sun Ra did keep his distance from the South, where his first encounters with racism had left both lasting hurt and anger. But Sonny's relationship to his hometown was much more complex than the outright renunciation many have read into his biography. To his bandmates and interviewers he spoke with admiration and enthusiasm of the bands of his youth; he praised his hometown as a wellspring of talent, and, like other Birmingham exports and expats, he enjoyed reunions and collaborations with players from home. In 1950s Chicago, he worked off and on with Paul Bascomb, arranging and producing several of his old friend's records. Another Birmingham cohort, guitarist and bandleader Banjo Bill Reese, had recently settled in Chicago, and Sun Ra visited his home more than once, hoping to recruit him to the Arkestra. (Bill respected Sonny's unique talent and vision but declined the invite, preferring to leave the "outer space music" to Sonny.)[25]

Sun Ra kept in touch, too, with Fletcher "Hootie" Myatt, his old Birmingham singer, in whose hands he left his band in 1946. A 1960 letter to Myatt from Alton Abraham shows Sun Ra looking for engagements in Birmingham. "Dear Fletch," Abraham began, revealing an established familiarity, "Here's hoping that this letter will find you in the best of health, wanting for nothing and having everything." Abraham inquired about lodging, meals, and venues and provided the Arkestra's rates ($800 for seven pieces, "a small variation" for a larger band) before signing off: "Sun Ra sends his best regards and states that he expects ten 'gigs' from you before the year is out." If a trip South did materialize, its details were not recorded, and Sonny himself in later years claimed he had not performed in Birmingham since he had left in the 1940s. The mere fact, however, that he was in touch with Myatt and seeking work in Birmingham, nearly fifteen years after he left the city, gives the lie to the notion that Sonny wanted nothing to do with his old home.[26]

Sun Ra's most vital link to the city was another of his old bandmates, the pianist and trumpeter Walter Miller. By 1962, Miller was recording with the Arkestra, and he was in and out of the band for the rest of Sonny's life. Other musicians noticed the ease of friendship and mutual respect that characterized Sun Ra's relationship with Miller; Sonny even performed his old friend's arrangements, an honor he did not bestow on other musicians. Miller also introduced Sun Ra to fresh young talent from home: in 1966, he brought Jothan Callins and trombonist Charles Stephens into the band, and he likely introduced Sun Ra to Arthur Doyle, an explosive free jazz saxophonist from Birmingham. Stephens played off and on with the band until 1979; Callins was in and out through the late 1960s, rejoining in 1989 and becoming one of Sonny's closest, most trusted associates in his final years.[27]

Like Erskine Hawkins, Sun Ra often alluded to Birmingham in the titles of his instrumental compositions; most notable was 1965's landmark album *The Magic City*, with its sprawling, experimental title track. Even for Sonny, *The Magic City* represented a music without precedent; "whatever one hears in Sun Ra's music before or after this period," John Szwed wrote, "it's clear that 1965 was a turning point, and that the recording of *The Magic City* was the clearest signal of the change." "If any one piece was intended to be Sun Ra's monument," added Robert Campbell, Sun Ra's painstaking discographer, "it is *The Magic City*." The piece, wrote Paul Youngquist, is "a miracle of musical invention . . . quite simply the most moving, evocative, and sustained group improvisation to come out of the sixties."[28]

Sun Ra and the band had moved to New York's East Village in 1961, entering a scene that swirled with bohemians, radicals, poets, and artists, a center for the development not only of avant-garde jazz but of socially conscious Black cultural movements. The Arkestra's members made their headquarters in a house they called the Sun Palace, and they rehearsed there endlessly, pushing the boundaries of the music further and further and honing their collaborative voice. *The Magic City* was an outgrowth of this process, an epic piece of collective improvisation, with Sun Ra directing his musicians through a series of solos, set pieces, and instrumental explosions. If Sun Ra had already played at the limits of jazz, he now stretched his soloists and listeners further into unmapped experience, particularly in the title track, which swallowed the entire first side of the record and sketched for nearly half an hour a sonic landscape that was, perhaps, part Birmingham and part outer space. "The Magic City" was its own kind of homecoming, but a homecoming on Sun Ra's unique terms, a cosmic re-visioning of the city in which the man and his music were born.

It is no surprise that Sonny's hometown might have been on his mind. The city had recently entered the forefront of the national consciousness, emerging as epicenter of the civil rights movement; the year 1963 had brought protests, marches, and arrests, along with shocking images of police brutality and a devastating, deadly church bombing. It may be possible to hear in Sun Ra's "Magic City" expressions of the grief, rage, and chaos the bandleader associated with his home. Or perhaps he was reclaiming the nickname for his own imagined, mythic metropolis, creating through his music a city far more magic than the one he had left behind. In a poem also titled "The Magic City," he evoked an alternate universe of "harmonic precision celestial being," of angels that "guard and watch . . . permit and limit." "This city is the magic of the Magi's thought," he wrote, and concluded, cryptically,

For the Magi is miracle Magic of it all
The Magi is all
The All-Magic citizen of the Magic City
Of the Magic universe.[29]

As Birmingham became linked forever to the civil rights movement, Sun Ra held himself aloof from the demonstrations that were shaking that city and the rest of the country. On one hand, his music and philosophy were in keeping with the times. From the beginning, he designed his music explicitly for Black listeners, offering through his composition and performance a celebration of Black identity and access to an alternative reality, a world apart from earthly oppression—not only the oppression of racial discrimination and violence but the ultimate oppression of death. "That's what I'm trying to do," he would say in a typical interview, "to play a superior type of music. Not music dealing with the body, not music dealing with the mind, but music dealing with the spirit—the way it should be. When you deal with music that deals with the spirit, you can encourage people to fight against the bad conditions on this planet. You can encourage them to change things, simply by the music."[30]

That notion—of music as a force for social transformation—was certainly prevalent in the 1960s, not only among jazz musicians but in folk, rock, and soul music circles and on the front lines of the civil rights and anti-war protests. But Sun Ra's space anthems and cosmic tones were far removed from the usual protest music, and he distanced himself from the philosophies and priorities of the era's Black leaders, rejecting outright the ambitions and methods of the civil rights movement. "They just go right on talking about freedom," he said of the movement's activists, "and they go right on talking about peace—and they go right on going to jail, and they go right on dying." To Sun Ra, this did not seem like a solution to anything.[31]

Integration, equality, and freedom were dead ends, the bandleader argued. "I'm talking about precision and discipline," he insisted; "human beings are talking about freedom and other things that don't concern me. I never had any freedom, and I never saw anybody else with any—I'm not interested in it." Instead of freedom, he promoted spiritual and artistic discipline; instead of integration, he offered visions of a Black utopia; instead of democracy, he advocated for what he called mythocracy. "Now you can take a myth," he explained, "and build a lot of things on it. The white race used the myth of white supremacy. They got a lot to show for it, you know—of course, it's a lie. But it makes no difference": whites had leveraged their mythology, their lie, to achieve real-world power. Black people, on the other hand, for all their commitment to righteousness and truth, had nothing to show, because "if they created something, the white race took it. So they don't own anything. . . . They've got to face facts, and see that facts are bad. They got to face the truth. And reject it." Or, as he put it on several occasions: "The possible has been tried and failed. Now it's time to try the impossible."[32]

What Black people needed was a new mythology, and Sun Ra—through his music, poetry, interviews, art, and example—would provide it. During his New York years, his Arkestra developed a live show that brought audiences into the performance itself, inviting them to partake in the expression of the myth. On Monday nights at Slug's—a seedy Village tavern that became ground zero for far-out jazz experimentation—the Arkestra performed all-night sets (often on the heels of all-day rehearsals) that incorporated homemade costumes, dancing, poetry, and Sun Ra's space chants. In 1968 the Arkestra moved again, this time to Philadelphia, where the band established the communal living and rehearsal space that became the center of Sun Ra's universe for the next three decades.

As Sun Ra pushed even past the wildest free jazz innovators, he threw himself equally into an exploration and reinvention of classic swing, reviving the work of those original "angels" he considered the essential creators of jazz in particular and of Black identity more broadly. Increasingly, when Sun Ra spoke to his bandmates and followers about the origins of jazz, he spoke with pride about the place where he had begun his own journey. "As far as creating jazz is concerned," he said, rejecting the usual narrative, "the center is Alabama, not New Orleans."[33]

Eventually, like many musicians of his generation, he would return to Alabama himself. In the meantime, the city of Birmingham, Sun Ra's original launching pad, was undergoing a transformation as dramatic as his own.

PART III

DOWN SOUTH IN BIRMINGHAM

One Sunday in May 1951, a fire ravaged Bob Williams's Little Savoy Café, Fourth Avenue's favorite night spot. Many believed the fire was a racially motivated attack: the next day, in nearby Fairfield, another fire broke out, and the homes of some forty Black families were laid to waste—while, the *New York Amsterdam News* reported, "a whole company of Birmingham firemen stood idly by, less than 200 yards away." The fire department refused to help until word came from its boss, the longtime police commissioner, fire chief, and "arrogant exponent of white supremacy," Eugene "Bull" Connor; so for four hours the firemen watched Black homes burn. "I don't know nothin' about it," Connor spat at reporters on the phone, even as the fire raged on.[1]

The Little Savoy suffered $25,000 in damages but rebuilt and reopened. Whether the fire was deliberately set—or whether there was any connection between it and the fire in Fairfield—was never determined; certainly, Bull Connor's police force would not have investigated the matter. The *New York Amsterdam News* simply added, as ominous postscript to its own report, that in the last two years "there have been 9 bombings of Negro homes" in Birmingham. Given the Savoy's significance to the Black community—it was a well-established hub of Black cultural life and had hosted formal and informal gatherings of civil rights leaders from across the state—it was no great stretch to suspect arson. In the last few years, Black spaces in Birmingham had increasingly become targets of violence. In 1947, a federal ruling had decreed the city's segregationist zoning laws unconstitutional, and as Black families began moving into middle-class, formerly all-white neighborhoods, angry vigilantes began setting fires to the newcomers' front doors, shooting out their windows, and planting bombs beneath their floorboards. The residential Center Street had been dividing line between the Black and white sections of Smithfield; by the start of the 1950s, the bombings there had gotten so common the street became known as Dynamite Hill. Birmingham itself had earned a new nickname, in the meantime: the Magic City had become "Bombingham."

In this context, Fourth Avenue remained an indispensable haven, the heart of Black Birmingham's social and political life. As it had now for decades, the street attracted members of every social class, and it inspired in observers an exuberant poetry. A writer for the local Black entertainment magazine *Glare* called it "Birmingham's Street of Dreams . . . where you're as big as the money in your wallet, whether you are a steel-worker or school teacher, hustler or square." Fourth Avenue was "the cat-walk of life," "a wilderness of Saturday night Tarzans, swinging from neon archway to neon archway bellowing their own personal cry to the world." It was a "proud street" that could "stick out its chest and boast," a worthy brother to Atlanta's Auburn Avenue or New Orleans's Rampart Street as a beacon for undiluted Black culture.[2]

In 1952, singer Del Thorne released on the Excello record label a jumping tribute to Fourth Avenue and its people. "Down South in Birmingham" was a kind of musical postcard from a scene packed with nightlife—"All the joints are jammed," its refrain exclaimed—and it invited travelers to check it out for themselves, even name-checking the district's most popular spot ("You buy all kinds of drinks," sang Thorne, "in little Bob's Savoy"). The tune had been written and recorded in Cleveland, created by Thorne's bandleader, Banjo Bill Reese, uprooted from his native Birmingham but still a champion of the scene that shaped him. The South was hipper than you'd think, Reese's lyrics declared—"All of them cats have been to jive school"—or, at any rate, hip had an outpost there. As racial tensions mounted through the region, Reese and Thorne's little travelogue offered a playful, if modest, reassurance—"The South ain't the worst, and it's not so bad"—inviting outsiders to see for themselves the swinging side of Birmingham, a buoyant culture they might not have suspected.[3]

Other venues sprung up, many on the outskirts of town, just beyond Bull Connor's jurisdiction. On a given night you might catch Ike Williams and the Miles College Collegians at the Downbeat Club in Ensley; John L. Bell or Lucky Leon Davis at the 401 Club in Powderly; Jimmy Chappell at the Grand Terrace; John Hayden and His Organettes at the 2728; or Westbrook Walker and His Vibratones at the Twelve Horsemen's Lounge in Fairfield. Singers Roszetta Scofield Johnson, Jesse Champion, and Hootie Myatt appeared all over town, and pianist Bonnie Mae Perine Samuels, organizer and performer of countless classical recitals, proved equally at home in any local jazz band. In one upstairs joint on Eighteenth Street, drummer "Cat Eye" Summerfield played the burlesque shows, and the Gaston Motel—famous as headquarters for Birmingham's civil rights strategy sessions—became a center for jazz activity, too, hosting the Cool Strings house band alongside major touring acts. When saxophonist Cannonball Adderly came to town, he would play the Gaston Lounge on Friday night and, the next day, offer up-and-coming musicians a jazz clinic in the same space.[4]

As for Bob's Savoy: for two decades that venue held its own on Fourth, but after a second fire broke out in 1958, Bob Williams closed its doors, foreshadowing the end of an era. Once again, Birmingham and its music made a home far from home: in the next decade, Williams opened a hotel in Monrovia, Liberia, bringing with him a piece of the Fourth Avenue sound. Local stalwarts Walter Miller, Melvin Caswell, and Newman Terrell became the house band for Liberia's newest hotel.[5]

In the 1950s and '60s, a new generation of teacher-musicians took root in Birmingham, many of them fresh from professional music careers. Especially influential were Amos Gordon and Frank Adams, both of whom had returned from work in major bands. For Gordon, the glamour of life on the road had worn thin. "I spent fourteen months with Louis Armstrong," he said, "eight months with Lucky Millinder and another eight months in other bands. I made big money. I made a movie with Billie Holiday and Louis Armstrong [1947's *New Orleans*] and played with Lena Horne but I got tired of traveling." There had been some backbreaking jumps: one especially miserable itinerary bounced the band from a string of shows in Canada all the way to Miami and then sent them through a snowstorm to Evansville, Indiana. When there was no time to bathe or do laundry, the musicians covered their shirts with talcum powder to keep them looking white and fresh. Then there were the racist indignities of travel: restaurant doors with signs that read "No Indians, No Dogs, No Niggers," or the threat of a roadside café cook's spit in a Black traveler's food. But the turning point for Gordon came on Christmas, 1946, when he knocked on the door of his family's New York apartment: "My son came to the door and he slammed it in my face. He didn't know anything about who Daddy was."[6]

"That put something on his heart," that son, drummer Hasan Shahid, later explained. Amos Gordon had himself grown up fatherless; as he heard his son run screaming from the door, he determined "he would be a father to *his* son." He moved the family back to Birmingham, taking a job in the

Councill Elementary band room. From there he moved to Western Olin High School, where he taught until 1977. With Armstrong he had been making $200 a week; in the Birmingham schools he started at $50 a month. No matter: when Armstrong invited him to rejoin the band in Paris, Gordon easily declined. "I told him I was tired of it."[7]

Frank Adams had graduated from Howard University, gigged around Washington, DC, and worked as a supplier, or fill-in musician, for Duke Ellington before he, too, came home. In 1950 he took a job at Lincoln grade school, where he replaced his own old bandmaster, William Wise Handy. (Handy in turn would open the first Black-operated music store in Birmingham, Music Service, which he ran until his death in 1977.) Adams stayed at Lincoln for twenty years and then served another twenty-seven as music director for all of Birmingham City Schools. In the meantime, he built up his own band on the side. He hooked up with a hard-drinking boogie-woogie pianist named Robert McCoy and developed a small combo, the kind of "bobtail band" that drew so much ire from Fess Whatley. For fourteen years, he played every weekend at the Woodland Club, an all-night dive past the outskirts of town. He married a schoolteacher, Doris "Dot" Williams, who became the singer in his band. As bassist, he hired the local patriarch, "old Pops Williams" himself, and on trumpet he featured Joe Guy, still living in exile from New York after his broken romance with Billie Holiday.

Guy remained, at his best, a powerful artist, and his playing attracted a cohort of local admirers, but he was haunted by his addiction. "Some of the things that Joe Guy played were beautiful," Adams said. "Most of them were—but there were nights that Joe would be *sickening*, because he'd hear these things in his head and he's got to go and get a fix to make it come out. He would try to get something that could make him climb to a level that wasn't natural for him to climb at that time." For all his difficulties, and despite his enormous fall, Guy carried himself with a dignity Adams never forgot, a kind of tragic nobility overlooked by those who saw only the shabby suits and addiction. Some nights at the Woodland Club, owner Red Hessler goaded the trumpeter mercilessly, asking how—if Guy had once been so great as they said—he had ended up in a "raggedy old place" like the Woodland. "It's better to be a *has-been*," Guy cooly replied, "than a *never-was*."[8]

But Guy's demons were unrelenting. He was in and out of rehab. In 1957, federal agents busted a Birmingham narcotics ring, arresting Guy and nine other men for forging stolen Treasury checks to purchase heroin. The local white press seemed dubious that one of the men might have once been something more than criminal: "Joe Guy claims he has played cornet with 'Fats' Waller, Charley Barnett, Coleman Hawkins and Lucky Millington,"

Birmingham musicians, 1950s. *Left to right:* siblings Charles (Chuck) Clarke and Mary Alice Clarke Stollenwerck, Joe Guy, and singer Jesse Evans. Courtesy Birmingham, Ala. Public Library Archives.

the *Birmingham News* noted, skeptically (misspelling *Barnet* and mangling *Millinder*). Guy was sentenced to another fifteen months' rehab at a federal hospital in Lexington, Kentucky, but as always the "cure" did not last, and he warned his bandmates not to get their hopes up. "Once a junkie, always a junkie," he said, and he implored Adams and other young musicians to never touch the stuff.[9]

Guy's celebrated ex, Billie Holiday, died in New York in 1959, at the age of forty-four. Guy died two years later in Birmingham, more than a decade after the world had passed him by. He was found in the Smithfield home he shared with his parents, lying on his bed in boxer shorts and socks, dead of an overdose. When unsuspecting family members arrived at the house, they were met by his mother in the yard. "Joe dead," were the only words she could muster. "Joe dead."[10]

He was forty-one years old.

All the while, Birmingham was inching toward a reckoning that had been decades in the making. Black southerners were protesting, more and more openly, the injustices of segregation and racial persecution, and their demands were increasingly met with violence from whites steeped in a belief in their own supremacy. The first major assaults on segregation—*Brown v. Board of Education* in 1954 and the Montgomery bus boycott, begun in December 1955—shook the foundations of the South's social order, offering glimpses of progress but stoking tensions between Black and white. "Almost overnight," wrote Birmingham's Geraldine Moore, describing the impact of *Brown*, "the attitudes of white people seemed to have changed appreciably," and "outbreaks of hostility toward Negroes" followed. "Bombingham" was ready to explode.[11]

Occasionally, musicians found themselves at the center of the drama, whether they wanted to be or not. Sometimes they became targets. Nat King Cole arrived in Birmingham in April 1956, scheduled for two nights at the Municipal Auditorium. In keeping with the city's segregationist policies, and to meet the demands of both white and Black fans, he would play separate shows on consecutive nights. A native of Montgomery, Cole had a huge white following across the country; later that year he would debut a prime-time TV show, short-lived but widely acclaimed and a landmark moment in television, the first show of its kind to feature a Black entertainer as host. Cole's earlier work as pianist-bandleader had helped popularize the sound of the classic jazz trio, but what made him a star was his voice, his elegant mastery of romantic pop ballads, and for that first night in Birmingham 4,000 white citizens filled the auditorium.

Cole was three songs into his performance when four men charged the stage and knocked him to the ground. A moment of chaos ensued. Police had been tipped off that there might be trouble, so a group of plainclothes cops rushed to intervene; uniformed officers mistook the plainclothesmen for additional assailants, and there was a flurry of confusion as both groups attempted to grab the real attackers. Cole was rushed offstage and the curtain fell, but he returned a few minutes later with a brief announcement to the agitated crowd: "I just came here to entertain," he said. "I thought that was what you wanted. . . . I cannot continue, because I have to go to a doctor." He left the stage and left the state.[12]

Cole's assailants belonged to the North Alabama Citizens' Council, a segregationist group founded by Klansman Asa Carter, who railed, loudly and often—through radio broadcasts, stump speeches, press interviews, and his own newsletter—against jazz, rock and roll, and any other form of "Negro music." The NAACP, Carter said, had "infiltrated" the masses of white southern teenagers through the dissemination of "Communistic" popular music—rock and roll in particular—which would "mongrelize America" in its irrevocable mixing of the races. Even Nat King Cole's gentle, crooning confections, Carter insisted, were "only a short step" from "the openly animalistic obscenity of the horde of rock'n'rollers." More threatening than the music itself was Cole's popularity with white women.[13]

The majority of Birmingham's white population supported segregation but drew a line at Carter's rhetorical crudity and denounced the violence of Cole's assailants. In the wake of the attack, the *Birmingham News* warned against the kind of "extremist passions and actions" witnessed at the auditorium, and many of the paper's white readers expressed their shock in letters to the editor. "You are not safe in Birmingham or Alabama, regardless of your beliefs, regardless of which side you are on in the segregation fight," one reader advised. "You are not safe because bigots are inflaming others into taking the law, your morals and your musical tastes in their own hands." Cole himself characterized his assailants as "hoodlums who thought they could hurt me and frighten me and [in] that way keep other Negro entertainers from the South. . . . But what they did has backfired on them because those thousands of white people in the audience could see how terrible it is for an innocent man to be subjected to such barbaric treatment." Civil rights organizations and the Black press, however, blasted Cole for agreeing, even after the incident, to play for segregated crowds. For his unwillingness to take a direct stance, he was denounced as an Uncle Tom, a traitor, and a coward. "It's foolish to think," Cole rejoined, "that a performer like me can go into a Southern city and demand that audiences be integrated. The Supreme Court is having a hard time integrating schools, so what chance do I have to integrate audiences?" The very notion that an entertainer could force a change in the law, he said, was "idiotic."[14]

Other Black performers, however, increasingly refused to play segregated events after the incident in Birmingham. If ordinary citizens in Montgomery could deny a segregationist system their business—the bus boycott was in its fourth month at the time of the Cole attack—then why shouldn't entertainers use their own, larger platforms to take a stand? Even the unassuming Erskine Hawkins expressed his new policy on Jim Crow venues: "The way I figure it is that when Negro musicians do play before such audiences, this only gives those who want to discriminate and hinder progress more reason to continue to discriminate. Our people are struggling too hard for dignity, equality and freedom for us in the music world not to do all we can to help in our own way." The last time he had played a segregated room, Hawkins added, had been in Birmingham, "just before the King Cole incident," at the very same auditorium, where he had played many times before. After that attack, he vowed he would never play a segregated show again, either in his hometown or anyplace else.[15]

On January 14, 1963, a new governor stood before the Alabama state capitol in Montgomery and addressed a crowd of supporters. George Wallace had become the state's most visible, powerful opponent of civil rights, and in his inaugural address he bellowed a vehement vow—"Segregation today, segregation tomorrow, segregation forever"—that was met with a wild rebel cheer. The author of that line was not Wallace himself but his chief speechwriter; Asa Carter, the man who engineered the attack on Cole, had now found a mouthpiece in the state's highest office.

The year ahead would define Birmingham for generations. In April, the Alabama Christian Movement for Human Rights and the Southern Christian Leadership Conference took direct action with a campaign to desegregate the city. There were mass meetings and boycotts of local businesses, sit-ins at lunch counters and the library, kneel-ins at local churches, and marches on government buildings. A state circuit court issued an injunction against the protests, and on April 12, Good Friday, some fifty peaceful marchers—including movement leaders Fred Shuttlesworth and Martin Luther King Jr.—were arrested for violating the injunction. From his cell, King wrote his famous "Letter from the Birmingham Jail," advocating nonviolent resistance to unjust laws and denouncing the gradualist approach to change.

Further protests followed. In May, more than 3,000 children streamed from the doors of the Sixteenth Street Baptist Church, marched in the streets, and were arrested by the hundreds, crowding the jails past capacity. The city locked the overflow in the fairgrounds stockade. In and around Kelly Ingram Park, just outside the church, a dramatic showdown unfolded as Bull Connor unleashed fire hoses and dogs on the protesters, producing prime-time and front-page images that shocked the nation.

Black Birmingham held a diversity of views on the movement and its tactics. Pops Williams, nearly as old as the city itself, compared the protesters to someone mixing a patty of dried manure with a stick: the real stench—whether of manure or of southern race relations—went unnoticed until somebody started "stirring things up." Williams was not one to do the stirring himself, but he did not subscribe, either, to the movement's insistence on nonviolence: among his varied occupations (musician, barber, house painter, herbalist) he worked as an undertaker, and he kept his embalming knife on him through the movement years in case he had to defend himself. He advised others to likewise keep some kind of weapon handy, even if just a stick; that way, he said, if you were attacked, you could fight back—as long as you remembered to "holler," loud. "You got to sound like *they're* hurting *you*," he advised, "but you *pound* them with that stick."[16]

Teachers were officially prohibited from endorsing the student protests; they were not, however, required to stop their pupils with force. Many, like Lincoln School's Frank Adams, literally looked the other way as their students left their classrooms. In his band room, Adams watched for his students' signal and then turned to write on the chalkboard. By the time he turned back to face the class, the room would be empty. There was no stopping those children, he said with pride. These were *band* kids, after all—and band kids were *made* to march.[17]

The Children's Crusade, as it came to be called, effectively shut down the city, paralyzing downtown commerce and forcing city leaders to negotiate. In the end, Birmingham's business and political leadership agreed to organizers' core demands: that summer, local department stores, lunch counters, restrooms, and water fountains were desegregated. The protests became a turning point for the movement, leading to the Civil Rights Act of 1964, which outlawed segregation nationwide. But the struggle in Birmingham was far from over, as each victory brought new incidents of retaliatory anti-Black violence. On September 15, 1963, four young girls—Addie Mae Collins, Denise McNair, Cynthia Wesley, and Carole Robertson—were killed when a bomb exploded in the basement of the Sixteenth Street Baptist Church. Two teenage boys, Johnny Robinson and Virgil Ware, were murdered the same day, Robinson by an officer of the law and Ware by a couple of joyriding Eagle Scouts with a Confederate flag and a gun. In a New Jersey studio that November, John Coltrane recorded a powerful, aching instrumental response to the nightmare the world had seen unfold in Birmingham. He called the composition "Alabama."

The integration of city schools began, uneasily, with the enrollment of two Black students at Graymont Elementary in the fall of 1963. Other schools followed through the 1960s, but the deep-seated culture of segregation was resistant to the change. Many white families left the city to send their children to neighboring all-white school systems. In Birmingham itself, enrollment plummeted and school resources dwindled. For students at Parker, Lincoln, and elsewhere, segregation remained a fact of life, long after it was legally outlawed. In 2007—107 years after its founding and nearly half a century after integration's official arrival in Birmingham—Parker High School graduated its first white senior, a milestone that reflected integration's failure.[18]

Change may have been slow in coming, but music and musicians created some of the first cracks in the foundations of the Jim Crow culture. "Music started integration," said bassist Cleve Eaton, born in Fairfield. "Jazz in particular, but music is what did it." Frank Adams began to see the first subtle shifts on weekends at the Woodland Club and other venues. "This jazz thing went beyond segregation, to a certain extent," he said. "When I was playing music in different clubs, I'd look up and there were a lot of whites that would come out to play. In jazz, you're always welcome. We learn something from you, and you learn something from us. Then the reputation goes around that, 'Hey. That guy is good. I want to play with him.' So late at night, regardless of segregation, they would come and play. At the Woodland Club, and different clubs, they would play."[19]

Adams continued:

> In other words, it's a thing that: "Hey, man, we play for different clubs and things, but when it comes to jamming and playing this music, this soul music, we get together on it; and we're brothers in this. We go our separate ways—but at *night*, when you're asleep, then we get together and work on this *jazz* music. We respect each other. We can't show this kind of love out in the open, because we've got so many that feel that this is crossing the line, that it shouldn't be that way. But the musicians: we're brothers. We don't show it, but we're just like each other. . . .
>
> In jazz, you always had this other little secret society. The white players would come out to Red's place. Sometimes they'd sneak you in to where they were playing. Or you'd meet up in the store and talk about music, about where you're playing and what you're doing. "Have you all played this number?" "Frank, have you heard this player?" That was a thing that existed in Birmingham. It was what I call a quiet brotherhood.[20]

Patrick Cather was one early, unlikely member of that brotherhood. By the time he turned sixteen, before he was shaving or driving a car, he was already an avid record collector, a blues and jazz researcher and writer, a burgeoning record producer, and the editor and publisher of his own music magazine. His boyhood dream was to be a late-night DJ on a Black radio station: he idolized local radio icon Shelley "The Playboy" Stewart and at night in his bedroom, alone, recorded reel-to-reel tapes in which he spun 45s and emulated between songs the Playboy's on-air style. Cather was at first glance an improbable champion of Black music in Birmingham. Against a backdrop of rigid segregation and violent racial conflict, he was a white boy hanging out in Black neighborhoods, tagging along with and learning from older Black musicians, sitting in with the band on the Woodland Club stage, and forging relationships that transcended both racial and generational divides.[21]

It started around 1960, when Cather was twelve years old, growing up in the Birmingham suburb of Homewood. One day, he watched his neighbors dump a stack of 78 rpm records into the trash. "I guess I had a collector's instinct all my life," he reflected, years later. "I went over and looked at these things—they were in a round metal garbage can, out on the street to be picked up—and I said, 'I'm not going to let those get thrown out.' It took me about three trips, but I took them all home."

He started with the records labeled "Fats Waller, Piano"—he had been taking lessons on that instrument since he was six—and was blown away by what he heard, not only by the virtuosity of Waller's playing but by the sheer fun of it all, the enormous good humor with which Waller tackled every tune. Next came Bessie Smith, a gutsy, evocative vocalist like none he had ever heard. Other records featured Louis Armstrong—but instead of the grandfatherly, gravel-voiced celebrity he knew from TV, Cather discovered a force of nature, thrilling and swinging, scaling impossible heights with his horn. He spent the day in his room, transfixed, spinning his favorite discs over and over. Then his father walked in: "If you really like that kind of music," he said, "then you need to meet Fess Whatley."

Patrick had met Whatley before—Fess was a frequent presence in the printing shop run by Cather's family—but he knew nothing of the man's music. It was the printing business that connected Patrick's father and Whatley, a trade that linked the men across the city's racial chasm. Cathers had been in the printing business since the 1860s; in the 1960s, Patrick's father ran white Birmingham's leading printing company, while Whatley, operating out of his classroom, handled the print needs of the city's Black community. As in all things, there were parallel businesses for parallel worlds, but behind the scenes the men shared occasional resources or traded jobs, forming a discreet partnership. Whatley brought projects to the elder Cather, whose company was equipped to undertake larger assignments; Cather in turn passed jobs to Whatley for his students to complete. After school and in the summer, Patrick spent many hours at the family business, and the next time Whatley came in, his father made a formal introduction. "He's been listening to a lot of Fats Waller and Louis Armstrong," his father said, and, to Patrick's astonishment, Whatley replied that he had known them both; his own students had even played on their records, and on those of Bessie

Smith, the same records that had held Patrick enthralled. Now, every time Whatley stopped by the shop, he regaled the boy with stories from the early days of jazz. "Well, come on," Fess finally said, about a year after their introduction, "and I'll take you for a ride in my Cadillac."

Whatley still had two Cadillacs, a new model and, most enchanting to Cather, a shining Black relic of the forties, still in pristine condition. He "had this woman that drove for him, kind of a female chauffeur, and he and I sat in the back" as Whatley narrated a tour through Black Birmingham history, pointing out the venues he had played and telling a story about each location. "So that just formed this friendship that was different than any other friendship I'd ever had. Because I was just a kid, and here's this guy that had all these experiences that fascinated me, taking the time to teach me a few things. And I will never get over that."

In the meantime, Cather was steadily growing his record collection. On weekends, his father would drive him to Salvation Army stores where the boy, armed with a five-dollar allowance, might walk away with a few dozen 78s. Soon he was placing classified ads in Black newspapers, looking to buy unwanted records. He rode along on errands with Sidney McDyles, a long-time Black employee of the Cather family, and McDyles drove him all over Smithfield on record-hunting expeditions. "Gradually I began to learn something about the old records: which ones were valuable, which ones weren't, what to look for, what to discard, how important condition was, this and that and the other." At thirteen, he had amassed an impressive, increasingly discerning collection. He started writing other collectors around the country, selling his duplicates by mail and tapping into a network of researchers, critics, record producers, and enthusiasts, sending out mimeographed lists of records for sale by auction. Soon he expanded the auction sheets into a full-fledged magazine, *Music Memories*, which he printed at the family business, fleshed out with profiles of blues and jazz pioneers and illustrated with old photos, some provided by Fess. In addition to his own research and writing, he published short articles by established critics he met through the mail. Patrick Cather was just a kid, but his home in the Birmingham suburbs became a regular stop for fellow researchers on their way through Alabama. Chris Strachwitz, president of Arhoolie Records, arrived from California in his Volkswagen bus; Sam and Ann Charters, on a mission from Folkways Records, arrived in theirs—*all* of the blues researchers, Cather observed, drove Volkswagen buses. Cather's mother would fix them sandwiches while they traded stories and leads and discussed their mutual enthusiasms.

It was jazz critic Rudi Blesh who sent Cather searching for survivors of Birmingham's once-thriving boogie-woogie piano tradition. Cather's first stop was Fess, but Whatley said he "never mixed with the alley players" ("I couldn't take piano players like that to the Birmingham Country Club," he explained). Fess rerouted the boy to Frank Adams, and Adams in turn recommended one of his own bandmates, the barrelhouse pianist Robert McCoy.

McCoy had made a few records in the 1930s, performing with Birmingham blues acts long forgotten by the sixties: Charlie Campbell and His Hot Peppers, Guitar Slim, and Peanut the Kidnapper (singer James Sherrill, recording under one of blues history's most wonderfully surreal pseudonyms). McCoy also wrote his own tunes, played a passable Fats Waller stride, and could fake his way through any requests, whatever the genre, improvising lyrics (and sometimes tunes) to any song he did not know. The first day they met, McCoy offered Cather a smoke and a drink, both of which Patrick—"still young and naive, probably thirteen, maybe fourteen"—declined. While every other Black person he had ever met called him "Mr. Patrick," a convention of the South's racial caste system, McCoy addressed him as "Patrick" or "Pat," chucking tradition and inviting a rare intimacy for the time and place. McCoy took him to neighborhood jook parties and taught him to play boogie-woogie piano. Soon Cather was spending his weekends in the Smithfield homes of Robert and Florence McCoy or Frank and Dot Adams, often setting up a recorder to capture the music that resulted. "I just felt like, for some reason, I'd been let into some sort of inner circle," he said. Those Smithfield days and nights were the happiest times of his youth.

Eventually Cather mailed a tape of McCoy to Rudi Blesh, who suggested they make an album but confessed it would be a year, maybe more, before he could schedule a session. "By then, Robert and I had become so close, and I'm thinking, *hell*: if they can put a record out, *I* can put a record out." So in November 1962 he rented time in a downtown studio, and at the end of a single day's recording, they had enough songs for an album, *Barrelhouse Blues and Jook Piano*, the first release on Patrick's new Vulcan record label. He sent the tapes to Nashville to have the records pressed, Cather Printing produced the front and back album covers, and workers at a local institute for the blind assembled the pieces. Production costs were low, bankrolled by the sale of old 78s. A first run of 200 copies quickly sold out; a second printing followed and sold out as well. The sales brought in enough cash that McCoy—who previously had to practice at his mother's house or on a piano his boss installed at the steel siding factory where he worked—was able to buy his own instrument.

In 1963, as the nation turned its eyes to Birmingham, the duo of Cather and McCoy returned, unnoticed, to that downtown studio to cut a second album, *Blues and Boogie Classics*. A few months later they were back with a full band, Robert McCoy and His Five Sins, to record a couple of R&B 45s. Frank Adams directed the group, which also included Pops Williams, Cat Eye Summerfield, and singer Marcus Ingram. "Marcus was blind," Cather recalled, "a good-looking guy, and between home and the studio he picked up two or three girl singers—or girls off the street that pretended to be singers. They weren't bad, but they were no Raelettes."

Cather himself sat in on a second piano. He was in heaven.

Birmingham, clearly, had underestimated its youth. No one expected hundreds of *kids* to break the back of segregation, taking to the streets and facing down the weight of Bull Connor's law. And no one was watching Patrick Cather and his smaller, more subtle rebellion. If he had been older, his comings and goings in Smithfield would have aroused more suspicion, even violence; but a young white boy tagging along for "errands" with his family's Black driver did not turn many heads in Birmingham. Cather's youth gave him cover for breaking the rules.

In many ways, Cather found himself an outsider, mystified by the world around him. In his own home the virulent rhetoric of the segregationists was altogether absent, and he could never relate to the hatred he witnessed in the news or heard spill from the mouths of his neighbors. As politicians railed against the mixing of the races, he spent his weekends in the company of Black men and women he admired and respected. Robert McCoy lived just off Dynamite Hill, Birmingham's most prominent site for white violence against Black lives; once, Sidney McDyles stopped the car to introduce the boy to Arthur Shores, the famous civil rights attorney and the Hill's most frequent target. They shook hands and stood in the yard, Cather doing a precocious teenager's best to apologize for the inhumanity of people who looked like him. On another occasion, McDyles pointed out a car trailing theirs and said they were likely being followed by the Klan. Eventually the car drove off, leaving them shaken but undisturbed.

Despite the gulf of race and age, Cather felt that a key to his friendship with McCoy, in particular, was a shared sense of living outside the larger society—Robert as a Black man in Birmingham, Patrick as "a young gay boy discovering himself in the sometimes-heartless heart of the Bible Belt." The music he loved, and the community he found through it, helped make sense of it all, offering both an escape and an unexpected sense of belonging. "If I could hold my heart right in my hand," Robert sang, "I would show everybody what my heart has had to stand"; somehow the poetry of the older man's blues seemed to echo between them. And as his adolescence unfolded,

Patrick discovered a purpose that increasingly drove his efforts in music: the desire to provide some small counter to the racism of his community, to explore and to celebrate local Black history and heritage, to learn from Black voices, to reach across the dividing lines of society and expand at least his own world.[22]

Once he turned sixteen, Patrick became a regular at the Woodland Club. He was obviously "way underage," but owner Red Hessler, who sold alcohol on Sundays in open defiance of the law, had paid off the cops and operated by his own rules. "The sheriff's deputies got to where they'd speak to me—and I could not have fooled anybody that I was over twenty-one." Occasionally Patrick joined the musicians onstage, sitting in on the organ. During the band's breaks, he followed the musicians to a back room, where they would "sit and smoke and drink and swap stories." It was a scene rich with personalities—above all, that of Pops Williams, now in his eighties, venerable grandfather of Birmingham jazz. "He'd drink straight bourbon, I think, and just kind of sip it," Cather said, "and he smoked a pipe and looked very professorial," recounting "amazing stories" from the dawning days of jazz.

Cather winced as the blustery Hessler came in, often drunk, draped his arm around the old man's shoulder, and spewed in his face flatly racist remarks. "Pops knew he was being talked down to and patronized, and yet he somehow came out on top," Cather said. "Pops just had this look on his face, like: 'I've lived a long life, and I'm listening to this shit, and it's not bothering me, because I know who I am.' Pops just had this serenity—even though he played a mean bass," and the impact stayed with Cather forever. "I still draw on that sometimes," he reflected, decades later. "When I think I should be mad: literally, I think back to Pops." More than anyone he ever met, he discovered in Williams a powerful, life-changing model for being oneself—for knowing, and owning, oneself—in the face of whatever insults and intolerance were hurled one's way.

In the fall of 1968, Cather started at Jacksonville State University in east Alabama; a few months later, he was expelled for criticizing George Wallace in a letter to the editor of the Birmingham News. He enrolled next at the University of Alabama at Birmingham, where he became active in student government and launched the school's first student newspaper. In 1969, he organized a "Battle of the Blues" concert on campus, bringing together a lineup that included Frank and Dot Adams, Robert McCoy, and "Slim Harpo"—a Slim Harpo, if not exactly the Slim Harpo—a local singer and harmonica player who claimed to be, but was not, the popular blues artist of that name. Cather cohosted with one of his boyhood idols, DJ Shelley

While the civil rights era's most dramatic battles raged in the streets, Birmingham musicians—unnoticed by the politicians or the press—challenged their city's strict segregationist culture on nightclub stages, after hours. Here, Patrick Cather sits in on organ with the Frank Adams band at the Woodland Club, 1960s. Also pictured are Frank Adams, saxophone, "Cat Eye" Summerfield, drums; Ivory "Pops" Williams, bass; and an organist remembered only as Lex. Vocalist Doris "Dot" Adams is at left, only her arm in the frame. Courtesy UAB Archives, University of Alabama at Birmingham.

the Playboy. Years later he learned the event was the first integrated dance on the school's campus.

By the late 1960s, the rock and roll explosion had persuaded more rebellious white teenagers to follow Cather's footsteps and head to Black venues like the Madison Night Spot or Grand Terrace to hear local acts like Poonanny and the Stormers or major touring stars like Chuck Berry and Ray Charles. It may have been a one-way street—Black fans did not yet have the luxury of attending white clubs without fear—but, little by little, boundaries were starting to dissolve, and the "quiet brotherhood" described by Frank Adams grew from a few musicians to music lovers more broadly, from players sitting in together to fans seeking out a shared experience that transcended the region's long history of segregation.[23]

Representations of the civil rights movement have long overlooked the interactions of Black and white in Birmingham nightclubs, focusing instead on the streets and parks, the lunch counters and churches; particularly absent from the historical memory of the movement is the intersection of diverse racial—as well as sexual—identities in the spaces where music was made. At the Sandridge Country Club, out on Oxmoor Road near the mining town of Ishkooda, Black, white, gay, and straight mingled together openly on the dance floor, even in the early 1960s, defying multiple Birmingham laws at once: city statutes forbade not only the public and private mixing of the races but a host of behaviors broadly deemed "lewd, lascivious, filthy, or pornographic"—a catchall description through which civic leaders decreed homosexuality a crime. One white visitor to the Sandridge was Howard Cruse, then a student at Birmingham-Southern College; his classic graphic novel *Stuck Rubber Baby*, published in 1995, would later fictionalize the experience of growing up gay in the thick of Birmingham's movement years. For that novel's protagonist, the AlleySax—a Black nightclub directly based on the Sandridge Country Club—proved a revelatory space in which interracial same-sex couples danced to the sounds of a local jazz band. By the late 1960s, young white gay men regularly attended the real-life Sandridge in drag, extending into the audience the same tradition of "female impersonation" that had long been a staple of vaudeville and nightclub stages. According to trumpeter Bo Berry, who played his first gigs there as a teenager, such dancers were a familiar, welcome part of the scene. Musicians, Berry explained, did not discriminate: all comers were free to be themselves.[24]

It is no surprise that this piece of Birmingham's history has been invisible. In her analysis of Cruse's *Stuck Rubber Baby*, historian Julie Buckner Armstrong has observed that "some of the more famous civil rights photographs happened because movement organizers staged protests to get media attention and, thus, national sympathy." By contrast, "many of Birmingham's LGBT rule breakers did not want media attention at all, especially if they were breaking racial codes as well." Regrettably, the secrecy of their subversion helped render it invisible not only to local law enforcement but also to historians; but "the absence of an iconic image," Armstrong notes, "does not signify the absence of a history." By the close of the sixties, the city's first gay bars became sites of both sexual freedom and racial integration, often supported by a live jazz soundtrack. At Tito's, Vic Cunningham led an integrated band; at the Gold Torch and other early gay bars, singer Nell Carter (Nell Ruth Hardy, in those days) performed some of her first gigs on integrated stages.[25]

Carter was a regular, too, at Society's Child, a downtown coffee shop that opened in 1968 and was pointedly named for the recent, surprising hit by singer-songwriter Janis Ian, a song that sparked nationwide controversy for its depiction of interracial romance. The venue's owner, David Walbert—barely twenty and the son of white civil rights workers—envisioned a listening room, inspired by the Greenwich Village coffeehouse scene, where Black and white could make and hear music together. The house band, the Renaissance Ensemble, consisted of Walbert on guitar and Carter on vocals, along with a (Black) congas player, James Cunningham; a (Black) flautist, Claude Kennedy; and a (white) bassist, Robert Alexander. Their repertoire was eclectic, blending jazz and classical and folk revival repertoires with more experimental excursions. A typical night's crowd mirrored the integrated makeup of the band. A couple of scowling policemen were usually on hand, uninvited, as well.[26]

There was a long way to go, but it was a beginning. The most fervent believers had no doubt that music could be an avenue to a better Birmingham. As the city sought to reimagine its identity and its future in the wake of the civil rights revolution, a handful of musicians turned explicitly to the local jazz tradition for answers. They need not conjure a new mythology, as Sun Ra maintained: Birmingham's past held the keys to its future, and Birmingham's music offered a vital, living heritage that could pave the way forward.

A good place to start was with Fess Whatley himself.

HERITAGE AND HOME

Fess Whatley's birthday had already become annual cause for celebration. When Whatley announced his retirement in 1956, a flurry of accolades followed. Social clubs, parents, and musicians organized a tribute, held at Parker High School and covered nationally in the pages of the *Pittsburgh Courier*. "Hundreds of telegrams, congratulatory messages and gifts were received by the honoree," the *Courier* noted, and "a special engraved citation was awarded by the Birmingham City Commission, signed by the Mayor and his associates." Fess passed the leadership of his dance orchestra to Ike "Bossman" Williams, founder of the Miles College band program, and Williams kept the group going into the 1970s. "So 'Fess' is retiring from active practice," wrote J. B. Sims, "but his name will live on forever through the thousands of fine musicians he has taught. He has turned over his baton to a younger group whom he hopes will carry on in the fine traditions that he maintained for so many years."[1]

Year after year, the tributes poured in. Area schools presented slideshows, biographical sketches, and musical acts in the old teacher's honor. Local 733 presented a yearly series of summer concerts in Fess's name, Amos Gordon directing local musicians and vocalists in a range of classical, spiritual, jazz, and pop performances. In 1960, the new John T. Whatley Elementary School opened its doors to students, adopting as its motto one of Whatley's creeds, "Discipline Is a 'Must'—Learning Is 'Compulsory,'" and selecting as alma mater an anthem set to the melody of "Danny Boy," one of Whatley's favorites. Mary Alice Clarke Stollenwerck, Fess's longtime pianist, wrote the arrangement, and Whatley himself provided lyrics ("We'll forever cherish all your golden rules," students sang to their school). International attention came with the publication of *Jazz Monthly*'s detailed profile in 1964. In the meantime, Whatley was documenting his own legacy in a scrapbook packed with photos, cards, typewritten notes, and ephemera, a collection that celebrated, in his own words, "A Few of the Many Students [Who] Have Succeeded in Their Upward Climb." The pages, he hoped, would serve as inspiration to the youth of the future: "I dedicate this History-Scrap Book," he wrote, "and pass it on to the few or many boys and girls who may see and read it." Before he died, he gave the book to J. L. Lowe, perhaps his most ardent disciple, instructing him to see the project completed. Lowe vowed he would do just that.[2]

John T. "Fess" Whatley died on January 19, 1972. His old friend and mentor Pops Williams, nearly ninety, came to see him in the hospital. "He held my hand when he was dying," Williams said. "Poor boy, I didn't want to see him blow his last out. I eased my hand out of his'n and . . . left.

"Tears were in my eyes; I cried."[3]

The victories of the civil rights years may have reshaped the city, but even Birmingham's progress brought new contradiction and challenge. Once brimming with life, Fourth Avenue struggled and sputtered, losing its force as a Black cultural stronghold. The city's entire downtown faced hardships familiar to communities across the country: in the 1960s and '70s, white flight to the suburbs, along with the development of the first shopping malls, sucked resources from the city's center. Black Birminghamians, no longer confined to a four-block commercial strip, looked beyond Fourth Avenue for their needs. The Masonic Temple housed fewer and fewer tenants and finally shuttered its doors. Across the street, the district's last surviving theater, the Carver, kept itself afloat screening X-rated films, then shut down altogether.

Tuxedo Junction showed even fewer traces of its former glory: the community of Ensley had been in decline well before the local steel economy dried up in the 1970s. In its prime, Ensley had boasted a population of more than 40,000; by the seventies that number had been reduced by more than half, and with the closing of the mills—US Steel pulled out in 1978—the town seemed doomed to extinction, its population dwindling to less than 4,000 in the new century. One of the old dance halls was rented out in the 1980s and '90s as a venue for punk rock shows, and a generation of white kids from the suburbs came of age in a venue still known as Tuxedo Junction Ballroom—despite parents' warnings against the "bad" side of town.

As a cultural force, jazz itself was in steady decline nationwide. But Birmingham kept pumping talent into the world: musicians who, in a previous generation, might have pursued careers in jazz turned to other, more popular sounds. Eddie Kendricks and Paul Williams left the Magic City for Motown, where they formed the Temptations (Dennis Williams, another Birmingham native, later joined the group); singer and multi-instrumentalist Frederick Earl "Shorty" Long also joined the Motown label, scoring hits with "Here Comes the Judge" and "Function at the Junction" (a tune which may have owed some inspiration to the famous Junction back home); Frederick Knight released a hit single, "I've Been Lonely for So Long," on Stax Records in 1972 and penned the disco chart-topper "Ring My Bell." Other performers who stayed close to home—like the somersaulting, back-flipping drummer Fletcher "Sputnick" Sheppard or the outrageous and raunchy Joe "Poonanny" Burns—mixed James Brown soul and funk with over-the-top showmanship (Poonanny would become, in time, a staple of "Southern Soul" and the Chitlin Circuit). Older musicians grumbled that the latest trends lacked the depth of discipline required by jazz, but even in the schools there was increasing tendency to promote music not as professional trade but as entertainment and extracurricular diversion: in Birmingham band rooms, music lost its purpose as an essential skill for survival.

Still, the jazz tradition continued, even if slowed to a trickle. Nell Carter became a celebrated singer and actress, first on Broadway (in the Fats Waller–themed musical, *Ain't Misbehavin'*) and then on prime-time network television. Deeply rooted in the Birmingham scene, she had first sung with the Parker High School choir, studied with local pianist Bonnie Mae Perine Samuels, and cut her professional teeth singing jazz standards and folk songs at Society's Child and the local gay bars. In the 1980s, at the height of her celebrity, she returned to perform for a new generation of students, backed by the Birmingham Heritage Band and the school choir's latest batch of singers. The resulting live album, appropriately titled *Take Me Home*, was sold exclusively as a fundraiser for the choir: "My way of saying 'Thank you,'" she explained, "of giving something back to my roots." "Try to hear the words," she told her student audience, as she introduced the title song. "It's about going home, down South, to the people who love you. Good God."[4]

One of the last great ambassadors of the Birmingham jazz tradition was bassist Cleveland "Cleve" Eaton, a formidable talent who arrived in Chicago in 1960 and quickly became entrenched in that city's scene. Eaton spent ten years with the Ramsey Lewis Trio, scoring two Grammys and multiple gold albums, from 1964's *Wade in the Water* to 1974's *Sun Goddess*. As a solo artist and leader of his own Garden of Eaton, he produced albums that blended jazz, disco dance grooves, and blistering funk. In 1979, Eaton joined the

Count Basie Orchestra, serving as Basie's final bassist and remaining with the group for seventeen years.[5]

Throughout, Eaton remained closely tied to Birmingham. Between his stints with Lewis and Basie, he mentored a group of Fairfield High School students who called themselves the Soul Controllers; in the 1970s and '80s, as simply the Controllers, the group recorded several R&B hits. Eaton coproduced their first single, "Right On, Brother—Right On," a funk-powered anthem that announced a bold new era ("Sisters sport their afros, while brothers do their thing / Shouting for equality, in every song they sing"). In the early 1980s, Eaton and his wife, Myra, opened a jazz club, Cleve's Place, just around the block from Tuxedo Junction, using his connections to bring in a host of national acts—including Basie, who celebrated his seventy-eighth birthday on Cleve's stage. Eaton's Birmingham bands—Cleveland Eaton & Co., the Cleveland Eaton Orchestra, the Alabama All-Stars—would remain local fixtures well into the twenty-first century.[6]

A small but significant circle of Birmingham musicians, meanwhile, joined the forefront of free jazz, spiritual jazz, and the avant-garde. Jothan Callins studied trumpet under Amos "Flash" Gordon at Jackson-Olin High and in 1965 joined the Lionel Hampton Orchestra; a year later, through Walter Miller's introduction, he fell into Sun Ra's New York orbit, absorbing the bandleader's philosophies of transcendent musical potentials. Callins also embraced, more broadly, the political and spiritual consciousness of New York's Village scene, creating music in conversation with Black history, Black art, and Black liberation. With his band, the Sounds of Togetherness, Callins envisioned Black music as "a shining light in the struggle for freedom, respect and dignity." That group's 1975 album, *Winds of Change*, now a coveted treasure among jazz collectors, presented "songs of life, jubilee and praise" alongside "songs that deal with present-day problems, ills, injustices and solutions." The album's final composition, "Call to Warriors," addressed the "concerned men and women, boys and girls" who committed themselves to triumph over evil.[7]

Amos Gordon's training produced other players on the cutting edge. In the early 1960s, Gordon assembled thirteen high school students into an Elks youth jazz band, and several of that group's alums enjoyed long-running, often overlapping careers. Trombonist Charles Stephens and saxophonist Arthur Doyle performed experimental music in New York's loft scene, appearing together on Doyle's explosive 1978 album, *Alabama Feeling*, a landmark of free jazz. For Doyle, the music was born of both the traumas and the hope of the civil rights era. "I feel it all went hand in hand," he said.

"The free jazz movement and people wanting to be free . . . All of this had an effect on me as a man and musician. The children killed in the church in Alabama and the killing of civil rights workers": it all found expression through his horn.[8]

Gordon's son, drummer Hasan Shahid (born Amos Gordon Jr.), was another member of the youth band directed by his father. The Sixteenth Street bombing was a turning point in his life, too: he went to school with those girls and watched his father carry his cousin Carole Robertson's casket. After the bombing, he gave up on the failed promises of both America and the dominant Christian religion. He devoted himself to civil rights work, converted to the Sunni Muslim faith, left the South, and found expression in the spiritual and free jazz movements. In 1969, his Black Unity Trio recorded the extraordinary, spirit-fueled *Al-Fatihah*, the band's only album, reissued to enormous acclaim in 2020. But Shahid's refusal to participate in the Vietnam War—he claimed conscientious objector status on the basis of his faith—led to a conviction of conspiracy against the United States, effectively squashing his career (and offering devastating parallel to Sonny Blount's case, more than two decades before). Shahid's federal probation required him to return to, and stay in, Alabama—where, he complained, "there was nobody playing the new music."[9]

Modern jazz had never taken much root in Birmingham, where big society bands and timeworn standards continued to dominate, long after they faded elsewhere. Ironically, the very forces that made Birmingham a powerful force in the swing years also helped instill a musical conservatism that stymied innovation and increasingly kept new developments at a distance. This conservatism surely weakened Birmingham's weight as a capital of jazz in the latter half of the twentieth century—and may help explain why the city, for all its contributions, has never received its due recognition as an essential jazz center. Frank Adams, a product himself of the swing years, hypothesized that there was something in the culture of Birmingham musicians that tended to keep them on the sidelines, an ingrained humility that prevented them from asserting themselves more fully. Even in the Hawkins band, a self-effacing modesty prevailed: Erskine himself had assumed leadership only reluctantly, and the group's star soloists, Dud Bascomb and Avery Parrish, likewise preferred to keep out of the spotlight. Haywood Henry described his own reluctance to strike out for himself in terms that reflected both his band's fundamental sense of community and the nature of his training: "I was a section man," he explained. "I wanted the whole thing together. I said, we can accomplish something *together*. And," he was quick to point out, "I was right."[10]

Haywood may have been right; but by the start of the 1970s, Hasan Shahid found the contemporary scene's lack of innovation suffocating. "I've got nothing against Duke Ellington," he said, "but they were still playing 'A Train' and 'Satin Doll.' I've played 'A Train' and 'Satin Doll' a thousand times. I don't want to play it no more." Even local beboppers, including a core of Joe Guy disciples, were still retreading bop's earliest developments.

"So," said Shahid, " I didn't mix well."[11]

J. L. Lowe, champion of the old tradition, had not forgotten his vow to Whatley. Lowe had always been a pusher of Birmingham talent. In countless interviews, articles, and public presentations, Lowe would advocate for Birmingham what he called a "musical patriotism," a sense of community pride rooted in the city's unique inheritance. Business and political leaders should harness that heritage, he said, as one of the place's chief cultural and economic resources. In the 1950s, he published effusive tributes to the hometown scene in the local *Glare* magazine; with input from a readers' poll, he designed a dream orchestra comprising the city's greatest stars, an "All-Time All-Birmingham Band," with Fess at the helm. After Whatley's death, Lowe's efforts to tell the city's jazz story took on new urgency: by the 1970s, Lowe feared that his city did not know its own history; that young people had never heard the *name* "Fess Whatley," let alone understood what it meant; that jazz itself—with its unique power to "promote culture," to create community, uplift, inspire, and transform—had lost its place in society. Swing-era musicians had lately been embraced by festivals and fan clubs overseas but were increasingly forgotten at home. Black people in Birmingham had been central to the creation of one of America's highest, most essential art forms—and nobody, not even in Birmingham, seemed to know it.[12]

And so, in 1976, Lowe assembled a supergroup of local talent, a real-life version of the dream team he had envisioned years ago in *Glare*. The band rehearsed in the evenings at Shields Elementary School, where Lowe served as principal, and made its debut at the city's celebration of the US bicentennial. Amos Gordon and Lowe's brother, Sammy, composed two tunes for the occasion, "Magic City Blues" and "Birmingham Is My Home" (Sammy, then living in New Jersey, would soon move back home himself, putting the latter song's lyrics into action). Even the name of the group, the Birmingham Heritage Band, announced its musicians' lineage and mission. "The makeup of the band," J. L. bragged, included veterans of the Ellington, Armstrong, Calloway, Hawkins, Millinder, "and even Sun Ra" bands; still others "were bandmasters in the metropolitan area, two [were] retired principals, and

The Birmingham Heritage Band, formed in 1976 to honor and perpetuate the local jazz tradition, included veterans of several major acts, including the Louis Armstrong, Duke Ellington, and Erskine Hawkins Orchestras; many of the band's members had retired from the road to build long and influential careers in Birmingham schools. At front are singer Henry Blankenship and conductor Amos Gordon; behind them (*left to right*) are J. L. Lowe, Newman Terrell, Chuck Clarke, Frank Davis, Ted Johnson, Ves Marable, Andre Barnett, Tolton Rosser, Hooper Abrams, Bo Berry, and Kenny Jerkins. Courtesy Birmingham, Ala. Public Library Archives.

four were [active] professional musicians." A showcase for the city's elder heroes, the group was also multigenerational by design, emphasizing the passing of a living tradition: the youngest member, trumpeter Daniel "José" Carr, was still in high school.

The Heritage Band was only one piece of a larger community vision. Working in collaboration with other local leaders and musicians, Lowe would also become the central force behind the developing Alabama Jazz Hall of Fame. In May of 1978, that organization inducted its first class of honorees, a group that included three longtime members of the Hawkins orchestra—Erskine himself, Haywood Henry, and Sammy Lowe—along with three beloved and influential music teachers: Fess Whatley (inducted posthumously), Amos Gordon, and Frank Adams. Each year, subsequent ceremonies would honor new classes of inductees: bandleaders, singers, educators, venue owners, promoters, and a long roster of sidemen. The "Alabama" in the hall of fame's name allowed for inductees from across the state—W. C. Handy of Florence, James Reese Europe of Mobile, Dinah Washington of Tuscaloosa, Nat King Cole of Montgomery—but the vast majority of inductees (there have been more than 215 at the time of this writing) have been from Birmingham, most of them products of Whatley or products of products of Whatley.

For the hall of fame's first headquarters, J. L. Lowe rented an unassuming office space on Seventeenth Street North, just off Fourth Avenue, outfitting its two rooms with a desk, a sagging secondhand couch, a few well-worn chairs, and a grungy green carpet. He created a makeshift museum, fixing to the walls old pictures of jazz pioneers, many of the photos literally torn from the pages of Fess Whatley's scrapbook and annotated directly on the wall with hand-painted captions. Like the Birmingham Heritage Band, the hall of fame was designed to commemorate the past while sustaining a tradition for the future: in the back room, Flash Gordon taught lessons, six days a week, at no charge. "ALL instruments" said the sign on the door.[13]

In 1979, a year after the hall of fame's founding, Birmingham elected its first Black mayor: Richard Arrington Jr., a city council member, biology professor, and former dean of Miles College, famous for taking on a police force still notorious in the Black community for its use of violence. The Birmingham Heritage Band played at the inauguration, a powerfully symbolic occasion for a new Birmingham; in the years that followed, that group would function as the city's unofficial house band, performing at seemingly every major civic event. Arrington had chaired the first organizing committee of the Alabama Jazz Hall of Fame and, as mayor, maintained a close working relationship with the local jazz community. As municipal leaders—including the city's first generation of Black elected officials—began to formally en-shrine the local civil rights history, Lowe, in particular, was insistent that the jazz heritage be part of the story. The Birmingham Civil Rights Institute opened in 1992, just across the street from both the Sixteenth Street Baptist Church and Kelly Ingram Park, sites of 1963's most climactic events. A year later, a greatly expanded Alabama Jazz Hall of Fame opened its doors in the renovated Carver Theater. The two facilities, conceived and developed together, helped establish the Birmingham Civil Rights District as a space where both locals and out-of-towners could engage the city's powerful lega-cies, confronting histories of segregation and racial injustice and exploring the long, continuing road to universal human rights.

The interconnected roots of the civil rights institute and jazz hall of fame reflected the entwined nature of the legacies those spaces sought to honor. Certainly, the confrontations of the 1960s had made Birmingham central to the movement; but a fuller understanding of the city's—and, indeed, of America's—civil rights history would also take into account the musical heritage pioneered there. Birmingham's jazz story was a compelling and empowering counter to the dominant stories the nation told about the city, or even to those Birmingham told about itself, and it offered a more nuanced understanding of the South's struggle for freedom. All along, the seeds of the movement had been planted and nourished in unlikely places, invisible to white America: in school band rooms, on the Masonic Temple dance floor and Tuxedo Junction bandstand, in the sweltering summer parades of Odd Fellows and Elks, at Smithfield Community Sings, in Sonny Blount's endless rehearsal sessions, in the cramped seats of Fess Whatley's gleaming Cadillacs. Birmingham jazz was forged in the fires of segrega-tion and shaped by a resilient and resourceful Black community; it was a testament to Black culture and identity and joy, but its message was also one that might transcend race. Music, Lowe and other leaders maintained, could create a bridge between Black and white. The local jazz story could exhilarate, inspire, and heal.

Lowe was unapologetically zealous in his devotion to the cause. For the hall of fame he edited a newsletter that publicized upcoming events and reported jazz-related news; in an editorial column, he riffed on his emphatic jazz philosophy. "In this world of violence," he wrote in the 1990s, "of Bosnia, of Somalia, of Haiti, of inexcusable crime all about us, in the streets, next door, a suitable objective of the Alabama Jazz Hall of Fame should be to do whatever is necessary to bring mankind to its senses—to stop the killing." It may have seemed "an odd objective," and an impossibly ambitious one, but jazz musicians had always been "ambassadors of peace" as they spread their music through the world, and their training uniquely equipped them to tackle society's problems. "To be a jazz musician requires complete dedication to the instrument as well as recognition that harmony must prevail." It was a message Fess Whatley and indeed Sun Ra might have preached: in its insistence on disciplined dedication and through its philosophy and practice of harmony, this music—this *Birmingham* music—could remake the world. The Alabama Jazz Hall of Fame could be a force for that change.[14]

Lowe was not the only musician on a mission. Jothan Callins, an essential cofounder of the Alabama Jazz Hall of Fame, had returned to Birmingham by the late 1970s, appointed Birmingham City Schools' first-ever Jazz Artist in Residence. Like Lowe, Callins was driven by a sense of musical patriotism, a spiritual-philosophical devotion to jazz, and a desire to uplift the youth through music. On his return to the city, he founded the nonprofit National Black Cultural Society, which sponsored a range of arts programs and served as parent organization for the developing hall of fame. For his master's thesis in ethnomusicology, awarded by the University of Pittsburgh in 1982, he developed the first scholarly treatment of the local tradition, drawing from original interviews with Pops Williams and other pioneers. In 1994, he launched the Birmingham Youth Jazz Ensemble, an intensive training ground for middle and high school students, providing instrumental instruction and performance experience while promoting a culture of character, achievement, and service. Callins's students became some of the city's most progressive and accomplished musicians—today, his protégés are professionally active across a broad spectrum of the arts, in Birmingham and beyond—and his own compositions would become local jam session standards.[15]

Callins proved critical in another sense, as well: he played a central role in bringing Sun Ra back to Birmingham, rejoining the Arkestra in 1989 and facilitating the intergalactic bandleader's renewed connection to his hometown.

In his last years on the planet, Sun Ra returned with increasing frequency to Alabama's Magic City. He was inducted in 1979 into the second class of the Alabama Jazz Hall of Fame, and a few months before the induction—inspired, perhaps, by that honor—he recorded three compositions whose titles alluded to the city and its neighborhoods. "Magic City Blue," "The Place of Five Points," and "West End Side of Magic City" seemed to mark a new preoccupation with the place of his youth. He incorporated into his live shows performances of "After Hours," the bluesy staple by his childhood friend Avery Parrish, which he also echoed and inverted in his own "Hours

After." Once Callins rejoined the band, Sun Ra adopted into his regular repertoire Callins's composition "Alabama."

He also breathed new life and meaning into the 1934 chestnut "Stars Fell on Alabama," investing the lyrics with a kind of tongue-in-cheek autobiography that only Alabama's most famous celestial visitor himself could provide. Sun Ra had long delighted in bringing cosmic meaning to old standards; tunes like "Stardust" and even "Somewhere over the Rainbow" (the latter of which he performed at his hall of fame induction) always meant something new when performed by his Arkestra. "I never planned in my imagination a situation so heavenly," he sang on "Stars Fell," his smile practically audible in the recording: "A fairy land where no one else can enter, and in the center just you and me." This was the kind of language Sun Ra understood and adored, Tin Pan Alley romance revealed as a code for otherworldly, transcendent experience. There was more to it, too, than joking reinvention of old lyrics; by the mid-1970s Sun Ra had explicitly turned to the music of his youth as a center for his performances. Like J. L. Lowe, he felt the world had lost something vital as it moved away from swing, and he revived the spirits of his idols—Fletcher Henderson, Duke Ellington, and others—by incorporating their music, as well as sweet old pop tunes, into the Arkestra's live performances.[16]

Long after the big bands had fallen from fashion, Sun Ra continued to sustain the tradition: not by offering musty replicas of bygone sounds but by creating something new from the music he cherished. As always, a desire to transform society drove him. He never forgot the impact the Black bands had had on him as a boy, how they served as a force for good in the community, how they celebrated Blackness itself, how they modeled for a young dreamer like himself other modes of existence. But things had changed since he had left Birmingham: for all his emphasis on an "Astro-Black Mythology," Sun Ra found that many of his most devoted followers, now, were white. Though he welcomed this unintended audience, it bothered him that Black people did not embrace his music and message more fully, and he openly chided Black America for its indifference.

At the same time, he drew accolades from unexpected sources—as in 1985 when he was honored by the Alabama Music Hall of Fame (founded in Muscle Shoals and unaffiliated with Birmingham's jazz hall) and presented an award by George Wallace himself. Confined to a wheelchair since an assassination attempt in 1972, Wallace was serving his fourth and final term as Alabama's governor; in recent years, he had publicly renounced his segregationist past, pleading for forgiveness and appointing record numbers of African Americans to state positions. "He sent for me," Sun Ra said of Wallace, "to come to his mansion"—and so, in full spaceways regalia, Sun Ra joined other honorees for "a little party," an afternoon tea at the governor's mansion in Montgomery, surely one of the most surreal summits in all of Alabama history, the intergalactic bandleader and representative of "the angel race" hobnobbing with the most lasting icon of the segregationist South. A ceremony was held at Birmingham's city auditorium—the same stage on which Nat King Cole had been attacked, three decades before—and Sun Ra received a key to the Magic City. "That's," he told doubters, "what Alabama did."[17]

And still, by his own account, he had not played in the state since he "ran off," years before. Finally, in August 1988, he brought the Arkestra to Birmingham for that now-legendary show at the Nick, the grungy rock club billed as "Birmingham's Dirty Little Secret," its xeroxed flyers proudly announcing from city telephone poles "THE VOYAGER RETURNS HOME / FOR ONE NIGHT ONLY." One audience member, writing as "Night Train" Jayne Layne, contributed an enthusiastic review to an underground fanzine, proclaiming that "the greatest thing about this magic show was the joy and love and wild enthusiasm with which the Arkestra played." As always, the band took in the full spectrum of blues and jazz history and cranked it back out as something new, something at once familiar and strange, full of explosive horn solos and dancing, while the aging bandleader, still in absolute control, directed the proceedings from his keyboard. "It was all very rhythmic, powerful, telekinetic, spiritual, tribal, and way-cool," wrote Jayne.[18]

Sun Ra described the gig differently. His booking agent, he told an interviewer, had "insisted" he return to Alabama but could not find a venue that would take him. "So he put me in a place, a hillbilly, redneck, motorcycle gang, Nazi, Ku Klux Klan place that was rough, and they had five pool tables in the back. Now, he put me in this place, on the edge of a Black neighborhood. Black people who knew about it, they weren't going in there." (Sun Ra's stories may have been often embellished or imbued with myth, but on this point he was accurate: the Nick was situated a block from a housing project whose many Black residents did not venture into the club, on that night or any other.) "So then they put me on a Tuesday night, which as you know is a slow night for night clubs, but the place was packed, standing room only, and when I got through playing there, the people surrounded me and said, 'Love is around you in Alabama.' And then they shouted my name for about fifteen minutes. Shouted, 'Ra! Ra!'" Sun Ra was not sure what to do with this sort of reception in this sort of venue. "I had to get out of there and go in the bus," he said, insisting, "Yes! The Ku Klux Klan and the rednecks too!" (His bandmates offered still another perspective on the night. Arkestra stalwarts Marshall Allen and Danny Ray Thompson recalled an unexpected visitor to the tour bus during intermission: Eddie Kendricks, founding member of the Temptations, had recently moved back to Birmingham himself and came to pay his respects.)[19]

Sun Ra was still wary of the city when he returned with Callins a few months later for a tribute at the Alabama Jazz Hall of Fame, but he came to marvel at the intensity of his Alabama fans. The next summer he was back, this time with the full Arkestra, to play Birmingham's first City Stages, a three-day outdoor festival that brought downtown local and national acts from across the musical spectrum. (Callins and J. L. Lowe both served on the festival's organizing board, and their fingerprints were clear in the lineup, which also included Erskine Hawkins and the Birmingham Heritage Band.) Sun Ra played central spectacle in an opening "Street Strut" parade, striding through the city like royalty, surrounded by enormous puppets—among them a papier-mâché sun and a giant double of Sun Ra himself. In addition to the City Stages performance, the band passed the hat for a playful afternoon concert at Southern Danceworks, a modern dance company. The following June, Sun Ra and the Arkestra were back for the second City Stages and a show at Grundy's Music Room, a downtown jazz club. At Sloss Furnaces—great rusty monument to Birmingham's industrial past, now remade as a concert stage—Sun Ra returned the music to its roots, performing a free show for students in the Birmingham school system. Finally, the Magic City had embraced him.[20]

Sonny's health, though, was failing. Later in 1990, he suffered a series of strokes but characteristically refused to stop working. When he next appeared in Alabama—in April 1992, for a three-night, sold-out engagement at the Chukker in Tuscaloosa—he was in obvious physical decline. During the days, he sat in his motel room, vaguely watching westerns on TV, the volume off, and talking to visitors about space. Appropriately, he was booked in the Moon Winx Lodge, a 1950s motor court over which a giant, neon-lit crescent moon grinned an unnerving, devilish smirk. Sun Ra sat in a wheelchair beneath the motel moon and spoke to a reporter about his Alabama childhood—"always running and leaping up to the trees, always thinking about space"—and humoring the interviewer's questions ("They say I was born in Birmingham," came the usual explanation, " . . . but I don't remember"). When his voice wore out, he alternately whispered his responses or scribbled them silently into a notebook. Asked why he had no wife or children, he wrote, "They neither marry nor is given in marriage but are like angels that shine forth like the sun." For each night at the Chukker, the Arkestra adopted a different theme: "Homage to Duke Ellington and Fletcher Henderson" celebrated Sonny's lifelong debt to the pioneers of

Magic City Sun: Sun Ra shares an embrace with his larger-than-life puppet likeness at Birmingham's inaugural City Stages music festival, 1989. Photo courtesy Philip Foster.

swing; "Homage to the Flowers and Trees" paid tribute to the natural world; and "From Saturn to Alabama: Travels in Outer Space" bridged the bandleader's cosmic and terrestrial homes. As biographer John Szwed observed, the series was "the closest thing to a retrospective Sun Ra would ever give."[21]

For the Birmingham jazz community, 1993 was a year of mourning and milestones. At the year's start, J. L. Lowe was busily preparing to unveil the Alabama Jazz Hall of Fame's new home in the Carver Theater, the fulfillment of a dream years in the making. But in the midst of the excitement, tragedy struck: on February 17, the Smithfield home shared by J. L.'s siblings, Sammy and Leatha, caught fire. Both brother and sister died in the flames. The city had lost two of its "pioneer musical figures," Mayor Arrington observed, and they had both been active to the end. Leatha had retired, barely a year before, from twenty-two years as music director at the A. G. Gaston Boys Club; the day of his death, Sammy had conducted a performance of the Heritage Band at Birmingham's central library. By the end of the year, the city would lose two more of its pioneers: even as the Alabama Jazz Hall of Fame opened its doors, enshrining the music's history, the departures of Sun Ra and Erskine Hawkins signified the end of an era.[22]

Sonny had come home to Birmingham that January, for good. "I guess that's where he came into this world and that's where he wanted to leave it," said John Gilmore, the Arkestra's longtime, legendary saxophonist. But Gilmore also indicated a less symbolic, more practical reason for the move: "We had no central heat," he said of the band's communal home; it was winter in Philadelphia and Sun Ra had just suffered another stroke. So Jothan Callins accompanied the bandleader by train to the city of his arrival, where he would live out his last days in the care of his sister.[23]

Mary Blount Jenkins was in poor health herself, and, her son Tom Jenkins explained, she took in Sonny "to the detriment of her own health." According to Jenkins, his mother could never come to terms with the fact that Sonny refused, all his life, to claim his earthly family—"but," Jenkins added, "she loved herself some Sonny," and she took her brother in, despite the personal and financial strain. Sun Ra's condition worsened steadily, and he spent his last months in the hospital. Callins kept him company and passed his musical requests to Jimmy Griffin, longtime salesman at the local Charlemagne Records and an avid Sun Ra devotee, who dubbed cassettes of whatever jazz heroes Sonny wanted to hear. (Sometimes, in his hospital bed, Sun Ra played along with the music on an invisible keyboard.) After further complications—pneumonia, heart attack, paralysis—Sun Ra departed this planet, on May 30, 1993.[24]

A homegoing service followed at Sixth Avenue Baptist Church, one of Birmingham's oldest and most prestigious Black churches. A small contingent of Arkestra members made the trip down and performed several selections—including a haunting a cappella "When There Is No Sun"—but in large part the service was a reflection of Sonny's deep Birmingham roots. Jothan Callins served as emcee; Walter Miller performed a tribute on the piano; Fletcher "Hootie" Myatt and Birmingham radio personality Roy Wood Sr. shared memories. There were gospel hymns and performances of Sun Ra's poetry. Singer Jesse Champion crooned "Somewhere over the Rainbow," backed by Birmingham bassist John Springer and members of the Arkestra. Midway through that tune, a screaming saxophone solo by Marshall Allen ripped through the room's sniffling stillness, shaking the living awake and effectively evoking the spirit of the departed. As mourners filed out, the Arkestra blasted a rousing "Space Is the Place," Sun Ra's signature anthem.[25]

A smaller gathering paid their last respects the next day at Elmwood Cemetery, where Sonny's body, decked in robes and cradling an Egyptian ankh, lay in a powder-blue coffin. "They banged the drum slowly," reported the *Birmingham News*, as Reverend John T. Porter offered a eulogy. "We gather," he said,

> to rededicate ourselves to music,
> the kind of music that will draw us all together,
> and to learn from the life [Sun Ra] lived
> that somehow *music* can do what nothing else can do for us.
> And we must hold fast to the art of music
> and give to it all that we possibly can,
> and pass it on to generations yet unborn,
> that they will know that *Sun Ra* walked among us.
> And we represent the tradition that he represented.

Barring a passing reference to Jesus Christ, the Baptist preacher's language blended easily with the language of Sun Ra's own cosmology; listeners could interpret the words as they saw fit. Concluding his remarks, the speaker invited mourners "to celebrate not only [Sun Ra's] journey, but his sailing—out into a land of peace and joy, and a fullness that he never knew in this world."[26]

"He'll come back in shining ships of gold," the Arkestra's members sang, their fingers pointed to the cosmos, and Sun Ra's corporeal form was laid finally to rest.

Erskine Hawkins comes home. The bandleader greets fans and friends at 1987's Function at the Junction, an annual birthday celebration at Tuxedo Junction Park—"right back where I belong." Photo by Bernard Troncale, courtesy Alabama Media Group.

In his own final years, Erskine Hawkins was widely embraced as one of Birmingham's favorite successes, treated with plaques and proclamations—"I have, let me see, one, two, three . . . I have about four keys" to the city, he joked—and he found himself in a new, somewhat awkward spotlight, "getting up in front of mayors and senators to make a speech." The University of Alabama at Birmingham named him an honorary professor, inviting him to give concerts and lectures, host workshops, and record his memories for posterity. In 1980, the city erected a historic marker at Tuxedo Junction, and Hawkins played the unveiling. Tuxedo Junction Park celebrated Hawkins's birthday in 1985 with the inaugural Function at the Junction, and each year until his death Hawkins returned for the party, backed by the Heritage Band. In 1988, the park was renamed in his honor.[27]

In 1992, J. L. Lowe conceived and cowrote, with actress and author Karma Ibsen, a musical based on Hawkins's hits, titled—naturally—*Tuxedo Junction*. Mercedes Ellington, granddaughter of Duke, came to Birmingham to direct and choreograph the show, which debuted on the UAB campus. A second run followed the next year, in the summer of 1993, with Hawkins himself performing a cameo; he appeared also that July at the annual Function, playing in the rain for his seventy-ninth birthday. With Haywood Henry he fronted a reunion show in the city that September, and the same month he cut the ribbon that signaled the opening of the new hall of fame. But it was a beginning and an end: a health scare landed him in the hospital the day after the ribbon-cutting, and the hall of fame's opening gala went on that night without him. A week later he mustered the strength to join the Heritage Band in a tribute to Sammy Lowe, but he was clearly suffering onstage. He entered a physician's care the next day and died on November 11.

"As a musician, I think Erskine Hawkins personified the spirit of Birmingham," Frank Adams told a reporter in the days that followed. "His style and his playing and his personality were all products of Birmingham, and he certainly will be forever missed." At the Guiding Light Baptist Church, Reverend J. L. Lowe *Jr.* preached the words of comfort, and the Birmingham Heritage Band performed in tribute. Between the church and cemetery, the hearse detoured to Ensley, trailed by a procession of mourners. The caravan lingered at the long-dormant Junction and then continued on its way.[28]

More than 100 years after Fess Whatley's Jazz Demons first appeared in the city, the tradition they launched is largely forgotten. Certainly, there are remnants: the Alabama Jazz Hall of Fame keeps the flame, hosting jam sessions, all-state band competitions, and live performances; offering music classes; and maintaining an instrument recycling program that refurbishes donated horns and puts them in the hands of students in need. The last weekend of August brings the annual Taste of Fourth Avenue Jazz Festival, and a Jazz in the Park series provides free outdoor concerts at more than two dozen area parks each year. (Purists complain it is almost all smooth jazz these days, but there is no denying that smooth jazz brings the crowds.) The Exposure Community Development Corporation—founded in 2019 by brothers Timothy and Wesley Huffman, former students of the late Frank Adams—provides free music clinics and camps to kids. The nonprofit Urban Impact, meanwhile, is working to restore Fourth Avenue's faded vitality, and the Prince Hall Masons anticipate, at the time of this writing, a major relaunch of the Masonic Temple, a restoration that deliberately honors both the history of the space and its ongoing potential for the city.

Similar community-driven efforts are underway in Ensley, where a revival of visual arts, poetry, and music—fueled largely by local Black youth—has begun taking shape.

The Function at the Junction still takes place each year at Erskine Hawkins Park. There is only a nod to jazz in the lineup anymore—one is more likely to hear R&B, gospel, even reggae—but the Birmingham Heritage Band, now in its fourth decade, still kicks things off, and "Tuxedo Junction" still makes at least the older folks move. In "Birmingham Is My Home"— the group's *other* theme song, this one unfamiliar to the world beyond this Function—the band swings its set to a joyous climax. On the chorus, the musicians stand as one, some a little stooped with age, and they sway side to side and they sing:

Birmingham!
Birmingham!
Birmingham is my home!

Birmingham!
Birmingham!
Birmingham is my home!

Where you going, daddy?
I don't want to roam.

EPILOGUE

n 1969, the critic Leonard Feather was combing Harlem for some vestige of its former jazz glory. Most of the great old nightspots had shut their doors, Feather lamented, or else had turned to R&B or rock; jazz was still being made, of course, in Manhattan and elsewhere, it had just abandoned Harlem. A rare holdout in the neighborhood was a place called the Baron Lounge, where Feather was greeted at the door by a familiar face: Teddy Hill's.[1]

Hill had remained at Minton's for nearly three decades, hosting jams, booking bands, and welcoming pilgrims who came in homage to one of American music's most legendary sites. But the thrill of experimentation was long gone by the sixties, and the music veered into bloodless imitations of sounds pioneered there, years before. Teddy confessed to Feather that he had moved to the Baron because it was "the only game in town"; just four months earlier, Minton's had stopped hosting live music altogether. And "any place where jazz has died," Teddy said, "that's where I don't belong."

Still, Hill was not exactly grieving. "It was a hell of a 29 years while it lasted," he said.

* * *

Dud Bascomb died suddenly of a heart attack on Christmas Day 1972, sitting beside his wife at the movies. He was fifty-six years old. One of the great trumpet soloists of the swing era, he had also been a bridge to the modern era, celebrated and imitated by a generation of musicians. To the rest of the world, his name had gone unknown.[2]

Like many another musician, Dud's brother Paul lived long enough to watch his popularity fade, his career in music supplanted by the need to make ends meet. By the 1970s, the original Bama State Collegian was working a garbage truck on the South Side of Chicago, pulling the heavy cans from the alleys for the younger guys to lift and empty into the trucks. Prodded by his coworkers, he would reminisce about his years on the music scene, hauling out a scrapbook loaded with photos in which he stood shoulder to shoulder, horn in hand, with seemingly every icon of jazz. Bascomb, who also served as precinct captain for the local Democratic Party, gladly mentored younger musicians, including a flock of amateur horn-players, white and Black, who applied for sanitation jobs just to work his ward yard. ("I still cherish the day," remembered one of these pupils, "when in chalk on a garage door, he wrote for me the changes to the famous chop buster 'Cherokee.'") His later years were spent in obscurity, punctuated too rarely by the honors due a pioneer and statesman. In 1978 he traveled to Nice, France, for its International Jazz Festival; the next year, he was inducted into the Alabama Jazz Hall of Fame. In 1982 Birmingham mayor Richard Arrington presented him a key to his hometown, and he was feted at another hall of fame ceremony—but a few months later, *Jet* magazine could report that "saxophonist Paul Bascomb, who achieved fame with bandleaders Erskine Hawkins and Count Basie, is hobbling [around] Chicago" after "a trash can injured his foot while he was working on a garbage truck." He made his last recordings the same year, sitting in with a group of reverent young Chicago musicians. On the "Garbage Man Blues," he provided both the tenor sax and vocals.[3]

● ● ●

Haywood Henry celebrated his eighty-first birthday—January 10, 1994—on the airwaves of New York radio station WKCR, a guest of the jazz DJ and historian Phil Schaap. Schaap's other guest, drummer Max Roach, was also celebrating a birthday, his seventieth, and for more than two hours the two men swapped stories on the air. Haywood boasted about his hometown, recounted his travels as a teenage Collegian, and marveled at the early genius of Jo Jones. The last survivor of the original Hawkins crew—Erskine and Sammy had both died in the previous year—Haywood remained sharp and spry, funny and warm. With Roach and Schaap he laughed over the endless youth of their mutual friend, "Mr. Driver," a mentor to them all, still going strong at ninety and tuned in to the broadcast from his Lenox Avenue apartment.[4]

To most of the listening audience, the name Wilson Driver would not have meant much. Like so many Birmingham musicians, Driver had worked his influence more or less anonymously. His greatest impact would be felt in the younger artists he influenced: as teacher and mentor and storyteller, as Jazz Demon and movie-house drummer, as Birmingham's longtime Harlem ambassador. Some piece of his legacy survived through the classic recordings of his mentee Jo Jones and—by extension—through the music of every Jo Jones emulator and imitator in the world. His drumming also lived on in the poetry of his daughter Sonia Sanchez, who had absorbed her father's music all her life. "I think that the rhythm that I have came from the music that was constantly played in our house," Sanchez said in 2011. "We were constantly exposed to jazz and blues, and I think that that is represented in my work, always. Even when I read my work, I am always attuned to the jazz of it, and that rhythm that I heard all those years, and listening to my father talk about music and explain music to me—that's all running in my poetry, and how I read my poetry.

"It is always there," the poet said. "It is never far from my tongue."[5]

. . .

"As long as God has given me a voice," Ethel Harper wrote in 1970, "I'll use it to make a better world."[6]

Harper hung up the Jemima apron and headscarf in 1958, stepping out of show business and settling thirty miles from New York in Morristown, New Jersey. Her final act was almost certainly her most rewarding, as she became a leading contributor to civic life in the region. Whoever Aunt Jemima might have been, Ethel Harper was a powerful personality: dignified, forward-thinking, creative, opinionated, and deeply engaged. She chaired the civil rights committee of the local League of Women Voters and the education committee of her area NAACP branch. For more than a decade she served as a field director to the Girl Scouts, the first Black woman to serve locally in such a role. She reentered the classroom at last, teaching in public and parochial schools and in adult education programs. As Jemima, she had preached a gospel of good nutrition; now she presented lectures on nutrition to groups of all ages. She developed and for a decade taught the county's first curriculum in Black history, and she championed the new multiculturalism movement in education. She coupled her service to the youth with an equal drive to serve the elderly: at sixty-nine, she became director of entertainment and outreach for Morris County senior citizens, she put on her old gowns and performed at nursing homes and retirement communities, and she served on the state's advisory commission on aging. She delivered for Meals on Wheels and volunteered at area hospitals, and she conceived and moderated a topical talk radio show, *Youth Speaks Out; Age Speaks Out; Are You Listening?*

A few months before she died, she mapped out her achievements on a pie chart, the sections of her life arranged chronologically into slices spanning the years 1903 to 1978: "The Pie of My Life," she called it, and she took obvious pride in each section. The final slice she labeled "Open for what lies ahead," and inside it she wrote this: "Plan for future: Return to theatre as a monologist."

Ethel Harper never stopped planning, never stopped hustling, never stopped looking toward the next adventure. Contemplating her legacy, her hopes were modest. "I wish to be remembered," she wrote, "for whatever good I have done; for whatever service I have rendered along the way."

* * *

It's a spring night in 2022 at trumpeter Daniel "José" Carr's long-running Tuesday night jam session.[7] Carr has been leading these sessions for more than three decades, migrating through the years from one club to the next. Some nights there are more than twenty musicians on hand, and fewer than half as many listeners. The musicians don't seem to mind the imbalance: they're playing for themselves more than the room. They're listening, working, refining their craft.

On other nights the place is packed, and recent sessions at True Story Brewing Company, the jam's latest home, have been drawing big crowds. Tonight Carr is feeding off the energy in the room. He dedicates one tune to the memory of his teacher at Jackson-Olin High School, the late Amos Gordon. Later in the set, he introduces a composition by another mentor, Jothan Callins; the tune is "Councill," a tribute to Ensley's Councill Elementary, which both Callins and Carr attended years ago.

There is significant diversity among the players: old and young, Black and white, male and female take turns improvising solos. Several of the musicians, notably trumpeter Collins "Bo" Berry, are longtime local stalwarts; others drive from across Alabama—from Tuscaloosa, Montgomery, Troy—to sit in at the best jam session in the state. Some of the younger players are visibly nervous, some visibly hungry for what this room has to offer. Musicians on the sidelines wait silently, studiously fingering their horns. Between solos, some of the old-timers offer encouragement and advice. They whisper tips, not just about the music but about the etiquette of the jam.

Carr is frustrated that jazz is no longer the force it once was in town. "Birmingham is still good for it," he says. "We just need to push more jazz in the schools." For now, these jams will have to do, filling the role performed, years ago, by the classroom. For his own part, Carr has no plans of slowing down. "All I'm trying to do," he says, "is pass the music down. Every day of my life. On my horn. And trying to be a role model for the kids."

"I like getting out playing with the cats, man," Bo Berry adds. "I like getting out and hanging with the *young* cats—just to play and tell them some things, and try to point some things out that they'll need along the way. And always *share*. Because it ain't about how great you are—it's if you're speaking the same language, and what kind of heart you have.

"That's the whole thing," he concludes, as musicians pack up for the night. "That's it. That's *it*. I'm telling you, man—I don't care how you look at it.

"*That's it.*"

ACKNOWLEDGMENTS

A long list of thank-yous must begin with Dr. Frank Adams, whom I knew as "Doc" (1928–2014). If we'd never met, I would have never imagined or attempted this book; more than that, I would have never found one of my life's most invaluable friends, mentors, collaborators, and inspirations.

Patrick Cather similarly deserves a universe of thanks: for all he's done to preserve Birmingham music and history, for sharing again and again his many extraordinary stories, and for his deep friendship, which extends well beyond the pages of this book.

I am forever indebted to the pioneering work of both Jothan Callins and J. L. Lowe, whose devoted efforts to document and perpetuate their community's tradition provided essential foundation and inspiration for my own research; to torch bearers Tolton Rosser and Tommy Stewart, for their invaluable input and insight; to Hasan Shahid, for the enlightening conversation; and to Bo Berry, José Carr, and the late Rickey Powell, for many nights of music and many answers to my questions. Thanks to writers Carol Ealons (*Tuxedo Junction: Right Back Where I Belong*) and Carolyn Marzette-Bolivar (*Swing Lowe: A Family's Dedication to Preserving Music in the Magic City*) and to filmmakers Sandy Jaffe (*Jazz in the Magic City*) and Matthew Bellisario (*So You Say You Play Jazz?*) for their own deep labors of love in researching, uplifting, and preserving local jazz voices and lives.

Huge thanks go to the Alabama Jazz Hall of Fame; its director, Leah Tucker; and its board members and staff for everything they do. I hope all who pick up this book will make it their business to schedule a visit to the jazz hall whenever they're in Birmingham.

Each musician and witness who made time for an interview (sometimes multiple interviews) has contributed to my understanding of this history and made this a better book. Because the book steps only briefly into the twenty-first century, several favorite players don't appear in these pages, but their music—and often their friendship—has nourished and inspired me throughout this process. You can still find great music in Birmingham, and there are many more stories left to tell.

There would be no story here, at all, without the teachers, and while this book introduces a few of the most influential, a whole community and lineage of school band directors has for more than a century shaped the course of Birmingham jazz. This city's musical life would not be the same without the legacies of them all: Hooper Abrams, Frank Adams, Jothan Callins, Daniel "José" Carr, Richard Clarke, Donald Crawford, Charles "Danny Boy" Daniels, Wilson Driver, Sam "High C" Foster, Amos "Flash" Gordon, William Wise Handy, George Hudson, Calvin Ivory, Jessie Larkin, John McAphee, Arthur Means, Dan Michael, Alvin Robertson, Wilton Robertson, Tolton Rosser, Awilda Smith, Benjamin Smith, John Springer, Newman Terrell, John T. "Fess" Whatley, and—still, always—more. Thanks go to those working in the schools today, still shaping and saving lives, making this community and the world better.

A separate history could be written of the venues alone. In the decade-plus that I've been working on this book, my life has been enriched by nights at Ona's Music Room, Marty's, Old Car Heaven, BOSS Ultra Bar and Lounge, Jazzi's on Third, Jazzy's on First, East Village Arts, and True Story Brewing. Any local reader will notice that many of those spaces have shut their doors in the years since I began this book, a fact that only underscores the urgency of their service. My gratitude goes to every venue owner who has worked to keep this music alive.

Essential support has been provided by the many generous donors to the *Lost Child* radio show and to the new, nonprofit Southern Music Research Center. Their contributions and kindness have fueled this work more than I can ever adequately express. For an expanded portrait of Birmingham's jazz story—including photos, ephemera, oral histories, and recordings—please visit the Southern Music Research Center's digital archive at southernmusicresearch.org.

For always expanding my musical mind—and for their devotion and promotion, in particular, of the Alabama avant-garde—I'm indebted to Jimmy Griffin and Lee Shook. My research has been facilitated greatly by the staffs of numerous libraries and archives—particularly the Alabama Department of Archives and History, the Alabama State University Archives, the Birmingham Public Library Archives, the Institute of Jazz Studies at Rutgers University, the Morristown and Morris Township Library, the University of Alabama at Birmingham Archives, and the University of Chicago Library. For providing access to the Masonic Temple and its history, I'm grateful to Urban Impact Inc. and the Most Worshipful Prince Hall Grand Lodge, F. & A. M. of Alabama. For his vast knowledge of Birmingham history and his heroic dedication to its preservation, a thousand thanks go to John Morse. His Bhamwiki is an astonishing, illuminating resource; I only wish every city had something like it.

Special thanks go to Robert Mugge, not only for his extraordinary film *Sun Ra: A Joyful Noise* but for access to interviews from his cutting-room floor and for his enthusiastic support throughout this book's long process. Big thanks go, too, to Guillaume Maupin and Pablo Guarise for breathing new life into Sun Ra's Birmingham and for the energizing conversations, collaboration, and friendship. My understandings of Sun Ra's music, philosophy, life, and legacy have been informed by a broad community of Sun Ra chroniclers, interpreters, superfans, and scholars. Thanks are due in particular to John Szwed, John Corbett, Robert L. Campbell, and Michael D. Anderson for their pioneering work in this field; to the Hinds Brothers, Peter and John, for all the years of *Sun Ra Research*; to Christopher Eaddy of the Sun Ra Arkive; and to Sun Ra's devoted following of Alabama fans, many of whom are my friends.

Multiple friends and colleagues contributed feedback on the work in progress. Conversations with David Hornbuckle helped refine this book in its early stages, and William Blackerby provided indispensable support in getting this thing to the finish line. At the University of North Carolina, Bill Ferris, Glenn Hinson, and Patricia Sawin lent their gracious guidance to a long-delayed master's thesis on Fess Whatley. A fellowship from the Alabama State Council on the Arts provided a significant boost in the final phases of this project. The readers and staff at UNC Press provided valuable direction. And the administration of Spain Park High School, particularly Larry Giangrosso, made possible a creative teaching schedule that allowed me both time in the classroom and time to write.

For the widest variety of contributions, conversations, leads, and encouragements, I am grateful to Rob Alley, Matt Baker, Carol Clarke, Ardie Colvin, Myra Eaton, Chad Fisher, Philip Foster, Yves François, Cassandra Griffen, Bart Grooms, Gary and Kim Hatfield, Wyteria Huffman, Emily Jack, Thomas Jenkins, Jessica Latten, Craig Legg, Roberta Lowe, Jud Mathews, Travis Morgan, George Mostoller, Kim Mowery, Nick Patterson, Connell Ruffin, Janet Simpson-Templin, Aaron Smithers, Will Stewart, Wilma Stewart, Charles Tortorici, Marnie Utz, Todd Utz, Katherine Webb-Hehn, and Paul Wilm.

I can never thank George and Betty Mathews, my parents, enough—for everything (!), including but not limited to a lifetime of encouragement. I'm grateful that since I began this book my family has expanded to include my wonderful in-laws, Pat and Wayne McLaughlin. Infinite love, appreciation, and admiration go to Norah Murphy, who makes life better, more fun, and certainly funnier. And the deepest debt of gratitude is due my best friend on the planet, an extraordinary human being, Glory McLaughlin, to whom this book is dedicated.

NOTES

INTRODUCTION

1. For Hawkins's homecoming, see Kathy Kemp, "Junction Function Too Hot for Rain to Cool," *Birmingham Post-Herald*, July 27, 1985.

2. The description of Sun Ra's performance at the Nick draws from author interviews with audience members, including George Mostoller, Jimmy Griffin, Charles Tortorici, and Craig Legg, as well from a recording of the event made by Joe Moudry. For other perspectives on this event, see chapter 23.

3. Sun Ra, "The Outer Darkness (1972, version 1)," in *Immeasurable Equation*, 294.

4. The unfinished manuscript of Sammy Lowe's memoir—"A Man from Tuxedo Junction (from Jazz to Swing to Rock to Soul): Diary of a Black Musician," housed in the archive of the Birmingham Public Library—consists of interview transcripts edited by hand, likely a project begun in collaboration with jazz historian Stanley Dance. Because the work blends and blurs the spoken and the written word, I've used such signifiers as "Lowe said" and "Lowe wrote" interchangeably when quoting this document.

CHAPTER 1: BEGINNINGS

1. Birmingham's Black and white community adopted the city's nickname early on. By 1876, Black residents had founded a short-lived newspaper, the *Magic City*, perhaps the city's first African American paper. Hornady, *Book of Birmingham*, 195.

2. Callins, "Birmingham Jazz Community," 35. For the early history of Birmingham and its music, I am deeply indebted to Callins's research and writing.

3. Hornady, *Book of Birmingham*, 100–103.

4. Quoted in Stearns and Stearns, *Jazz Dance*, 24.

5. Hornady, *Book of Birmingham*, 111.

6. Handy, *Father of the Blues*, 8.

7. Handy, *Father of the Blues*, 22–23.

8. Handy, *Father of the Blues*, 23–26.

9. Callins, "Birmingham Jazz Community," 42.

10. Adams and Mathews, *Doc*, 190. The following portrait of Pops Williams draws from multiple interviews with Frank Eaton Adams Sr. (conducted between 2008 and 2012) and Patrick Cather (conducted between 2010 and 2016).

11. Jaffe, *Jazz in the Magic City*.

12. Unless otherwise noted, biographical details on Williams appear in Callins, "Birmingham Jazz Community," 42–44.

13. Jaffe, *Jazz in the Magic City*.

14. Nearly a century later, Williams remembered his first bandmates as Gus Lawson (banjo), "B" Riley (fiddle), and, on drums, a player they simply called "Long Tall."

15. Hornady, *Book of Birmingham*, 269–71.

16. Adams and Mathews, *Doc*, 191.

17. See Watkins, *Showman*; and Handy, *Father of the Blues*, 66. For Lowery's "Hustleth" quote, see Watkins, front matter.

18. Callins, "Birmingham Jazz Community," 42.

19. Callins, "Birmingham Jazz Community," 44. For the significance of New Orleans's Colored Waif's Home for Boys, see Teachout, *Pops*, 34–39; for the Jenkins Orphanage, see Chilton, *Jazz Nursery*.

CHAPTER 2: AN INDUSTRIAL EDUCATION

1. John T. "Fess" Whatley and J. L. Lowe Scrapbook, Birmingham Public Library, Department of Archives and Manuscripts (hereinafter BPL).

2. Whatley and Lowe Scrapbook, BPL.

3. Bertrand Demeusy, "John Tuggle 'Fess' Whatley, a Maker of Musicians," *Jazz Monthly*, August 1966, 6.

4. "Fess Whatley's Band to Make Tour of Eastern States," *Chicago Defender*, June 23, 1934; Murray, *Murray Talks Music*, 39.

5. Demeusy, "John Tuggle 'Fess' Whatley," 8.

6. "Returns from Long Western Trip in His Brand New 1941 Cadillac," *Weekly Review*, July 4, 1941; Adams and Mathews, *Doc*, 58; Whatley Scrapbook, BPL.

7. Adams and Mathews, *Doc*, 51–52, 62; Patrick Cather, interview with the author, October 23, 2010; Jaffe, *Jazz in the Magic City*; John L. Mitchell, "Birmingham, Ala.," *Pittsburgh Courier*, January 29, 1927 ("She climbs to the middle of the steering wheel," the *Courier* says of Whatley's poodle, "watching with unblinking gravity the traffic lights"); Marzette-Bolivar, *Swing Lowe*, 37; Demeusy, "John Tuggle 'Fess' Whatley."

8. Tommy Stewart, interview with the author, February 3, 2011.

9. See, for example, James Chisum, "'Fess' Whatley's World of Music Slipping Away," undated article, c. 1968, Whatley and Lowe Scrapbook, BPL; Jesse Champion, interview by Horace Huntley, November 1, 1995, Civil Rights Oral History Project, Birmingham Civil Rights Institute. The same story is told of Capt. Walter Dyett, legendary music director of Chicago's Wendell Phillips and DuSable High Schools. Singer Marshall Thompson said of Dyett, "He was one of the greatest musicians in the world. He'd throw that stick at you if you played the wrong note. He'd throw that stick right at your face. It was amazing, we had a thirty-piece orchestra and he could tell who was playing wrong" (quoted in A. Cohen, *Move On Up*, 8).

10. Demeusy, "John Tuggle 'Fess' Whatley," 6; Callins, "Birmingham Jazz Community," 45–46. For a history of the Tuggle Institute, see Feldman, *Sense of Place*, 172–75.

11. Callins, "Birmingham Jazz Community, 45–46.

12. Callins, "Birmingham Jazz Community," 46; Chisum, "'Fess' Whatley's World of Music Slipping Away."

13. Gaston, *Green Power*, 27–28. Gaston's civil rights legacy has long been a source of debate. To some, he was an overcautious accommodationist, his activism compromised by his deference to the white business community; but Gaston was a critical player behind the scenes of the movement, contributing essential funds and providing meeting space in his Gaston Motel, which in turn became a prominent target for violence. That motel, and its Gaston Supper Club, also became a resource for the jazz community, hosting live music and workshops from visiting artists.

14. Whatley Scrapbook, BPL.

15. Whatley Scrapbook, BPL.

16. For a history of Industrial/Parker High School, see Feldman, *Sense of Place*, 120–34.

17. Feldman, *Sense of Place*, 126–27; James Saxon Childers, "Where Pupils Study Books and Brooms," *Birmingham News Age-Herald*, May 28, 1933.

18. "Negro High School with Booker T. Washington Purpose," *Christian Science Monitor*, October 11, 1932.

19. John Temple Graces, "This Morning," *Birmingham Age-Herald*, April 4, 1930; "Excellent Work Which Is Being Done by the Negro High School," *Birmingham News*, May 30, 1903.

20. "Folk Songs of Negroes Praised by Dr. Phillips," *Birmingham News*, May 31, 1914.

21. For a detailed look at Wilkerson, see Abbott and Seroff, *To Do This*, 116–24.

22. Abbott and Seroff, *To Do This*, 120–21; Adams and Mathews, *Doc*, 56–57; Parker, *Dream That Came True*, 61; "Tibbett Says Songs by Negroes Here His Greatest Experience," *Industrial High School Record*, vol. 12, no. 5 (May 1931), reprinted in Abbott and Seroff, *To Do This*, 121; Byron S. Dozier, "Parker High Long Way from Single Room," *Birmingham News*, May 24, 1985; Sammy Lowe, "A Man from Tuxedo Junction (from Jazz to Swing to Rock to Soul): Diary of a Black Musician," part 1, 37–38 (unpublished manuscript, n.d.), ARR1137, BPL.

23. Quoted in Parker, *Dream That Came True*, 59–62.

24. Quoted in Parker, *Dream That Came True*, 60.

25. Quoted in Parker, *Dream That Came True*, 37.

26. Undated article, Whatley Scrapbook, BPL.

27. Oscar Adams, "Local News," *Birmingham Reporter*, March 16, 1918; Marzette-Bolivar, *Swing Lowe*, 28.

28. Adams and Mathews, *Doc*, 56; Jaffe, *Jazz in the Magic City*.

CHAPTER 3: MAKER OF MUSICIANS

1. David Lawrence, "Democrats Condemn, While Republicans Give Praise to Harding's Speech Here," *Birmingham News*, October 27, 1921. Harding was no fan of the growing jazz fad, however; a few months before his Birmingham speech, an article appeared in the *Birmingham Reporter* with the headline "No Jazz for Harding: President Does Not Care for Modern Syncopators" (May 14, 1921).

2. Dave Payton, "The Musical Bunch," *Chicago Defender*, November 3, 1928; Adams and Mathews, *Doc*, 57.

3. Jesse Champion, interview by Horace Huntley, November 1, 1995, Civil Rights Oral History Project, Birmingham Civil Rights Institute, Birmingham, AL; Greer quoted in Bertrand Demeusy, "John Tuggle 'Fess' Whatley, a Maker of Musicians," *Jazz Monthly*, August 1966, 8. See also Lloyd, "Life and Legacy of Frank Terry Greer."

4. Marzette-Bolivar, *Swing Lowe*, 29; Sammy Lowe, "A Man from Tuxedo Junction (from Jazz to Swing to Rock to Soul): Diary of a Black Musician," part 1, 110 (unpublished manuscript, n.d.), ARR1137, BPL; Chip Stern, "Wilson Driver: Driver Man, Reflections of an Urban Griot," Chipstern.com, accessed June 17, 2011, https://www.chipstern.com/chip_tribal_wilson.htm (site discontinued).

5. Jaffe, *Jazz in the Magic City*; Marzette-Bolivar, *Swing Lowe*, 30; Tommy Stewart, interview with the author, June 3, 2011.

6. Lowe, "Man from Tuxedo Junction," part 1, 87; Adams and Mathews, *Doc*, 51.

7. "Even the way he walked," said J. L. Lowe: "it was with rhythm in his mind. One, two, three, four. It was always like that with him" (quoted in Marzette-Bolivar, *Swing Lowe*, 42–43); Lowe, "Man from Tuxedo Junction," part 1, 88; Adams and Mathews, *Doc*, 64.

8. Adams and Mathews, *Doc*, 64, 53; Lowe, "Man from Tuxedo Junction," part 1, 88–89.

9. Adams and Mathews, *Doc*, 62.

10. Joos, "Natchez Fire," 36–38.

11. Stern, "Wilson Driver."

12. Adams and Mathews, *Doc*, 54.

13. J. L. Lowe interview, June 20, 1994, Behind the Veil Oral History Project, John Hope Franklin Research Center for African and African American History and Culture, David M. Rubenstein Rare Book and Manuscript Library, Duke University, Durham, NC; Marzette-Bolivar, *Swing Lowe*, 39.

14. Stern, "Wilson Driver."

15. Lowe, "Man from Tuxedo Junction," part 1, 19–20; Adams and Mathews, *Doc*, 43–45; Tolton Rosser, interviews with the author, April 19, 2016, and June 30, 2020. In her memoir

of growing up in 1960s Birmingham, Condoleezza Rice remembered the centrality of music, and music teachers, to the culture of Birmingham's Black schools. In the days before integration, she wrote, music activities were not "extracurricular or add-ons": "They were an essential part of transforming students into more cultured people with well-developed artistic talents," each performance serving as opportunity "for the community to come together." An aspiring concert pianist reared in the middle-class Black community of Titusville, Rice would grow up to become national security advisor and secretary of state; as a student at Lane Elementary School, she played bells in the marching band. Though she gave up plans for a career in music, Rice remained an accomplished pianist; she has performed onstage with both Aretha Franklin and Yo-Yo Ma and played for Queen Elizabeth II. Rice, *Ordinary, Extraordinary People*, 56–58.

16. Advertisements, *Birmingham News*, November 20, 1921, and November 22, 1921; Jay Sims, "The 'Fess Whatley Story,'" *Huntsville Mirror*, February 4, 1956. For Whatley's sponsorship of student bands, see Bob Rusch, "Sun Ra: Interview," *Cadence*, June 1978, 5; and advertisement, *Kingsport (TN) Times*, October 12, 1934.

17. "Fess Whatley and Band Hit in the South," *Chicago Defender*, July 7, 1934; "Fess Whatley's Band to Make Tour of Eastern States," *Chicago Defender*, June 23, 1934.

18. Newspaper advertisement, undated, author's collection; Rosser, interview with the author, June 30, 2020.

19. Adams and Mathews, *Doc*, 62.

20. Stern, "Wilson Driver." As Driver indicates, the rules were especially strict when white people were involved; for more on this, see chapter 7.

21. For discussions of the "sweet" and "hot," see Hart, "Jazz Jargon"; Webb, "Slang of Jazz"; and Wilkerson, "Hot and Sweet."

22. Rosser, interview with the author, June 30, 2020; Patrick Cather, interview with the author, October 23, 2010. See Gayle Dean Wardlow, "Black Birds of Paradise," *78 Quarterly* 2 (1968), reprinted in Wardlow, *Chasin' That Devil Music*, 80.

23. Lowe, "Man from Tuxedo Junction," part 1, 99–100; Stern, "Wilson Driver."

24. Tyina Steptoe's study of the Houston schools and their musical legacies provides an especially valuable parallel to the Birmingham story (*Houston Bound*, 156–71).

25. Callins, "Birmingham Jazz Community," 47–48; Tolton Rosser, interview with the author, July 1, 2020; Adams and Mathews, *Doc*, 136; Whatley Scrapbook, BPL. As with other aspects of society, there would be two parallel unions in Birmingham for decades, until the two merged in 1969 to form Local 256–733.

26. Adams, interview with the author, c. 2012.

CHAPTER 4: SMITHFIELD

1. Lofton, *Voices from Alabama*, 339.

2. Marzette-Bolivar, *Swing Lowe*, 12; Frank Eaton Adams Sr., interview with the author, May 15, 2010.

3. For a history of Smithfield's development and the rise of its Black middle-class community, see Feldman, *Sense of Place*.

4. Feldman, *Sense of Place*, 29–31.

5. For Italian-Black relations in Birmingham, see Fede, "Interdependence of Blacks and Italians."

6. "Haywood Henry Meets Max Roach Birthday Broadcast," January 9, 1994, Birthday Broadcasts, Phil Schaap Jazz, www.philschaapjazz.com.

7. Frank Eaton Adams Sr., interview with the author, September 19, 2009.

8. Frank Adams, foreword to *Swing Lowe*, by Marzette-Bolivar, xi.

9. Frank Eaton Adams Sr., interview with the author, May 22, 2010.

10. Sammy Lowe, "A Man from Tuxedo Junction (from Jazz to Swing to Rock to Soul): Diary of a Black Musician," part 1, 12–13 (unpublished manuscript, n.d.), ARR1137, BPL.

11. Adams and Mathews, *Doc*, 9; Lowe, "Man from Tuxedo Junction," part 1, 6.

12. In *Behind the Ebony Mask*, author Geraldine Moore ("Speaking for Birmingham") offered an overview of Chambliss's career and identified the leaders of several prominent private music schools in Birmingham: Jessica Divers Hayden, Mrs. Gregory Durr White, Savannah Crews Jones, Essie Heath Bennett, and Jessie Heath Robinson (91–93). Jazz bassist Cleve Eaton's older sister LaVergne Eaton Comer was another popular teacher. Activist Angela Davis, who grew up on Smithfield's Dynamite Hill, recalled her own piano lessons without enthusiasm: "Once a week I trudged over to Mrs. Chambliss's house, dutifully played my scales and compositions, suffering the humiliations of being screamed at if I made a mistake" (*Autobiography*, 84–85).

13. Lowe, "Man from Tuxedo Junction," part 1, 95.

14. Lowe, "Man from Tuxedo Junction," part 1, 6; Davenport quoted in Mike Rowe, liner notes, *Cow Cow Davenport: Complete Recorded Works in Chronological Order, Volume 1*, Document Records DOCD-5141, 1992. In the community of Woodlawn, on the east side of Birmingham, young Edwin Witt was enough enamored of the piano to take up lessons, at twenty-five cents an hour, with a typical private instructor—"short, dark, bespectacled, very quiet, polite"—but he quit after his baseball pals taunted him for the music book he carried under his arm to practice. "Sis-ay, sis-ay, sis-ay," they sang, and Witt's piano career ended (Witt, *Witt's End*, 211). The instrument's association with femininity—and male homosexuality—was in no way unique to Birmingham. In Mobile, trombonist Fred Wesley Jr. recalled that "all the good piano players I knew of were girls or like a girl." The only exception was Wesley's father, a music teacher, bandleader, and boogie-woogie pianist who "must have learned [piano] by himself," since he never absorbed a feminine style (Wesley, *Hit Me*, 9). "When a man played piano," Jelly Roll Morton of New Orleans recalled, "the stamp was on him for life—the femininity stamp." Morton took a proactive approach to that stamp: he made sure his early songs were "kinda smutty a bit," cutting off the "sissy" charge before it could stick (*Jelly Roll Morton: The Complete Library of Congress Recordings by Alan Lomax*, Rounder 11661-1889-2, 2006).

15. Shawn Ryan, "Blues' Meaning Varies according to Memories," undated article, author's collection; Lowe, "Man from Tuxedo Junction," part 1, 11, 24.

16. Lowe, "Man from Tuxedo Junction," part 1, 85.

17. Lowe, "Man from Tuxedo Junction," part 1, 27.

18. Lowe, "Man from Tuxedo Junction," part 1, 25.

19. Lowe, "Man from Tuxedo Junction," part 1, 25–26; Marzette-Bolivar, *Swing Lowe*, 25–26; Frank Adams, interview with the author, July 29, 2009.

20. "Haywood Henry, Musician," 121; Marzette-Bolivar, *Swing Lowe*, 25.

21. "Haywood Henry, Musician," 127.

22. "Haywood Henry, Musician," 127

23. "Haywood Henry, Musician," 123–24.

CHAPTER 5: FOURTH AVENUE STOMP

1. "Southern Artists to Make Records," *Birmingham News*, July 12, 1927; see also R. Kennedy, *Jelly Roll*, 175–77; and Burgin Mathews, "The Birmingham Sessions: Gennett Records and the Sounds of 1920s Alabama," *Old-Time Herald*, January 2017, 24–36.

2. "Southern Artists to Make Records"; "Gennett Recording Expedition in Birmingham, Ala.," *Talking Machine World*, July 1927, 34d.

3. "Southern Artists to Make Records"; "Gennett Record Laboratory Established in Birmingham," *Talking Machine World*, August 1927, 8.

4. Stan Diel, "Fourth Avenue Business District, Booming under Segregation, Still Works to Rebound 50 Years Later," AL.com, March 15, 2013, https://www.al.com/business/2013/03/fourth_avenue_business_distric.html; Adams and Mathews, *Doc*, 92; Marcel Hopson, interview by Steve McCallum, February 7, 1985, Working Lives Oral History Project, University of Alabama Libraries Special Collections, Tuscaloosa, AL.

5. Nathan Ben Young, "Eighteenth Street (Birmingham): An Anthology in Color," in Johnson, *Ebony and Topaz*, 37–38.

6. Judge Nathan B. Young, interview by Richard Resh, July 15, 1970, Oral History Collection, State Historical Society of Missouri, www.shsmo.org; Nathan Ben Young, "These 'Colored' United States," *The Messenger*, March 1925, 124, 140.

7. Adams and Mathews, *Doc*, 10. For a history of African American fraternal organizations, see Skocpol, Liazos, and Ganz, *What a Mighty Power*; for a history of the Knights of Pythias in Birmingham, see Peebles, *Alabama Knights of Pythias*.

8. Erected in 1913, the space had first served as home to the Alabama Penny Savings Bank, one of the first Black-owned banks in the nation, and it continued to stand as symbol of independent economic achievement, a source for local Black pride.

9. *Birmingham Reporter*, December 22, 1923. See also Mary Stanton, "Birmingham's Most Worshipful Prince Hall Grand Lodge," *Alabama Heritage*, Winter 2017, 26–35.

10. Dance notices from Katherine Kent Lambert's "Birmingham News" column for the *Chicago Defender*: January 7, 1928; March 7, 1925; January 31, 1925. Jones, *Rifftide*, 38; Adams and Mathews, *Doc*, 46. See Brothers, *Louis Armstrong's New Orleans*, 211–16, for a discussion of the fraternal orders' influence on the jazz culture of New Orleans, particularly on that city's celebrated tradition of funeral parades.

11. Steptoe, *Houston Bound*, 163; Brothers, *Louis Armstrong's New Orleans*, 21. Protests like Handy's had parallels in other schools; see Steptoe, 164, for a Houston educator's resistance to his own city's "Black Band in the Back" tradition.

12. J. L. Lowe, interview, June 20, 1994, Behind the Veil Oral History Project, John Hope Franklin Research Center for African and African American History and Culture, David M. Rubenstein Rare Book and Manuscript Library, Duke University, Durham, NC; Sammy Lowe, "A Man from Tuxedo Junction (from Jazz to Swing to Rock to Soul): Diary of a Black Musician," part 1, 95 (unpublished manuscript, n.d.), ARR1137, BPL; Erskine Hawkins, interview by Leonard Goines, February 6, 1982, 27, 31, Jazz Oral History Project, Institute of Jazz Studies, Rutgers University (hereinafter JOHP).

13. Hardy with Turner, *Sweetest Harmony*, 5. Jo Jones summed up segregation with the same story: "You might think it's a lie. Years ago the white folks would laugh first, and now you niggers laugh after that. That's where the laughing bell came in. You didn't get to laugh until after the white folks got to laugh" (Jones, *Rifftide*, 39).

14. *Birmingham Reporter*, March 30, 1918.

15. Quoted in Albertson, *Bessie*, 113–14. So ingrained was the minstrelsy tradition in America's popular culture that, in the early twentieth century, even in Black-controlled spaces, some Black comedians continued to appear in the burnt cork or greasepaint of blackface. The result was a complex web of appropriated and exaggerated identities, Black imitations of white imitations of Blackness. Many of the most popular Black comedians, like the duo of Butterbeans and Susie, dispensed with the paint but drew nonetheless from the mannerisms and tropes of the blackface tradition.

16. Lowe, "Man from Tuxedo Junction," part 1, 10.

17. "New Queen Theatre Birmingham Ala.," *Indianapolis Freeman*, July 29, 1916, quoted in Abbott and Seroff, *Original Blues*, 172.

18. Lowe, "Man from Tuxedo Junction," part 1, 9.

19. Charles O'Neal, "In Old Kaysee," *Chicago Defender*, October 31, 1925.

20. Even in the logbooks, the Triangle Harmony Boys were rendered anonymous: the Gennett files listed only Murray Harper by name (John Wilby, liner notes, *Gennett Rarities*, Jazz Oracle BDW 8009, 1998, CD).

21. Wardlow, "The Black Birds of Paradise," in *Chasin' That Devil Music*, 77–78; on Gennett's payment policies to Birmingham artists, see also R. Kennedy, *Jelly Roll*, 180; and Mathews, "Birmingham Sessions," 35.

CHAPTER 6: FAMOUS RHYTHM

1. Sammy Lowe, "Man From Tuxedo Junction (from Jazz to Swing to Rock to Soul): Diary of a Black Musician," part 1, 9 (unpublished manuscript, n.d.), ARR1137, BPL; "To Give Lectures," *Birmingham News*, February 17, 1924; "Addresses Negroes," *Birmingham News*, February 18, 1924.

2. Chip Stern, "Wilson Driver: Driver Man, Reflections of an Urban Griot," Chipstern.com, accessed June 17, 2011, https://www.chipstern.com/chip_tribal_wilson.htm (site discontinued); Sonia Sanchez, interview with the author, June 18, 2011; Lowe, "Man from Tuxedo Junction," part I, 114.

3. Stern, "Wilson Driver."

4. Stern, "Wilson Driver."

5. Stern, "Wilson Driver."

6. Stern, "Wilson Driver."

7. Korall, *Drummin' Men*, 118; Jones, *Rifftide*, 28.

8. Ralph Ellison to Albert Murray, October 22, 1955, in Murray and Callahan, *Trading Twelves*, 98; Sanchez, interview with the author.

9. Murray and Callahan, *Trading Twelves*, 98; Paul Devlin, introduction to *Rifftide*, by Papa Jo Jones, 8; Korall, *Drummin' Men*, 120.

10. "Retold and embellished": see, for example, the 2014 movie *Whiplash*, in which a brutal drumming instructor recounts the tale of how "Jones nearly decapitate[d]" Parker by throwing a cymbal at his head.

11. Korall, *Drummin' Men*, 131.

12. Korall, *Drummin' Men*, 126–27.

13. Korall, *Drummin' Men*, 128.

14. Chip Stern, "Papa Jo Jones," *Modern Drummer*, January 1984, 12.

15. Korall, *Drummin' Men*, 128.

16. Korall, *Drummin' Men*, 130; David Gonzalez, "Toe to Toe over a Checkerboard," *New York Times*, December 7, 1991; Jones, *Rifftide*, 109.

17. Korall, *Drummin' Men*, 130, 128.

18. Stern, "Wilson Driver."

19. Stern, "Wilson Driver"; Korall, *Drummin' Men*, 129.

20. Stern, "Wilson Driver"; Jones, *Rifftide*, 75.

21. Jo Jones, *The Drums*, Jazz Odyssey JO 008, 1974, LP.

22. Stern, "Wilson Driver"; Devlin, introduction to *Rifftide*, by Jones, 8.

23. Stern, "Wilson Driver"; Korall, *Drummin' Men*, 129.

24. Stern, "Wilson Driver."

25. Korall, *Drummin' Men*, 129.

26. Stern, "Wilson Driver."

CHAPTER 7: A CITY APART

1. Walling Keith, "Birmingham's Harlem Is City Apart," *Birmingham News*, September 13, 1936.

2. Keith, "Birmingham's Harlem Is City Apart."

3. For frequent coverage of the Midnight Reviews—advertisements, accolades, and the demise of the series—see the *Birmingham News*, December 17, 1924, through January 10, 1925.

4. Two headlines in the January 10, 1924, edition of the *Birmingham News* reflect the split between white audiences and the city government: "'Midnight Show' Pleases Audience" and "Midnight Shows Seen as Menace."

5. O. Cohen, *Dark Days*, 4; O. Cohen, *Black and Blue*, 3.

6. J. L. Lowe, interview, June 20, 1994, Behind the Veil Oral History Project, John Hope Franklin Research Center for African and African American History and Culture, David M. Rubenstein Rare Book and Manuscript Library, Duke University, Durham, NC.

7. Frank Eaton Adams Sr., interview with the author, October 17, 2010; Adams and Mathews, *Doc*, 220.

8. "Haywood Henry, Musician," 124.

9. "Jazz and Suicide," *Birmingham Age-Herald*, April 23, 1924.

10. Jack Linx to Bill Dean-Myatt, February 20, 1961, reprinted in liner notes for *Jack Linx and Maurice Sigler*, Jazz Oracle BDW 8018, 2000, CD.

11. Lowe interview, Behind the Veil Oral History Project.

12. Lofton, *Voices from Alabama*, 312; Adams and Mathews, *Doc*, 216; "Plans Made for Huge Celebration of President's Birthday," *Cullman (AL) Banner*, January 21, 1938; "Stage Set for Cullman's Big Party Saturday Night," *Cullman Banner*, January 28, 1938. For a history of sundown towns, see Loewen, *Sundown Towns*; on Cullman's reputation as a sundown town, see Ben Windham, "Cullman's 'Sundown Town' Image Worthy of Study," *Tuscaloosa News*, March 5, 2006.

13. Adams and Mathews, *Doc*, 216. Arnold Dwight "Gatemouth" Moore—the charismatic blues singer turned gospel evangelist who broadcast on Birmingham radio stations during the 1950s and once staged his own Easter weekend death and resurrection at Fourth Avenue's Masonic Temple—was similarly famous for his Cadillacs. Moore once told folklorist Bill Ferris that he traveled with a chauffeur's cap for the same reason as Whatley; if he was pulled over, he would claim to be a driver for "Mr. Moore" (author conversation with Ferris, June 30, 2020). In fact, the strategy was widespread in Jim Crow's America. Professor O. C. Nix of Jarvis Christian College told his students the same story, from his own experience: to emphasize his point, Jarvis walked into his classroom with a chauffeur's cap on his head, placed the cap on a table, and asked his students to explain its significance. After dismissing a few mystified guesses, Nix finally explained that "wearing this cap saved lives" (Pilgrim, *Understanding Jim Crow*, 29–30). In her history of Black travel in America, author Candacy Taylor relates her stepfather Ron Buford's personal version of the story: "'Everybody had one,' he said, referring to the chauffeur's cap. 'And you always kept it in the car.'" Taylor adds that "during the Jim Crow era, the chauffeur's hat was the perfect cover for every middle-class black man pulled over and harassed by the police" (Taylor, *Overground Railroad*, 8–10).

14. The following story appears in Sammy Lowe, "A Man from Tuxedo Junction (from Jazz to Swing to Rock to Soul): Diary of a Black Musician," part 1, 101 (unpublished manuscript, n.d.), ARR1137, BPL.

15. Lofton, *Voices from Alabama*, 312; Adams, interview with the author, November 29, 2009; John S. Johnson, "Why Negroes Buy Cadillacs," *Ebony*, September 1949, 34. For more on the significance of Cadillacs and other luxury cars in midcentury African American life, see Sorin, *Driving while Black*, 63–69.

16. Marzette-Bolivar, *Swing Lowe*, 29.

17. The following story appears in Lowe, "Man from Tuxedo Junction," part 1, 91–92.

18. Chip Stern, "Wilson Driver: Driver Man, Reflections of an Urban Griot," Chipstern. com, accessed June 17, 2011, https://www.chipstern.com/chip_tribal_wilson.htm (site discontinued).

19. Stern, "Wilson Driver"; Lowe, "Man from Tuxedo Junction," part 1, 100.

20. Lowe, "Man from Tuxedo Junction," part 1, 101.

21. The story that follows is from Sonia Sanchez, interview with the author, June 18, 2011.

CHAPTER 8: THE GREAT WIDE WORLD

1. John T. (Fess) Whatley and J. L. Lowe Scrapbook, BPL. McCord played Bombay's burgeoning jazz scene as a member of the Leon Abbey Orchestra, 1935–36; for a fascinating glimpse into this unlikely jazz outpost, see Fernandes, *Taj Mahal Foxtrot*.

2. Sammy Lowe, "A Man from Tuxedo Junction (from Jazz to Swing to Rock to Soul): Diary of a Black Musician," part 1, 44 (unpublished manuscript, n.d.), ARR1137, BPL, emphasis added.

3. Wells, *Night People*, 31, 143.

4. Roi Ottley, "Are You Listenin'?," *New York Amsterdam News*, June 28, 1933.

5. Barbarin and Charlie Holmes quoted in Chilton, *Ride, Red, Ride*, 58–59.

6. Johnson quoted in Dance, *World of Swing*, 246; Coleman, *Trumpet Story*, 91.

7. Percival Outram, "Activities among Union Musicians," *New York Age*, June 23, 1932; "Shrine to Musicians Erected," *Pittsburgh Courier*, February 18, 1933; "Newsy Newsettes," *Pittsburgh Courier*, March 11, 1933; "Teddy Hill New Rhythm Club Boss," *Chicago Defender*, March 11, 1933. For the Rhythm Club's significance as a source for musicians' employment, see Shapiro and Hentoff, *Hear Me Talkin'*, 167–68.

8. "Becton Is Off to a Good Start in Thirty-Day Revival Service at 16th St. Baptist Church," *Birmingham Reporter*, January 14, 1928; "Becton Is Sweeping Birmingham—Thousands Flock to Meeting—They Try to Explain His Power but Can't," *Birmingham Reporter*, January 21, 1928; "Dr. Becton Grips Harlem; People Crying for More," *Birmingham Reporter*, April 4, 1931.

9. Various headlines, *Birmingham Reporter*, September 1930–April 1931.

10. Hughes, *Big Sea*, 275–78.

11. Adams and Mathews, *Doc*, 28–29.

12. Lowe, "Man from Tuxedo Junction," part I, 30–32.

13. Marvel Cooke, "Becton—Saint or Charlatan? Mysterious Death of Minister as Dramatic as the Life He Lived," *New York Amsterdam News*, December 2, 1939; "Names Powell for 'Gang Busters,' Asks Him to Solve Becton Murder," *Chicago Defender*, January 18, 1941; "12,000 at Becton Rites," *New York Amsterdam News*, May 31, 1933.

14. For Ellington's 1933 southern tour, see H. Cohen, *Duke Ellington's America*, 129–36.

15. Ralph Ellison, "Homage to Ellington on His Birthday," *Washington Sunday Star*, April 27, 1969, reprinted in Ellison, *Going to the Territory*, 220–21.

16. Adams and Mathews, *Doc*, 33–34.

17. Lowe, "Man from Tuxedo Junction," part 1, 105–7.

18. Lowe, "Man from Tuxedo Junction," part 1, 11.

19. "Haywood Henry, Musician," 138.

20. Hampton with Haskins, *Hamp*, 7–8.

21. Hampton with Haskins, *Hamp*, 3–4.

22. Hampton with Haskins, *Hamp*, 3. One other memory from Birmingham stood out in Hampton's memory: his older sister's graduation from Industrial High School. "It was the first ceremony I'd ever been to outside church, and I was impressed. . . . Professor Parker, the founder, gave a thundering speech about the rights of colored people. . . . An orchestra played, and all sorts of Black dignitaries, mainly ministers were present" (*Hamp*, 6).

CHAPTER 9: ERSKINE

1. Erskine Hawkins to Erskine Ramsay, 1938, Charities: Namesakes—January 1, 1921–October 21, 1952, Erskine Ramsay Papers, BPL.

2. James L. Baggett, "Erskine Ramsay's Many Namesakes," *Alabama Heritage*, Winter 2011, 8–10.

3. Baggett, "Erskine Ramsay's Many Namesakes," 8–10.

4. Hawkins to Ramsay, 1938, BPL. Hawkins later discovered that his birth certificate read Erskine *Johnny* Hawkins and that his mother legally changed the middle name, sometime later, to Ramsay (Erskine Hawkins, interview by Leonard Goines, February 6, 1982, 296–97, JOHP).

5. Correspondence, Erskine Ramsay to Erskine Hawkins, Charities: Namesakes—January 1, 1921–October 21, 1952, Erskine Ramsay Papers, BPL.

6. See, for example, *Pittsburgh Courier*, August 12, 1939, 21.

7. Deffaa, *In the Mainstream*, 149; Hawkins, interview by Goines, JOHP, 260, 262.

8. Hawkins, interview by Goines, JOHP, 15–16; Erskine Hawkins, interview by Ann Elizabeth Adams, December 31, 1986, Oral History Collection, Mervyn H. Sterne Library, University of Alabama at Birmingham. "My grandfather and uncles," Hawkins pointed out, also "built Professor Whatley's house." Though Hawkins was not himself one of Fess's students, his family and Whatley were close; because of their shared connection to High C Foster, Fess took special interest in the boy and recruited him for occasional jobs. "So that's how I had my little in" (Hawkins, interview by Goines, JOHP, 15).

9. Hawkins, interview by Goines, JOHP; Hawkins, interview by Adams, Oral History Collection.

10. Hawkins, interview by Adams, Oral History Collection; Hawkins, interview by Goines, JOHP, 7–8.

11. Hawkins, interview by Goines, JOHP, 3.

12. Hawkins, interview by Goines, JOHP, 20–21.

13. Gretchen Weaver, "Melodious Hot Man," *Band Leaders*, January 1946, 24.

14. Hawkins, interview by Goines, JOHP, 31, 52.

15. Advertisement, *Birmingham Reporter*, July 28, 1928; Hawkins, interview by Goines, JOHP, 17, 25.

CHAPTER 10: COLLEGIANS

1. Stewart, *Bama State Collegians*, 21–22.

2. Eric Townley, "The Man from Birmingham: An Interview with Paul Bascomb," *Storyville* 84 (August–September 1979), 210.

3. Townley, "Man from Birmingham," 212.

4. Stewart, *Bama State Collegians*, 32–33.

5. Stewart, *Bama State Collegians*, 21–23, 43.

6. Stewart, *Bama State Collegians*, 10.

7. Stewart, *Bama State Collegians, 1935–1939*, 15–19.

8. Tommy Stewart, interview with the author, February 3, 2011.

9. "Alabama Singers Coming," *Pittsburgh Courier*, August 30, 1930.

10. "Haywood Henry, Musician," 125. This assessment by Henry—"that we were the first band to play jazz . . . in a marching band"—should be taken with a grain of salt. But it is worth noting that, though they might cite different moments in history, many Birmingham musicians made similar claims, stating that this or that student band was the *first* marching band to incorporate jazz into its repertoire. Most likely this development, while still rare enough to be considered a novelty, occurred in multiple places around the same time; but

it is significant that so many Birmingham players at least perceived this to be one of their community's achievements.

11. "Haywood Henry, Musician," 126. Later Jimmy Mitchell added an *e* to the end of his last name, and he is often identified by that spelling, *Mitchelle*.

12. Erskine Hawkins, interview by Leonard Goines, February 6, 1982, JOHP. According to Sammy Lowe, "I remember times when we'd hear about a new Louis Armstrong record that somebody had, and we would walk 2–3 miles to that person's home to hear this record. That was the influence that Louis Armstrong had on young trumpet players in those days" (Sammy Lowe, "A Man from Tuxedo Junction [from Jazz to Swing to Rock to Soul]: Diary of a Black Musician," part 1, 44 [unpublished manuscript, n.d.], ARR1137, BPL).

13. Hawkins, interview by Goines, JOHP, 83–84.

14. Katherine Kent Lambert, "Alabama State News," *Chicago Defender*, January 2, 1932.

15. Erskine Hawkins, interview with Ann Elizabeth Adams, December 31, 1986, Oral History Collection, Mervyn H. Sterne Library, University of Alabama at Birmingham; "Haywood Henry, Musician," 128.

16. "Bama Band Plays 505 Dances," *Atlanta Daily World*, January 8, 1934; "Alabama's Schoolboy Band Hits," *Chicago Defender*, July 1, 1933; "America's Greatest Collegiate Band," *Chicago Defender*, September 2, 1933.

17. A box labeled "Orchestra Correspondence" in the President Harper Councill Trenholm Collection at the Alabama State University archives is testament to this remarkable achievement, showcasing the president's deep immersion into the minutiae of running three bands, and a college, at once.

18. Lucius L. Jones Jr., "What a Band—That Bama Crew!," *Atlanta Daily World*, September 27, 1932.

19. "Belton Bows to Ala. Collegians," *Pittsburgh Courier*, June 2, 1934; "Bama State Collegians Overwhelm Syncopators in Torrid Jazz Battle," *Norfolk New Journal and Guide*, May 12, 1934.

20. "Fess Whatley Loses," *Atlanta Daily World*, August 11, 1935.

21. "Haywood Henry, Musician," 130.

22. "Haywood Henry, Musician," 130.

23. Hawkins, interview by Goines, JOHP, 51, 31; Dance, *World of Earl Hines*, 78; Erskine Hawkins, interview by Ann Elizabeth Adams. Once Erskine was established at New York's Savoy Ballroom, his aunt came for every Sunday matinee dance, armed with a sweet potato pie. "I guess that's the reason why I'm so heavy" (Hawkins, interview by Goines, JOHP, 295).

24. "Haywood Henry, Musician," 126.

CHAPTER 11: EFFLORESCENCE

1. Callins, "Birmingham Jazz Community," 69.

2. Katherine Kent Lambert, "What's Happening in Birmingham, Ala.," *Chicago Defender*, October 11, 1936; Adams and Mathews, *Doc*, 91. Across the South, local night spots borrowed the names of the urban North's most celebrated entertainment venues: in and around Birmingham, the Grand Terrace, the Cotton Club Casino, and the Little Savoy all paid homage to their more famous namesakes in Chicago and New York.

3. Katherine Kent Lambert, "Alabama State News," *Chicago Defender*, December 5, 1936, 10.

4. Fay Young, "Through the Years," *Chicago Defender*, January 9, 1943.

5. Klima, *Willie's Boys*, 26–27. So long as it was the city's only Black social district, Fourth Avenue attracted a cross-section of Birmingham's Black community, but within its borders distinct social groups carved out their own separate spaces. "There were the four corners of Fourth Avenue and 17th Street," one resident remembered of her youth in the 1950s, "and

each of those corners had a different clientele." The northwest corner, by the Masonic Temple, "is where the professionals met. The doctors, the dentists, school teachers—after work, they would come and wait there on the corner in the drug store or in one of the clubs upstairs." Across the street, on the southeast corner, stood the Carver Theater, where young people—primarily high school students—gathered. "Transient" types loitered in front of the Little Savoy, at the northeast corner, while "a group of older, ne'er-do-wells"—out-of-work vagrants and drunks—gathered on the remaining corner, in front of the Famous Theater. "You didn't have to identify it, but everybody seemingly knew his 'turf.' . . . Everybody had his corner, there, and I always found that fascinating" (Valerie Lockett and Evelyn Howard, interview by Peggy Hamrick, Working Lives Oral History Project, September 1, 1984, University of Alabama Libraries Special Collections, Tuscaloosa).

6. Young, "Through the Years."

7. "'Cotton Club' Charged with Hiring 'Scab Bands,'" *Atlanta Daily World*, April 2, 1937.

8. Sammy Lowe, "A Man from Tuxedo Junction (from Jazz to Swing to Rock to Soul): Diary of a Black Musician," part 1, 35–36 (unpublished manuscript, n.d.), ARR1137, BPL. Sims and Thompson's band was called the Moonlight Serenaders and also included drummer Alton "Snooky" Davenport and saxophonist Cornelius Aiken. Aiken had started a version of the Serenaders in high school with Haywood Henry and others.

9. Lowe, "Man from Tuxedo Junction," part 1, 19, 33.

10. For Lowe's memories of the Calloway tour, see "Man from Tuxedo Junction," part 1, 44–74. Cab Calloway *did* in fact have a bandleader sister, Blanche, and a baton-wielding brother named Elmer, both of whom capitalized on the family name; other "family" bandleaders seemed to pop up everywhere, making more dubious claims. In addition to Jean, there were "brothers" Dick, Walter, and Cal—"and to date," Cab joked, "I know of about 50 cousins" (James Aswell, "My New York," *Brooklyn Times Union*, February 17, 1933).

11. Lowe, "Man from Tuxedo Junction," part 1, 66.

12. Lowe, "Man from Tuxedo Junction," part 1, 76.

13. Lowe, "Man from Tuxedo Junction," part 1, 40–42, 83, 98, 102.

14. Frank Eaton Adams Sr., interview with the author, May 22, 2010.

15. Carol Clarke, interview with the author, July 23, 2022.

16. Harper, *Autobiography*, 13.

17. Harper, *Autobiography*, 26.

18. Harper, *Autobiography*, 27, 34–37, 44; "'Heaven Bound' Pleases Large Audience First Night," *Birmingham Reporter*, February 6, 1932; "Pageant Closes Book Week Here," *Birmingham Reporter*, February 27, 1932; Oscar W. Adams, "What Negroes Are Doing," *Birmingham News*, February 28, 1932.

19. Harper, *Autobiography*, 44–45; "Alabama State News," *Chicago Defender*, August 18, 1934; *New York Age*, June 15, 1935; *New York Age*, June 22, 1935.

20. Harper, *Autobiography*, 45.

CHAPTER 12: THE MAGIC CITIZEN

1. Lock, *Blutopia*, 47.

2. Ira Steingroot, "Sun Ra's Magical Kingdom," *Reality Hackers*, Winter 1988, 51.

3. Steingroot, "Sun Ra's Magical Kingdom," 51.

4. Sun Ra, undated broadsheet, Alton Abraham Collection of Sun Ra, Hanna Holborn Gray Special Collections Research Center, University of Chicago Library.

5. Kathy Kemp, "Aboard the Spaceship Sun Ra," *Kudzu* (*Birmingham Post-Herald* supplement), April 17, 1992. Built in 1909, the majestic Terminal Station was demolished in 1969, amid the protests of preservationists and many other locals; its destruction is frequently cited in Birmingham today by those who seek to preserve the city's history from shortsighted

development. In 2016, at the entrance to a downtown walking trail, the local Rotary Club erected a new "Magic City" sign, modeled on the original.

6. Steingroot, "Sun Ra's Magical Kingdom," 50; Bob Rusch, "Sun Ra: Interview," *Cadence*, June 1978, 7. Sonny may also have been conscious that the rhythmless "Blount" (pronounced "blunt") carried the baggage of what Malcolm X—born Malcolm Little—called a "slave name," provided by a previous generation's oppressor in place of a true ancestral name. Alabama history is rich with prominent white Blounts: Blount County took its name from the Tennessee governor who dispatched Andrew Jackson to defeat Alabama's Creeks in 1813, and in the twentieth century Wynton Blount emerged as one of the state's most successful business leaders, a US postmaster general, a candidate for the US Senate, and a celebrated patron of the arts. None of these associations would have impressed Sun Ra.

7. Kemp, "Aboard the Spaceship Sun Ra."

8. Rusch, "Sun Ra: Interview," 3.

9. Adams and Mathews, *Doc*, 82.

10. Rusch, "Sun Ra: Interview," 5; Walter Miller, unpublished interview with Robert Mugge, July 26, 1978, courtesy Robert Mugge.

11. "Sun Ra Interview: Hearing Legendary Blues & Jazz Bands," Sun Ra, *The Eternal Myth Revealed*, disc 5, Transparency TRANS 316CD, CD; Sun Ra, *Immeasurable Equation*, 470.

12. "Sun Ra Interview: Hearing Legendary Blues & Jazz Bands."

13. Sun Ra, "My Music Is Words," in Sun Ra, *Immeasurable Equation*, 470; Rusch, "Sun Ra: Interview," 5.

14. "Sun Ra Interview: Hearing Legendary Blues & Jazz Bands"; Rusch, "Sun Ra: Interview," 5.

15. Rusch, "Sun Ra: Interview," 5.

16. "Sun Ra Interview: Remembers How Musicians Used to Dress," Sun Ra, *The Eternal Myth Revealed*, disc 1.

17. Sun Ra, *Immeasurable Equation*, 476.

18. Tam Fiofori, "Sun Ra's Space Odyssey," *DownBeat*, May 14, 1970, 14.

19. Rusch, "Sun Ra: Interview," 7.

20. Rusch, "Sun Ra: Interview," 3; Sun Ra, interview by Phil Schaap, WKCR, New York City, April 1987, https://www.youtube.com/watch?v=JXjh7BFxV2g.

21. Sun Ra interview by John Hinds, March 5, 1990, *Sun Ra Research CD 1*, track 4, Sun Ra Research SRR001, 2004, CD.

22. Rusch, "Sun Ra: Interview," 3; *Kingsport Times*, October 12, 1934; *Pittsburgh Courier*, November 3, 1934; *Pittsburgh Courier*, December 1, 1934. Other members for the tour included Alvin Robinson, Ellis McClure, John Reed, William Reed, Jessie Larkin, Melvin Caswell, James Bates, Ivy [Iva] Williams, Jerry Reed, Bayford Woods, and Nathanial Atkins. Sadly, no reporters offered detailed descriptions of the dancing.

23. Lucius Jones, "Okay Realmites," *Atlanta Daily World*, February 21, 1935; Lucius Jones, "Society Slants," *Atlanta Daily World*, March 6, 1935.

24. Lucius Jones, "Troubadours versus Sonny Blount!," *Atlanta Daily World*, March 4, 1935; Lucius Jones, "Sonny Blount Engages Troubadours in Jazz Contest," *Atlanta Daily World*, March 6, 1935; Lucius Jones, "Sonny Blount Here; Set for War," *Atlanta Daily World*, March 7, 1935; Lucius Jones, *Atlanta Daily World*, July 31, 1935.

25. Rusch, "Sun Ra: Interview," 5.

26. Sun Ra, interview by Phil Schaap, WKCR, New York City, December 2, 1988, WKCR Radio Archives, accessed 2013, www.philschaapjazz.com.

27. Sun Ra, interview with the Hinds Brothers, "IV: Sun Ra, 03.05.1990, San Francisco, Birmingham years / musical destiny," *Sun Ra Research CD 1*, SRR001, 2004, CD.

28. Szwed, *Space Is the Place*, 29; Francis Davis, "Sun Ra, Himself," *Philadelphia Inquirer*, February 16, 1990; "Dance Due Friday at High School," *Huntsville Times*, November 19, 1935;

"Hi-Y Club Dance Set for Friday," *Huntsville Times*, December 5, 1935. This early encounter with the aliens was not the only "spaceways" connection Sun Ra traced to A&M: in the 1950s, NASA would begin developing its Saturn series of rocket ships at Huntsville's Marshall Space Flight Center, just a few miles from the A&M campus. To Sonny, the area was a unique center for contact between humanity and the cosmos. Speaking to filmmaker Robert Mugge in 1980, Sun Ra explained that the various iterations of his Arkestra developed in locations with distinct cosmic resonances: his current band "was started in Chicago, at the same time they were developing the atomic bomb. And the other was started in Normal, Alabama, when I was going to school there, at the same time they were developing rocket ships. . . . [Technically, the rocket ships came a bit later, but *time* for Sun Ra was never linear or literal.] Each time, I was a few miles from space things, doing my thing, too." Sun Ra, unpublished interview by Robert Mugge, August 3, 1980, courtesy Robert Mugge.

CHAPTER 13: ARRIVAL

1. "Bama State Collegian," *Storyville* 77 (June–July 1978): 183–84; "Haywood Henry, Musician," 132.

2. "Haywood Henry, Musician," 133.

3. "Haywood Henry, Musician," 133; Erskine Hawkins, interview by Leonard Goines, February 6, 1982, JOHP.

4. Hawkins, interview by Goines, JOHP, 134; "Haywood Henry, Musician," 134.

5. "Haywood Henry, Musician," 134.

6. Stewart, *Bama State Collegians*, 41; Hawkins, interview by Goines, JOHP, 74; "Alabama State Will Give Hawkins Scroll," *New York Amsterdam News*, June 14, 1947.

7. Sid Ross, "Clip Joints," *Salt Lake Tribune*, February 19, 1950; Walter Winchell, "Winchell on Broadway," *Tampa Times*, November 15, 1939; Mark Hellinger, "All in a Day," *Springfield (MO) Leader and Press*, October 18, 1930; Jim Bishop, "Feet Edson, Nervy Guy," *Dubois (PA) Courier-Express*, September 13, 1969.

8. Sammy Lowe, "A Man from Tuxedo Junction (from Jazz to Swing to Rock to Soul): Diary of a Black Musician," part 2, 2 (unpublished manuscript, n.d.), ARR1137, BPL.

9. Wilson Driver, filling in as guest writer for J. B. Sims's column "Round the Blocks," *Weekly Review*, September 5, 1941; Sims himself often bragged about this role in his own column and elsewhere. Dance, *World of Swing*, 193–94.

10. "Haywood Henry, Musician," 143; Gold, *Sittin' In*, 33.

11. "Haywood Henry, Musician," 134.

12. "Haywood Henry, Musician," 143.

13. "Alabama State Collegians to Go on Dance Tour Shortly," *Pittsburgh Courier*, October 26, 1935.

14. Erskine Hawkins, interview by Ann Elizabeth Adams, December 31, 1986, Oral History Collection, Mervyn H. Sterne Library, University of Alabama at Birmingham; "Bama State Collegian," *Storyville* 77, 185; "Original Bama State Band Is Coming Here," *Atlanta Daily World*, November 12, 1935.

15. "Bama State Collegian," *Storyville* 77, 186–87.

16. Hawkins, interview by Goines, JOHP, 81–82, 97.

17. "Rugcutters Find Harlem 'Heaven': Ladies Night at Savoy Ballroom Colorful in Thorough Mixing of Racial Elements," *New York Amsterdam News*, April 8, 1939.

18. Haywood Henry swore the Hawkins band only ever lost three battles at the Savoy, mostly due to cocky overconfidence (Dance, *World of Swing*, 210). Some battle outcomes were hotly debated. "Savoy Actually Smokes after Sunday's Battle of Jazz Bands," the *New York Amsterdam News* reported after a furious bout between the Hawkins and Lionel Hampton bands. "Whether Hampton 'took' Hawkins or whether the 'Hawk' 'cut' Hampton is a moot

question and one still being debated in the candy stores, drugstores, hotel lobbies, school locker rooms and on the street" (March 28, 1942).

19. Hawkins, interview by Goines, JOHP, 177. Describing the Savoy's dancers, one regular recalled, "Man, those jitterbugs [were] just loose as a goose. Feet going all which-ways, hands flapping and waving, partners sliding between the other's legs, frontwards, backwards, bodies tossed in the air, legs straight up, clothes flying—Lord, they were *fast*. New steps. Old steps. Impossible steps" (Clyde E. B. Bernhardt and Sheldon Harris, "The Memoirs of a Jazzman," *New York Times*, June 1, 1986).

20. Hawkins, interview by Goines, JOHP, 260.

21. Lowe, "Man from Tuxedo Junction," part 1, 108, 115, 124, 128.

22. Lowe, "Man from Tuxedo Junction," part 1, 129.

CHAPTER 14: UP FROM DOWN SOUTH

1. Adams and Mathews, *Doc*, 141.

2. Korall, *Drummin' Men*, 130.

3. Korall, *Drummin' Men*, 134.

4. Korall, *Drummin' Men*, 131.

5. Korall, *Drummin' Men*, 156.

6. Basie, *Good Morning Blues*, 150.

7. Richard J. Smith, "Jazz Festival Tonight: The Reno Club Reunion," *Star Sunday Magazine of the Kansas City Star*, April 29, 1973; Driggs and Haddix, *Kansas City Jazz*, 137; Basie, *Good Morning Blues*, 160.

8. Korall, *Drummin' Men*, 141, 143.

9. "Haywood Henry Meets Max Roach Birthday Broadcast," January 9, 1994, Birthday Broadcasts, Phil Schaap Jazz, www.philschaapjazz.com.

10. Hammond with Townsend, *John Hammond on Record*, 172.

11. Gioia, *History of Jazz*, 154.

12. Korall, *Drummin' Men*, 145.

13. Sammy Lowe, "A Man from Tuxedo Junction (from Jazz to Swing to Rock to Soul): Diary of a Black Musician," part 2, 2–4 (unpublished manuscript, n.d.), ARR1137, BPL.

14. Chilton, *Roy Eldridge*, 65; Leonard Feather, "Earl Hines Recalls . . . When Gangsters Ran the Jazz World," *Melody Maker*, September 10, 1949. The Hill musicians in question were Roy Eldridge and Teddy Wilson.

15. "Haywood Henry, Musician," 135.

16. Maurice Zolotow, "Harlem's Great White Father," *Saturday Evening Post*, September 1941, 40.

17. "Haywood Henry, Musician," 136.

18. "Haywood Henry, Musician," 136; Erskine Hawkins, interview by Leonard Goines, February 6, 1982, JOHP.

19. Harper, *Autobiography*, 49.

20. Harper, *Autobiography*, 47.

21. Harper, *Autobiography*, 47; "Bama School 'Marm' Wins Amateur Hour: High School Teacher Captures Apollo Audience," *New York Amsterdam News*, June 20, 1936.

22. "Bama School 'Marm' Wins Amateur Hour"; Joe Bostic, "Radiograph," *New York Age*, June 27, 1936.

23. Harper, *Autobiography*, 47–48.

24. Harper, *Autobiography*, 49

25. Harper, *Autobiography*, 50.

26. Harper, *Autobiography*, 50–51.

27. Harper, *Autobiography*, 51.

28. Mordden, *Sing for Your Supper*, 201.

29. Harper, *Autobiography*, 52.

CHAPTER 15: BLUE RHYTHM FANTASY

1. "Teddy Hill Still Tops over Radio," *Chicago Defender*, July 27, 1935.

2. "Teddy Hill Honored by Birmingham, Ala. School," *New York Age*, August 10, 1935; Percival Outram, "Among Union Musicians," *New York Age*, August 10, 1935.

3. Percival Outram, "Among the Musicians," *New York Age*, October 5, 1935.

4. Otis Ferguson, "Breakfast Dance, in Harlem," *New Republic*, February 12, 1936, reprinted in Ferguson, *In the Spirit of Jazz*, 59–60.

5. Gillespie with Fraser, *To Be, or Not*, 33.

6. Shipton, *Groovin' High*, 35–36; Wells, *Night People*, 104; Hill quoted in Gillespie with Fraser, *To Be, or Not*, 66. Hill recalled that Dizzy, babysitter or not, "was very fond of my little daughter, Gwendolyn, who was five or six years old; he'd wallow all over the floor, tell her candy wasn't good for her, then eat if all himself. Still a big kid" (Gillespie with Fraser, *To Be, or Not*, 66).

7. Hugues Panassié, "They Like Teddy Hill in France," *Pittsburgh Courier*, July 17, 1937; John T. (Fess) Whatley and J. L. Lowe Scrapbook, BPL; Howard Rye, "Visiting Firemen, 6: Teddy Hill and the Cotton Club Revue," *Storyville* 100 (April 1982): 144–46. Frankie Manning, who performed with the team of Lindy Hoppers, gave an account of the tour in his memoir (with Cynthia R. Millman), *Frankie Manning*, 134–37.

8. Porter Roberts, "Praise and Criticism," *Pittsburgh Courier*, October 16, 1937.

9. "Teddy Hill Packs Up and Goes Home," *Pittsburgh Courier*, October 9, 1937.

10. Shapiro and Hentoff, *Hear Me Talkin'*, 346; Gillespie with Fraser, *To Be, or Not*, 88; Shipton, *Groovin' High*, 45.

11. Gillespie with Fraser, *To Be, or Not*, 88; Billy Jones, "Stars That Shine," *Chicago Defender*, April 30, 1938; "Bonnie Davis Clicks," *Norfolk New Journal and Guide*, April 3, 1943.

12. Leon James, quoted in Stearns and Stearns, *Jazz Dance*, 325.

13. Russell, *Bird Lives!*, 133; Gillespie with Fraser, *To Be, or Not*, 87; Leonard Feather, "Be-Bop??!!—Man, We Called It Klook-Mop!," *Metronome*, April 1947, 21. It is hard to pinpoint the origin of a nickname or a new piece of slang, and it is hard to believe that Teddy Hill was responsible for every coinage ascribed to him. It does, however, deserve to be noted that Hill has been credited with giving both "Dizzy" and "Klook-mop" their names, and with being the first to call the new music "bebop."

14. Gillespie with Fraser, *To Be, or Not*, 87.

15. Gitler, *Swing to Bop*, 55.

16. Hennessey, *Klook*, 194,

17. Dance, *World of Swing*, 196; Manning and Millman, *Frankie Manning*, 160.

18. Gillespie with Fraser, *To Be, or Not*, 89.

CHAPTER 16: DANCE THE NIGHT AWAY

1. Erskine Hawkins, interview by Leonard Goines, February 6, 1982, JOHP, 190, 116; "Bama State Collegian," *Storyville* 77 (June–July 1978): 188; Dance, *World of Swing*, 196.

2. Hawkins, interview by Goines, JOHP, 301–3.

3. "Hawkins Plays Here Sunday," *Oakland Tribune*, October 30, 1942; Sammy Lowe, "A Man from Tuxedo Junction (from Jazz to Swing to Rock to Soul): Diary of a Black Musician," part 3, (unpublished manuscript, n.d.), ARR1137, BPL; Gitler, *Swing to Bop*, 79–80; Steve Voce, "Big Band, Sore Hand," *Jazz Journal*, December 1968; Deffaa, *In the Mainstream*, 142.

4. Lowe, "Man from Tuxedo Junction," part 3, 54; Deffaa, *In the Mainstream*, 142.

5. Lowe, "Man from Tuxedo Junction," part 3, 61.

6. Quoted in Dance, *World of Swing*, 210.

7. Quoted in Dance, *World of Swing*, 211; Fernett, *Swing Out*, 83.

8. Joe Bostic, "Seeing the Show," *New York Age*, August 1, 1936; "Footlight Flickers," *Norfolk New Journal and Guide*, January 9, 1937; *Variety*, January 24, 1940.

9. Quoted in Dance, *World of Swing*, 220.

10. Quoted in Fernett, *Swing Out*, 83.

11. Lowe, "Man from Tuxedo Junction," part 3, 2.

12. Hawkins, interview by Goines, JOHP, 92–93; "Haywood Henry, Musician," 137; Lowe, "Man from Tuxedo Junction," part 3, 27.

13. Lowe, "Man from Tuxedo Junction," part 3.

14. Jothan Callins, drawing from his own interview with Williams, identifies the trumpeter as "Shorty" and the tune as "Shorty's Blues." "Erskine always requested that [tune] because he liked it," Williams told Callins, recalling the young Hawkins's visits to the Junction. (Callins, "Birmingham Jazz Community," 48.) Frank Adams heard the same story from Williams, but when Adams repeated it to me, the trumpeter's name was "Trigg." (Adams and Mathews, *Doc*, 191–92.)

15. Frank Eaton Adams Sr., interview with the author, October 17, 2010. A surviving broadcast from the Apollo Theater includes "Down in Titusville," another Hawkins tribute to a Birmingham-area community.

16. Hawkins, interview by Goines, JOHP, 150; Lowe, "Man from Tuxedo Junction," part 3, 52.

17. Stewart, *Bama State Collegians*; Gitler, *Swing to Bop*, 79–80; Dan Morgenstern, "Framework for Blowing: The Dizzy Gillespie Quintet," *DownBeat*, June 17, 1965, 23; Steve Voce, "Clark Terry Talks to Steve Voce," *Jazz Journal*, December 1986, reprinted at http://www.ellingtonweb.ca/Hostedpages/Voce/removed201100807–1112-Voce.html; Von Freeman, interview by Steve Coleman, May 23–24, 2000, 38, 46, Smithsonian Jazz Oral History Program, Archives Center, National Museum of American History, https://jazzday.com/media/AC0808_Freeman_Von_Transcript.pdf.

18. Deffaa, *In the Mainstream*, 145–46.

19. R. L. Larkin, "Are Colored Bands Doomed as Money Makers?," *DownBeat* 7, December 1, 1940, 2.

20. "Negro Bands Are Not Doomed Says Millinder," *New York Amsterdam News*, December 21, 1940.

21. "The Battle of 'Tuxedo Junction,'" *Pittsburgh Courier*, February 24, 1940.

22. Deffaa, *In the Mainstream*, 145–46; "Erskine Hawkins Seeks a 'Junction' Built around Another Town," *Chicago Defender*, July 13, 1946. Nothing seemed to come of the hometown competition, but Hawkins did try to follow up on the success of "Junction" with related titles "Junction Blues" (1940) and "Function at the Junction" (1953).

23. "Erskine Hawkins Recalls 'Tuxedo Junction,'" *Birmingham News*, May 10, 1972.

24. Bill Bennett, "Tuxedo Junction, Ensley's Corner with Theme Song, Is Reaping Nickel Harvest," *Birmingham Post*, July 24, 1940.

25. Emory O. Jackson, "10,000 See Steel Bowl Battle," *Atlanta Daily World*, January 2, 1941; Ric Roberts, "Money Was Made in the 'Steel Bowl,'" *Atlanta Daily World*, January 12, 1941; Ric Roberts, "'Tuxedo Junction' a Keener Number When One's in Birmingham," *Atlanta Daily World*, September 15, 1940.

CHAPTER 17: THE ROAD

1. "Do You Know," *Weekly Review*, July 24, 1943; Frank Eaton Adams Sr., interview with the author, October 30, 2010.

2. Erskine Hawkins, interview by Leonard Goines, February 6, 1982, JOHP.

3. Hawkins, interview by Goines, JOHP, 57.

4. Hawkins, interview by Goines, JOHP, 39–45; Sammy Lowe, "A Man from Tuxedo Junction (from Jazz to Swing to Rock to Soul): Diary of a Black Musician," part 3, 6, 39–45 (unpublished manuscript, n.d.), ARR1137, BPL.

5. "Hawkins Quells Riot by Playing the National Anthem: Quick Thinking of Maestro Is Commended," *Norfolk New Journal and Guide*, September 11, 1943; Carrie Miller, "Backstage," *California Eagle* (Los Angeles), September 16, 1943; Lowe, "Man from Tuxedo Junction," part 3, 30.

6. Lowe, "Man from Tuxedo Junction," part 3, 8.

7. Lowe, "Man from Tuxedo Junction," part 3, 8–9.

8. Lowe, "Man from Tuxedo Junction," part 3, 1.

9. Lowe, "Man from Tuxedo Junction," part 3.

10. "Fear Mounts: Police Chief Kills Man in North Carolina," *Pittsburgh Courier*, June 14, 1947.

11. Quoted in Dance, *World of Swing*, 198.

12. Lowe, "Man from Tuxedo Junction," part 3, 34–36.

13. Lowe, "Man from Tuxedo Junction," part 3, 34–36.

14. Quoted in Lowe, "Man from Tuxedo Junction," part 3, 3.

15. Hawkins, interview by Goines, JOHP, 109–10.

16. Lowe, "Man from Tuxedo Junction," part 3, 26.

17. Alan McMillan, "Hi Hattin' in Harlem," *Chicago Defender*, November 16, 1935; Lowe, "Man from Tuxedo Junction," part 3, 23–24.

18. "Birmingham's Glamour Girl Captures Broadway," *Chicago Defender*, August 13, 1938.

19. Ida James returned briefly to the Hawkins band after Dolores Brown married; Brown resumed her singing career after the death of her husband, Marcellus Green.

20. *Pittsburgh Post-Gazette*, November 8, 1941.

21. "She Sang the Blues the Hard Way," *Birmingham News*, July 28, 1979.

22. Reese, *Angels along the Way*, 166.

23. Reese, *Angels along the Way*, 166–68.

24. Lowe, "Man from Tuxedo Junction," part 3, 65–66.

25. Quoted in Dance, *World of Swing*, 209.

26. Hawkins, interview by Goines, JOHP, 282–83.

27. Sammy Lowe, "Man from Tuxedo Junction," part 3.

28. The following story appears in Gentry, *Echoes out of the Burton*, 144–46.

CHAPTER 18: WAR

1. "Negro Draftees March Off to Serve Uncle Sam," *Weekly Review*, December 13, 1940.

2. Other Birmingham musicians in the 313th included Rushton Miller, Thomas Miller, Afton Lee, Alvin Robertson, and Wilton Robertson.

3. For the war's effect on Black swing musicians, see DeVeaux, *Birth of Bebop*, 236–53.

4. Brian Case, "Buddy Tate and the President," *Melody Maker*, December 1, 1979, 37.

5. For Lester Young's military experience, see Delannoy, *Pres*, 134–48; and Daniels, *Lester Leaps In*, 250–64. See also Jones, *Rifftide*, 60; and Chip Stern, "Wilson Driver: Driver Man, Reflections of an Urban Griot," Chipstern.com, accessed June 17, 2011, https://www.chipstern.com/chip_tribal_wilson.htm (site discontinued).

6. Delannoy, *Pres*, 148. For a challenge to the long-standing narrative that Young's army experience forever altered his trajectory as an artist, see, for example, Daniels, *Lester Leaps In*, 264.

7. Korall, *Drummin' Men*, 157–58.

8. Harper, *Autobiography*, 62.

9. Harper, *Autobiography*, 62–65; William Forest Couch, dir., *Keep Smiling* (1943), posted on YouTube by Reelblack One on October 23, 2019, https://www.youtube.com /watch?v=mU4jSxHPUPQ.

10. Harper, *Autobiography*, 64–65.

11. Harper, *Autobiography*, 65–68.

12. Quoted in Erenberg, *Swingin' the Dream*, 191.

13. Quoted in Erenberg, *Swingin' the Dream*, 209, 193.

14. Sammy Lowe, "A Man from Tuxedo Junction (from Jazz to Swing to Rock to Soul): Diary of a Black Musician," part 3, 75 (unpublished manuscript, n.d.), ARR1137, BPL.

15. Lowe, "Man from Tuxedo Junction," part 3, 79–80.

16. Lowe, "Man from Tuxedo Junction," part 3, 79–80.

17. Lowe, "Man from Tuxedo Junction," part 3, 80.

18. Lowe, "Man from Tuxedo Junction," part 1, 81; "Hawkins Bandsman Is Laid to Rest," *Atlanta Daily World*, August 15, 1942.

19. "Hawkins Player Killed in Accident," *New York Amsterdam News*, August 15, 1942.

20. "Erskine Hawkins Ork in Highway Accident; One Killed, 4 Injured," *New York Age*, August 15, 1942.

21. Lowe, "Man from Tuxedo Junction," part 3.

22. Lowe, "Man from Tuxedo Junction," part 3, 81, 84; Alvin Robertson, interview, Civil Rights Oral History Project, Birmingham Civil Rights Institute, Birmingham, AL.

23. Hawkins, interview by Leonard Goines, JOHP, 268–73.

24. The following story appears in Lowe, "Man from Tuxedo Junction," part 3, 93.

25. Dance, *World of Swing*, 209, 198; "Rumors All Wrong—Avery Parrish Is Alive!," *California Eagle*, August 12, 1943.

26. Quoted in Dance, *World of Swing*, 197.

27. Ritz, *Respect*, 43; Ferris, *Blues from the Delta*, 124. On her 1974 recording "Just Right Tonight," Aretha Franklin revisited and reclaimed "After Hours" for herself: Billy Preston performed the Parrish part, Quincy Jones added a big band arrangement, and Franklin improvised lyrics to the expanded piece. "She's making up the words as she goes along," said Preston. "She's moaning low. And before long, she's screaming, she's soaring, she turns in the best straight-up blues singing I've heard since Ray Charles" (quoted in Ritz, *Respect*, 264–65). Buddy Feyne, who created lyrics to "Tuxedo Junction," also added words to "After Hours," but they never caught on.

28. Erenberg, *Swingin' the Dream*, 207–8.

29. Erenberg, *Swingin' the Dream*, 207–8; Andy Razaf, "'Guilty' Savoy," *People's Voices*, May 8, 1943, 26; Alvarez, *Power of the Zoot*, 123–26.

CHAPTER 19: TEDDY'S HILL, BILLIE'S GUY

1. Curley J. Parrish, "Bama on Broadway," *Alabama Voice*, November 15, 1946.

2. Parrish, "Bama on Broadway."

3. Sonia Sanchez, interview with the author, June 18, 2011; Chip Stern, "Wilson Driver: Driver Man, Reflections of an Urban Griot," Chipstern.com, accessed June 17, 2011, https://www.chipstern.com/chip_tribal_wilson.htm (site discontinued).

4. Sanchez, interview with the author.

5. "Teddy Hill Drawing 'em at Minton's," *New York Amsterdam News*, February 15, 1941; Ellison, "The Golden Age, Time Past," in *Shadow and Act*, 210; Williams quoted in Shapiro and Hentoff, *Hear Me Talkin'*, 341.

6. Kelley, *Thelonious Monk*, 124.

7. Nat Hentoff, "Just Call Him Thelonious," *DownBeat*, July 25, 1956, 15–16.

8. Ellison, "Golden Age, Time Past," 209–10.

9. Shapiro and Hentoff, *Hear Me Talkin'*, 339.

10. DeVeaux, *Birth of Bebop*, 219.

11. Shapiro and Hentoff, *Hear Me Talkin'*, 337–38.

12. Asked in 1972, "Where did the term be-bop come from?" Kenny Clarke responded, "That was an old expression of Teddy Hill's, picked up by Jerry Newman. . . . Before the war it wasn't called be-bop, it was called 'that music they're playing up at Minton's.' When I came home from the war I heard all this be-bop business. I really didn't understand what they meant by it." Kenny Clarke, interviewed by Arthur Taylor, *Courier-Journal* (Louisville, KY), July 9, 1972, 212. For a history of Minton's, see DeVeaux, *Birth of Bebop*, 217–35; Kelley, *Thelonious Monk*, 60–75; and Shapiro and Hentoff, *Hear Me Talkin'*, 335–58.

13. Because Newman's acetate disc recorder could capture up to fifteen minutes at a stretch, the recordings—in contrast to the typical three-minute commercial release—offered unique access to the extended improvisations at the heart of the developing jazz culture. The American Federation of Musicians recording strike of 1942–44 made such access all the more rare, further adding to the bebop mystique.

14. Herbert Nichols, "Jazz Milieu," *Music Dial*, August 1944.

15. Adams and Mathews, *Doc*, 187.

16. Adams and Mathews, *Doc*, 198.

17. Gillespie with Fraser, *To Be, or Not*, 157–58.

18. Kelley, *Thelonious Monk*, 69–70.

19. Holiday with Dufty, *Lady Sings the Blues*, 121.

20. Burns and Ward, *Ken Burns' Jazz*.

21. Greene, *Billie Holiday*, 90; Clarke, *Billie Holiday*, 214.

22. Michael Levin, "Don't Blame Show Biz!," *DownBeat*, June 4, 1947, reprinted in Holiday, *Last Interview*, 16. "Joe Guy, Bean's regular trumpet player, had just gotten married to Billie Holiday," Miles Davis wrote. "Sometimes, they'd be so high off heroin and be fucking so good that Joe would miss his gig. So would Billie. So, Hawk would use me when Joe didn't show up" (Davis with Troupe, *Miles*, 66–67).

23. Quoted in Clarke, *Billie Holiday*, 216, 226.

24. Quoted in Clarke, *Billie Holiday*, 256.

25. Holiday with Dufty, *Lady Sings the Blues*, 123.

26. Holiday with Dufty, *Lady Sings the Blues*, 123, 127; "Billie Holiday Breaking Records," *Chicago Defender*, September 15, 1945; "Songstress Billie Holiday, Joe Guy's Ork Hit Road, Sept. 1," *Pittsburgh Courier*, August 18, 1945.

27. Quoted in Shapiro and Hentoff, *Hear Me Talkin'*, 200. After a show at the Howard Theatre, Holiday claimed she received a premonition her mother was dead. "Goddamit you better be good to me," she told Guy, "because you're all I've got now" (Holiday with Dufty, *Lady Sings the Blues*, 124).

28. "Billie Holiday's Hubby or Is He Bea's Spouse?," *New York Amsterdam News*, October 20, 1945.

29. Online auction listing, "Billie Holiday Heartfelt Autographed Letter Signed to Joe Guy in a Framed Display (1947.) Written While Both Were Serving Time . . . ," Heritage Auctions, accessed April 29, 2019, https://entertainment.ha.com/itm/music-memorabilia /autographs-and-signed-items/billie-holiday-heartfelt-autographed-letter-signed-to-joe -guy-in-a-framed-display-1947-written-while-both-were-serving-time/a/7176-89514.s. Spellings and punctuation appear as in original document. In April 2018, this letter sold at auction online for $6,875.

30. *The Property of a Distinguished American Private Collector Part I*, auction catalog, December 18, 2012, 242, Profiles in History, https://profilesinhistory.com/wp-content

/uploads/2012/12/Historical54-FINAL-updated-112812lo.pdf. Spellings and punctuation appear as in original document.

31. "Billie Holiday's Mate Freed," *New York Amsterdam News*, September 20, 1947; Yanow, *Bebop*, 81; Scott Yanow, "Joe Guy," All Music, https://www.allmusic.com/artist/joe -guy-mn0000784260; Clarke, *Billie Holiday*, 262.

32. "Billie Holiday's Mate Freed"; "Billie Holiday Out of Prison," *New York Amsterdam News*, March 20, 1948; "Billie Holiday Reported Freed from U.S. Jail," *Chicago Defender*, April 3, 1948, 3. A column in the *New York Amsterdam News* included a brief mention, on April 3, of Guy performing with his band in New York before he finally disappeared from the city for good.

CHAPTER 20: IF IT'S IN YOU

1. Szwed, *Space Is the Place*, 32–33.

2. Advertisements, *Birmingham News*, December 5, 1943.

3. Advertisement, *Birmingham News*, August 23, 1935; Henry McCellons and Sun Ra, "Alone with Just a Memory of You," manuscript music score, music by Sonny Blount, words by Henry McCellons, 1936, Library of Congress; Sun Ra, "My Sweet," manuscript music score, words and music by Herman "Poole" Blount, 1940, Library of Congress; Sun Ra, "That's the Way I Feel Today," manuscript music score, words and music by Herman Poole Blount, 1941, Library of Congress.

4. Abbott and Seroff, *To Do This*, 396; email correspondence with Doug Seroff, January 2019.

5. Advertisements, *Birmingham News*, April 9, 10, and 11, 1939; "Ripple Rhythm Four Gets Contract," *Weekly Review*, October 25, 1940; advertisement, *Birmingham News*, September 14, 1941.

6. "Ripple Rhythm Four Gets Contract"; "They Do Jive Differently," *Weekly Review*, July 24, 1943.

7. Walter Miller, unpublished interview with Robert Mugge, July 26, 1978, courtesy Robert Mugge.

8. Miller, interview with Mugge.

9. "Esquire Dance Tonight at Elk's Rest" and "Society Slants," *Birmingham World*, January 3, 1941.

10. "Sonny Blount Jumps Tonight at Sunset," *Atlanta Daily World*, August 1, 1941. Also in the band's lineup, that paper pointed out, was Jimmy Hawkins, "brother of the famous Erskine."

11. Notices for Club Congo appear regularly in the *Weekly Review* beginning November 14, 1941.

12. Chip Stern, "Wilson Driver: Driver Man, Reflections of an Urban Griot," Chipstern. com, accessed June 17, 2011, https://www.chipstern.com/chip_tribal_wilson.htm (site discontinued); Szwed, *Space Is the Place*, 41.

13. Sgt. N. H. Bronner, "News of Mighty Fort Benning," *Atlanta Daily World*, July 14, 1945; Szwed, *Space Is the Place*, 39–40.

14. Szwed, *Space Is the Place*, 40–41.

15. "Negro Orchestra Leader Held under Draft Laws," *Birmingham News*, December 30, 1942, 14.

16. Szwed, *Space Is the Place*, 41–45.

17. Szwed, *Space Is the Place*, 46.

18. Adams and Mathews, *Doc*, 70, 73.

19. Frank Eaton Adams Sr., interview with the author, May 13, 2012.

20. Frank Adams, interviews with the author, January 30, 2010, and March 6, 2010; Adams and Mathews, *Doc*, 76–77, 254; Szwed, *Space Is the Place*, 285.

21. Adams and Mathews, *Doc*, 77–79; "Dan Michael on WBRC for Pizitz Every Sunday at 12:45 P.M.," *Weekly Review*, March 2, 1946. A typical broadcast, highlighted in the *Weekly Review*, presented the teenage Walter Miller in performances of "Body and Soul" and "Stardust," members of the Parker High School band, and Fletcher "Hootie" Myatt's orchestra.

22. Adams and Mathews, *Doc*, 70–71; Sun Ra, interview by Phil Schaap, WKCR, New York City, December 1988, WKCR Radio Archives, www.philschaapjazz.com.

23. Stern, "Wilson Driver"; Tommy Stewart interview, June 3, 2011; J. B. Barker to the *Weekly Review*, July 22, 1944; Jay Sims, "Round the Blocks," *Weekly Review*, July 8, 1944; Jay Sims, "Round the Blocks," *Weekly Review*, May 13, 1944.

24. Adams and Mathews, *Doc*, 73.

25. Adams and Mathews, *Doc*, 73; Adams, interview with the author, January 30, 2010.

26. Weekly advertisements for Sonny Blount at the Grand Terrace appear, with photographs of the crowds, in the *Weekly Review*, late October 1943 through August 1944.

27. Miller, interview with Mugge.

28. Fletcher Myatt at Sun Ra memorial service, June 5, 1993, video courtesy of Wilma Stewart.

29. Jay Sims, "Round the Blocks," *Weekly Review*, February 20, 1942; Glass, *Life and Death*, 290–96. For more on the history of police shootings in Birmingham, see the podcast *Unjustifiable*, particularly "Chapter Three: The Shoebox," Reckon Radio, 2020.

30. "Youth Congress in Anniversary Celebration," *Weekly Review*, February 6, 1942; "Erskine Hawkins Spurs Campaign for Swimming Pool at Tuxedo Park," *Weekly Review*, August 7, 1943; "Bandleader Aids Swim Pool Drive," *Pittsburgh Courier*, August 28, 1943.

31. "Fund Approved for Negro Unit in Tuxedo Park," *Weekly Review*, April 1, 1944; "A Negro Swimming Pool," *Birmingham News*, March 29, 1944; "City Votes $3,600 for Pool for Negroes," *Birmingham News*, March 26, 1944; Jay Sims, "Round the Blocks," *Weekly Review*, August 26, 1944.

32. "Swimming Pool Now Open," *Weekly Review*, August 26, 1944.

33. "Tuxedo Swim Pool Official Dedication," *Weekly Review*, August 19, 1944; "Swimming Pool Open," *Weekly Review*, August 26, 1944.

34. Rev. John Goodgame and A. G. Gaston, "Another Swimming Pool Is Need [*sic*] for Negroes," *Birmingham News*, August 20, 1952; "Swimming Pool Open."

35. Szwed, *Space Is the Place*, 23; Adams and Mathews, *Doc*, 68–69.

36. Sims, "Round the Blocks," *Weekly Review*, November 15, 1940; "Hits and Bits," *Atlanta Daily World*, February 2, 1945. In addition to his work with the parks department, Briskey was celebrated in white Birmingham as a barbershop quartet leader and as director of the Twenty-Five Black Dots, a blackface minstrelsy troupe. He later became the first director of the Birmingham Zoo but was fired when a secretary accused him of indecent exposure.

37. Adams and Mathews, *Doc*, 69.

38. Advertisements in the *Birmingham News*, March 5, 1945, September 23, 1945, and October 13, 1945. In 1982's "Nuclear War," Sun Ra—with characteristic humor but uncommon profanity—repeatedly crooned, for nearly eight minutes, "Nuclear war, it's a motherfucker . . . If they push that button, your ass got to go."

39. Adams and Mathews, *Doc*, 80.

CHAPTER 21: SWING ON TRIAL

1. Adams and Mathews, *Doc*, 65, 93.

2. Dud Bascomb quoted in Dance, *World of Swing*, 201. Haywood Henry also worked briefly in Ellington's band and was likewise struck by the contrast to Hawkins's group. After two

tours with Ellington, Haywood explained, "It was nothing that he could offer me to want to stay in the band. . . . I said, 'I'd rather be with the guys [the Hawkins orchestra], and feel a bit free, than going through the torture of begging for solos or playing with some guy that don't want you to play.'" "Haywood Henry Meets Max Roach Birthday Broadcast," January 9, 1994, Birthday Broadcasts, Phil Schaap Jazz, www.philschaapjazz.com.

3. "Things Look Better for Musicians Says Hawkins," *New York Amsterdam News*, June 26, 1948; "Erskine Hawkins Breaking Records," *California Eagle*, May 27, 1948; "Swing's on Trial at Apollo; Erskine Hawkins for Defense," *Chicago Defender*, February 26, 1949; "We Cop the Bop but Swing's the Thing," *Chicago Defender*, March 5, 1949.

4. Erskine Hawkins, interview by Leonard Goines, February 6, 1982, JOHP, 166–67.

5. Quoted in Dance, *World of Swing*, 222; Sammy Lowe, interview with the National Black Culture Society, 1979, reprinted in Ealons, *Tuxedo Junction*, 104.

6. Quoted in Dance, *World of Swing*, 211.

7. Quoted in Dance, *World of Swing*, 202.

8. Sammy Lowe in Ealons, *Tuxedo Junction*, 108.

9. "Erskine Hawkins Blows Sweet Sounds in Catskills," *New York Times*, April 10, 1988; Deffaa, *In the Mainstream*, 149.

10. Hawkins, interview with Goines, JOHP, 198–200; Stanley Dance, liner notes, *Erskine Hawkins and His Orchestra Reunion! Live at Club Soul Sound*, Stang ST 1014, 1971.

11. George Avakian, liner notes, *Ellington at Newport*, Columbia CL 934, 1956, LP; Ellington, *Music Is My Mistress*, 241. The original pressing of the classic *Newport* album includes on its back cover, beside a photo of Ellington, an image of Jones, its caption asking, "Unsung hero?"

12. Chip Stern, "Wilson Driver: Driver Man, Reflections of an Urban Griot," Chipstern. com, accessed June 17, 2011, https://www.chipstern.com/chip_tribal_wilson.htm (site discontinued); Sonia Sanchez, interview with the author, June 18, 2011; Sanchez, "Last recording session/for papa Joe," *Collected Poems*, 180.

13. Harper, *Autobiography*, 69–70.

14. Harper, *Autobiography*, 73–83.

15. For a history of Aunt Jemima, see Manring, *Slave in a Box*; for Nancy Green and the birth of the "living Jemimas," see Manring, 77–78.

16. Harper, *Autobiography*, 83.

17. Harper, *Autobiography*, 84; Baldwin, *Notes of a Native Son*, 27.

18. Harper, *Autobiography*, 85.

19. Harper, *Autobiography*, 90–93.

20. Harper, *Autobiography*, 90–91.

21. "Friends Downplay Aunt Jemima Role at Ethel Harper Funeral Services," *Passaic (NJ) Herald-News*, April 9, 1979. Harper's attitude toward the job echoed that of Ione Brown, another of the era's "living Jemimas." Speaking to her local newspaper, Brown described her job as a chance to present a positive image of African Americans. "I'm a public representative of my race," she said. "I get the opportunity to meet little white children, children in small towns who have never ever seen a Negro before. I try to leave them with the best impression I can" and to impart "a little touch of Christianity," singing "church hymns and spirituals" wherever she went. Brown's granddaughter, author and journalist Michele Norris, was at first bewildered to discover this piece of her grandmother's past, remembering Brown for her "style and polish," eloquent speech, and "crownlike" braided hair. In her 2010 memoir, Norris confronts this complex reality, along with another family "secret": a white policeman's 1946 shooting of her father, a World War II veteran on his way to a party at Birmingham's Pythian Temple. Norris, *Grace of Silence*, 21–35, 85–102.

22. For more on the naming of the Arkestra, see Szwed, *Space Is the Place*, 94–95.

23. Sun Ra, "THE POOR LITTLE RICH ONE: THE PRINCE OF THIS WORLD...," reprinted in Corbett, *Wisdom of Sun Ra*, 102. John Corbett has compiled many of Sun Ra's Chicago-era broadsheets and leaflets in the collection *The Wisdom of Sun Ra*. For further analysis of these writings, see Youngquist, *Pure Solar World*, 42–61.

24. Sun Ra, "WHAT MUST NEGROES DO TO BE SAVED?," reprinted in Corbett, *Wisdom of Sun Ra*, 126–28.

25. Brenda Ross, daughter of Banjo Bill Reese, interview with the author, July 11, 2022; thanks to music researcher Matt Baker for helping piece together the history of Banjo Bill.

26. Alton Abraham to Fletcher Myatt, December 1, 1960, Alton Abraham Collection of Sun Ra, Hanna Holborn Gray Special Collections Research Center, University of Chicago Library.

27. According to Sun Ra bandmate and discographer Michael D. Anderson, Miller's were the only arrangements Sun Ra played besides his own; in his last years on the planet, Sun Ra also would perform arrangements by Callins (Anderson, interview with the author, June 17, 2013; Szwed, *Space Is the Place*, 371).

28. Szwed, *Space Is the Place*, 212; "Best Reissues of 2017," The End of All Music website, December 3, 2017, https://theendofallmusic.com/best-reissues-of-2017; Youngquist, *Pure Solar World*, 182, 186. Whatever Sun Ra's extraterrestrial ties, longtime Arkestra member Danny Ray Thompson maintained "He was Birmingham all the way. That's why he wrote that song 'Magic City.'" Interview with the author, 2016.

29. Sun Ra, "The Magic City," in *Immeasurable Equation*, 232–33.

30. Sun Ra, interview by Deborah Ray, *Detroit Black Journal*, Detroit Educational Television Foundation, 1981, posted to YouTube by ukvibeorg on March 21, 2011, https://www.youtube.com/watch?v=mNgwzYoKzlM.

31. Sun Ra, lecture, "The Black Man in the Cosmos," University of California, Berkeley, 1971, on Sun Ra, *The Creator of the Universe*, Transparency 0301, CD.

32. Sun Ra, interview by Ra.

33. Sun Ra interview, Sun Ra Research, October 2, 1986, SoundCloud, www.soundcloud.com/hinds-brothers.

CHAPTER 22: DOWN SOUTH IN BIRMINGHAM

1. "Firemen Let 39 Homes Burn; Refuse Aid to Victims of Big Fire," *New York Amsterdam News*, May 26, 1951; "Birmingham Firemen Stand By as Fire Destroys Town," *New Journal and Guide* (Norfolk, VA), May 26, 1951.

2. *Glare*, April 1953, 9.

3. Del Thorne and Her Trio, "Down South in Birmingham," Excello, 1952; Brenda Ross, daughter of Banjo Bill Reese, interview with the author, July 11, 2022.

4. Author interviews with George Washington, Collins "Bo" Berry, Tolton Rosser, and Donald Crawford Jr., 2016–2022. Issues of the *Birmingham Mirror* and *Glare* magazine from the 1950s and 1960s provide additional coverage of Black nightlife in this era.

5. Mayo Teal Furniss, "Birmingham Spotlight," *Pittsburgh Courier*, June 27, 1964; Christopher Caswell-Rice, interview with the author, October 12, 2022.

6. Hasan Shahid, interview with the author, February 16, 2022; Jeff Hardy, "He Teaches ALL Instruments and All That jazz," *Kudzu* (*Birmingham Post-Herald* supplement), undated clipping, vertical files, "Musicians—B'ham—Black," BPL.

7. Shahid, interview with the author; Hardy, "He Teaches ALL Instruments." Western Olin was renamed P. D. Jackson–Olin High School in 1973.

8. Adams and Mathews, *Doc*, 198, 200–201.

9. "10 Jailed on Dope, Mail Theft Charges," *Birmingham News*, February 4, 1957; Adams and Mathews, *Doc*, 197; Washington, interview with the author.

10. Bernith Guy, interview with the author, April 17, 2019.

11. Moore, *Behind the Ebony Mask*, 29.

12. Quoted in Ward, "Civil Rights and Rock and Roll," 21.

13. Quoted in Ward, 21–22.

14. "Outrageous Attack," *Birmingham News*, April 11, 1956, 10; "Voice of the People," *Birmingham News*, April 13, 1956, 14; "Cole Says Attack Integration Aid," *Huntsville Times*, April 12, 1956, 1, 8.

15. Quoted in Nat Hentoff, "American Airmail," *New Musical Express*, December 27, 1957, 9.

16. Quoted in Adams and Mathews, *Doc*, 194.

17. Adams and Mathews, *Doc*, 223–24.

18. "White High School Grad Makes History," NPR, June 1, 2007, npr.org.

19. Quoted in Millard, *Magic City Nights*, 109–10; Adams and Mathews, *Doc*, 234.

20. Adams and Mathews, *Doc*, 234–35.

21. All details in this section derive from the author's interviews with Cather, 2010–2022, unless otherwise noted.

22. Patrick Cather, liner notes, Robert McCoy, *Bye Bye Baby* (reissue), Delmark DE-759, 2002, CD.

23. Millard, *Magic City Nights*, 99–100.

24. Cruse, *Stuck Rubber Baby*; Armstrong, "*Stuck Rubber Baby* and the Intersections of Civil Rights Historical Memory," 124–26; Collins "Bo" Berry, interview with the author, January 24, 2023.

25. Armstrong, "*Stuck Rubber Baby* and the Intersections of Civil Rights Historical Memory," 126.

26. David Walbert, interview with the author, May 19, 2023.

CHAPTER 23: HERITAGE AND HOME

1. "'Fess' Whatley Honored," *Birmingham News*, March 11, 1956; Hattie B. Witt, "Magic City Society," *Pittsburgh Courier*, March 21, 1956; Jay Sims, "The 'Fess Whatley Story,'" *Huntsville Mirror*, February 4, 1956.

2. Geraldine Moore, "What Negroes Are Doing—Musicians Local to Open Annual Concerts on Tuesday," *Birmingham News*, July 22, 1962; "Concerts Slated Here This Week," *Birmingham News*, June 30, 1963; "New York Beat," *Jet*, March 12, 1964, 64; *John Tuggle Whatley Elementary School*, undated pamphlet, author's collection; John T. (Fess) Whatley and J. L. Lowe Scrapbook, BPL.

3. Jaffe, *Jazz in the Magic City*.

4. *Take Me Home: A. H. Parker High School Presents Nell Carter in Concert with the A. H. Parker High School Choir*, private press, 1983, LP.

5. Lee Shook, "Cleve's Place," *B-Metro*, April 2019, 40–44.

6. Shook, "Cleve's Place," 40–44.

7. Jothan Callins, liner notes, Jothan Callins and The Sounds of Togetherness, *Winds of Change*, Triumph Records 006, 1975.

8. Roy Morris, "Arthur Doyle: A Short Talk," *Cadence*, December 1995, 17.

9. Pierre Crépon, "The Blistering Cosmic Music of The Black Unity Trio," *The Wire*, March 2020, https://www.thewire.co.uk/in-writing/interviews/the-black-unity-trio-cleveland-ohio-1968–1969-interviews-hasan-shahid-pierre-crepon.

10. Frank Adams, interview with the author, January 16, 2011; "Haywood Henry Meets Max Roach Birthday Broadcast," January 9, 1994, Birthday Broadcasts, Phil Schaap Jazz, www.philschaapjazz.com.

11. Cisco Bradley, "Hasan Shahid and the Return of Al-Fatihah," Jazz Right Now, October 22, 2020, www.jazzrightnow.com/artist-feature-hasan-shahid.

12. Tommy Black, "J. L. Lowe's Dream: Jazz Hall of Fame," *Birmingham News*, January 27, 1980; Sonia Carpenter, "Preserving Fading Notes of Jazz," *Kudzu* (*Birmingham Post-Herald* supplement), October 14, 1988, 6–7; Kate Pierce, "Jazzy Yesterdays," *Birmingham*, c. 1984, 63–65; Bob Carlton, "Yesterday's Gone: What Will It Take to Bring It Back?" undated article, c. 1984, *Birmingham News*, author's collection.

13. Kate Pierce, "Jazzy Yesterdays," *Birmingham Magazine*, June 1984, 63–65; Larry Ragan, "Jazz Man," *Birmingham Magazine*, November 1989, 34–38.

14. J. L. Lowe, "Stop the Killing—Be a Jazz Musician," Alabama Jazz Hall of Fame newsletter, c. 1993, author's collection.

15. Jothan Callins, "The Alabama Hall of Fame—Shame," *Birmingham World*, September 16–22, 1993; Birmingham Youth Jazz Ensemble website, accessed 2019, www.jothancallins byje.com (site discontinued).

16. "Stars Fell on Alabama," lyrics by Mitchell Parish (1934), performed by Sun Ra on *Purple Night*, A&M Records 75021 5324 2, 1990.

17. Sun Ra, interview by Jennifer Rycenga, San Francisco, 1988, Sun Ra—Stories (website), www.geocitiessites.com/brian_zimmerman/sunra/stories. At the Alabama Music Hall of Fame ceremony, fellow inductee Tammy Wynette serenaded Wallace with her signature "Stand by Your Man," a performance that drew praise from Sun Ra. "Sun Ra was a fan of *all* music," explained Arkestra member Danny Ray Thompson, "as long as it was pure." Marshall Allen and Danny Ray Thompson, unpublished interview by Lee Shook, February 2016, courtesy Lee Shook.

18. "Night Train" Jayne Layne, aka Craig Legg, "Space Is the Place!," review in *Live Shots!* fanzine, September 1988.

19. Sun Ra, interview by Rycenga. In the same interview, Sun Ra explained that "the South is still an empire. It's not part of the United States, really. And it never did give up, because they still got the Confederate flag. Now . . . when a nation is defeated, they take their flag down. Confederate flag is still the flag of Alabama."

20. Some things, though, had not changed in the South. After the Arkestra's triumphant shows in Birmingham and a gig in nearby Tuscaloosa, the band made a pitstop in small-town Oxford, Alabama, where police arrested one of the musicians on suspicions of drug possession. Sun Ra railed against the sheriff, warning him, "Don't try that Rev. King stuff on me!" and protesting, as one of Alabama's own: "I don't like the way you disgrace this state." When Sun Ra finished his harangue, the police released the musician and the Arkestra got back on the road (Szwed, *Space Is the Place*, 371). On Sun Ra's Alabama fans, see Sun Ra interview, Sun Ra Research, April 4, 1989, SoundCloud, www.soundcloud.com/hinds-brothers.

21. Ludovic Goubet, interview with the author, c. 2014; Kathy Kemp, "Aboard the Spaceship Sun Ra," *Kudzu* (*Birmingham Post-Herald* supplement), April 17, 1992; Szwed, *Space Is the Place*, 375.

22. "Fire Claims Life of Jazz Leader and His Sister," *Birmingham World*, February 25, 1993; Steve Joynt, "Two Will Be Missed," *Birmingham Post-Herald*, February 19, 1993.

23. Tony Norman, "Space Is the Place," *Pittsburgh Post-Gazette*, October 24, 1993; Corbett, *Extended Play*, 173.

24. Tom Jenkins, interview with the author, June 8, 2013.

25. Video of Sun Ra memorial and graveside service, courtesy Wilma Stewart.

26. Sun Ra memorial and graveside service.

27. Erskine Hawkins, interview by Leonard Goines, February 6, 1982, JOHP.

28. "Jazzman Remembered for Modesty," *Montgomery Advertiser*, November 14, 1993.

EPILOGUE

1. This scene appears in Leonard Feather, "Jazz's Spiritual Home Revisited—A Last Lament for Harlem," *Los Angeles Times*, December 14, 1969, 597.

2. "Trumpeter Dud Bascomb Dies of a Heart Attack," *Jet*, January 11, 1973, 53. The movie was the grisly Harlem crime drama *Across 110th Street*.

3. Recalling his experience working Chicago's South Side sanitation trucks, writer and musician Guy Senese notes that "the Black guys on the crew were especially conscientious to 'carry' an elderly man named Paul Bascomb. Occasionally, 'carrying' was a service provided for a ward yard dignitary. . . . Paul 'pulled' cans, the 55 gallon drums, out from the alley fences. We would lift them into the truck. . . . I couldn't believe a guy that accomplished could 'wind up on the garbage.' . . . He was an educated man, in more ways than one" (*Throwing Voices*, 81–83). *Jet*, April 11, 1983.

4. "Haywood Henry Meets Max Roach Birthday Broadcast," January 9, 1994, Birthday Broadcasts, Phil Schaap Jazz, www.philschaapjazz.com.

5. Sonia Sanchez, interview with the author, June 18, 2011.

6. Details in this section come from the Ethel Ernestine Harper Papers, Morristown and Morris Township Library, Morristown, NJ.

7. The following scene is a composite, grounded in a particular 2022 session at True Story Brewing Company (April 26, 2022) but drawing also from other nights at both True Story and its predecessor, BOSS Ultra Bar and Lounge. Quotes in this section are from author interviews with José Carr (August 15, 2015) and Bo Berry (July 15, 2011). Carr's jam sessions are also the subject of a documentary film, *So You Say You Play Jazz? José Carr's True Story*, directed by Matthew Bellisario (BellisarioSonic Arts, 2023).

BIBLIOGRAPHY

PRIMARY SOURCES
Author Interviews
Frank Eaton Adams Sr.
Michael D. Anderson
Collins "Bo" Berry
Daniel "José" Carr
Christopher Caswell-Rice
Patrick Cather
Carol Clarke
Donald Crawford Jr.
Cleveland Eaton
Ludovic Goubet
Jimmy Griffin
Bernith Guy
Thomas Jenkins
Craig Legg
George Mostoller
Rickey Powell
Brenda Ross
Tolton Rosser
Sonia Sanchez
Hasan Shahid
Tommy Stewart
Danny Ray Thompson
Charles Tortorici
David Walbert
George Washington

Newspapers and Magazines
Alabama Heritage
Alabama Voice
Atlanta Daily World
Band Leaders
Birmingham Age-Herald
Birmingham Magazine
Birmingham News
Birmingham News Age-Herald
Birmingham Post
Birmingham Post-Herald
Birmingham Reporter
Birmingham World
B-Metro
Brooklyn Times Union

Cadence
California Eagle (Los Angeles)
Chicago Defender
Christian Science Monitor
Cullman (AL) Banner
DownBeat
Dubois (PA) Courier-Express
Ebony
Glare
Huntsville Mirror
Huntsville Times
Indianapolis Freeman
Jazz Journal
Jazz Monthly
Jet
Kingsport (TN) Times
Los Angeles Times
Melody Maker
Messenger
Metronome
Modern Drummer
Montgomery Advertiser
Music Dial
New York Age
New York Amsterdam News
New York Times
Norfolk New Journal and Guide
Oakland Tribune
Passaic (NJ) Herald-News
Philadelphia Inquirer
Pittsburgh Courier
Pittsburgh Post-Gazette
Reality Hackers
Salt Lake Tribune
Saturday Evening Post
Springfield (MO) Leader and Press
Star Sunday Magazine of the Kansas City Star
Storyville
Talking Machine World
Tampa Times
Tuscaloosa News
Variety
Weekly Review

Archival Collections

Alabama State University, Levi Watkins
Learning Center, Montgomery, AL
    Bama State Collegians Collection
    President Harper Councill Trenholm
    Collection
    Tommy Stewart Collection
Birmingham Civil Rights Institute,
Birmingham, AL
    Civil Rights Oral History Project
Birmingham Public Library, Department
of Archives and Manuscripts,
Birmingham, AL
    Erskine Ramsay Papers
    J. L. Lowe, Photographs
        Documenting Birmingham's
        Black Jazz Musicians
    John T. (Fess) Whatley and J. L.
    Lowe Scrapbook
    Sammy Lowe, "A Man from Tuxedo
    Junction (from Jazz to Swing
    to Rock to Soul): Diary of a
    Black Musician" (unpublished
    manuscript, n.d.), ARR1137
College of Charleston, School
of the Arts, Charleston Jazz
Initiative, Charleston, SC
    St. Julian Bennett Dash Collection
Duke University, John Hope Franklin
Research Center for African and
African American History and
Culture, David M. Rubenstein
Rare Book and Manuscript
Library, Durham, NC
    Behind the Veil Oral History Project
Emory University, Stuart A. Rose
Manuscript, Archives, and Rare
Book Library, Atlanta, GA
    Oscar W. Adams Papers
Library of Congress, Washington, DC,
Performing Arts Reading Room
Morristown and Morris Township
Library, Morristown, NJ
    Ethel Ernestine Harper Papers
Rutgers University, Institute of
Jazz Studies, Newark, NJ
    Jazz Oral History Project
University of Alabama Libraries Special
Collections, Tuscaloosa, AL
    Working Lives Oral History Project

University of Alabama at
Birmingham, Mervyn H. Sterne
Library, Birmingham, AL
    Oral History Collection
University of Chicago Library, Hanna
Holborn Gray Special Collections
Research Center, Chicago, IL
    Alton Abraham Collection of
    Sun Ra

Books

Adams, Frank, and Burgin Mathews. *Doc: The Story of a Birmingham Jazz Man*. Tuscaloosa: University of Alabama Press, 2012.

Baldwin, James. *Notes of a Native Son*. Boston: Beacon Press, 1955.

Basie, Count, as told to Albert Murray. *Good Morning Blues: The Autobiography of Count Basie*. Cambridge, MA: Da Capo, 1985.

Cohen, Octavus Roy. *Black and Blue*. New York: Little, Brown, 1926.

———. *Dark Days and Black Knights*. New York: Dodd, Mead, 1923.

Coleman, Bill. *Trumpet Story*. London: Macmillan, 1990.

Cruse, Howard. *Stuck Rubber Baby*. New York: Paradox Press, 1995.

Davis, Angela. *An Autobiography*. Chicago: Haymarket Books, 2021.

Davis, Miles, with Quincy Troupe. *Miles: The Autobiography of Miles Davis*. New York: Simon and Schuster, 1989.

Dreams Come True: Industrial Education for Black Youth in Alabama, 1881–1939. Birmingham: Birmingham Public Library, 1985. Pamphlet.

Ellington, Duke. *Music Is My Mistress*. New York: Da Capo, 1973.

Ellison, Ralph. *Going to the Territory*. New York: Random House, 1986.

———. *Shadow and Act*. New York: Vintage, 1953.

Ferguson, Otis. *In the Spirit of Jazz: The Otis Ferguson Reader*. Edited by Dorothy Chamberlain and Robert Wilson. New York: Da Capo, 1997.

Gaston, Arthur George. *Green Power: The Successful Way of A. G. Gaston*.

Birmingham: Southern University Press, 1968.

Gentry, Helen H. *Echoes out of the Burton*. Bloomington: AuthorHouse, 2011.

Gillespie, Dizzy, with Al Fraser. *To Be, or Not . . . to Bop*. Minneapolis: University of Minnesota Press, 1979.

Hammond, John, with Irving Townsend. *John Hammond on Record*. New York: Ridge Press / Summit Books, 1977.

Hampton, Lionel, with James Haskins. *Hamp: An Autobiography*. New York: Warner Books, 1989.

Handy, William Christopher. *Father of the Blues*. New York: Macmillan, 1941.

Hardy, Evelyn Starks, with Nathan Hale Turner Jr. *The Sweetest Harmony: Evelyn Starks Hardy and the Original Gospel Harmonettes*. Jonesboro, AR: GrantHouse Publishers, 2009.

Harper, Ethel Ernestine. *The Autobiography of Ethel Ernestine Harper*. N.p.: n.p., 1970.

Holiday, Billie. *Billie Holiday: The Last Interview and Other Conversations*. Brooklyn: Melville House, 2019.

Holiday, Billie, with William Dufty. *Lady Sings the Blues*. New York: Doubleday, 1956.

Hughes, Langston. *The Big Sea*. New York: Hill and Wang, 1940.

Johnson, Charles S., ed. *Ebony and Topaz: A Collectanea*. New York: National Urban League, 1927.

Jones, Papa Jo. *Rifftide: The Life and Opinions of Papa Jo Jones*. Minneapolis: University of Minnesota Press, 2011.

Manning, Frankie, and Cynthia R. Millman. *Frankie Manning: Ambassador of Lindy Hop*. Philadelphia: Temple University Press, 2007.

Murray, Albert. *Murray Talks Music: Albert Murray on Jazz and Blues*. Edited by Paul Devlin. Minneapolis: University of Minnesota Press, 2016.

Murray, Albert, and John F. Callahan, eds. *Trading Twelves: The Selected Letters of Ralph Ellison and Albert Murray*. New York: Modern Library, 2000.

Norris, Michele. *The Grace of Silence: A Memoir*. New York: Pantheon, 2010.

Parker, Arthur H. *A Dream That Came True: Autobiography of Arthur Harold Parker*. Birmingham: Industrial High School, 1932–33.

Reese, Della. *Angels along the Way: My Life with Help from Above*. New York: Berkley Boulevard Books, 1997.

Rice, Condoleezza. *Ordinary, Extraordinary People: A Memoir of Family*. New York: Three Rivers Press, 2010.

Sanchez, Sonia. *Collected Poems*. Boston: Beacon Press, 2021.

Senese, Guy. *Throwing Voices: Five Autoethnographies on Postradical Education and the Fine Art of Misdirection*. Charlotte: Information Age Publishing, 2007.

Shapiro, Nat, and Nat Hentoff. *Hear Me Talkin' to Ya: The Story of Jazz as Told by the Men Who Made It*. New York: Dover, 1955.

Stearns, Marshall, and Jean Stearns. *Jazz Dance: The Story of American Vernacular Dance*. Cambridge, MA: Da Capo, 1994.

Sun Ra. *The Immeasurable Equation: The Collected Poetry and Prose*. Edited by James L. Wolf and Hartmut Geerken. Wartaweil, Ger.: Waitawhile, 2005.

Wells, Dicky, as told to Stanley Dance. *The Night People: The Jazz Life of Dicky Wells*. Washington: Smithsonian Institution Press, 1991.

Wesley, Fred. *Hit Me, Fred: Recollections of a Sideman*. Durham: Duke University Press, 2002.

Witt, Edwin T. *Witt's End: Fulfilling the American Dream*. Victorville, CA: E & C Publishers, 1997.

SECONDARY SOURCES

Abbott, Lynn, and Doug Seroff. *The Original Blues: The Emergence of the Blues in African American Vaudeville, 1889–1926*. Jackson: University Press of Mississippi, 2017.

———. *To Do This, You Must Know How: Music Pedagogy in the Black Gospel*

Quartet Tradition. Jackson: University Press of Mississippi, 2013.

Albertson, Chris. *Bessie*. New Haven: Yale University Press, 2003.

Alvarez, Luis. *The Power of the Zoot: Youth Culture and Resistance during World War II*. Berkeley: University of California Press, 2008.

Anderson, James D. *The Education of Blacks in the South, 1860–1935*. Chapel Hill: University of North Carolina Press, 1988.

Armstrong, Julie Buckner. "*Stuck Rubber Baby* and the Intersections of Civil Rights Historical Memory." In *Redrawing the Historical Past: History, Memory, and Multiethnic Graphic Novels*, edited by Martha J. Cutter and Cathy J. Schlund-Vials, 106–28. Athens: University of Georgia Press, 2018.

Brothers, Thomas. *Louis Armstrong's New Orleans*. New York: Norton, 2006.

Burns, Ken, and Geoffrey C. Ward. *Ken Burns' Jazz: The Story of America's Music*. New York: Sony Music Entertainment, 2000.

Callins, Jothan McKinley. "The Birmingham Jazz Community: The Role and Contributions of Afro-Americans (up to 1940)." Master's thesis, University of Pittsburgh, 1982.

Chilton, John. *A Jazz Nursery: The Story of the Jenkins' Orphanage Bands of Charleston, South Carolina*. London: Bloomsbury Book Shop, 1980.

———. *Ride, Red, Ride: The Life of Henry "Red" Allen*. London: Continuum, 1999.

———. *Roy Eldridge: Little Jazz Giant*. London: Continuum, 2002.

Clarke, Donald. *Billie Holiday: Wishing on the Moon*. Cambridge, MA: Da Capo, 2000.

Cohen, Aaron. *Move On Up: Chicago Soul Music and Black Cultural Power*. Chicago: University of Chicago Press, 2019.

Cohen, Harvey G. *Duke Ellington's America*. Chicago: University of Chicago Press, 2010.

Corbett, John. *Extended Play: Sounding Off from John Cage to Dr. Funkenstein*. Durham: Duke University Press, 1994.

———, ed. *The Wisdom of Sun Ra: Sun Ra's Polemical Broadsheets and Streetcorner Leaflets*. Chicago: WhiteWalls, 2006.

Dance, Stanley. *The World of Earl Hines*. New York: Da Capo, 1977.

———. *The World of Swing*. New York: Da Capo, 1974.

Daniels, Douglas Henry. *Lester Leaps In: The Life and Times of Lester "Pres" Young*. Boston: Beacon Press, 2002.

DeBarros, Paul. *Jackson Street after Hours*. Seattle: Sasquatch Books, 1993.

Deffaa, Chip. *In the Mainstream: 18 Portraits in Jazz*. Metuchen, NJ: Scarecrow, 1992.

Delannoy, Luc. *Pres: The Story of Lester Young*. Translated by Elena B. Odio. Fayetteville: University of Arkansas Press, 1993.

DeVeaux, Scott. *The Birth of Bebop: A Social and Musical History*. Berkeley: University of California Press, 1997.

Driggs, Frank, and Chuck Haddix. *Kansas City Jazz: From Ragtime to Bebop—A History*. Oxford: Oxford University Press, 2005.

Ealons, Carol P. *Tuxedo Junction: Right Back Where I Belong*. Brownsboro, AL: Ardent Press, 2011.

Erenberg, Lewis A. *Swingin' the Dream: Big Band Jazz and the Rebirth of American Culture*. Chicago: University of Chicago Press, 1998.

Fairclough, Adam. *A Class of Their Own: Black Teachers in the Segregated South*. Cambridge, MA: Belknap Press of Harvard University Press, 2007.

Fede, Frank Joseph. "Interdependence of Blacks and Italians in Birmingham." In *Italians in the Deep South: Their Impact on Birmingham and the American Heritage*, 235–42. Montgomery: Black Belt Press, 1994.

Feldman, Lynn B. *A Sense of Place: Birmingham's Black Middle-Class Community, 1890–1930*. Tuscaloosa: University of Alabama Press, 1999.

Fernandes, Naresh. *Taj Mahal Foxtrot: The Story of Bombay's Jazz Age*. New Delhi: Roli Books, 2012.

Fernett, *Swing Out: Great Negro Dance Bands*. New York: Da Capo, 1993.

Ferris, William. *Blues from the Delta*. New York: Da Capo, 1978.

Gioia, Ted. *The History of Jazz*. Oxford: Oxford University Press, 2011.

Gitler, Ira. *Swing to Bop: An Oral History of the Transition in Jazz in the 1940s*. Oxford: Oxford University Press, 1985.

Glass, Jay M. *Life and Death in the Magic City: A Coroner's Perspective of Jefferson County, Alabama in the Early 20th Century*. Birmingham: Media Mint Publishing, 2020.

Gold, Jeff. *Sittin' In: Jazz Clubs of the 1940s and 1950s*. New York: Harper Design, 2020.

Greene, Meg. *Billie Holiday: A Biography*. Westport, CT: Greenwood, 2007.

Hart, James D. "Jazz Jargon." *American Speech* 7, no. 4 (April 1932): 241–54.

"Haywood Henry, Musician." *Artist and Influence* 11 (1992): 120–43.

Hennessey, Mike. *Klook: The Story of Kenny Clarke*. Pittsburgh: University of Pittsburgh Press, 1994.

Hornady, John R. *Book of Birmingham*. New York: Dodd, Mead, 1921.

Jaffe, Sandy, dir. *Jazz in the Magic City*. Birmingham, Alabama, 1985. Film.

Joos, Vincent. "The Natchez Fire: A Profile of African American Remembrance in a Small Mississippi Town." Master's thesis, University of North Carolina at Chapel Hill, 2011.

Kelley, Robin D. G. *Thelonious Monk: The Life and Times of an American Original*. New York: Free Press, 2009.

Kennedy, Al. *Chord Changes on the Chalkboard: How Public School Teachers Shaped Jazz and the Music of New Orleans*. Lanham, MD: Scarecrow Press, 2005.

Kennedy, Rick. *Jelly Roll, Bix, and Hoagy: Gennett Studios and the Birth of Recorded Jazz*. Bloomington: Indiana University Press, 1994.

Klima, John. *Willie's Boys: The 1948 Birmingham Black Barons, the Last Negro League World Series, and the Making of a Baseball Legend*. Hoboken: John Wiley and Sons, 2009.

Korall, Burt. *Drummin' Men: The Heartbeat of Jazz; The Swing Years*. Oxford: Oxford University Press, 1990.

Lloyd, Michael. "The Life and Legacy of Frank Terry Greer and His Influence on Historically Black College and University Bands." Master's thesis, University of Florida, 2016.

Lock, Graham. *Blutopia: Visions of the Future and Revisions of the Past in the Work of Sun Ra, Duke Ellington, and Anthony Braxton*. Durham: Duke University Press, 1999.

Loder-Jackson, Tondra L. *Schoolhouse Activists: African American Educators and the Long Birmingham Civil Rights Movement*. Albany: SUNY Press, 2015.

Loewen, James W. *Sundown Towns: A Hidden Dimension of American Racism*. New York: New Press, 2005.

Lofton, J. Mack, Jr. *Voices from Alabama: A Twentieth-Century Mosaic*. Tuscaloosa: University of Alabama Press, 1993.

Manring, M. M. *Slave in a Box: The Strange Career of Aunt Jemima*. Charlottesville: University of Virginia Press, 1998.

Marzette-Bolivar, C. *Swing Lowe: A Family's Dedication to Preserving Music in the Magic City*. New York: Vantage Press, 2001.

McCarthy, Albert. *Big Band Jazz*. New York: Carter Lash Cameron Limited, 1974.

Millard, Andre. *Magic City Nights: Birmingham's Rock 'n' Roll Years*. Middletown: Wesleyan University Press, 2017.

Moore, Geraldine. *Behind the Ebony Mask: What American Negroes Really Think*. Birmingham: Southern University Press, 1961.

Mordden, Ethan. *Sing for Your Supper: The Broadway Musical in the 1930s*. New York: St. Martin's Press, 2005.

Peebles, Marilyn T. *The Alabama Knights of Pythias of North America, South America, Europe, Asia, Africa, and Australia: A Brief History*. Lanham, MD: University Press of America, 2012.

Pilgrim, David. *Understanding Jim Crow: Using Racist Memorabilia to Teach*

Tolerance and Promote Social Justice. Oakland: Ferris State University and PM Press, 2015.

Ritz, David. *Respect: The Life of Aretha Franklin.* New York: Little, Brown, 2014.

Robertson, David. *W. C. Handy: The Life and Times of the Man Who Made the Blues.* Tuscaloosa: University of Alabama Press, 2009.

Russell, Ross. *Bird Lives! The High Life and Times of Charlie (Yardbird) Parker.* New York: Da Capo, 1996.

Shipton, Alyn. *Groovin' High: The Life of Dizzy Gillespie.* New York: Oxford University Press, 1999.

Sites, William. *Sun Ra's Chicago: Afrofuturism and the City.* Chicago: University of Chicago Press, 2020.

Skocpol, Theda, Ariane Liazos, and Marshall Ganz. *What a Mighty Power We Can Be: African American Fraternal Groups and the Struggle for Racial Equality.* Princeton: Princeton University Press, 2006.

Sorin, Gretchen. *Driving while Black: African American Travel and the Road to Civil Rights.* New York: Liveright Publishing, 2020.

Steptoe, Tyina L. *Houston Bound: Culture and Color in a Jim Crow City.* Oakland: University of California Press, 2016.

Stewart, Thomas W. *The Bama State Collegians, 1929–1934.* Gadsden, AL: Thomasina Publishing Company, 1993.

———. *The Bama State Collegians, 1935–1939.* Gadsden, AL: Thomasina Publishing Company, 1993.

Stowe, David W. *Swing Changes: Big Band Jazz in New Deal America.* Cambridge, MA: Harvard University Press, 1994.

Szwed, John. *Space Is the Place: The Lives and Times of Sun Ra.* New York: Pantheon, 1997.

Taylor, Candacy. *Overground Railroad: The Green Book and the Roots of Black Travel in America.* New York: Abrams Press, 2020.

Teachout, Terry. *Pops: A Life of Louis Armstrong.* Boston: Mariner Books, 2010.

Ward, Brian. "Civil Rights and Rock and Roll: Revisiting the Nat King Cole Attack of 1956." *OAH Magazine of History* 24, no. 22 (April 2010): 21–24.

Wardlow, Gayle Dean. *Chasin' That Devil Music.* San Francisco: Miller Freeman Books, 1998.

Watkins, Clifford Edward. *Showman: The Life and Music of Perry George Lowery.* Jackson: University of Mississippi Press, 2003.

Webb, H. Brook. "The Slang of Jazz." *American Speech* 12, no. 3 (October 1937): 179–84.

Wilkerson, Christopher. "Hot and Sweet: Big Band Music in Black West Virginia before the Swing Era." *American Music* 21, no. 2 (Summer 2003): 159–79.

Yanow, Scott. *Bebop.* San Francisco: Miller Freeman Books, 2000.

Youngquist, Paul. *A Pure Solar World: Sun Ra and the Birth of Afrofuturism.* Austin: University of Texas Press, 2016.

INDEX

Page numbers in italics indicate illustrations.

Basie, Count, 4, 62, 63, 71, 74, 78, 107, 152–53, 154–57, 168, 190, 194, 195, 235, 239, 274, 291

Bates, Bernice, 122, 125

"Bear Mash Blues," 173, 174–75

bebop, 4, 7, 41, 175, 202, 207, 208, 209, 210, 217, 218, 234, 236, 238, 312n13, 316n13

Becton, George Wilson, 96–98, 102, 143, 144, 211

Bell, John L., 122, 254

Bentley, Gladys, 147

Berry, Collins "Bo," 269, 277, 293–94

Berry, Chu, 164

Berry, Chuck, 268

Bessemer, AL, 15, 58, 59, 67, 86, 132

Birmingham Black Barons, 121

Birmingham Civil Rights Institute, 279

Birmingham Heritage Band, 10, 273, 276–78, 277, 283, 285, 287, 288, 289

"Birmingham Is My Home," 276, 289

Birmingham Jubilee Singers, 220, 221

Birmingham-Southern College, 80, 269

Birmingham Youth Jazz Ensemble, 280

Black and Tan Syncopators, 122, 123

Black Birds of Paradise, 45, 58

Black Herman, 130

Black press, 6, 117, 121, 199, 229, 259, 297n1

Black Unity Trio, 275

Blankenship, Henry, 277

Blanton, Jimmy, 151

Blesh, Rudi, 264, 265

Blevins, J. William, 135

Blount, Herman "Sonny." See Sun Ra

blues music, 52–53, 57, 58, 66, 72, 100–101, 102, 112, 188, 202, 292

Bob's Savoy, 121–22, 253, 254, 255, 307n2, 308n5

boogie-woogie piano, 52–53, 112, 264–66, 301n14

Britton, Joseph "Joe," 68, 69, 70

Broadway, 24, 82, 160–61, 195, 205, 237, 240, 273

Brown, Dolly, 222

Brown, Dolores, 186, 188, 314n19

Brown, Eddie, 159

Brown, James, 237, 273

Bunch, Carl, 68, 69

Bunch, Frank, 69, 92. See also Frank Bunch and His Fuzzy Wuzzies

Burns, Joe "Poonanny," 268, 273

Burton, Wayne, 66

Butterbeans and Susie, 78, 80, 302n15

Callins, Jothan, 10, 274, 280, 293; dissertation quoted, 13, 16–17, 120, 313n14; and Sun Ra, 246, 281, 283, 285–86, 320n27

Calloway, Cab, 4, 62, 63, 114, 147, 194, 308n10

Calloway, Jean, 123, 308n10

Cannon, Richard, 223

Carmichael, Hoagy, 201

Carr, Daniel "José," 278, 293–94

Carter, Asa, 258–59, 260

Carter, Benny, 69, 125, 158

Carter, Nell, 269–70, 273

Carver Theater, 65, 272, 279, 285, 308n5

Caswell, Melvin, 136, 151, 226, 255, 309n22

Cather, Patrick, 262–68, 268

Catlett, Sid, 206

Chambliss, Minnie, 51–52, 53

Champion, Jesse, 38, 254, 286

Chappell, Jimmy, 254

Charles, Ray, 221, 268, 315n27

Children's Crusade (Children's March), 5, 260, 261

"Chocolate Avenue," 136, 219

Christian, Charlie, 161, 217

Chukker (venue), 283–84

church music, 15, 16, 31, 51, 52, 55, 96–98, 101, 109, 125, 132, 139, 220

circus bands, 6, 17, 20, 139, 153. See also Lowery, P. G.

City Stages festival, 283, 284

civil rights movement, 61, 241, 247, 248, 255, 260–61, 270, 274–75, 298n13; historical representations of, 5, 269, 279

Clarke, Arthur "Babe," 124, 192

Clarke, Charles "Chuck," 124, 192, 257, 277

Clarke, Kenny, 168–69, 190, 208–9, 210, 212, 312n13, 316n12

Clarke, Mary Alice, 125, 126, 257, 271

Clarke, Pete, 124, 143

Clarke, Richard "Dick," 124, 143

Cleve's Place, 274

Club Congo, 223, 228

Club DeLisa, 223, 244

Cohen, Octavus Roy, 62, 80–82

Cole, Nat King, 187, 205, 258–59, 278, 282

Coleman, Jaybird, 58

Coltrane, John, 261
Community Sings, 33–34, 51, 71, 140, 279
Connor, Eugene "Bull," 231, 253, 254, 260, 266
Cotton Club Casino (Birmingham), 121, 307n2
Councill Elementary, 256, 293
Cox, Ida, 79, 132
Cruse, Howard, 269
C. S. Belton's Society Syncopaters, 116, 118
Cullman, AL, 85
Cunningham, James, 270
Cunningham, Vic, 269

Dash, Julian, 146, 172, 173, 184
Davenport, Alton "Snooky," 55, 192, *193*, 223, 308n8
Davenport, Charles "Cow Cow," 52–53
Davis, Frank, *277*
Davis, Lucky Leon, 254
Davis, Miles, 154, 175–76, 213
"Dixie," 87, 89–90
Dobbins, Lynette, 185–86
"Dolomite," 175
Dolomite, AL, 59, 175
Downbeat Club (Ensley), 254
Downbeat Club (New York), 213
"Down South in Birmingham," 254
Doyle, Arthur, 7, 246, 274–75
Dozier, Jack, 108
Driskell, Clarence, *220*
Driver, Wilson, 40–41, 44, 45, 88, 89–90, 153, 190, 194, 205–6, 223, 239, 291–92
Dunham Jubilee Singers (Dunham Jazz Singers), 58
Dyett, "Captain" Walter, 46, 298n9
Dynamite Hill, 254, 266, 301n12

Earl, George, 19, 72, 110
Eaton, Cleveland "Cleve," 7, 262, 273–74, 301n12
Eaton, LaVergne, 301n12
Eaton, Myra, 274
Edson, Hyman "Feets," 145–46, 147, 157, 158
education: industrial philosophy of, 28–30; and music training in Birmingham, 4, 21. *See also* Industrial High School; teachers
Eldridge, Roy, 164, 207, 212, 311n14

Elks, 60, 63, 64, 65, 113, 114, 120, 122, 222, 223, 279; Elks youth jazz band, 274–75
Ellington, Duke, 63, 116, 147, 151, 186, 212, 238–39, 281, 283, 288, 319n11; in Birmingham, 62, 98–100, 102, 222; Birmingham musicians performing with, 4, 8, 69, 125, 205, 256, 276, 277; compared to Hawkins Orchestra, 107, 170, 235, 318n2
Ellington, Mercedes, 288
Ellison, Ralph, 73, 99, 208
Englund, Leon, 143, 157
Enon Ridge, 107–8
Ensley, AL, 59, 109–10, 132, 174, 179, 254, 272, 288, 289
Erskine Hawkins Orchestra, 7, 49, 100, 158, 227, 244, 291; family atmosphere of, 107, 171–72, 203, 235, 275, 318n2; female vocalists in, 185–87, 314n19; later years of, 235–36, 238; performance style of, 170–73; as quintessential Birmingham band, 7, 105, 107; returns to Birmingham, 180, 182, 198, 211; tours of, 180–85; at the Savoy Ballroom, 204, 310n18; and "Tuxedo Junction," 173–79, 238; and World War II, 197–201, 203. *See also* Bama State Collegians
Ethel Harper's Rhythm Boys, 127–28, 136
Europe, James Reese, 278
Evans, Jesse, 257
Exposure Community Development Corporation, 288

Fair, Andrew Curtis, 112, 117
Fairfield, AL, 59, 253, 254, 262, 274
Famous Theater, 65, 71, 72, 76, 78, 153, 308n5
Feather, Leonard, 165, 290
female impersonators, 147, 228, 269
female vocalists, 124–25, 159, 185–87. *See also* Harper, Ethel
Fess Whatley's Jazz Demons, 71, 92, 288, 292
Fess Whatley's Sax-o-Society Orchestra, 63, 82, 103, 118, 133, 192
Fess Whatley's Vibra-Cathedral Orchestra, 125, 244
Feyne, Buddy, 178, 315n27
Fisk Jubilee Singers, 30–31
Fitzgerald, Ella, 158, 177, 186

Printed in the USA
CPSIA information can be obtained
at www.ICGtesting.com
CBHW020224210524
8864CB00002B/36

9 781469 676883